THE
BRASS CHECK

A Study of American Journalism

by
Upton Sinclair

Ayer Company Publishers, Inc.

Reprinted Edition 1993

Ayer Company Publishers, Inc.
P.O. Box 958
Salem, NH 03079

Reprinted from a copy furnished by the
Manchester Public Library
Manchester, New Hampshire.

ISBN 0-405-01696-4 (Hard Cover Edition)
ISBN 0-88143-153-2 (Paper Back Edition)

THE
BRASS CHECK

A Study of
American Journalism

BY
UPTON SINCLAIR

Revised Edition
with Index

PUBLISHED BY THE AUTHOR
PASADENA, CALIFORNIA.

First Edition	Paper	February, 1920	23,000 Copies
Second Edition	Paper	February, 1920	20,500 Copies
Third Edition	Cloth	April, 1920	16,500 Copies
Fourth Edition	Paper	June, 1920	15,000 Copies
Fifth Edition	Paper	July, 1920	12,000 Copies
Sixth Edition	Cloth	August, 1920	12,500 Copies
Seventh Edition	Paper	August, 1920	15,000 Copies
Eighth Edition	Paper	October, 1920	30,000 Copies
Ninth Edition	Paper	January, 1928	5,000 Copies
" "	Cloth	January, 1928	2,500 Copies
Tenth Edition	Cloth	April, 1931	1,100 Copies
" "	Paper	April, 1931	900 Copies

A LETTER FOR THE TIME

VILLENEUVE, SWITZERLAND,
Monday, Oct. 6, 1919.

My Dear Confrère:

I am happy to see you always so burning with energy, but your next book prepares for you some rude combats. It requires a bold courage to dare, when one is alone, to attack the monster, the new Minotaur, to which the entire world renders tribute: the Press.

I return to Paris in a few weeks. Reaction there holds the center of the walk. It speaks already as master, and perhaps it will be master before the end of the winter. The wave of counter-revolution, of counter-liberty, passes over the world. It will drown more than one among us, but it will retire, and our ideas will conquer.

Very cordially I press your hand.

ROMAIN ROLLAND.

CONTENTS

THE INVADERS

CONTENTS

PART I

THE EVIDENCE

PART II

THE EXPLANATION

PART III

THE REMEDY

INTRODUCTORY

The social body to which we belong is at this moment passing through one of the greatest crises of its history, a colossal process which may best be likened to a birth. We have each of us a share in this process, we are to a greater or less extent responsible for its course. To make our judgments, we must have reports from other parts of the social body; we must know what our fellow-men, in all classes of society, in all parts of the world, are suffering, planning, doing. There arise emergencies which require swift decisions, under penalty of frightful waste and suffering. What if the nerves upon which we depend for knowledge of this social body should give us false reports of its condition?

The first half of this book tells a personal story: the story of one man's experiences with American Journalism. This personal feature is not pleasant, but it is unavoidable. If I were taking the witness-chair in a court of justice, the jury would not ask for my general sentiments and philosophic opinions; they would not ask what other people had told me, or what was common report; the thing they would wish to know—the only thing they would be allowed to know—is what I had personally seen and experienced. So now, taking the witness-stand in the case of the American public versus Journalism, I tell what I have personally seen and experienced. I take the oath of a witness: the truth, the whole truth, and nothing but the truth, so help me God. After this pledge, earnestly given and earnestly meant, the reader must either believe me, or he must exclude me from the company of civilized men.

My motive in writing this book is not to defend myself. We live in a time of such concentrated agony and peril that a man who would waste ink and paper on a defense of his own personality would be contemptible. What I tell you is: "Look! Here is American Journalism! Here is what it did to one man, systematically, persistently, deliberately, for a period of twenty years. Here are names, places, dates—such a mass of material as you cannot doubt, you cannot evade. Here is the whole thing, inside and out. Here are your sacred names, the very highest of your gods. When you have read this story, you will know our Journalism; you will know the body and soul of it, you will know it in such a way that you will not have to be told what it is doing to the movement for industrial freedom and self-government all over the world."

In the second half of the book you will hear a host of other witnesses—several score of them, the wisest and truest and best people of our country. They are in every part of our country, in every class and every field of public life; and when you have heard their experiences, told for the most part in their own words, you must grant my claim concerning this book—that it is a book of facts. There are no mistakes in it, no guesses, no surmises; there are no lapses of memory, no inaccuracies. There are only facts. You must understand that I have had this book in mind for twenty years. For twelve years I have been deliberately collecting the documents and preserving the records, and I have these before me as I write. In a few cases of personal experiences I have relied upon my memory; but that memory is vivid, because the incidents were painful, they were seared into my soul, and now, as I recall them, I see the faces of the people, I hear their very tones. Where there is any doubt or vagueness in my recollection, or where there is hearsay testimony, I state the fact explicitly; otherwise I wish the reader to understand that the incidents happened as I say they happened, and that upon the truth of every statement in this book I pledge my honor as a man and my reputation as a writer.

One final word: In this book I have cast behind me the proprieties usually held sacred; I have spared no one, I have narrated shameful things. I have done this, not because I have any pleasure in scandal; I have not such pleasure, being by nature impersonal. I do not hate one living being. The people I have lashed in this book are to me not individuals, but social forces; I have exposed them, not because they lied about me, but because a new age of fraternity is trying to be born, and they, who ought to be assisting the birth, are strangling the child in the womb.

P. S. to ninth edition, 1926: The circulation of "The Brass Check," prior to the present edition, amounts to 144,000 copies, exclusive of translations.

PART I

THE EVIDENCE

CHAPTER I

THE STORY OF THE BRASS CHECK

Once upon a time there was a little boy; a nice little boy, whom you would have liked if you had known him—at least, so his mother says. He had been brought up in the traditions of the old South, to which the two most important things in the world were good cooking and good manners. He obeyed his mother and father, and ate his peas with a fork, and never buttered the whole slice of his bread. On Sunday mornings he carefully shined his shoes and brushed his clothes at the window, and got into a pair of tight kid gloves and under a tight little brown derby hat, and walked with his parents to a church on Fifth Avenue. On week-days he studied hard and obeyed his teachers, and in every field of thought and activity he believed what was told him by those in authority. He learned the catechism and thought it was the direct word of God. When he fell sick and the doctor came, he put himself in the doctor's hands with a sense of perfect trust and content; the doctor knew what to do, and would do it, and the little boy would get well.

The boy's grandfather had been a Confederate naval officer, drowned at sea. The boy's father had spent his youth in Virginia during the agonies of the Civil War, thus missing most of his education. After the war the family was ruined, and the father had to enter into competition with Yankee "hustle," handicapped by a Southern gentleman's quaint notions of dignity, and also by a Southern gentleman's weakness for mint-juleps. So the last week's board bill was generally a matter of anxiety to the family. But always, no matter how poor the family might be, the little boy had a clean white collar, and a copy of the "New York Sun" every morning. This paper was beautifully printed, smooth and neat; the little boy knew all its peculiarities of type, and he and his father and his mother accepted every word they read in it, both the news-columns and the editorial page, precisely as they accepted the doctor's pills and the clergyman's sermons, the Bible and the multiplication table and Marian Harland's cookbook.

The "New York Sun" was edited by one of the bitterest cynics that ever lived in America. He had been something of a radical in his early days, and had turned like a fierce wolf upon his young ideals. He had one fixed opinion, which was that everything new in the world should be mocked at and denounced. He had a diabolical wit, and had taught a tradition to his staff, and had infected a good part of American Journalism with the poison of his militant cynicism. Once every twenty-four hours the little boy absorbed this poison, he took it for truth, and made all his ideas of it.

For example, there were women who were trying to be different from what women had always been. There was a thing called "Sorosis." The boy never knew what "Sorosis" was; from the "Sun" he gathered that it was a collection of women who wanted to have brains, and to take part in public affairs—whereas the "Sun" acidly considered that woman's place was the home. And the boy found it easy to agree with this. Did not the boy's grandmother make the best ginger-cakes of any grandmother in the whole city of Baltimore? Did not his mother make the best chocolate-cake and the best "hot short-cake"—that is, whenever the family could escape from boarding-houses and have a little kitchen of its own. The boy was enormously fond of chocolate-cake and short-cake, and of course he didn't want women neglecting their duties for fool things such as "Sorosis."

Also there were the Populists. The little boy had never seen a Populist, he had never been given an opportunity to read a Populist platform, but he knew all about the Populists from the funny editorials of Charles A. Dana. The Populists were long-haired and wild-eyed animals whose habitat was the corn-fields of Kansas. The boy knew the names of a lot of them, or rather the nick-names which Dana gave them; he had a whole portrait-gallery of them in his mind. Once upon a time the "Sun" gave some statistics from Kansas, suggesting that the Populists were going insane; so the little boy took his pen in hand and wrote a letter to the editor of the "Sun," gravely rebuking him. He had never expected to read in the columns of the "Sun" a suggestion that Populists might *go* insane. And the "Sun" published this feeble product of its own "smartness."

Later on the boy discovered the "New York Evening Post," the *beau ideal* of a gentleman's newspaper, and this became for years his main source of culture. The "Evening Post" was edited by E. L. Godkin, a scholar and a lover of righteousness, but narrow, and with an abusive tongue. From him the boy learned that American politics were rotten, and he learned the cause of the rottenness: First, there was an ignorant mob, composed mainly of foreigners; and second, there were venal politicians who pandered to this mob. Efforts were continually being made by gentlemen of decency and culture to take the government away from these venal politicians, but the mob was too ignorant, and could not be persuaded to support a clean government. Yet the fight must be kept up, because conditions were going from bad to worse. The boy witnessed several "reform campaigns," conducted mainly by the "Evening Post" and other newspapers. These campaigns consisted in the publication of full-page exposures of civic rottenness, with denunciations of the politicians in office. The boy believed every word of the exposures, and it never occurred to him that the newspapers might be selling more copies by means of them; still less did it occur to him that anybody might be finding in these excitements a means of diverting the mind of the public from larger and more respectable forms of "graft."

There was a candidate for district attorney, William Travers Jerome by name; a man with a typical "Evening Post" mind, making an ideal "Evening Post" candidate. He conducted a "whirlwind" campaign, speaking at half a dozen meetings every evening, and stirring his audience to frenzy by his accounts of the corruption of the city's police-force. Men would stand up and shout with indignation, women would faint or weep. The boy would sit with his finger-nails dug into the palms of his hands, while the orator tore away the veils from subjects which were generally kept hidden from little boys.

The orator described the system of prostitution, which was paying its millions every year to the police of the city. He pictured a room in which women displayed their persons, and men walked up and down and inspected them, selecting one as they would select an animal at a fair. The man paid his three dollars, or his five dollars, to a cashier at the window, and received a brass check; then he went upstairs, and paid this check to the woman upon receipt of her favors. And suddenly the orator put his hand into his pocket and drew forth tne bit of metal. "Behold!" he cried. "The price of a woman's shame!"

To the lad in the audience this BRASS CHECK was the symbol of the most monstrous wickedness in the world. Night after night he would attend these meetings, and next day he would read about them in the papers. He was a student at college, living in a lodging-house room on four dollars a week, which he earned himself; yet he pitched in to help this orator's campaign, and raised something over a hundred dollars, and took it to the "Evening Post" candidate at his club, interrupting him at dinner, and no doubt putting a strain on his patience. The candidate was swept into office in a tornado of excitement, and did what all "Evening Post" candidates did and always do—that is, nothing. For four long years the lad waited, in bewilderment and disgust, ending in rage. So he learned the grim lesson that there is more than one kind of parasite feeding on human weakness, there is more than one kind of prostitution which may be symbolized by the BRASS CHECK.

CHAPTER II

THE STORY OF A POET

The boy, now become a youth, obtained a letter of introduction from his clergyman to the editor of his beloved "Evening Post," and at the age of sixteen was given a trial as reporter. He worked for a week collecting odd scraps of news, and when the week was over he had earned the generous sum of two dollars and sixty-seven cents. This was his first and last experience as newspaper reporter, and it confirmed his boyish impression of the integrity of the journalistic profession. His work had consisted of compiling obituary notices about leading citizens who had died. "John T. McGurk, senior partner of McGurk and Isaacson, commission-merchants of 679 Desbrosses Street, died yesterday of cirrhosis of the liver at his home, 4321 George Washington Avenue, Hoboken. Mr. McGurk was 69 years of age, and leaves a widow and eleven children. He was a member of the Elks, and president of the North Hoboken Bowling Association." And these facts the "Evening Post" printed exactly as he had written them. In a book which will not have much to say in favor of American Journalism, let this fidelity to truth, and to the memory of the blameless McGurk, have its due meed of praise.

The youth took to writing jokes and jingles, at which he earned twice as much as the "Evening Post" had paid him. Later on he took to writing dime-novels, at which he made truly fabulous sums. He found it puzzling that this cheap and silly writing should be the kind that brought the money. The editors told him it was because the public wanted that kind; but the youth wondered—might not at least part of the blame lie with the editors, who never tried giving anything better? It was the old problem—which comes first, the hen or the egg?

We have spoken jestingly of the traditions of the old South, in which the youth was brought up; but the reader should not get a false impression of them—in many ways they were excellent traditions. For one thing, they taught the youth to despise a lie; also to hate injustice, so that wherever in his life he encountered it, his whole being became a blaze of excitement. Always he was striving in his mind to discover the source of lies and injustice—why should there be so much of them in the world? The newspapers revealed the existence of them, but never seemed to know the causes of them, nor what to do about them, further than to support a reform candidate who did nothing but get elected. This futility in the face of the world's misery and corruption was maddening to the youth.

He had rich relatives who were fond of him, so that he was free to escape from poverty into luxury; he had the opportunity to rise quickly in the world, if he would go into business, and devote his attention thereto. But would he find in business the ideals which he craved? He talked with business men, also he got the flavor of business from the advertisements in the newspapers—and he knew that this was not what he was seeking. He cultivated the friendship of Jesus, Hamlet and Shelley, and fell in love with the young Milton and the young Goethe; in them he found his own craving for truth and beauty. Here, through the medium of art, life might be ennobled, and lifted from the muck of graft and greed.

So the youth ran away and buried himself in a hut in the wilds of Canada, and wrote what he thought was the great American novel. It was a painfully crude performance, but it had a new moral impulse in it, and the youth really believed that it was to convert the world to ways of love and justice. He took it to the publishers, and one after another they rejected it. They admitted that it had merit, but it would not sell. Incredible as it seemed to the youth, the test by which the publishers judged an embryo book and its right to be born, was not whether it had vision and beauty and a new moral impulse; they judged it as the newspapers judged what they published—would it sell? The youth earned some money and published the book himself, and wrote a preface to tell the world what a wonderful book it was, and how the cruel publishers had rejected it. This preface, together with the book, he sent to the leading newspapers; and thus began the second stage of his journalistic experiences!

Two newspapers paid attention to his communication—the "New York Times," a respectable paper, and the "New York American," a "yellow" paper. The "American" sent a woman

reporter, an agreeable and friendly young lady, to whom the
author poured out his soul. She asked for his picture, saying
that this would enable her to get much more space for the
story; so the author gave his picture. She asked for his wife's
picture; but here the author was obdurate. He had old-
fashioned Southern notions about "newspaper notoriety" for
ladies; he did not want his wife's picture in the papers. There
stood a little picture of his wife on the table where the interview
took place, and after the reporter had left, it was noticed
that this picture was missing. Next day the picture was
published in the "New York American," and has been published in the "New York American" every year or two since.
The author, meantime, has divorced his first wife and married
a second wife—a fact of which the newspapers are fully
aware; yet they publish this picture of the first wife indif-
ferently as a picture of the first wife and of the second wife.
When one of these ladies says or does a certain thing, the
other lady may open her paper in the morning and receive
a shock!

Both the "New York Times" and the "New York
American" published interviews with the young author. It had
been his fond hope to interest people in his book and to cause
them to read his book, but in this he failed; what both the
interviews told about was his personality. The editors had
been amused by the naïve assumption of a young poet that
he might have something of importance to say to the world;
they had made a "human interest" story out of it, a journalistic
tidbit to tickle the appetites of the jaded and worldly-wise.
They said scarcely anything about the contents of the book,
and as a result of the two interviews, the hungry young author
sold precisely two copies!

Meantime he was existing by hack-work, and exploring
the world in which ideas are bought and sold. He was having
jokes and plots of stories stolen; he was having agreements
broken and promises repudiated; he was trying to write
worth-while material, and being told that it would not sell;
he was trying to become a book-reviewer, and finding that the
only way to succeed was to be a cheat. The editor of the
"Independent" or the "Literary Digest" would give him half
a dozen books to read, and he would read them, and write
an honest review, saying that there was very little merit in
any of them: whereupon, the editor would decide that it was

not worth while to review the books, and the author would get nothing for his work. If, on the other hand, he wrote an article about a book, taking it seriously, and describing it as vital and important, the editor would conclude that the book was worth reviewing, and would publish the review, and pay the author three or four dollars for it.

This, you understand, was the "literary world," in which ideas, the most priceless possession of mankind, were made the subject of barter and sale. In every branch of it there were such petty dishonesties, such tricks of the trade. There were always ten times as many people trying to get a living as the trade would support. They were clutching at chances, elbowing each other out of the way; and their efforts were not rewarded according to their love of truth and beauty, but according to quite other factors. They were dressing themselves up and using the "social game," they were posing and pretending, the women were using the sex-lure. And everywhere, when they pretended to care about literature and ideas, they were really caring about money, and "success" because it would bring money. Everywhere, above all things else, they hated and feared the very idea of genius, which put them to shame, and threatened with annihilation their petty gains and securities.

From these things the youth fled into the wilderness again, living in a tent with his young wife, and writing a story in which he poured out his contempt upon the great Metropolis of Mammon. This was "Prince Hagen," and he sent it to the "Atlantic Monthly," and there came a letter from the editor, Professor Bliss Perry, saying that it was a work of merit and that he would publish it. So for weeks the young author walked on the top of the clouds. But then came another letter, saying that the other members of the "Atlantic" staff had read the story, and that Professor Perry had been unable to persuade them to see it as he saw it. "We have," said he, "a very conservative, fastidious and sophisticated constituency."

The young author went back to his "pot-boiling." He spent another winter in New York, wrestling with disillusionments and humiliations, and then, fleeing to the wilderness for a third summer, he put his experience into "The Journal of Arthur Stirling," the story of a young poet who is driven to suicide by neglect and despair. The book was given to the world as a genuine document, and relieved the tedium of a

literary season. Its genuineness was accepted almost everywhere, and the author sat behind the scenes, feeling quite
devilish. When the secret came out, some critics were cross,
and one or two of them have not yet forgiven the writer.
The "New York Evening Post" is accustomed to mention the
matter every once in a while, declaring that the person who
played that trick can never receive anyone's confidence. I
will not waste space discussing this question, save to point out
that the newspaper reviewers had set the rules of the game—
that love and beauty in art were heeded only in connection
with personalities and sensation; so, in order to project love
and beauty upon the world, the young author had provided
the personalities and sensation. As for the "Evening Post"
and its self-righteousness, before I finish this book I shall tell
of things done by that organ of Wall Street which qualify
decidedly its right to sit in judgment upon questions of honor.

CHAPTER III

OPEN SESAME !

My next effort was "Manassas," a novel of the Civil war. I poured into it all my dream of what America might be, and inscribed it: "That the men of this land may know the heritage that has come down to them." But the men of this land were not in any way interested in the heritage that had come down to them. The men of this land were making money. The newspapers of this land were competing for advertisements of whiskey and cigars and soap, and the men who wrote book-reviews for the literary pages of these newspapers were chuckling over such works of commercial depravity as "The Letters of a Self-Made Merchant to His Son." They had no time to tell the public about "Manassas"; though Jack London called it "the best Civil War book I've read," and though it is my one book which no severest critic can say has any propaganda motive. Charlotte Perkins Gilman told me a story of how she persuaded an old Civil War veteran to read it. The old fellow didn't want to read any book about the war by a youngster; he had been through it all himself, and no youngster could tell him anything. But Mrs. Gilman persisted, and when she met him again she found him with shining eyes and a look of wonder on his face. "It's the War!" he cried. "It's the War—and he wasn't even born!"

It happened that at this time Lincoln Steffens was publishing his terrible exposés of the corruption of American civic life. Steffens did for the American people one specific service. He knocked out forever the notion, of which E. L. Godkin and his "New York Evening Post" were the principal exponents, that our political corruption was to be blamed upon "the ignorant foreign element." Steffens showed that purely American communities, such as Rhode Island, were the most corrupt of all; and he traced back the corruption, showing that for every man who took a bribe there was another man who gave one, and that the giver of the bribe made from ten to a thousand times as much as he paid. In other words, American political corruption was the buying up of legislatures and assemblies to keep them from doing the people's will and protecting the people's interests; it was the exploiter entrenching himself in power, it was financial autocracy undermining and destroying political democracy.

Steffens did not go so far as that in the early days. He just laid bare the phenomena, and then stopped. You searched in vain through the articles which he published in "McClure's" for any answer to the question: What is to be done about it? So I wrote what I called "An Open Letter to Lincoln Steffens." I cannot find it now, but I recall the essence of it well enough.

"Mr. Steffens, you go from city to city and from state to state, and you show us these great corporations buying public privileges and capitalizing them for tens and hundreds of millions of dollars, and unloading the securities upon the general investing public. You show this enormous mass of capital piling up, increasing at compound interest, demanding its toll of dividends, which we, the people who do the hard work of the world, who produce the real wealth of the world, must continue forever to pay. I ask you to tell us, what are we to do about this? Shall we go on forever paying tribute upon this mass of bribery and fraud? *Can* we go on paying it forever, even if we want to? And if not, what then? What will happen when we refuse to pay?"

I sent this letter to Steffens, to see what he thought about it. He replied that it was the best criticism of his work that he had seen, and he tried to persuade "McClure's" to publish it, but in vain. I forget whether it was he or I who sent it to "Collier's Weekly"; but anyway, the article was read and accepted, and Robert J. Collier, the publisher, wrote and asked me to come to see him.

Picture me at this moment, a young writer of twenty-five who has been pleading with the American public to remember its high traditions, and has seen his plea fall flat, because the newspapers and magazines overlooked him; also—a painful detail, but important—who has been supporting a wife and baby on thirty dollars a month, and has been paid only five hundred dollars for two years work on a novel. A friend who knows the literary world tells me that this is the chance of my life. "Collier's" is run "on a personal basis," it appears; a sort of family affair. "If Robbie likes you, your fortune is made," says my friend. "This is your 'open sesame' to the public mind."

Well, I go to see Robbie, and it appears that Robbie likes me. I am young and ascetic-looking; the tension under which I have worked has given me dyspepsia, so my cheeks are hollow and my skin is white and my eyes have a hectic shine. Robbie, no doubt, is moved to sympathy by these phenomena; he himself is a picture of health, florid and jolly, a polo-player, what is called a "good fellow." He asks me, will I come to dinner at his home and meet some of his friends and his editorial staff? I answer that of course I will.

My worldly-wise friend insists that I shall invest my spare savings in a dress-suit, but I do not take this advice. I go to Robbie's palatial home in my old clothes, and Robbie's velvet-footed butler escorts me upstairs to Robbie's dressing-room, where Robbie's valet is laying out his things on the bed. And while Robbie is dressing, he tells me again how much he admires my article. It is the most illuminating discussion of present-day problems that he has ever read. He and his friends don't meet many Socialists, naturally, so I am to tell them about Socialism. I am to tell them everything, and needn't be afraid. I answer, quite simply, that I shall not be in the least afraid.

The evening was spoiled because Robbie's father came in. Old Peter Collier was a well-known character in New York "society"; but as not all my readers have been intimate in these circles, I explain that he had begun life as a pack-peddler, had started "Collier's Weekly" as an advertisement sheet, and by agents offering books as premiums had built up a tremendous circulation. Now he was rich and important; vulgar, ignorant as a child, but kind-hearted, jovial—one of those nice, fatherly old fellows who put their arms about you, no matter who you are.

And here he had come in to dinner with his son, and found his son entertaining a Socialist. *"What?* What's this?" he cried. It was like a scene in a comedy. He would hear one sentence of what I had to say, and then he would go up in the air. "Why—why—that's perfectly outrageous! Who ever heard of such a thing?" He would sputter for five or ten minutes, to the vast amusement of the rest of the guests.

Presently he heard about the "Open Letter to Lincoln Steffens." "What's this? You are going to publish an article like that in my magazine? *No, sir!* I won't have it! It's preposterous!" And there sat Robbie, who was supposed to

be the publisher; there sat Norman Hapgood, who was supposed to be the editor—and listened to Old Peter lay down
the law. Norman Hapgood has since stated that he does not
remember this episode, that he never knew Peter Collier to
interfere with the policy of the magazine. Well, the reader
may believe that the incident was not one that I would forget
in a hurry. Not if I should live to be as old as Methuselah
will I forget my emotions, when, after the dinner, the old
gentleman got me off in a corner and put his arm around
my shoulders. "You are a nice boy, and I can see that you've
got brains, you know what you're talking about. But what
you ought to do is to put these ideas of yours into a book.
Why do you try to get them into my magazine, and scare
away my half million subscribers?"

I went home that evening feeling more sick at heart than
I like to remember. And sure enough, my worst fears were
justified. Week after week passed, and my Open Letter to
Lincoln Steffens did not appear in the columns of "Collier's
Weekly." I wrote and protested, and was met with evasions;
a long time afterwards, I forget how long, "Collier's" graciously condescended to give me back the article, without asking the return of the two hundred dollars they had paid me.
The article was rejected by many other capitalist magazines,
and was finally published in some Socialist paper, I forget
which.

Such is the picture of a magazine "run on a personal basis."
And see what it means to you, the reader, who depend upon
such a magazine for the thoughts you think. Here is Lincoln
Steffens, taking his place as America's leading authority on the
subject of political graft; and here am I, making what Steffens
declares is the best criticism of his work. It is accepted and
paid for, and a date is set to give it to you, the reader; but
an ignorant and childish old pack-peddler steps in, and with
one wave of his hand sweeps it out of your sight. Sixteen
years have passed, and only now you hear about it—and most
of you don't hear about it even now!

But here is a vital point to get clear. The old pack-peddler
wiped out my discussion of the question, but he did not wipe
out the question. To-day the question is cried aloud from the
throats of a hundred and eighty million people in Russia, and
the clamor of it spreads all over Europe, a deafening roar
which drowns out the eloquence of statesmen and diplomats.

It is the question of the hour in America, and America must find the answer under penalty of civil war. Sixteen years ago the answer was given to Robert Collier, and if he had had the courage to stand out against his father, if Norman Hapgood had been what he pretended to be, an editor, they would have taken up the truth which I put before them, they would have conducted a campaign to make the American people see it—and to-day we should not be trying to solve the social problem by putting the leaders of the people's protest into jail.

CHAPTER IV

THE REAL FIGHT

There was a strike of the wage-slaves of the Beef Trust in Chicago, and I wrote for the "Appeal to Reason" a broadside addressed to these strikers, trying to point out to them the truth which Peter Collier had concealed from his precious half million subscribers. This broadside was taken up by the Socialists of the Stockyards district, and thirty thousand copies were distributed among the defeated strikers. The "Appeal to Reason" offered me five hundred dollars to live on while I wrote a novel dealing with the life of those wage-slaves of the Beef Trust; so I went to Packingtown, and lived for seven weeks among the workers, and came home again and wrote "The Jungle."

Now so far the things that had been done to me by the world of American Journalism had been of a mocking nature. I had been a sort of "guy"; a young poet—very young—who believed that he had "genius," and kept making a noise about it. So I was pigeon-holed with long-haired violinists from abroad, and painters with fancy-colored vests, and woman suffragists with short hair, and religious prophets in purple robes. All such things are lumped together by newspapers, which are good-naturedly tolerant of their fellow fakers. The public likes to be amused, and "genius" is one of the things that amuse it: such is the attitude of a world which understands that money is the one thing in life really worth while, the making of money the one object of grown-up and serious-minded men.

But from now on you will see that there enters into my story a new note. The element of horse-play goes out, and something grim takes its place. And what is the reason for this change? Was there any change in me? Did I suddenly become dissipated, dishonest, self-seeking? No, there was no change in me; I was the same person, living the same life. But I ceased to oppose social wickedness with the fragile weapon of poetry, with visions and inspirations and consecrations; instead, I took a sharp sword of contemporary fact, and thrust it into the vitals of one of those monstrous parasites which are sucking the life-blood of the American people. That was the difference; and if from now on you find in this story a note of fierce revolt, please understand that you are listening to a man who for fourteen years had been in a battle, and has seen his cause suffering daily wounds from a cruel and treacherous foe.

My first experience, it happened, was with "Collier's Weekly." But it was not a dinner-party experience this time, there was no element of friendliness or sociability in it.

"The Jungle" was appearing serially, and was causing a tremendous lot of discussion; it occurred to me that it might be possible to persuade "Collier's" to take up the matter, so I wrote an article, telling quite simply some of the things that were going on in the packing-houses of Chicago. I had been there, and had seen—and not as a blundering amateur, as the packers charged. It happened that I had met in Chicago an Englishman, Mr. Adolph Smith, the world's greatest authority on packing-houses. He had studied methods of meat-packing all over Great Britain, and all over the continent of Europe, for the "London Lancet," the leading medical paper of Great Britain. He had come, as authorized representative of the "Lancet," to investigate conditions in America. I had his backing in what I wrote; I also had the backing of various State and Federal authorities; I had the text of the Federal meat-inspection law, which had been written by the packers to enable them to sell diseased meat with impunity.

I took all these facts to Norman Hapgood and Robert Collier. I offered them the opportunity to reap the fame and profit which I subsequently reaped from the book-publication of "The Jungle," and incidentally to do a great public service. They were interested, but not convinced, and they employed a United States army-officer, Major Louis L. Seaman, who went out to Chicago and accepted the hospitality of the packers, and reported that all my charges were exaggerated, and most of them entirely false. And Collier and Hapgood accepted Major Seaman's word against my word and the authorities I offered.

That was all right; I had no complaint against that; they used their editorial judgment. My complaint was of the way they handled the story. In their preliminary announcement (April 15, 1905) they said:

Some very brilliant articles have been sent us about the un-hygienic methods of the Beef Trust. In order not to run any risk of wronging that organization we engaged Major Seaman to go to Chicago, and his first report will appear next week.

So, you see, they were going to give an illustration of editorial fairness, of scrupulous regard for exact truth; and having thus prepared their readers, on April 22, 1905, they presented their material—a long article by Major Seaman, praising the Chicago Stockyards, and pretending to refute all my charges. At the same time they published only three paragraphs of my charges—the great bulk of my articles they left unpublished! They gave their readers a few paragraphs from the "London Lancet," but so far as concerned me, the readers got only the answers of Major Seaman, and an introductory editorial condemnation of me, explaining that I had submitted my articles to the editors, and they, "desirous of securing the unexaggerated facts," had sent Major Seaman to Chicago, and now gave his findings.

And this not being enough, they added a discussion of the matter on their editorial page. This editorial they headed, "Sensationalism"; and they subtly phrased it to give the impression that the paragraphs they were publishing constituted all I had to say: "Mr. Sinclair's article, published alone, would have produced much more of a sensation than it will produce as mitigated by the report of Major Seaman . . . . Having some doubt, however, about the real facts, we induced Major Seaman to make the trip to Chicago. This incident will serve as an example of the policy mapped out for the conduct of this paper."

How dignified and impressive! And how utterly and un-speakably knavish! And when I wrote to them and protested, they evaded. When I demanded that they publish my entire article, they refused. When I demanded that they publish my letter of protest, they refused that. And this was done by Norman Hapgood, who posed as a liberal, a lover of justice; a man who spent his editorial time balancing like a tight-rope walker on the narrow thread of truth, occupying himself like a medieval schoolman with finding the precise mathematical or metaphysical dead centre between the contending forces of conservatism and radicalism. A friend of mine talked with him about his treatment of me and reported him as saying, with a smile: "We backed the wrong horse." The truth was, he had backed the horse of gold, the horse that came to his office loaded down with full-page advertisements of packing-house products.

"Collier's" calls itself "The National Weekly," and has obtained a reputation as a liberal organ, upon the strength of several useful campaigns. It attacked spiritualist fakers and land-fraud grafters; also it attacked dishonest medical advertising. It could do this, having arrived at the stage of security where it counts upon full-page advertisements of automobiles and packing-house products. But when it was a question of attacking packing-house advertisements—then what a difference!

Robert J. Collier was a gentleman and a "good fellow"; but he was a child of his world, and his world was a rotten one, a "second generation" of idle rich spendthrifts. The running of his magazine "on a personal basis" amounted to this: a young writer would catch the public fancy, and Robbie would send for him, as he sent for me; if he proved to be a possible person—that is, if he came to dinner in a dress-suit, and didn't discuss the socialization of "Collier's Weekly"—Robbie would take him up and introduce him to his "set," and the young writer would have a perpetual market for his stories at a thousand dollars per story; he would be invited to country-house parties, he would motor and play golf and polo, and flirt with elegant young society ladies, and spend his afternoons loafing in the Hoffman House bar. I could name not one but a dozen young writers and illustrators to whom I have seen that happen. In the beginning they wrote about America, in the end they wrote about the "smart set" of Fifth Avenue and Long Island. In their personal life they became tipplers and café celebrities; in their intellectual life they became bitter cynics; into their writings you saw creeping year by year the subtle poison of sexual excess—until at last they became too far gone for "Collier's" to tolerate any longer, and went over to the "Cosmopolitan," which takes them no matter how far gone they are.

And now young Collier is dead, and the magazine to which for a time he gave his generous spirit has become an instrument of reaction pure and simple. It opposed and ridiculed President Wilson's peace policies; it called the world to war against the working-class of Russia; it is now calling for repression of all social protest in America; in short, it is an American capitalist magazine. As I write, word comes that it has been taken over by the Crowell Publishing Company, publishers of the "Woman's Home Companion," "Farm and Fireside," and the "American Magazine." I shall have something to the point to say about this group of publications very soon.

P. S.—A well known journalist writes me that he feels I do an injustice to Norman Hapgood in telling the above story, and in failing to give credit to Hapgood for other fine things he has done. The writer brings facts, and I am always ready to give place to the man with facts. I quote his letter:

"Do you know the circumstances of Hapgood's break with Collier? Hapgood was the highest paid editor of any periodical in the country. The business side was encroaching on the editorial—demanding that advertising be not jeopardized, and with it the commissions that were its part. Collier, as you know, for years had mixed his whiskey with chorus girls, and needed all the property could milk to supply his erratic needs. So the business office had his ear. And Hapgood left—and made his leaving effective. He took Harper's and gave the country some of the most important exposés it had. Do you know the story of the Powder Trust treason? I wrote it. It was drawn from official records, and could not be contradicted, that the Powder Trust had once made a contract with a German military powder firm—in the days when military smokeless powder was the goal of every government—to keep it informed as to the quantity, quality, etc., of the smokeless powder it furnished to our government. And this was in the days when we were in the lead in that department. The Powder Trust jumped Hapgood hard. He could have had anything he wanted by making a simple disavowal of me, any loophole they would have accepted—and do you have any doubt that he could have named his own terms? He declined point blank, and threw the challenge to the heaviest and most important client his weekly could have had. That he guessed wrong and 'backed the wrong horse' in the 'Jungle' may be true. But isn't it fair to assume, in the light of his final challenge to the Collier advertising autocracy, that he was meeting problems inside as best he could—and that he could not tell you at the time of all the factors involved in the Collier handling of the stockyards story?"

CHAPTER V

THE CONDEMNED MEAT INDUSTRY

"The Jungle" had been accepted in advance by the Macmillan Company. Mr. Brett, president of the company, read the manuscript, and asked me to cut out some of the more shocking and bloody details, assuring me that he could sell ten times as many copies of the book if I would do this. So here again I had to choose between my financial interest and my duty. I took the proposition to Lincoln Steffens, who said: "The things you tell are unbelievable. I have a rule in my own work—I don't tell things that are unbelievable, even when they are true."

Nevertheless, I was unwilling to make the changes. I offered the book to four other publishers, whose names I do not now remember; then I began preparations to publish it myself. I wrote to Jack London, who came to my help with his usual impetuous generosity, writing a resounding call to the Socialists of the country, which was published in the "Appeal to Reason." The result was that in a couple of months I took in four thousand dollars. The Socialists had been reading the story in the "Appeal," and were thoroughly aroused.

I had the book set up and the plates made, when some one suggested Doubleday, Page and Company, so I showed the work to them. Walter H. Page sent for me. He was a dear old man, the best among business-men I have met. There were several hustling young money-makers in his firm, who saw a fortune in "The Jungle," and desperately wanted to publish it. But Page was anxious; he must be sure that every word was true. We had a luncheon conference, and I was cross-questioned on every point. A week or two passed, and I was summoned again, and Herbert S. Houston of the firm explained that he had a friend, James Keeley, editor of the "Chicago Tribune," to whom he had taken the liberty of submitting my book. Here was a letter from Keeley—I read the letter—saying that he had sent his best reporter, a trusted man, to make a thorough report upon "The Jungle." And here was

the report, thirty-two typewritten pages, taking up every statement about conditions in the yards, and denying one after
another.

I read the report, and recall one amusing detail. On page
one hundred and sixteen of "The Jungle" is a description of
the old packing-houses, their walls covered with grease and
soaked with warm moist steam. "In these rooms the germs of
tuberculosis might live for two years." The comment upon
this statement was: "Unproven theory." So it was necessary
for me to consult the text-books on bacteriology, and demonstrate to Doubleday, Page and Company that unicellular para-
sitic organisms are sometimes endowed with immortality!

I said: "This is not an honest report. The thing you have
to do, if you really wish to know, is to send an investigator of
your own, somebody in whom you have confidence." They
decided this must be done, and picked a young lawyer, McKee
by name, and sent him to Chicago. He spent some time there,
and when he came back his verdict was that I had told the
truth. I went to dinner at McKee's home and spent the
evening hearing his story—incidentally getting one of the
shocks of my life.

McKee had done what I had urged him not to do: he had
gone first to the packers, to see what they had officially to show
him. They had placed him in charge of a man—I do not recall
the name, but we will say Jones—their publicity agent, a
former newspaper man, who served as host and entertainer to
inquiring visitors. He had taken McKee in charge and shown
him around, and in the course of their conversation McKee
mentioned that he was looking into the charges made in a
novel called "The Jungle." "Oh, yes!" said Jones. "I know
that book. I read it from beginning to end. I prepared a
thirty-two page report on it for Keeley of the 'Tribune'."

So here was a little glimpse behind the curtain of the newspaper world of Chicago! James Keeley was, and still is the
beau ideal of American newspaper men; I have never met him,
but I have read articles about him, the kind of "write-ups"
which the capitalist system gives to its heroes. He had begun
life as a poor boy and risen from the ranks by sheer ability
and force of character—you know the "dope." Now he was
one of the high gods of newspaperdom; and when it was a
question of protecting the great predatory interest which subsidizes all the newspapers of Chicago and holds the govern-

ment of the city in the hollow of its hand, this high god sent to Armour and Company and had a report prepared by their publicity-agent, and sent this report to a friend in New York as the result of a confidential investigation by a trusted reporter of the "Chicago Tribune" staff!

And maybe you think this must be an unusual incident; you think that capitalist Journalism would not often dare to play a trick like that! I happen to be reading "Socialism versus the State," by Emile Vandervelde, Belgian Minister of State, and come upon this paragraph:

> It will be remembered, for example, that the "London Times" published, a few years ago, a series of unsigned articles, emanating, it was said from an impartial observer, against the municipal lighting systems in England. These articles made the tour of Europe. They furnish, even today, arguments for the opponents of municipalization. Now, a short time after their publication, it was learned that the "impartial observer" was the general manager of one of the big electric light and power companies of London.

Doubleday, Page and Company published "The Jungle," and it became the best-selling book, not only in America, but also in Great Britain and its colonies, and was translated into seventeen languages. It became also the subject of a terrific political controversy.

The packers, fighting for their profits, brought all their batteries to bear. To begin with, there appeared in the "Saturday Evening Post" a series of articles signed by J. Ogden Armour, but written, I was informed, by Forrest Crissey, one of the staff of the "Post." The editor of this paper, George Horace Lorimer, was for nine years an employee of the Armours; he is author of "The Letters of a Self-Made Merchant to His Son," a text-book of American business depravity. From first to last his paper was at the service of the packers, as it has always been at the service of every great financial interest.

Some of the statements made under Armour's signature made me boil, and I sat down to write an answer, "The Condemned Meat Industry." I had the facts at my fingers ends, and wrote the article in a few hours, and jumped on the train and came up to New York with it. I took it to the office of "Everybody's Magazine" and asked to see E. J. Ridgway, the publisher. I was wise enough by this time to understand that it is the publisher, not the editor, you need to see. I read the article to Ridgway, and he stopped the presses on which "Everybody's Magazine" was being printed, and took out a short story and shoved in "The Condemned Meat Industry."

"Everybody's Magazine" at this time was on the crest of a wave of popularity. It had finished Tom Lawson's exposé of Wall Street, upon the strength of which it had built up a circulation of half a million. Its publishers, Ridgway and Thayer, were advertising men who had bought a broken-down magazine from John Wanamaker, and had made the discovery that there was a fortune to be made by the simple process of letting the people have the truth. They wanted to go on making fortunes, and so they welcomed my article. It gave the affidavits of men whom the Armours had employed to take condemned meat out of the destructors and sell it in Chicago. It told the story of how the Armours had bribed these men to retract their confessions. It gave the reports of State health authorities, who showed how the Armours had pleaded guilty to adulterating foods. It was a mass of such facts fused in a white heat of indignation. United States Senator Beveridge told me that he considered the article the greatest piece of controversial writing he had ever read.

You may find it in the library, "Everybody's" for May, 1906. Whatever you think of its literary style, you will see that it is definite and specific, and revealed a most frightful condition in the country's meat supply, an unquestionable danger to the public health. It was therefore a challenge to every public service agency in the country; above all, it was a challenge to the newspapers, through which the social body is supposed to learn of its dangers and its needs.

It was my first complete test of American Journalism. Hitherto I had tried the newspapers as a young poet, clamoring for recognition; they had called me a self-seeker, and although I felt that the charge was untrue, I was powerless to disprove it to others. But now I tried them in a matter that was obviously in the public interest—too obviously so for dispute. I was still naïve enough to be shocked by the result. I had expected that every newspaper which boasted of public spirit would take up these charges, and at least report them; but instead of that, there was silence—silence almost complete! I employed two clipping-bureaus on this story, and received a few brief items from scattered papers here and there. Of all

the newspapers in America, not one in two hundred went so
far as to mention "The Condemned Meat Industry."

Meantime "The Jungle" had been published in book form.
I will say of "The Jungle" just what I said of the magazine
article—whatever you may think of it as literature, you must
admit that it was packed with facts which constituted an appeal
to the American conscience. The book was sent to all American
newspapers; also it was widely advertised, it was boosted by
one of the most efficient publicity men in the country. And
what were the results? I will give a few illustrations.

The most widely read newspaper editor in America is
Arthur Brisbane. Brisbane poses as a liberal, sometimes even
as a radical; he told me that he drank in Socialism with his
mother's milk. And Brisbane now took me up, just as Robbie
Collier had done; he invited me to his home, and wrote one
of his famous two-column editorials about "The Jungle"— a
rare compliment to a young author. This editorial treated me
personally with kindness; I was a sensitive young poet who had
visited the stockyards for the first time, and had been horrified
by the discovery that animals had blood inside them. With a
fatherly pat on the shoulder, Brisbane informed me that a
slaughter-house is not an opera-house, or words to that effect.

I remember talking about this editorial with Adolph Smith,
representative of the "London Lancet." He remarked with
dry sarcasm that in a court of justice Brisbane would be entirely safe; his statement that a slaughter-house is not an
opera-house was strictly and literally accurate. But if you
took what the statement was meant to convey to the reader—
that a slaughter-house is necessarily filthy, then the statement was false. "If you go to the municipal slaughter-houses
of Germany, you find them as free from odor as an opera-
house," said Adolph Smith; and five or six years later, when
I visited Germany, I took the opportunity to verify this statement. But because of the kindness of American editorial
writers to the interests which contribute full-page advertisements to newspapers, the American people still have their meat
prepared in filth.

Or take the "Outlook." The "Outlook" poses as a liberal
publication; its editor preaches what he calls "Industrial
Democracy," a very funny joke. I have dealt with this organ
of the "Clerical Camouflage" in five sections of "The Profits
of Religion"; I will not repeat here, except to quote how the

pious "Outlook" dealt with "The Jungle." The "Outlook" had no doubt that there were genuine evils in the packing-plants; the conditions of the workers ought of course to be improved, BUT—

To disgust the reader by dragging him through every conceivable horror, physical and moral, to depict with lurid excitement and with offensive minuteness the life in jail and brothel—all this is to over-reach the object . . . . Even things actually terrible may become dis-torted when a writer screams them out in a sensational way and in a high pitched key . . . . More convincing if it were less hysterical.

Also Elbert Hubbard rushed to the rescue of his best advertising clients. Later in this book you will find a chapter dealing especially with the seer of East Aurora; for the present I will merely quote his comments on my packing-house revel-ations. His attack upon "The Jungle" was reprinted by the Chicago packers, and mailed out to the extent of a million copies; every clergyman and every physician in the country received one. I have a copy of his article, as it was sent out by a newspaper syndicate in the form of "plate-matter." It occupies four newspaper columns, with these head-lines:

ELBERT HUBBARD LASHES THE MUCK-RAKER CROWD.

Says "The Jungle" Book is a Libel and an Insult to Intelligence, and that This Country is Making Headway as Fast as Stupidity of Reformers Will Admit.

After which it will suffice to quote one paragraph, as follows:

Can it be possible that any one is deceived by this insane rant and drivel?

And also the friend of my boyhood, my beloved "New York Evening Post"! This organ of arm-chair respectability—I have reference to the large leather receptacles which you find in the Fifth Avenue clubs—had upbraided me for a harmless prank, "The Journal of Arthur Stirling." Now comes "The Jungle"; and the "Evening Post" devotes a column to the book. It is "lurid, overdrawn . . . . If the author had been a man who cared more for exact truth," etc. Whereupon I sit my-self down and write a polite letter to the editor of the "Evening Post," asking will he please tell me upon what he bases this injurious charge. I have made patient investigations in the stockyards, and the publishers of "The Jungle" have done the same. Will the "Evening Post" state what investigations *it* has made? Or does it make this injurious charge against my book without investigation, trusting that its readers will accept its word, and that it will never be brought to book?

This is a fair question, is it not? The organs of arm-chair respectability ought not to make loose charges against radicals, they ought not condemn without knowledge. So I appeal to my beloved "Evening Post," which I have read six times per week for ten or twelve years; and the answer comes: "It is not our custom to permit authors to reply to book-reviews, and we see no reason for departing from our practice in order to permit you to advertise your book and to insult us." And so the matter rests, until a couple of months later, the President of the United States makes an investigation, and his commission issues a report which vindicates every charge I have made. And now what? Does the "Evening Post" apologize to me? Does it do anything to make clear to its readers that it has erred in its sneers at "The Jungle"? The "Evening Post" says not one word; but it still continues to tell the public that I am unworthy of confidence, because I once played a harmless joke with "The Journal of Arthur Stirling"!

CHAPTER VI

AN ADVENTURE WITH ROOSEVELT

I was determined to get something done about the Condemned Meat Industry. I was determined to get something done about the atrocious conditions under which men, women and children were working in the Chicago stockyards. In my efforts to get something done, I was like an animal in a cage. The bars of this cage were newspapers, which stood between me and the public; and inside the cage I roamed up and down, testing one bar after another, and finding them impossible to break. I wrote letters to newspaper editors; I appealed to public men, I engaged an extra secretary and ran a regular publicity bureau in my home.

It happened that I had occasion to consult the record of the congressional investigations held after the Spanish-American War, into the quality of canned meat furnished by the Chicago packers. Here was Theodore Roosevelt on the witness-stand, declaring: "I would as soon have eaten my old hat." And now Theodore Roosevelt was president of the United States, with power to help me if he would! In a moment of inspiration I decided to appeal to him.

He had already heard about "The Jungle," as I learned later; his secretary, Loeb, told me that he had been receiving a hundred letters a day about the book. Roosevelt now wrote, saying that he had requested the Department of Agriculture to make an investigation. I replied that nothing could be expected from such an investigation, because the Department of Agriculture was itself involved in my charges. If he wanted to get the truth, he must do what Doubleday, Page and Company had done, get an independent report. He wrote me to come to Washington, and I had several conferences with him, and he appointed two of his trusted friends to go out to Chicago and make a "secret" investigation. Three days after this decision was made I forwarded a letter to Roosevelt from a working-man in the Chicago stockyards, saying that it was known all over the yards that an investigation was to be made by the government, and that a mad campaign of cleaning up was in progress.

Roosevelt asked me to go with his commission. I was too busy to do this, but I sent Mrs. Ella Reeve Bloor, a Socialist lecturer, and her husband as my representatives, paying the cost out of my own pocket. I knew that they would be trusted by the workers who had trusted me, and thought they might be able to get at least a few of the facts to Roosevelt's commission. As a matter of fact, they were not able to do very much, because they were shadowed during the entire time by detectives of the packers, and every workingman knew that it would cost him his job to be seen near the commission's rooms. I found the Socialists of Chicago bitterly distrustful of the commission, and disposed to ridicule me for trying to work with it.

The news of what was going on soon leaked into the newspapers of Chicago. They had already published vicious attacks upon "The Jungle"; and upon me. One paper—I forget the name—had remarked that it was quite evident that I knew more about the inside of the brothels of Chicago than I knew about the stockyards. This, you understand, in a book-review! I replied to this that possibly the editor might be interested to know the exact facts in the case: I had spent seven weeks patiently investigating every corner of the stockyards, and I have never been inside a brothel in my life.

Now there began to be dispatches from Washington, so phrased as to turn the investigation against me instead of against the packers. Finally there appeared in the "Tribune" a column or two from Washington, signed by Raymond Patterson, editor of the paper. This dispatch stated in specific and precise detail that President Roosevelt was conducting a confidential investigation into the truth of "The Jungle," intending to issue a denunciation and annihilate a muck-raking author. On the day when this story appeared in the "Chicago Tribune," I received seventeen telegrams from friends in Chicago!

One of the telegrams—from A. M. Simons—declared that the author of the "Tribune" dispatch was Roosevelt's personal friend. So, of course, I was considerably disturbed, and spent the day trying to get Roosevelt on the telephone from Princeton, not an easy achievement. First he was at a cabinet session, then he was at luncheon, then he had gone horseback riding; but finally, after spending my day in the telephone-office in Princeton, I heard his voice, and this is what he said: "Mr.

Sinclair, I have been in public life longer than you, and I will give you this bit of advice; if you pay any attention to what the newspapers say about you, you will have an unhappy time." So I went home to bed. The next time I saw Roosevelt he told me that he had not seen Raymond Patterson, nor had he said anything about his intentions to anyone. "I don't see how Patterson could have done such a thing," was Roosevelt's comment.

The commissioners came back to Washington, and I went down to see them. They were amazingly frank; they told me everything they had seen, and everything that was in their report to the President, nor did they place any seal of confidence upon me. I realized that I was dealing with people who desired publicity, and I had sufficient worldly tact to know that it would be better not to mention this point, but simply to go ahead and do what all parties concerned wanted done.

The report was known to be in the President's hands, and he had summoned the chairmen of the agricultural committees of the House and Senate, and was holding the report as a threat over their heads to force them to amend the Federal meat inspection law. The newspaper reporters all knew what was going on, and were crazy for news. I returned to my little farm at Princeton, and packed up a suit-case full of documents, letters, affidavits and official reports, and came to New York and called up the offices of the Associated Press.

Here was a sensation, not only nation-wide, but international; here was the whole world clamoring for news about one particular matter of supreme public importance. There had been an investigation by the President of the United States of one of America's greatest industries, and I had been tacitly commissioned to make the results known to the public, for the benefit of the public, whose physical health was at stake. I came to the great press association, an organization representing at that time some seven hundred newspapers, with scores of millions of readers, hungry for news. The Associated Press was the established channel through which the news was supposed to flow; and in this crisis the channel proved to be a concrete wall.

I was about to describe the thickness of the wall, but I stop myself, remembering my pledge to tell the exact facts. I do not know the thickness of this wall, because I have never been able to dig through it. I only know that it is as thick

as all the millions of dollars of all the vested interests of
America can build it. I first telephoned, and then sent a
letter by special messenger to the proper officials of the Associated Press, but they would have absolutely nothing to do
with me or my news. Not only on that day, but throughout
my entire campaign against the Beef Trust, they never sent
out a single line injurious to the interests of the packers, save
for a few lines dealing with the Congressional hearings, which
they could not entirely suppress.

It is the thesis of this book that American newspapers as a
whole represent private interests and not public interests. But
there will be occasions upon which exception to this rule is
made; for in order to be of any use at all, the newspapers
must have circulation, and to get circulation they must pretend
to care about the public. There is keen competition among
them, and once in a while it will happen that a "scoop" is too
valuable to be thrown away. Newspapermen are human, and
cannot be blamed by their owners if now and then they yield
to the temptation to publish the news. So I had found it
with "Everybody's Magazine," and so now I found it when I
went with my suit-case full of documents to the office of the
"New York Times."

I arrived about ten o'clock at night, having wasted the day
waiting upon the Associated Press. I was received by C. V.
Van Anda, managing editor of the "Times"—and never before
or since have I met such a welcome in a newspaper office. I
told them I had the entire substance of the confidential report
of Roosevelt's investigating committee, and they gave me a
private room and two expert stenographers, and I talked for
a few minutes to one stenographer, and then for a few minutes
to the other stenographer, and so the story was dashed off in
about an hour. Knowing the "Times" as I have since come
to know it, I have often wondered if they would have published
this story if they had had twenty-four hours to think, and to
be interviewed by representatives of the packers. But they
didn't have twenty-four hours, they only had two hours. They
were caught in a whirlwind of excitement, and at one o'clock
in the morning my story was on the press, occupying a part
of the front page and practically all of the second page.

The question had been raised as to how the story should
be authenticated. The "Times" met the problem by putting the
story under a Washington "date-line"—that is, they told their

readers that one of their clever correspondents in the capital had achieved this "scoop." Being new to the newspaper game, I was surprised at this, but I have since observed that it is a regular trick of newspapers. When the Socialist revolution took place in Germany, I happened to be in Pasadena, and the "Los Angeles Examiner" called me up to ask what I knew about the personalities in the new government. So next morning the "Examiner" had a full description of Ebert and a detailed dispatch from Copenhagen!

The "New York Times," having put its hand to the plough, went a long way down the furrow. For several days they published my material. I gave them the address of the Bloors, and they sent a reporter to Delaware to interview them, and get the inside story of the commission's experiences in Chicago; this also went on the front page. All these stories the "Times" sold to scores of newspapers all over the country—newspapers which should have received them through the Associated Press, had the Associated Press been a news channel instead of a concrete wall. The "Times," of course, made a fortune out of these sales; yet it never paid me a dollar for what I gave it, nor did it occur to me to expect a dollar. I only mention this element to show how under the profit-system even the work of reform, the service of humanity, is exploited. I have done things like this, not once but hundreds of times in my life; yet I read continually in the newspapers the charge that I am in the business of muck-raking for money. I have read such insinuations even in the "New York Times"!

Also I had another experience which threw light on the attitude of the great metropolitan newspapers to the subject of money. It is the custom of publishers to sell to newspaper syndicates what are called the "post-publication serial rights" of a book. "The Jungle" having become an international sensation, there was keen bidding for these serial rights, and they were finally sold to the "New York American" for two thousand dollars, of which the author received half. Forthwith the editorial writers of both the Hearst papers in New York, the "American" and the "Evening Journal," began to sing the praises of "The Jungle." You will recall the patronizing tone in which Arthur Brisbane had spoken of my charges against the Chicago packers. But now suddenly Brisbane lost all his distrust of my competence as an authority on stockyards. In the "Evening Journal" for May 29, 1906, there

appeared a double-column editorial, running over into another
double column, celebrating "The Jungle" and myself in emphatic capitals, and urging the American people to read my
all-important revelations of the infamies of the Beef Trust:

In his book—which ought to be read by at least a million
Americans—Mr. Sinclair traces the career of one family. It is a
book that does for modern INDUSTRIAL slavery what "Uncle
Tom's Cabin" did for black slavery. But the work is done far better
and more accurately in "The Jungle" than in "Uncle Tom's Cabin."
Mr. Sinclair lived in the stockyards. He saw how the men that
work there are treated, how the people that buy dreadful, diseased
products are treated. HE TOLD THE TRUTH SIMPLY AND
CONVINCINGLY. He went there to study life, not merely to tell
a story.
As a result of the writing of this book, of the horror and the
shame it has aroused, there is a good prospect that the Beef Trust
devilries will be CHECKED at least, and one hideous phase of modern
life at least modified. . . . .
Meanwhile, the public should be thankful to Mr. Sinclair for the
public service he is rendering, and his book "The Jungle" should sell
as no book has sold in America since "Uncle Tom's Cabin."

And then on May 31st, two days later, appeared another
editorial of the same character, conveying to the readers of
the "Evening Journal" the fact that they might read this
wonderful novel in the Hearst newspapers; the first chapter
would be published in both the "Evening Journal" and the
"American," and after that the complete story would run in
the "American." The ordinary capitals used by Mr. Brisbane
in his editorials were not sufficient in this crisis; he used a
couple of sizes larger—almost an advertising poster. I quote
the closing paragraphs from his editorial:

It will please our readers to know that for the right to publish
Mr. Sinclair's book serially in our newspapers—which includes no
interest whatever in its publication in book form—we pay to him an
amount of money exceeding all that he has been able to earn in six
years of hard literary work.
This newspaper, which has opposed the Beef Trust and its iniquities for years, and which first published the facts and the affidavits
that form part of Mr. Sinclair's indictment, rejoices that this young
man should have had the will, the courage and the ability to write a
work that HAS FORCED NATIONAL ATTENTION, including the
attention of the President of the United States. . . . .
We urge that you read the first installment of Mr. Sinclair's
book in this newspaper to-day, and that you continue reading it daily
as the various installments appear in THE AMERICAN.

CHAPTER VII

JACKALS AND A CARCASE

Roosevelt had hoped to get the new inspection bill through Congress without giving out the report of his commission. But the packers and their employes in Congress blocked his bill, and so finally the report was given out, and caused a perfect whirlwind of public indignation. The packers, fighting for their profits, made their stand in the Agricultural Committees of the House, which apparently they owned completely. Courteous hearings were granted to every kind of retainer of the Beef Trust, while the two representatives of the President were badgered on the witness-stand as if they had been criminals on trial. I sent a telegram to Congressman Wadsworth of New York, chairman of the committee, asking for a hearing, and my request was refused. I then wrote a letter to Congressman Wadsworth, in which I told him what I thought of him and his committee—which letter was taken up later by his democratic opponents in his district, and resulted in his permanent removal from public life.

But meantime, Wadsworth was king. In the fight against him, I moved my publicity bureau up to New York, and put three stenographers at work. I worked twenty hours a day myself—nor was I always able to sleep the other four hours. I had broken out of the cage for a few weeks, and I made the most of my opportunity. I wrote articles, and sent telegrams, and twice every day, morning and evening, a roomful of reporters came to see me. Some of these men became my friends, and would tell me what the packers were doing in the New York newspaper-offices, and also with their lobby in Washington. I recall one amusing experience, which gave me a glimpse behind the scenes of two rival yellow journals, the "New York Evening World" and the "New York Evening Journal."

The "Evening Journal" sent a reporter to see me. Would I write an article every day, telling what I knew about conditions among working-girls in New York? I signed a contract with the "Journal" for a month or two, and that same evening all the wagons which delivered papers for the "journal" were out with huge signs over them: "Upton Sinclair will write, etc., etc." Then next day came my friend William Dinwiddie, representing the "Evening World." Would I write a series of articles for the "Evening World"? Certainly I would, I said, and signed a contract for a number of articles at five cents a word; so all the wagons of the "World" appeared with the announcement that I would tell in the "World" what I knew about conditions in the packing-houses of New York. And the editorial writers of the "Evening World," who had hitherto ignored my existence, now suddenly discovered that I was a great man. They put my picture at the top of their editorial page, celebrating me in this fashion:

A BOOK THAT MADE HISTORY

Not since Byron awoke one morning to find himself famous has there been such an example of world-wide celebrity won in a day by a book as has come to Upton Sinclair.

Yesterday unknown, the author of "The Jungle" is to-day a familiar name on two continents. Paris, London and Berlin know him only less well than New York and Boston. They know about him even in far-off Australia.

Forthwith came the man from the "Journal," all but tearing his hair with excitement. What unspeakable treachery was this I had committed? Was it true that I had promised to write for the "World," as well as for the "Journal"? I answered that it was, of course. "But," said this man, "you gave me an exclusive contract." "I gave you nothing of the sort," I said, and pulled out the contract to prove it. "But," said he, "you promised me personally that it would be an exclusive contract." "I promised you nothing of the sort," I said. "I never thought of such a thing." But he argued and insisted—I must have known, my common-sense must have told me that my stories for them were of no value, if at the same time I was writing for their deadly rival. I was rather shocked at that statement. Were they entirely interested in a "scoop," and not at all in the working girls of New York? "To hell with the working girls of New York!" said the Hearst reporter; whereat, of course, I was still more shocked.

For three days this man from the "Journal" and other men from the "Journal" kept bombarding and besieging me; and I, poor devil, suffered agonies of embarrassment and distress, being sensitive, and not able to realize that this was an every-day matter to them—they were a pack of jackals trying to tear a carcase away from another pack of jackals. But when I stood by my contract with the "Evening World," the "Journal" dropped its contract, and lost its interest, not merely in the working-girls of New York, but also in the sins of the Chicago packers.

The lobbyists of the packers had their way in Washington; the meat inspection bill was deprived of all its sharpest teeth, and in that form Roosevelt accepted it and prepared to let the subject drop. I was bitterly disappointed, the more so because he had made no move about the matter which lay nearest my heart. I had made a remark about "The Jungle" which was found amusing—that "I aimed at the public's heart and by accident I hit it in the stomach." It is a fact that I had not been nearly so interested in the "condemned meat industry" as in something else. To me the diseased meat graft had been only one of a hundred varieties of graft which I saw in that inferno of exploitation. My main concern had been for the fate of the workers, and I realized with bitterness that I had been made into a "celebrity," not because the public cared anything about the sufferings of these workers, but simply because the public did not want to eat tubercular beef.

I had objected to Roosevelt that he was giving all his attention to the subject of meat-inspection, and none to the subject of labor-inspection. His answer was that he had power to remedy the former evils, but no power to remedy the latter. I tried to persuade him to agitate the question and obtain the power; but I tried in vain. "The Jungle" caused the whitewashing of some packing-house walls, and it furnished jobs for a dozen or two lady-manicurists, but it left the wage-slaves in those huge brick packing-boxes exactly where they were before. Ten years later the war broke out, and as these wage-slaves became restive, an investigation was made. Here are a few paragraphs describing the adventures of the Federal investigators:

The first four homes brought expressions of horror from the women of the party, dark, insanitary, pest-ridden rooms and foodless kitchens.

Mrs. Belbine Skupin. Working in the yards. The six Skupin children in their home at 4819 Laflin Street, hugging the stove and waiting for "mother to return." "I didn't think such things existed outside the books," said one indignant young lady visitor, Miss Walsh.

In one home, seven children found. Youngest, a baby of fourteen

months; oldest, a boy of eight years. Baby "mothered" by girl of
four. Father and mother work in stock-yards. Children had no shoes
or stockings and flimsy underwear. No food in house except pot
of weak coffee, loaf of rye bread and kettle containing mess of
cabbage. But in the basement was a 'conservation' card, bearing the
motto "Don't waste food."

I look back upon this campaign, to which I gave three years
of brain and soul-sweat, and ask what I really accomplished.
Old Nelson Morris died of a broken conscience. I took a few
millions away from him, and from the Armours and the
Swifts—giving them to the Junkers of East Prussia, and to
Paris bankers who were backing enterprises to pack meat in the
Argentine. I added a hundred thousand readers to "Everybody's Magazine," and a considerable number to the "New
York Times." I made a fortune and a reputation for Doubleday, Page and Company, which immediately became one of
the most conservative publishing-houses in America—using
"The Jungle" money to promote the educational works of
Andrew Carnegie, and the autobiography of John D. Rockefeller, and the obscene ravings of the Reverend Thomas Dixon,
and the sociological bunkum of Gerald Stanley Lee. I took
my next novel to Doubleday, Page and Company, and old
Walter Page was enthusiastic for it and wanted to publish it;
but the shrewd young business-men saw that "The Metropolis"
was not going to be popular with the big trust companies and
insurance companies which fill up the advertising pages of the
"World's Work." They told me that "The Metropolis" was
not a novel, but a piece of propaganda; it was not "art." I
looked them in the eye and said: "You are announcing a new
novel by Thomas Dixon. Is *that* 'art'?"

Quite recently I tried them again with "King Coal," and
they did not deny that "King Coal" was "art." But they said:
"We think you had better find some publisher who is animated
by a great faith." It is a phrase which I shall remember as
long as I live; a perfect phrase, which any comment would
spoil. I bought up the plates of "The Jungle," which Doubleday, Page and Company had allowed to go out of print—not
being "animated by a great faith." I hope some time to issue
the book in a cheap edition, and to keep it in circulation until
the wage-slaves of the Beef Trust have risen and achieved
their freedom. Meantime, it is still being read—and still being
lied about. I have before me a clipping from a Seattle

paper. Some one has written to ask if "The Jungle" is a true book. The editor replies, ex cathedra, that President Roosevelt made an investigation of the charges of "The Jungle," and thoroughly disproved them all!

And again, here is my friend Edwin E. Slosson, literary editor of the "Independent," a man who has sense enough to know better than he does. He reviews "The Profits of Religion" in this brief fashion:

> The author of "The Jungle" has taken to muck-raking the churches—with similar success at unearthing malodorous features and similar failure to portray a truthful picture.

I write to Slosson, just as I wrote to the "New York Evening Post," to ask what investigation he has made, and what evidence he can produce to back up his charge that "The Jungle" is not a "truthful picture"; and there comes the surprising reply that it had never occurred to Slosson that I myself meant "The Jungle" for a truthful picture. I had not portrayed the marvelous business efficiency of the Stockyards, their wonderful economies, etc.; and no picture that failed to do that could claim to be truthful! That explanation apparently satisfied my friend Slosson, but it did not satisfy the readers of the "Independent"—for the reason that Slosson did not give them an opportunity to read it! He did not publish or mention my protest, and he left his readers to assume, as they naturally would, that the "Independent" considered that I had exaggerated the misery of the Stockyards workers.

> *Note:* The "Congressman Wadsworth" referred to on page 45 is not the present Senator Wadsworth, but his father.

CHAPTER VIII

THE LAST ACT

I am telling this story chronologically, but in dealing with a subject like "The Jungle" it seems better to skip ahead and close the matter up. There was a last act of this Packingtown drama, about which the public has never heard. The limelight had been turned out, the audience had gone home, and this act was played in darkness and silence.

A year had passed and I was living at Point Pleasant, New Jersey, when W. W. Harris, editor of the Sunday magazine-section of the "New York Herald," came to call on me, and explained a wonderful idea. He wanted me to go to Chicago secretly, as I had gone before, and make another investigation in the Stockyards, and write for the "New York Herald" an article entitled "Packingtown a Year Later."

He was a young editor, full of enthusiasm. He said: "Mr. Sinclair, I know enough about the business-game to feel quite sure that all the reforms we read about are fakes. What do you think?"

I answered, "I know they are fakes, because not a week passes that I don't get a letter from some of the men in Packingtown, telling me that things are as bad as ever." And I showed him a letter, one sentence of which I recall: "The new coat of whitewash has worn off the filthy old walls, and the only thing left is the row of girls who manicure the nails of those who pack the sliced dried beef in front of the eyes of the visitors!"

"Exactly!" said the editor. "It will make the biggest newspaper story the 'Herald' has ever published."

"Possibly," said I. "But are you sure the 'Herald' will publish it?"

"No worry about that," said he. "I am the man who has the say."

"But where is Bennett?"

"Bennett is in Bermuda."

"Well," said I, "do you imagine you could sign a contract

with me, and put such a job through, and get such a story on the 'Herald' presses without Bennett's getting word of it?"

"Bennett will be crazy for the story," said the editor. "Bennett is a newspaper man."

"Well, you have to show me."

I explained that I was writing another novel, and was not willing to stop, but my friend Mrs. Ella Reeve Bloor, who had represented me with Roosevelt's investigating committee, would do the work. Let the "Herald" send Mrs. Bloor and one of its own reporters, to make sure that Mrs. Bloor played the game straight; and when the investigation was made, I would write an introductory statement, which would lend my name to the articles, and make them as effective as if I had gone to Packingtown myself. But first, before I would trouble Mrs. Bloor, or do anything at all about the matter, the editor must put it before Bennett and show me his written consent to the undertaking. "I am busy," I said. "I don't care to waste my time upon a wild goose chase." The editor agreed that that was reasonable, and took his departure.

James Gordon Bennett, the younger, was the son of the man who had founded the "New York Herald," establishing the sensational, so-called "popular" journalism which Pulitzer and Hearst afterwards took up and carried to extremes. Bennett, the elder, had been a real newspaper man; his son had been a debauché and spendthrift in his youth, and was now in his old age an embittered and cynical invalid, travelling in his yacht from Bermuda to the Riviera, and occasionally resorting to the capitals of Europe for fresh dissipations. He had made his paper the organ of just such men as himself; that is to say, of cosmopolitan café loungers, with one eye on the stock-ticker and the other on their "scotch and soda." And this was the publisher who was to take up a new crusade against the Beef Trust!

But to my surprise, the editor came back with a cablegram from Bennett, bidding him go ahead with the story. So I put the matter before Mrs. Bloor, and she and the "Herald" reporter went out to the Stockyards and spent about two months. Mrs. Bloor disguised herself as a Polish woman, and both she and the reporter obtained jobs in half a dozen different places in the yards. They came back, reporting that conditions were worse than ever; they wrote their story, enough to fill an eight-page Sunday supplement, with numerous photographs of the scenes described. There was a conference of the editorial staff of the "Herald," which agreed that the story was the greatest the paper had ever had in its history. It must be read by Mr. Bennett, the staff decided. So it was mailed to Bermuda—which was the last ever seen or heard of it!

Week after week I waited for the story to appear. When I learned that it was not to appear I was, of course, somewhat irritated. I threatened to sue the "Herald" for payment for the time I had spent writing the introduction, but I found myself confronting this dilemma: the enthusiastic young editor was a Socialist, and if I made trouble, he was the one who would be hurt. So I decided to forego my money-claim on the "Herald." But I would not give up the story—that was a public matter. The public had been fooled into believing that there had been reforms in Packingtown; the public was continuing to eat tubercular beef-steaks, and I was bound that somehow or other the public should get the facts. I wrote up the story and submitted it to other newspapers in New York. Not one would touch it. I submitted it to President Roosevelt, and he replied that he was sorry, but was too busy to take the matter up. "Teddy" was a shrewd politician, and knew how hard it is to warm up dead ashes, how little flavor there is in re-cooked food.

I knew, of course, that I could publish the story in the Socialist papers. That has always been my last recourse. But I wanted this story to reach the general public; I was blindly determined about it. There was a big Socialist meeting at the Hippodrome in New York, and I went up to the city and asked for fifteen minutes at this meeting. I told the story to an audience of five or six thousand people, and with reporters from every New York paper in front of me. Not a single New York paper, except the Socialist paper, mentioned the matter next morning.

But still I would not give up. I said: "This is a Chicago story. If I tell it in Chicago, public excitement may force it into the press." So I telegraphed some of my friends in Chicago. I planned the most dramatic thing I could think of —I asked them to get me a meeting in the Stockyards district, and they answered that they would.

Mind you, a little over a year before I had put Packingtown on the map of the world; I had made Packingtown and its methods the subject of discussion at the dinner-tables of many countries; and now I was coming back to Packingtown for the first time since that event. There was a big hall, jammed to the very doors with Stockyards workers. You will pardon me if I say that they made it clear that they were glad to have me come there. And to this uproarious audience I told the story of the "New York Herald" investigation, and what had been discovered. I stood, looking into the faces of these workingmen and women, and said: "You are the people who know about these matters. Are they true?" There was a roar of assent that rocked the building. I said: "I know they are true, and *you* know they are true. Now tell me this, ought they be made known to the American people? Would you like them to be made known to the American people?" And again there was a roar of assent.

Then I looked over the edge of the platform to a row of tables, where sat the reporters looking up, and I talked to them for a while. I said: "You are newspaper men; you know a story when you see it. Tell me now—tell me straight—is not this a story?" The newspaper men nodded and grinned. They knew it was a "story" all right. "The public would like to read this—the public of Chicago and the public of all the rest of America—would they not?" And again the newspaper men nodded and grinned. "Now," said I, "play fair with me; give me a square deal, so far as you are concerned. Write this story just as I have told it tonight. Write it and turn it in and see what happens. Will you do that?" And they pledged themselves, the audience saw them pledge themselves. And so the test was made, as perfect a test as anyone could conceive. And next morning there was just one newspaper in Chicago which mentioned my speech in the Stockyards district—the "Chicago Socialist." Not one line in any other newspaper, morning or evening, in Chicago!

A little later I happened to be on the Pacific coast, and made the test once more. I was putting on some plays, and it happened that a newspaper had played me a dirty trick that morning. So in my curtain-speech I said what I thought of American newspapers, and told this Chicago story. Just one newspaper in San Francisco published a line about the matter, and that was the "Bulletin," edited by Fremont Older, who happened to be a personal friend, and one of the few independent newspaper editors in America. Excepting for

Socialist papers, the "Bulletin" has the distinction of being the only American newspaper which has ever printed that story.

I say the only American newspaper; I might say the only newspaper in the world. Some time afterwards there was a scandal about American meat in England, and the "London Daily Telegraph" requested me to cable them "without limit" any information I had as to present conditions in Packingtown. I sent them a couple of thousand words of this "New York Herald" story, but they did not publish a line of it. They had, of course, the fear that they might be sued for libel by the "Herald." It is no protection to you in England that you are publishing the truth, for the maxim of the law of England is: "The greater the truth the greater the libel." Also, no doubt, they were influenced by newspaper solidarity—a new kind of honor among thieves.

POSTSCRIPT TO THE 8TH EDITION:

The above statement concerning the English law was disputed by an Englishman, and the writer made careful investigation. It appears that the truth is now a defense, if a public motive can be shown; but motives are notoriously difficult of proof. This is the most serious error of statement which has been pointed out in "The Brass Check." About a dozen minor errors were pointed out, and were corrected in the next edition. For example, Mr. Gimbel of Gimbel Brothers, Philadelphia, was arrested in New York, not in Philadelphia, as stated originally on page 227; and it was the chief of police of Spokane, not of Seattle, who was shot (page 188). At the present time, September, 1920, "The Brass Check" has been before the public for seven months; nearly a hundred thousand copies have been sold, and it seems worth while to call attention to the fact that not one of its more serious allegations has been challenged, nor has a single one of the newspapers and individuals who have been attacked ventured to accept the book's invitation to a libel suit.

CHAPTER IX

AIMING AT THE PUBLIC'S HEART

The publication of "The Jungle" had brought me pitiful letters from workingmen and women in others of our great American slave-pens, and I went to Ridgway of "Everybody's" with the proposition to write a series of articles dealing with the glass industry, the steel industry, the coal-mines, the cotton-mills, the lumber-camps. I offered to do all the work of investigating myself; my proposition was accepted and I set to work.

I went first to the glass-works of South Jersey, where I saw little children working all night in eleven-hour shifts, carrying heavy trays of red-hot glass bottles. Other children worked at the same tasks in the blazing heat of summer, and sometimes they fainted and had their eyes burned out by hot glass. When the State child-labor inspector came, he was courteous enough to notify the superintendent of the glass-works in advance, and so the under-age children were collected in the passageway through which fresh air was blown to the furnaces. I told the story of one little Italian boy who had to walk several miles on the railroad-track to his home after his all-night labors. He fell asleep from exhaustion on the way and the train ran over him. I submitted this article to "Everybody's," who sent one of their editors to check up my facts. I recall one remark in his report, which was that he could not see that the little boys in the glass-factories were any worse off than those who sold newspapers on the streets of New York. My answer was that this was not a reason for altering the glass-article; it was a reason for adding an article about the news-boys!

Meantime I was investigating the steel-mills of Alleghany County. I spent a long time at this task, tracing out some of the ramifications of graft in the politics and journalism of Pittsburgh. The hordes of foreign labor recruited abroad and crowded into these mills were working, some of them twelve hours a day for seven days in the week, and were victims of every kind of oppression and extortion. An elaborate system of spying crushed out all attempt at organization. I talked with the widow of one man, a Hungarian, who had had the misfortune to be caught with both legs under the wheels of one of the gigantic travelling cranes. In order to save his legs it would have been necessary to take the crane to pieces, which would have cost several thousand dollars; so they ran over his legs and cut them off and paid him two hundred dollars damages.

This article also I brought to "Everybody's," and watched the process of the chilling of their editorial feet. What influences were brought to bear to cause their final break with me, I do not know; but this I have observed in twenty years of watching—there are few magazines that dare to attack the Steel Trust, and there are no politicians who dare it. Our little fellows among the corporations, our ten and hundred million dollar trusts, are now and then fair game for some muck-raker or demagogue; but our billion dollar corporation is sacred, and if any one does not know it, he is taught it quickly.

While I am on the subject of "Everybody's," I might as well close my account with them. They had gained the purpose of their "muck-raking" campaign—that is, half a million readers at two dollars per year each, and one or two hundred pages of advertising each month at five hundred dollars a page. So year by year one observed their youthful fervors dying. They found it possible to discover good things in American politics and industry. They no longer appreciate my style of muck-raking; they do not stop their presses to put on my articles. Again and again I have been to them, and they are always friendly and polite, but they always turn me down. Three or four years ago, I remember, they published an editorial, telling what wonderful people they were; they had been over their files, and gave a long list of the campaigns which they had undertaken for the benefit of the American people. Whereupon I wrote them a letter, asking them to take up this list and test it by the one real test that counted. From the point of view of a magazine, of course, it suffices if the public is told it is being robbed. That brings readers to the magazine; but what good does it do the public, if the robbery continues, and if the magazine drops the subject, and makes no move to get back the stolen money, or even to stop the future stealings? Let "Everybody's" apply the one test that had any meaning—let them point out one instance where their exposures had resulted in changing the ownership of a dollar from the hands of predatory exploiters to the hands of their victims!

I was in position to bear witness in one of the cases cited by "Everybody's Magazine." I knew that the condemned meat industry was still flourishing, I knew that the wage-slaves of Packingtown were still being sweated and bled. I knew also that the campaign of Tom Lawson had brought no result. "Everybody's" had clamored for laws to prevent stock-gambling and manipulation, but no such laws had been passed, and "Everybody's" had dropped the subject. What had the magazine to say about the matter? Needless to add, the magazine had nothing to say about it; they did not answer my letter, they did not publish my letter. They have been taken over by the Butterick Publishing Company, and are an adjunct of the dress-pattern trade, not an organ of public welfare. For years I continued to look over the magazine month by month, lured by vain hopes; it has been several years since I have found an article with any trace of social conscience. They have just finished a series of articles on After-the-War Reconstruction, which for futility were unexampled; after glancing over these articles, I removed "Everybody's" from that small list of magazines whose contents repay the labor of turning over the pages.

CHAPTER X

A VOICE FROM RUSSIA

For the sake of consecutiveness in this narrative, I have put off mention of a newspaper sensation which occurred during my "Jungle" campaign, and which I happened to observe from the inside. I am glad to tell this story, because it gives the reader a chance to hear about the troubles of another man than Upton Sinclair.

First, picture to yourself the plight of the Russian people in the spring of 1906: one or two hundred million people held down by the most brutal tyranny of modern times, all knowledge withheld from them, their leaders, their best brains and consciences systematically exiled, slaughtered, tortured to death in dungeons. The people had been led into an imperialist war with Japan, and after a humiliating defeat were making an effort at freedom. This effort was being crushed with constantly increasing ferocity, and the cry of despair of the Russian people now echoed throughout the whole of civilization.

Among these enslaved masses was one man who by titanic genius had raised himself to world fame. Nor had fame spoiled or seduced him; he stood a heroic figure, championing the rights of his people before the world. He came to America to plead for them, and to raise funds for their cause. Never since the days of Kossuth had there been an appeal which should have roused the American people to greater enthusiasm than this visit of Maxim Gorky.

A group of American Socialists went out on the revenue-cutter "Hudson" to meet Gorky's steamer in the harbor; among them I remember Gaylord Wilshire, Abraham Cahan, Leroy Scott. There were also reporters from all the newspapers, and on the way down the bay a reporter for the "World" came to Wilshire and asked if he had heard a report to the effect that the lady who was coming as Gorky's wife, Madame Andreieva, was not legally his wife. Wilshire answered by explaining to the reporter the situation existing in Russia: that marriage and divorce there were a graft of the orthodox

58

church. It cost a good deal to get married, and it cost still more to get a divorce; the money you paid went to the support of fat and sensual priests, who were occupied in conducting pogroms, and keeping the peasantry of the country in superstition and slavery. Naturally, all Russian revolutionists repudiated this church, and paid it no money, for marriage or divorce or any other purpose. The revolutionists had their own marriage code which they recognized. Gorky had complied with this code, and regarded Madame Andreieva as his wife, and everybody who knew him regarded her as his wife, and had no idea that she was not his wife. The reporters of other papers had gathered about, listening to this explanation, and they all agreed that the American public had no concern with the marriage customs of Russia, and that this story had nothing to do with Gorky's present mission.

Gorky went to the Hotel Belleclaire, as Wilshire's guest. From the moment of his arrival he was the object of several different intrigues. In the first place there was the embassy of the Tsar, who was hanging and shooting Gorky's partisans in Russia, and naturally spared no labor or treasure to destroy him in America. A spy of the embassy afterwards confessed that it was he who took the story about Gorky's unorthodox marriage to the New York newspapers, and who later on succeeded in persuading the "World" to make use of it.

Then there were representatives of the various newspaper syndicates and magazines and publishing-houses, which wanted Gorky's writings, and were besieging his friends. And then there were two different groups of radicals, competing for his favor—the "Friends of Russian Freedom," settlement-workers and folks of that sort, many of whom have since become Socialists, but who in those days were carefully bourgeois and painfully respectable, confining their revolutionary aims strictly to Russia; and the American Socialists, who knew that Gorky was an internationalist like themselves, and wished to use his prestige for the benefit of the American movement, as well as for the Russian movement.

It happened that at this time Moyer and Haywood were being tried for their lives, and this case was the test upon which the right and left wings were dividing. Gaylord Wilshire, who was then publishing a Socialist magazine in New York, drafted a telegram of sympathy to Moyer and

Haywood, and submitted it to Madame Andreieva, proposing that Gorky should sign it. Which, of course, threw the "Friends of Russian Freedom" into a panic. If Gorky supported Moyer and Haywood, he would get no money from the liberal millionaires of New York, the Schiffs and the Strausses and the Guggenheims and the rest, who might be persuaded to subsidize the Russian revolution, but who had no interest in industrial freedom for America! The matter was explained to Gorky, and he gave his decision: he was an international Socialist, and he would protest against the railroading of two radical labor leaders to the gallows. He signed the telegram, and it was sent, and next morning, of course, the New York newspapers were horrified, and the Russian Embassy got busy, and President Roosevelt cancelled a reception for Gorky at the White House!

But the worst mistake that Gorky made was in his contracts for his writings. He fell into the very same trap that I have told about in Chapter VII—he signed a contract with the "New York Journal," and thereby incurred the furious enmity of the "New York World"! So then the editors of the "World" remembered that story which they had got from the Russian Embassy; or maybe the Embassy reminded them of it again. By this story they could destroy entirely the news-value of Gorky's writings; they could render worthless the contract with their hated rival! That incidentally they would help to hold one or two hundred million people in slavery and torment for an indefinite number of years—that weighed with the staff of the "World" not a feather-weight.

Next morning the "World" came out with a scare-story on the front page, to the effect that Maxim Gorky had insulted the American people by coming to visit them and introducing his mistress as his wife. And instantly, of course, the news-channels were opened wide—the Russian Embassy saw to that. (Do you recollect the fact that the general manager of the Associated Press went to Russia and received a decoration from the Tsar?)

From Maine to California, American provincialism quivered with indignation and horror. That night Gorky and his "mistress" were invited to leave the Hotel Belleclaire. They went to another hotel, and were refused admittance there. They went to an apartment-house and were refused admittance there. They spent a good part of the small hours of the morning wandering about the streets of New York, until friends picked them up and whisked them away to a place which has never been revealed. And next morning all this shameful and humiliating story was flaunted on the front page of the newspapers—especially, of course, the "New York World."

A perfect flood of abuse was poured over the head of poor, bewildered Gorky; the clergy began to preach sermons about him, and our great, wise, virtuous statesmen, who were maintaining a "House of Mirth" in Albany, and high-class houses of prostitution in every State capital and in the National capital, joined in denunciations of this display of "foreign licentiousness." So Gorky's mission fell absolutely flat. His writings were scorned, and all he had to send to his heroic friends in Russia was the few dollars he himself was able to earn. I saw him several times during the year or two he stayed in America, first on Staten Island and then in the Adirondacks: a melancholy and pitiful figure, this Russian giant who had come to make his appeal to the heart of a great and liberal people, and had been knocked down and torn to pieces by the obscene vultures of commercial journalism. Even now the story is raked up, to serve the slave-drivers of the world. Gorky is defending his revolution against allied world-capitalism; the United States Senate is officially collecting scandal concerning the Bolsheviki; and Senator Knute Nelson, aged servant of privilege from Minnesota, puts these words on the Associated Press wires: "That horrible creature Maxim Gorky—he is about as immoral as a man can be."

CHAPTER XI

A VENTURE IN CO-OPERATION

The next experience with which I have to deal is the Helicon Home Colony. I will begin by telling very briefly what this was: an attempt to solve the problem of the small family of moderate means, who have one or two children and are not satisfied with the sort of care these children get from ignorant servant-maids, nor with the amount of play-space they can find in a city apartment. I wrote an article in the "Independent," pointing out that the amount of money which these people spent in maintaining separate kitchens and separate nurseries would, if expended in co-operation, enable them to have expert managers, and a kindergartner instead of a servant-girl to take care of their children. I proposed that a group of forward-looking people should get together and establish what might be called a home-club, or a hotel owned and run by its guests. There was nothing so very radical about this idea, for up in the Adirondacks are a number of clubs whose members rent cottages in the summertime and eat their meals in a club dining-room. Why might there not be in the same community a school, owned and run by the parents of the children?

The economic importance of the idea, if it could be made to work, would be beyond exaggerating. There are twenty million families in America, maintaining twenty million separate kitchens, with twenty million stoves and twenty million fires, twenty million sets of dishes to be washed, twenty million separate trips to market to be made. The waste involved in this is beyond calculation; I believe that when our system of universal dog-eat-dog has been abolished, and the souls of men and women have risen upon the wings of love and fellowship, they will look back on us in our twenty million separate kitchens as we look upon the Eskimos in their filthy snow-huts lighted with walrus-blubber.

Here was a man who had made thirty thousand dollars from a book, risking the whole of it, and giving all his time to an effort to demonstrate that fifty or sixty intelligent people might solve this problem, might learn to co-operate in their housekeeping, and save a part of their time for study and play. Here were the newspaper-editors of New York City, who were supposed to report the experiment, and who behaved like a band of Brazilian Indians, hiding in the woods about Helicon Hall and shooting the inmates full of poisoned arrows. Upton Sinclair and his little group of co-workers became a public spectacle, a free farce-comedy for the great Metropolis of Mammon. The cynical newspaper editors, whose first maxim in life is that nothing can ever be changed, picked out their cleverest young wits and sent them to spy in our nursery, and eavesdrop in our pantry, and report all the absurdities they could see or hear or invent.

The procedure was so dishonest that even the reporters themselves sickened of it. There was one young man who used to come every Sunday, to write us up in Monday's "New York Sun"; for, you see, on Mondays there is generally a scarcity of news, and we served as comic relief to the sermons of the Fifth Avenue clergy. The "Sun," of course, treated us according to its tradition—as in the old days it had treated "Sorosis" and the "Populists." "Mr. Sinclair," said this young reporter, "you've got an awfully interesting place here, and I like the people, and feel like a cur to have to write as I do; but you know what the 'Sun' is." I answered that I knew. "Well," said the reporter, "can't you think of something amusing that I can write about, that won't do any harm?" So I thought. I had brought a collie dog from my farm at Princeton, and three times this dog had strayed or been stolen. "You might write about the dog instead of about the people," I said. So next morning there were two or three columns in the "New York Sun," making merry over this latest evidence of the failure of co-operative housekeeping! Upton Sinclair's dog refused to stay at Helicon Hall!

And then there was the famous adventure with Sadakichi Hartmann. One day there arrived a post-card, reading: "Sadakichi Hartmann will call." The announcement had a sort of royal sound, and I made inquiry and ascertained that I ought to have known who Sadakichi Hartmann was. Just about dinner-time there appeared two men and a girl, all three clad in soiled sweaters. One of the men was the Japanese-German art-critic, and the other was Jo Davidson, the sculptor, a lovable fellow, who made sketches of us and kept us entertained. But Hartmann had evidently been drinking, and when he told us that he had come to spend the night, we assured him quite truthfully that we had no room and could not accommodate him. There happened to be a meeting of the executive committee that night, with important problems to be settled; and when I came out from the committee-room at eleven o'clock, I found the art-critic making preparations to spend the night on one of the couches in our living-room. He was told politely that he must leave, whereupon there was a scene. He spent a couple of hours arguing and denouncing, and next day he wrote a letter to all the newspapers, telling how he and his companions had been turned out of Helicon Hall at one o'clock in the morning, and had spent the night wandering about on the Palisades.

And then there was a gentleman from Boston via Montmartre, Alvan F. Sanborn by name. He had written a book about the revolutionists of Paris, looking at them through a microscope as if they had been so many queer kinds of bugs; and now he came to turn his microscope on us. He proved to be a gentleman with a flowing soft necktie and a sharp suspicious nose. He accepted our hospitality, and then went away and criticized the cooking of our beans. His article appeared in the "Evening Transcript" of Boston, a city which is especially sensitive on the subject of beans. Mr. Sanborn found our atmosphere that of a bourgeois boarding-house. I have no doubt it was a different atmosphere from that of the Quartier Latin, where Mr. Sanborn's standards of taste had been formed.

Also there were the two Yale boys who ran away from college and came to tend our furnaces, and then ran back to college and wrote us up in the "New York Sun." They were Allan Updegraff and Sinclair Lewis, both of whom have grown up to be novelists. What they wrote about us was playful, and I would have shared in the fun, but for the fact that some of our members had their livings to think about. For example, there was a professor of philosophy at Columbia. Once or twice a week he had to give lectures to the young ladies at Barnard, and the Dean of Barnard was a lady of stern and unbending dignity, and after those articles had appeared our professor would quiver every time he saw her. We were trying in Helicon Hall not to have servants, in the sense of a separate class of inferior animals whom we put off by themselves in the basement of the building. We tried to treat our workers as human beings. Once a week we had a dance, and everybody took part, and the professor of philosophy danced with the two pretty Irish girls who waited on the table. The fact that his wife was present ought to have made a difference, even to a Dean, but the stories in the "Sun" did not mention the wife.

So before long we began to notice dark hints in the newspapers; such esoteric phrases as "Sinclair's love-nest." I have since talked with newspaper men and learned that it was generally taken for granted by the newspaper-world that Helicon Hall was a place which I had formed for the purpose of having many beautiful women about me. Either that, or else a diseased craving for notoriety! I remember Ridgway of "Everybody's" asking the question: "Couldn't you find some less troublesome way of advertising yourself?"

Now, I was still naïve about many things in the world, but I assure the reader that I had by this time learned enough to have kept myself securely on the front pages of the newspapers, if that had been my aim in life. A group of capitalists had come to me with a proposition to found a model meat-packing establishment; they had offered me three hundred thousand dollars worth of stock for the use of my name, and if I had accepted that offer and become the head of one of the city's commercial show-places, lavishing full-page advertisements upon the newspapers, I might have had the choicest and most dignified kind of publicity, I might have been another Nicholas Murray Butler or George Harvey; I might have been invited to be the chief orator at banquets of the Chamber of Commerce and the National Civic Federation, and my eloquence would have been printed to the extent of columns; I might have joined the Union League Club and the Century Club, and my name would have gone upon the list of people about whom no uncomplimentary news may be published under any circumstances. At the same time I might have kept one or more apartments on Riverside Drive, with just as many beautiful women in them as I wished, and no one would have criticized me, no newspaper would have dropped hints about "love-nests." I have known many men, prominent capitalists and even prominent publishers and editors, who have done this, and you have never known about it—you would not know about it in ten thousand life-times, under our present system of predatory Journalism.

But what I did was to attack the profit-system—even the profit in news. I refused to go after money, and when money came to me, I spent it forthwith on propaganda. So it comes about that you think of me—at best as a sort of scarecrow, at worst as a free-lover and preacher of sexual riot.

So far as Helicon Hall was concerned, we were a gathering of decent literary folk, a number of us not Socialists or cranks of any sort, several of the ladies coming from the South, where standards of ladyhood are rigid. There were Professor William Noyes of Teachers' College and his wife; Prof. W. P. Montague of Columbia, and his wife; Edwin Björkman, the critic, editor of the Modern Drama Series, and during the war director of the government's propaganda in Scandinavian countries; his wife, Frances Maule Björkman, a well-known suffrage worker; Mrs. Grace MacGowan Cooke, the novelist, and her sister Alice MacGowan; Edwin S. Potter, now assistant editor of the "Searchlight on Congress," and his wife; Michael Williams and his wife. Williams has since turned into a Roman Catholic, and has written an autobiography, "The High Romance," in which he pokes fun at our Socialist colony, but he is honest enough to omit hints about "free love."

What our people did was to work hard at their typewriters, and spend their spare time in helping with our community problems. We had many, and we didn't solve them all, by any means; it was not easy to find competent managers, and we were all novices ourselves. We had only six months to work in, and that was not time enough. But we certainly did solve the "servant-problem"; from first to last those who did the monotonous household work of our colony conducted themselves with dignity and sympathy. Also we solved the problem of the children; we showed that the parents of our fourteen children could co-operate. Our children had a little world of their own, and did their own work and lived their own community life, and were happier than any fourteen children I have seen before or since. Also we had a social life, which no one who took part in will forget. Such men as William James and John Dewey came to see us frequently, and around our big four-sided fireplace you heard discussions by authorities on almost every topic of present-day importance. But nobody read about these discussions in the newspapers; the publishers of newspapers were not selling that sort of news.

I look back on Helicon Hall to-day, and this is the way I feel about it. I have lived in the future; I have known those wider freedoms and opportunities that the future will grant to all men and women. Now by harsh fate I have been seized and dragged back into a lower order of existence, and commanded to spend the balance of my days therein. I know that the command is irrevocable, and I make the best of my fate— I manage to keep cheerful, and to do my appointed task; but nothing can alter the fact in my own mind—I have lived in the future, and all things about me seem drab and sordid in comparison. I feel as you would feel if you were suddenly taken back to the days when there was no plumbing and when people used perfume instead of soap.

CHAPTER XII

THE VILLAGE HORSE-DOCTOR

At three o'clock one morning in March there came a fire and wiped out the Helicon Home Colony. Everybody there lost everything, but that did not save us from dark hints in the newspapers, to the effect that some of our members had started the fire. The colony had just purchased ropes to be used as fire-escapes from some remote rooms on the third floor of the building. It was not mentioned by the newspapers that the managing committee had been discussing the need of those ropes for three or four months. For my part I escaped from my room in the tower of the building with my night-clothing burned, and part of my hair singed off, and my feet full of broken glass and burning brands, which laid me up for two or three weeks.

The "American Magazine" printed an editorial based on the rumor that the fire had been caused by leaking gas. The fact that we had defective gas-pipes and not enough fire-escapes proved to the "American Magazine" that industrial co-operation was an impossibility! They gave me space to answer that there was absolutely no evidence that the fire had been caused by gas-leaks, and that for years the authorities of the town had allowed Helicon Hall to be conducted under the profit-system as a boarding-school for boys, with no provision for fire-escapes whatever. They did not allow me to state that at the time the mysterious fire took place I had in the building the data of many months of secret investigation into the armor-plate frauds, whereby the Carnegie Steel Company had robbed the United States government of a sum which the government admitted to be seven hundred thousand dollars, but which I could have proven to be many millions. I had, for example, the precise designation of a certain plate (A.619) in the conning-tower of the battleship "Oregon," which was full of plugged up blow-holes, and would have splintered like glass if struck by a shell. I had the originals of the shop-records of many such plates, which had been doctored in the hand-writings of certain gentlemen now high in the counsels of the Steel Trust. I had enough evidence to have sent these prominent gentlemen to the penitentiary for life, and I myself came very near being burned along with it. I put a brief account of these matters into "The Money-changers," and some of the heads of the Steel Trust announced that they were going to sue me for libel, but thought better of it. I shall give some details about the matter later on, in telling the story of "The Money-changers" and its adventures.

There was a coroner's inquest over the body of one man who lost his life in the Helicon Hall fire. This inquest I attended on crutches, and was cross-questioned for a couple of hours by the village horse-doctor. Two or three members of the jury were hostile, and I couldn't understand it, until near the end of the session it came out. We had had two organizations at Helicon Hall; the company, which owned the property, and the colony, a membership corporation or club, which leased the property from the company. We had made this arrangement, because under the law it was the only way we could keep the right to decide who should have admittance to the colony. If we had had one corporation, anybody who bought our stock would have had the right to come and live with us. But now it appeared that the village horse-doctor and the village barber and the village grocer suspected the colony of a dire plot to keep from paying its just debts in the locality! I made haste to assure these gentlemen that my own credit was behind the bills, and that everything would be paid—except the account of one painter who had contracted to do a job for three hundred dollars and had rendered a bill for seven hundred.

Also they questioned us closely about moral conditions in the colony, and brought out some sinister facts, which were spread on the front pages of the "New York Evening World" and the "New York Evening Journal." It appeared that we had not had enough bed-rooms at Helicon hall, and on the third floor there was a huge studio which had served for the drawing-classes of the boys' school. It was proposed to convert this studio into bed-rooms, but first it would be necessary to raise the roof, and this would cost more money than we had to spare. Our architect had advised us that the same lumber which would be needed for this work might serve temporarily to partition off compartments in the studio, which would serve for sleeping-quarters with curtains in front. So here at last the newspapers had what they wanted! Here was something "suggestive," and a coroner's jury thrust-ing into it a remorseless probe!

As it happened, in those curtained-off compartments there had slept an elderly widow who had begged to be allowed to work for us in order to educate her sixteen-year-old son—who slept in the compartment next to her. Also there was an old Scotchman, an engineer who had come all the way across the continent to take charge of our heating-plant; also a young carpenter who was working on the place, and one or two others whose names I forget, but all quite decent and honest working-people whom we had come to know and respect. It is perfectly obvious that if people wish to be decent, curtains are sufficient; whereas, if they wish to be indecent, the heaviest doors will not prevent it: just as a woman can behave herself in a scanty bathing-suit, or can misbehave herself though clad in elaborate court-costume. These considerations, however, were not presented to the readers of the "New York Evening World" and the "New York Evening Journal." What they got were the obscene hints of a village horse-doctor, confirming their impression that Socialists are moral lepers.

There were forty adults at Helicon Hall, and they did not live together six months without some gossip and some unpleasantness. There was a young workingman who spouted crude ideas on sex, to the indignation of our two pretty Irish girls, and he was asked to shut up or to leave. There was a certain doctor, not a Socialist, but an entirely conventional capitalist gentleman, who left of his own accord after asking one of the pretty Irish girls to visit his office. Also there was a man who fell in love with another man's wife. You cannot run a hotel—not even a co-operative hotel—without such things happening. Every hotel-manager knows it, and counts himself lucky indeed if nothing worse happens. I was told by one of those in charge of the Waldorf-Astoria in New York that there sits on every floor a woman-clerk whose duty it is to see who goes into whose room. Quite recently I had dinner in a certain gorgeous and expensive leisure-class hotel in Southern California, and heard some young men of the world, guests of the hotel, discussing what was going on there: the elderly ladies of fashion who were putting paint on their cheeks and cutting their dresses half-way down their backs, and making open efforts to seduce these young men; the young matrons of the hotel, who disappeared for trips into the mountain canyons near by; the married lady of great wealth, who had been in several scandals, who caroused all night with half a dozen soldiers and sailors, supplying them with all the liquor they wanted in spite of the law, and who finally was asked to leave the hotel—not because of this carousing, but because she failed to pay her liquor bills.

All this goes on in our fashionable resorts, from California to Florida via Lake Michigan and Newport. It goes on, and everybody in the hotels knows that it is going on, including the management of the hotels; but do you read anything about it in the newspapers? Only when it gets into the law-courts; and then you get only the personal details— never the philosophy of it. Never are such facts used to prove that the capitalist system is a source of debauchery, prostitution, drunkenness and disease; that it breaks up the home, and makes true religion and virtue impossible!

For the most part what you read about these leisure-class hotels in the newspapers is elaborate advertisements of the hotels and their attractions, together with fatuous and servile accounts of the social doings of the guests: columns and columns of stuff about them, what they eat and what they drink and what they wear, what games they play and what trophies they win, how much money they have, and what important positions they fill in the world, and their opinions on every subject from politics to ping-pong. They are "society"; they are the people who own the world, and for whom the world exists, and in every newspaper-office there is a definite understanding that so long as these people keep out of the law-courts, there shall be published no uncomplimentary news concerning them.

I will finish with the subject of Helicon Hall while I am on it. Seven years later I found myself involved in the Colorado coal-strike, fighting to break down the boycott of the capitalist newspapers. A group of young radicals endeavored to tell the story of the Ludlow massacre at a street meeting in Tarrytown, New York, the home of the Rockefellers. They were arrested and thrown into jail, and I started a campaign in Tarrytown to set them free. Under these circumstances I became the object of venomous attacks by the local paper, the "Tarrytown News"; in one of its editorials the "News" declared that my home in Englewood, New Jersey, had been raided by the police on account of "free-love" practices; and this statement was reprinted by other papers. I was pretty cross at the time, because of a series of outrages which I had witnessed, so I caused the arrest of the editors of the "Tarrytown News" for criminal libel. By a curious coincidence I found myself involved once more with a village horse-doctor—not the horse-doctor of Englewood, New Jersey, but the horse-doctor of Tarrytown, New York. Readers of "King Coal" will find him portrayed as the justice of the peace with whom the hero has an interview.

This judicial horse-doctor issued warrants, and appointed the day of the trial, and a number of my Helicon Hall friends agreed to come. But one was ill and another was called away, and my lawyer arranged with the lawyers of the other side for a week's postponement. Such agreements between lawyers are always considered matters of honor with the profession, but in this case, when we appeared before the judicial horse-doctor to have the postponement arranged, the lawyers of the other side repudiated their agreement. So we found ourselves in a trap—ordered to proceed to trial without a single witness. Of course we refused to proceed, and the defendants were discharged.

However, I still had the right of civil action, and of this right I prepared to avail myself. The attorneys for the "News"—as they afterwards told me themselves—made a thorough search of my life, and found nothing to help them. So they were willing to publish a retraction and an apology. There was no doubt that I could have made the "News" pay a very pretty price; but I had not brought the suit for money, and I agreed to let them off. The retraction was published on the front page of the "News," but of course it was not published anywhere else, and there are probably not a dozen people today who know about it. Mark Twain, I believe, is author of the saying that a lie can run all the way round the earth while the truth is putting on its shoes.

I find that wherever people still remember Helicon Hall, it is some of these old newspaper falsehoods they remember, and never our earnest effort to show the economies of domestic co-operation. Even the genial O. Henry—who, being an American, got his ideas about life from the newspapers. "Say, do I look like I'd climbed down one of them missing fire-escapes at Helicon Hall?" inquires the sarcastic James Turner, cleaner of hats, in the story, "What you Want."

On my desk there lies a copy of the "Moving Picture World" for April 19, 1919. Somebody has produced a moving picture film out of a book by the Irreverend Thomas Dixon, and the magazine tells the managers of moving picture theaters how to work up interest and make a "clean-up" on this film. "Put up red flags about the town and hire soldiers to tear them down, if necessary," advises the "Moving Picture World." This picture, "Bolshevism on Trial," has a sublime patriotic motive. "Columbia's sword is unsheathed to keep Bolshevism from the Land of the Free," proclaims the article. And it furthermore informs us that the picture "promises to be one of the clean-up pictures of the season." The "Moving Picture World" thinks that it "might profitably be given Government support, for it is a powerful argument in controverting the dream-talk of the Socialists." It advises you to "get local patriotic societies to help." "Work all of the crowd stunts," it urges; and in giving elaborate details of a press campaign, it says:

Work gradually to the contention that Socialism will not be possible in this or the succeeding generation because people are not yet prepared for liberty such as Socialism aims at. Later work in allusion to the feature of the limited experiment made by Upton Sinclair some years ago at Halycon Hall, where the community idea fell because all wanted to live without working. All of this should be worked under a pseudonym.

The above, you must understand, is not an advertisement, but is reading matter in the country's leading motion picture journal. It gives you a fair idea of the intellectual attainments and moral standards of the men who supply the material by which our children's imaginations are stimulated and developed.

CHAPTER XIII

IN HIGH SOCIETY

I had written a book showing what was going on at one end of the social scale. It now occurred to me to write a book showing what was going on at the other end. Who spent the money wrung from the wage-slaves of the Stock-yards, and what did they spend it for? So came "The Metropolis," whose adventures I have next to tell.

The dramatization of "The Jungle" had brought me into touch with a play-broker, Arch Selwyn, who has since become a well-known producer of plays. We were having lunch at some hotel on Broadway, talking about our play-business, when I happened to mention the new novel I was writing. "Say! That's the real thing!" said Arch. "What you want to do is to get on the inside of that society game. Get a job in one of those Long Island country homes, and treat them to a real muck-raking!" We spent some time "joshing" one another over this idea. I was to get a job as steward on Howard Gould's yacht! Arch, who had a tendency toward stoutness, was to assist me by butlering in one of the Vander-bilt palaces!

Arch was chummy with a man named Rennold Wolf, who wrote gossip for the "Morning Telegraph," organ of the "Tenderloin" and the sporting world of New York. To my consternation, there appeared in the "Telegraph" next morning a news-item with these headlines:

UPTON SINCLAIR PUTS ON LIVERY
Other Servants at "The Breakers," the Vanderbilt Home in Newport, Catch Him Taking Notes

"JUNGLE'S" AUTHOR EJECTED

And in the detailed story which followed it was set forth that I had also been employed as a steward on Howard Gould's yacht. The concluding sentence read:

He says that he was ready to leave, inasmuch as he already had absorbed the salient features of Newport culture.

Now there are three or four main press-agencies whereby

news from New York goes out to the rest of the world. I have shown how in the case of the "condemned meat industry" these news-channels became a concrete wall. Here suddenly this concrete wall collapsed and became a channel. In Vancouver and Buenos Aires, in Johannesburg and Shanghai and Auckland, people read next morning that the author of "The Jungle" had been listening at the keyhole on board the private yacht of an American millionaire. I wrote an indignant letter to the "Morning Telegraph," denouncing the story and demanding that they should publish a retraction. They published it—in an obscure corner. I took the trouble myself to forward this letter to all the press agencies which had sent out the story; but the news channels had again become concrete walls.

To show what our press has done to my literary work, let me say that in small countries such as Norway and Denmark and New Zealand I have more readers than in the whole of the United States. A single book of mine, "Sylvia's Marriage," which in America sold two thousand copies in five years, sold in Great Britain forty-three thousand copies in two years. And sometimes I wonder what all these people abroad must think about me, after fifteen years' operation of the news channel and concrete wall!

I wonder—and then there comes to me the memory of an incident which happened in Holland. I had rented the home of a peasant-family in the country, and was much troubled by fleas, due to a custom of the Hollanders of keeping their cattle and goats in the rear portions of their homes during the winter. I tried insect powders and sulphur fumes in vain, and finally decided upon a desperate remedy. I went to an apothecary and told him that I wanted five pounds of cyanide of potassium and a couple of quarts of sulphuric acid. I remember well his look of dismay. "My dear sir! What—what—" I told him that I was aware of the danger, and would seal up the house for several days, and take all due precautions. They are a polite people, these Hollanders, the most considerate I have ever met, and the apothecary's comment was a beautiful combination of terseness and tact. "Here in Holland," said he, "we should say that was a characteristically American procedure." —And so I suppose it must be with my readers abroad. They would not expect a European author to go prying at key-holes on board a private yacht; but when they read it in a dispatch from New

York, they say what the Dutch chemist said about cyanogen gas as a remedy for fleas.

The charge has been made so many times that "The Metropolis" is a book of servants' gossip that it might be well to state that there is no detail in the book which was derived in any such way. The newspapers which labored so desperately to discredit the book pointed out that while it was possible for anyone to go into the Stockyards and see what was going on, it was not possible for anyone to go into "society." They saw fit to overlook the fact that I myself had been brought up in what is called "society"—or at least on the edge of it, with the right to enter whenever I chose. My earliest boyhood recollections have to do with young ladies being prepared for début parties or for weddings, discussing the material for costumes, and the worldly possessions of various "eligible" young men, and whether so and so's grandfather was a grocer. I cannot remember the time that I was too young to abhor "society," its crass materialism, its blindness to everything serious and truly sacred in life.

Also, contrary to the general impression, it is not in the least difficult to meet the New York "smart set," if you happen to be a celebrity. As the late John L. Sullivan remarked about Grover Cleveland: "A big man is a big man. It don't matter if he is a prize-fighter or a president." I remember once asking Arthur Brisbane how he managed to hobnob with the Long Island "smart set," when he was attacking their financial interests so frequently. He answered that they esteemed success, and cared very little how it had been gained.

You must understand that the members of this "smart set" are bored most of the time. They go hunting wild animals all over the world; they fly in airplanes, and break their necks chasing imitation foxes; they collect porcelains and postage stamps, Egyptian scarabs and Japanese prints; they invite prize-fighters and vaudeville artists and European noblemen—anything in the world to escape boredom. Do you suppose they would resist the temptation of a novelist whose bloody horrors had sent shudders along their spines?

You have read how hunters on the plains are accustomed to draw antelope to them. They stand on their heads and kick their heels in the air, and the timid, curious creatures peer wonderingly, and come nearer and nearer to gaze at the startling spectacle. And precisely so it was with me; after "The Jungle" came out, and even after it was known that I was writing "The Metropolis," I used to see the sharp ears and soft brown eyes of timid and curious society antelopes peering at me through the curtained windows of Fifth Avenue mansions and Long Island country-places. All I had to do was to go on kicking my heels in the air, and they would come out of their hiding-places and draw nearer and nearer—until at last I might leap to my feet and seize my rifle and shoot them.

I can say truly that I did not break any game-laws in "The Metropolis." The ladies whom I drew from real life— for example, "Mrs. Vivie Patton" and "Mrs. Billy Alden"— were ladies who let me understand that they were "game"; they lived to be conspicuous, and they would not be distressed to have it rumored that they figured in my novel.

Moffat, Yard & Company, who were to publish "The Metropolis," opened negotiations with the "New York Times," offering to give them the exclusive story of this sensational book. Van Anda, managing editor of the "Times," is a newspaper man, and made preparations for another big scoop, as in the case of the "condemned meat industry." But this time, alas, he reckoned without his owner! Mr. Adolph Ochs happened in at one o'clock in the morning, and discovered a three or four column story about "The Metropolis" on the front page of the "Times." It was not so bad for Upton Sinclair to attack a great industry of Chicago, but when it came to the sacred divinities of New York, that was another matter. The story was "killed"; and incidentally, Upton Sinclair was forbidden ever again to be featured by the "New York Times." The law laid down that night has been enforced for twelve years!

Some extracts from "The Metropolis" were published serially in the "American Magazine." The editors expected to create a sensation, but they were not prepared for the storm of abuse which fell upon "The Metropolis," and upon them for publishing it. I was surprised myself by the way in which those who posed as men of letters dropped their literary camouflage, their pretenses of academic aloofness, and flung themselves into the class-struggle. It is a fact with which every union workingman is familiar, that his most bitter despisers are the petty underlings of the business world, the poor office-clerks, who are often the worst exploited of proletarians, but who, because they are allowed to wear a white collar and to work in the office with the boss, regard themselves as members of the capitalist class. In exactly the same way I now discovered that every penny-a-liner and hack-writer in newspaperdom regarded himself or herself as a member of "society," and made haste to prove it by pouring ridicule upon "The Metropolis." Mrs. Corra Harris, a Southern authoress of rigid propriety, wrote an article about me in "The Independent," in which she hailed me as the "buzzard novelist," and went on to say that I had listened at the key-hole on Howard Gould's yacht. "The Independent" printed my answer, which was that I had been following my career as "buzzard novelist" for many years, and had yet to be accused of a falsehood, but that Mrs. Harris, at the very opening of her career as buzzard critic, had repeated a grotesque falsehood which I had denied again and again.

I am not proud of "The Metropolis" as a work of art; I was ill and desperately harassed when I wrote it, and I would not defend it as literature. But as a picture of the manners and morals of the "smart set" of New York, I am prepared to defend it as a mild statement of the truth. I have been charged with exaggeration in the prices I quoted, the cost of the orgies of the "smart set." These prices I had verified, not from the columns of the yellow journals, but by the inspection of bills. I was accused of crudeness in mentioning prices, because in "society" it is not good form to mention them. I would answer that this is one of the shams which "society" seeks to impose upon the wondering multitude. I have never anywhere heard such crude talk about the prices of things and the worldly possessions of people as I have heard among the idle rich in New York. And even if "society" were as austere and free from vulgarity as it wishes the penny-a-liners and hack-writers to believe, that would make no difference to me; for if people are squandering the blood and tears of the poor in luxury and wantonness, it does not seem to me such a great virtue that they avoid referring to the fact.

Also the critics were cross with the hero of the novel; they said he was a prig; he ought to have been really tempted by the charms of the lovely "Mrs. Winnie Duval." Well, I don't know. I planned the book as the first of a trilogy, meaning to show the real temptations to which men are exposed in the Metropolis of Mammon. It happened to me, not once, but several times, to meet with an experience such as I have portrayed in the "Mrs. Winnie" scene, and I never found it any particular temptation. The real temptation of the great Metropolis is not the exquisite ladies with unsatisfied emotions; it is that if you refuse to bow the knee to the Mammon of its Unrighteousness you become an outcast in the public mind. You are excluded from all influence and power, you are denied all opportunity to express yourself, to exercise your talents, to bring your gifts to fruition. One of the reasons "The Metropolis" had a comparatively small sale was because I had refused to do the conventional thing—to show a noble young hero struggling in the net of an elegant siren. The temptation I showed was that of the man's world, not of the woman's; the temptation of Wall Street offices, not of Fifth Avenue boudoirs. It was a kind of temptation of which the critics were ignorant, and in which the public, alas, was uninterested.

POSTSCRIPT TO THE TENTH EDITION

In the first nine editions of "The Brass Check" it was stated that the "American Magazine" arranged with the "New York Times" for the publication of the new story about "The Metropolis." This proved to be a lapse of memory on my part; it was Moffat, Yard & Company, the publishers of the book, who handled the matter. The "New York Times" has denied the truth of my account, declaring editorially: "In every particular Mr. Sinclair's statement in 'The Brass Check' is false. No such incident ever occurred." Upon reading this editorial (March 29th, 1921) I wired the "Times," asking if they would publish an affidavit from the man who was city editor of the "Times" in the year 1907, declaring that no such incident had occurred; also if they would agree to publish such evidence as I could produce, provided the space did not exceed 500 words. To this the "Times" made no reply. I have a letter from Mr. W. D. Moffat, then president of Moffat, Yard & Company, stating: "I remember the incident about the New York 'Times' story, and our chagrin on the morning when we expected to find the story in the 'Times' and did *not* find it." I have also a telegram from Mr. Robert Sterling Yard, who handled the negotiations with the "Times," reading: "I recall article was prepared about 'Metropolis' for 'Times' to publish, but that it was not published, which greatly disappointed us all."

Readers of "The Brass Check" are invited to send to the author for a free pamphlet, "The Crimes of the Times."

CHAPTER XIV

THE GREAT PANIC

My investigations for "The Metropolis" had brought me several permanent friendships; for there are true and gracious people in New York "society," as everywhere else. One of them was Edmond Kelly, who was not only a thinker and writer of distinction, but an international lawyer, known in all the capitals of Europe, and up to the time of his death the only American who had received the cross of the Legion of Honor in France. Kelly had been counsel for Anna Gould in her famous divorce suit, and told me the incredible story of Count Boni de Castellane. "The Metropolis" was being published in Paris, and causing a sensation there; as I read the eulogies of the French critics, I used to smile to myself, wondering what they would have said if I had made a book about the manners and morals of French "society," as seen through the eyes of Edmond Kelly!

It happened that I was in New York in the fall of 1907, and was in Kelly's study late one evening. I had to wait an hour or two for him, and he came in, deeply moved, and told me that he had just left the home of an old friend, Charles T. Barney, President of the Knickerbocker Trust Company, who was in dire distress. I had been reading in the papers for a couple of days wild rumors of trouble in this institution, which had built itself a miniature Greek temple at the corner of Thirty-fourth Street and Fifth Avenue. Now I got the inside story of what was going on. It appeared that the masters of high finance in New York, of whom the late J. P. Morgan was king, had determined to break these new institutions, the independent trust companies which were creeping in upon their preserves. Morgan had deliberately led Barney into entanglements, and had given him definite promise of support. That night, when called upon by Barney, he had repudiated his pledge; so the Knickerbocker Trust Company was doomed, several other trust companies would go with it, and the whole financial structure of New York would be shaken to the foundations. Kelly had promised even that late at night to make appeals in Barney's behalf, so I left him. Next morning I read in the paper that an hour or two after Kelly had parted from him, the President of the Knickerbocker Trust Company had shot himself through the body.

So came the panic of 1907. Pierpont Morgan, having deliberately brought it on to tighten his hold upon the credit of the country, discovered that it was getting beyond his control, and by desperate efforts stopped it—for which action he became the hero of Capitalist Journalism in America. It happened that from two other independent sources I got the story, every part of which dove-tailed together. So I went about the streets of New York, knowing that this mighty master of finance, who was being crowned as a deliverer, was in fact a greedy old ruffian who had deliberately brought ruin to thousands of small business-men, and misery and want to millions of workers.

I had Kelly's permission to tell the story in the form of a thinly veiled allegory, the meaning of which no one could possibly miss. I took the proposition to the "American Magazine," which signed a contract with me to publish the story as a serial. I set to work to write it, but meantime the "American Magazine" must have begun to hear from Wall Street. It was not very long before John S. Phillips, editor of the magazine, was sending for me and pleading with me as a personal favor to let him off from this contract. I did so, and so ends the chapter of my dealings with another of our great organs of publicity.

I know no more pitiful story in the history of our Journalism than that of the "American Magazine." It was founded because Lincoln Steffens, Ida Tarbell, Ray Stannard Baker and Finley Peter Dunne found they were no longer permitted to tell the truth in "McClure's." They purchased the "American," assuming a debt of four hundred thousand dollars. Soon afterwards one of the assistant editors told me that they were having trouble in meeting their interest payments; and then came a crisis, plainly revealed in their columns. The magazine had begun the publication of a sensational series of articles, "Barbarous Mexico," by John Kenneth Turner. These articles, since published in book form, and a second time suppressed, gave an intimate, first-hand account of the ferocities of the Diaz régime, under

6

which American "dollar diplomats" were coining enormous fortunes. The "American" began the publication with a grand hurrah; it published two or three of the articles, and then suddenly it quit, with a feeble and obviously dishonest excuse—and poor Turner had to take his articles to that refuge of suppressed muck-rakers, the "Appeal to Reason."

There must have been some crisis in the office of the magazine. Somebody had evidently had a "show-down," the editors had been "taught their place." Ever since then they have been a theme for tears. Ida Tarbell, who had torn the wrappings off the infamies of Standard Oil, has forgotten the subject, while Standard Oil, after a sham reorganization, has almost doubled the value of its stock, and more than doubled its plundering of the public. Ray Stannard Baker, who exposed the financial knaveries of the Beef Trust, shed his muck-raker skin and metamorphosed himself into "David Grayson," a back-to-the-land sentimentalist—and this while the Beef Trust has multiplied four times over the profits it takes out of the necessities of a war-torn world! Finley Peter Dunne, who contributed the satires of Mr. Dooley and that withering ridicule of the idle rich under the name of "Mr. Worldly-Wise Man," has apparently fallen silent from shame. Lincoln Steffens, the one man who stood by his convictions, quit the magazine, and now cannot get his real opinions published anywhere. The "American Magazine," which started out to reclaim the industrial and political life of our country, is now publishing articles about how a little boy raises potatoes in a cigar-box, and how a man can become a millionaire by cobbling his own shoes.

I write these words in anger; but then I remember my pledge—the exact facts! So I go to the library and take down the first bound volume my hand touches. Here are the titles of a few "special articles" and "feature stories" from the "American Magazine" for January, 1918: "How We Decide When to Raise a Man's Salary." "What to Do with a Bad Habit." "Are You Going Somewhere—or Only Wandering Around?" "The Comic Side of Trouble." "Do You Laugh at the Misfortunes of Others?" "The Business-Woman and the Powder Puff: The personal story of one who has made a success and thinks she knows the reason why." "What I Have Seen Booze Do." "Interesting People:

A Wonderful Young Private Secretary." "A Barber Who Uses His Head." "The Star in a 'One-Girl Show'." "From Prize-Fighter to Parson."

Now I ask you: could any muck-raker in a rage make up a list of titles more completely expressive of vulgarity, commercialism and general "bunk" than the above real ones?

I was at this time planning the sequel to "The Metropolis," called "The Money-changers." The story of the 1907 panic fitted perfectly into my purposes, and so I made it the basis of this novel. Needless to say, I couldn't get the "American Magazine" or any other magazine to publish it serially, nor could I get any respectable publishing-house to take up the book. I was forced to go to a fifth-rate concern, which afterwards went into bankruptcy. By the literary reviewers I was now practically boycotted; I had written a book of scandal, I had declassed myself as a man-of-letters. The fact that every word I had written was the truth, and that the men I pilloried were the plunderers of a great nation, made no difference whatever to the austere guardians of our literary traditions.

Since the year 1908, when "The Money-changers" was published, it has been the rule of American literary authorities that in discussions of American novelists my name is not mentioned. In 1914 Georg Brandes, the greatest of living critics, visited America, and to reporters at the steamer he made the statement that there were three American novelists whom he found worth reading, Frank Norris, Jack London, and Upton Sinclair. Every New York newspaper except one quoted Dr. Brandes as saying that there were *two* American novelists he found worth reading, Frank Norris and Jack London. Dr. Brandes was puzzled by this incident, and asked me the reason; when I told him, he consented to write a preface to my next novel, "King Coal." He spoke so highly of the book that I refrain from quoting him. But did his praise make any difference to American critics? It did not.

All the publicity "The Money-changers" got was from our "yellow" journals. The reader will understand that I despise these "yellows"; they are utterly without honor, they are vulgar and cruel; and yet, in spite of all their vices, I count them less dangerous to society than the so-called "respectable" papers, which pretend to all the virtues, and set the smug and pious tone for good society—papers like the "New York

Tribune" and the "Boston Evening Transcript" and the
"Baltimore Sun," which are read by rich old gentlemen and
maiden aunts, and can hardly ever be forced to admit to their
columns any new or vital event or opinion. These are "kept"
papers, in the strictest sense of the term, and do not have
to hustle on the street for money. They serve the pocket-
books of the whole propertied class—which is the meaning of
the term "respectability" in the bourgeois world. On the
other hand the "yellow" journals, serving their own pocket-
books exclusively, will often print attacks on vested wealth,
provided the attacks are startling and sensational, and provided
the vested wealth in question is not a heavy advertiser. An
illustration of what I mean is the following, which appeared
in the "New York American" for September 6, 1908:

U. S. NAVY ADMITS ROTTEN ARMOR

Carnegie Co.'s Profit, $700,000

ADMIRAL MASON SAYS OREGON NOW CARRIES 400 TONS

Indiana, Massachusetts, New York and Others Also Have Defective
Plates

FACTS HIDDEN 15 YEARS

Revelations in Upton Sinclair's New Novel Are Fully Verified

Washington, Sept. 5—Rear-Admiral W. P. Mason, Chief of the
Bureau of Ordnance, in an interview to-day admitted that the battleship Oregon, once the pride of the United States Navy, has carried
since the day she was built 400 tons of defective armor plate.

In addition the naval authorities reluctantly told that the conning
tower of the Oregon, which by expert testimony nearly fifteen years
ago was shown to be full of blowholes, is still on this vessel, which
may any day be called in defending the country against an enemy.

It is also known that the armor manufactured by the Carnegie
Steel Company, Limited, up to the latter part of 1893, which Hilary A.
Herbert, then Secretary of the Navy, recommended be stripped from
the Indiana, New York, Massachusetts and several other smaller
vessels has never been removd.

The investigation made by the "American" was prompted by the
assertion in Upton Sinclair's new book, "The Money-changers," that
"there are ships in our navy covered with rotten armor plate that was
sold to the Government for four or five times what it cost."

Referring to the investigation in 1893-94, which resulted in the
celebrated armor plate scandal, the author says: "Nothing much was
ever done about it. The Government could not afford to let the real
facts get out. But, of course, the insiders in the navy knew about it,
and the memory will last as long as the ships last."

This part of the book is a bitter attack on several well-known
men who have been connected for years with the steel industry, and

whose identity it is easy to trace. It charges that at the time of the armor plate scandal they bought out the Democratic party and secured the support of a President of the United States.

And here is part of a second dispatch, which appeared in the "New York World" the following day. It is amusing to note how these two rivals, the "World" and the "American," follow each other up!

Lake Placid, N. Y., Sept. 6—In an interview given by him today, after he had been informed by his publishers and a representative of the "World" of a report from Pittsburgh that William E. Corey, President of the U. S. Steel Corporation, is to proceed against him for libel, basing his action on charges contained in his new novel, Upton Sinclair, who is spending the summer at Lake Placid, defied the "Steel Crowd," as he designated Mr. Corey and his associates, to do their worst.

Mr. Sinclair declared he would welcome legal action on the part of Mr. Corey, because it would give him an opportunity to place on record evidence which he declares is in his possession concerning alleged fraudulent acts of the steel men.

"I have not as many documents as I once had," said Mr. Sinclair; "I have not been able to replace some that were burned at Helicon Hall; but I have more than Mr. Corey would care to see in print, I fancy."

Mr. Sinclair said that among other documents in his possession before the destruction of Helicon Hall by fire, were affidavits and other papers pertaining to alleged fraudulent practices in connection with the manufacture of steel rails.

"I took the trouble," said he "to go out to Pittsburgh. I spent a couple of weeks investigating. I had affidavits to prove that these practices prevailed in the case of steel rails, a year or two before E. H. Harriman gave out his statement as to the wretched quality of rails which the Steel Trust was selling his railroads. I can tell Mr. Harriman, too, that his own purchasing officials were not ignorant about it."

All this, of course, had little to do with literature. But it had something to do with Journalism, had it not? It had to do with matters of vital importance to the American people—battle-ships that could not fight, and steel rails that cracked and caused train-wrecks. How came it that all our organs of "respectability" kept silence, and left these grave matters to the despised "yellow" press?

P. S. to ninth edition: The character of the Baltimore "Sun" has been improved—the one improvement I know in American Journalism.

CHAPTER XV

SHREDDED WHEAT BISCUIT

I had all but ruined my health by overwork, and I now went to California for a winter's rest. I rested a couple of months, and then wrote three one act plays. Having received a couple of thousand dollars from "The Money-changers," I decided to try out a plan which had haunted me for many years, that of establishing a Socialist theatrical enterprise. There were fifteen hundred Socialist locals throughout the United States, some of them large organizations. Would not they welcome a little travelling company, voicing the ideas which were barred from the commercial stage? I began to organize and rehearse such a company in San Francisco. And so came new adventures with the newspapers.

First, the famous Adventure of the Shredded Wheat Biscuit. It must be explained that I was trying queer ideas in diet; I have always been of an experimental temperament, and was willing to try anything in the hope of solving the health problem, which I have since realized is insoluble— there being no diet or system of any sort which will permit a man to overwork with impunity. In California I was living on raw food, and had written some articles about it in "Physical Culture." When I had to eat in San Francisco hotels I could not get raw food, of course, but at least I wanted whole wheat bread, or failing that, Shredded Wheat Biscuit. All of which, needless to say, was highly amusing to hotel proprietors and newspaper reporters.

I was staying at the St. Francis, and I ordered a meal in the restaurant, from a menu which specified "One Shredded Wheat Biscuit with cream, 25c; Two Shredded Wheat Biscuit with cream, 40c." I ordered One Shredded Wheat Biscuit, and after I had eaten it I wanted another, so I told the waiter to make it two. When I received the bill it showed fifty cents, and I pointed out to the waiter that this was an error, it should have been forty cents; I had had only one portion of cream. The waiter consulted and returned with the information that inasmuch as the order had been placed in the form of two orders, the bill was twenty-five cents each. I paid the bill without further comment, but going out into the lobby I reflected that it was rather preposterous to charge twenty-five cents for a Shredded Wheat Biscuit, when you could go around the corner to a grocery-store and buy a dozen in a box for ten or fifteen cents. My abnormal sense of equity vented itself in a brief note to the management, stating that I had been charged fifty cents for two Shredded Wheat Biscuit, when the price on the menu was forty cents, and I would appreciate having my extra ten cents returned to me. This note I handed to the clerk, and there my knowledge of the matter ends. I am not in position to say that the management of the Hotel St. Francis turned over my note to the "San Francisco Examiner." I can only say that I did not mention the matter to anyone, and that all I did was to write the note, seal it in an envelope, and hand it to the clerk at the desk.

I understand, of course, that hotels have to have publicity. People are arriving in the city by thousands every day, and the problem of what hotels they go to depends upon what hotels they hear about. If a great soap-magnate or lard-king is visiting the St. Francis, the management makes haste to notify the reporters, and there is published a dignified interview with the soap-magnate or lard-king, giving his opinion of the market-prospects for soap or lard, and the need of a higher tariff on such commodities. If a notorious Socialist muck-raker is visiting the St. Francis, and it is discovered that he orders Waldorf salads and Shredded Wheat Biscuit and such-like foods for monkeys and squirrels—why, then the management perceives an opportunity for publicity of a gay and cheerful nature. San Francisco, you understand, prides itself upon being a place of Bohemianism, of bonhomie; San Francisco had more saloons in proportion to its population than any other city in America, and more venereal disease than Paris—so I was told by a Stanford professor. San Francisco must have its little jokes.

Next morning there appeared in the "San Francisco Examiner" a "feature story" to the effect that Upton Sinclair had ordered two Shredded Wheat Biscuit in the dining-room of the Hotel St. Francis, and when rendered a bill for twenty-five cents had refused to pay it and had raised a disturbance in the dining-room. Immediately, of course, the great concrete

wall turned into a news-channel once again, and people in
Vancouver and Buenos Aires, in Johannesburg and Shanghai
and Auckland, who had last heard of Upton Sinclair as working as a steward on Howard Gould's yacht, now heard of him
as raising a disturbance over Shredded Wheat Biscuit in a
hotel dining-room. "Upton Sinclair Rages," runs the headline in the "Los Angeles Examiner." An actress by the name
of Rose Stahl was playing up in Seattle, and her publicity
man must have seen an opportunity to "get in on the game."
In the afternoon paper there appeared a story to the effect
that Rose Stahl had telegraphed me twenty-five cents with
which to pay for my Shredded Wheat Biscuit. Rose Stahl
did not actually send me the twenty-five cents; at any rate
I never received it; she merely gave out the story that she
was sending it, and the concrete wall remained a news-channel
long enough to convey this report.

I stop and wonder: will my readers find it possible to
believe these tales? So many, many things happening to
one man! There is something suspicious about it—where
there is so much smoke, surely there must have been at least
one tiny spark of fire! Did I not really raise a disturbance,
just the tiniest little bit of a disturbance—such as would have
caused the people at the next table to desist from their conversation and look at me?

All that I can do is to remind the reader of the pledge I
gave at the beginning of this book: I am telling the truth,
the whole truth, and nothing but the truth. Not only did I
not raise a disturbance in the dining-room of the Hotel St.
Francis, I never in my life raised a disturbance in a public
dining-room, nor in any other public place so far as I can
recollect. The one act that might be called a "disturbance"
was that which I performed in front of the office of John
D. Rockefeller, Jr., during the Colorado coal-strike; it consisted of walking up and down in absolute silence with a
band of crepe around my arm. On several other occasions
I have made Socialist speeches, and the newspapers have seen
fit to write these up as if they were disturbances; but I have
never in my life engaged in any sort of altercation or controversy in a public place. I am by instinct shy, and I don't
go into public at all, except I am carried by some conviction.
As a little boy I got into one or two fights, and got a bloody
nose each time, but since the age of eleven or twelve I have

never struck a human being, and can only remember threatening to do so on one occasion—in a public park, when I saw an old bootblack beating a very small boy. As for raising a disturbance with a waiter, I can only say that when a poor wage-slave in a leisure-class hotel brings me an improper bill, my impulse is to give him, not a scolding, but an I. W. W. tract. My anger is reserved for the management of the hotel which is robbing me, and I give vent to this anger in a polite letter, which causes the management to rob me still further. As Shakespeare says:

> Who steals my purse steals trash;
> But he that filches from me my good Name,
> Robs me of that which not enriches him,
> And leaves me poor indeed.

My wife reads this story, and laughs; she says the world will find me comical, defending myself so very solemnly against a comical charge. Well, I am not without a sense of humor; I look back in retrospect, and have not a little fun over my "monkey diet" days. But I am serious in this book, and if you will bear with me to the end, you will see why; you will see this same predatory Journalism, which made a "monkey" out of me, engaged in blasting the best hopes of mankind, and perpetuating slavery and torment for hundreds of millions of people.

CHAPTER XVI

AN INTERVIEW ON MARRIAGE

Two or three days after the Shredded Wheat episode, there called on me a pleasant lady who introduced herself as a friend of an old friend of mine. She wanted to ask me some questions; and as I was just going in to lunch and had an engagement immediately afterwards, I asked this lady to lunch with me. It appeared that a man and woman in the city had announced the completion of a five or ten years' "trial marriage." Would I say what I thought about this couple, and about "trial marriages" in general? I have always been willing to say what I thought about any subject, so I explained that while I was not an advocate of "trial marriages," it was apparent that this couple were sincere, and one must respect people who stood by their convictions in the face of prejudice and ridicule.

I went on to talk to this lady on the subject of modern marriages. I cannot, of course, state word for word what I said, but I know my views, which have not changed in any way, so I can practically duplicate the interview.

In any competitive society, woman is necessarily condemned to a position of inferiority by the burdens of maternity; so, either she has to suppress her love-nature and her desire for children, or she must find some man who will take care of her. In a society whose standards are pecuniary, that is to say, whose members are esteemed in proportion to the amount of their worldly possessions, the average woman is forced into a mercenary attitude toward love and marriage. In weighing the various men who offer themselves, she will generally have to balance money against love; and the more corrupt the society becomes—that is to say, the greater the economic inequality—the more mercenary will become the attitude of women, the more they will weigh money in the balance, and the less they will weigh love. This is particularly true of the older women, who know the world and the ways of the world, and who seek to control the marriages made by their young.

In the course of this abstract discourse I gave some instances. I told of a couple of mothers I had watched, marrying off their daughters to what they called "eligible" men—that is to say, men who could support the daughters in luxury. I said: "Those girls were practically sold." I told of a young girl being married to a hard and dull old business man. I told of another young girl being married to a rich man who had syphilis. I told of another young girl, who happened to be intimately known to myself and my wife, who had been in the plight of a school-teacher—that is to say, facing a life-time of drudgery, and the ultimate breakdown of her health—and who had married a middle-aged corrupt politician. We had watched the progress of this marriage. We knew that the husband was unfaithful to his wife, and we knew that the wife knew it, and we knew that for the sake of a home and fashionable clothes she was parting with the finer qualities of her nature. Said I: "We have seen this woman's character deteriorating stage by stage; and when we see things like that, it almost makes us feel ashamed of being married."

Now, of course, this was a foolish remark; but it was no worse than foolish, was it? It wasn't precisely criminal. But see what was done with it!

I parted from the lady who had been my guest at lunch, and next morning, January 30, 1909, a member of my little theatrical company called me up in excitement and distress of mind, to ask had I seen that morning's "Examiner." I obtained a copy, and on the front page I saw a picture of myself and a picture of my wife—that stolen picture about which I have previously told. The story had a scare head-line reading:

UPTON SINCLAIR SORRY HE WED. SAYS CEREMONY IS
FARCE

Underneath the pictures was the caption:

Upton Sinclair and the wife he declared yesterday he is sorry that he married.

I will quote a few paragraphs from the article; you will appreciate the jolly tone of it:

Upton Sinclair says he's sorry he's married.
He said it right out in a calm, matter-of-fact tone of voice, and the waiter almost dropped the butter-plate, well trained as the particular

waiter who happened to be leaning over the back of Mr. Sinclair's chair with this particular butter-plate happened to be.

As Mr. Sinclair talked he threw a handful of California raisins into his dish of Waldorf salad and watched with evident pleasure the contrast of the dull purple of the raisins with the pale silver of the celery and the gold of the aspic mayonnaise.

"Why am I so prejudiced against marriage? Why shouldn't I be prejudiced against it? You might as well ask me why I am so prejudiced against slavery—or against thievery—or if it comes to that against murder either. Marriage in this day is nothing but legalized— slavery; that's the most polite word to call it, I fancy. The average married woman is bought and sold just exactly as much as any horse or any dog is bought. Marriage—ough! It really isn't a subject to be discussed at the table!"

Needless to say, here was another occasion where the concrete wall became a news-channel. This story was tele-graphed to all the Hearst newspapers, and published with the same photographs in New York, Boston, Chicago, Atlanta, and Los Angeles. The substance of it was telegraphed abroad and laid before the readers of my books, not merely in England and France and Germany and Norway and Sweden, but in South Africa and Australia, in Yokohama and Hong Kong and Bombay. Please do not think that I am just giving you a geography lesson; I made a memorandum at the time con-cerning this particular story, which hurt me more than any-thing that had ever happened to me.

It chanced that my three one-act plays were to have their opening performance in San Francisco that evening. So when I was called on the stage to make a speech, I spread out a copy of the "Examiner" and told what had happened. Next morning the "Examiner" took up the cudgels, and published an article by "Annie Laurie," the interviewing lady, upbraid-ing me for "playing the cry-baby" and refusing to stand by the words that I had spoken. Thinking the matter over, I realized that quite possibly "Annie Laurie" was partly sincere; she may have thought that the interview she wrote represented me! She was so vulgar that she saw no difference between the phrases I had used and the twist she had given to them.

This misquotation by ignorant and vulgar reporters hap-pens not merely to muck-rakers and Socialist agitators; it happens to the most respectable persons. For example, here is Professor J. Laurence Laughlin, of Chicago University; he hides himself in the shade of his classic elms, and does his best to preserve his dignity, but in vain. In an address to a

graduating class he urged the class "to seek a sense of form
—in dress, manners, speech and intellectual habits. In antith-
esis it was pointed out that we had lived too long in a kingdom
of slouch." The New York papers got it by telegraph in this
fashion:

> The wiggling, swaying movements of American women on the
> streets and the stage have made them the ridicule of all Europe.
> They have a glide and a wiggle that makes them both undignified
> and ungraceful.

Whereupon the horrified professor writes to the "New
York Nation":

> Of course, I never said any such thing, but papers in all parts
> of the country could not know that the report was stupid fiction,
> and that the quotation marks were absolutely false. Yet in this form
> the above vulgar paragraphs have gone the length and breath of
> the country as my utterances.

To understand such incidents you must know the economics
of reporting. The person who misquoted Professor Laughlin
was probably a student, scratching for his next week's board-
bill, and knowing that he would get two or three dollars for
a startling story, and nothing at all for a true story—it would
be judged "dull," and would be "ditched." In my own case, the
person to blame was a "star writer"; she was working on
a fancy salary, earned by her ability to cook up sensations, to
keep her name and her picture on the front page. If this
"star" had gone back to her city editor and said, "Upton
Sinclair is a good fellow; he gave me an interesting talk about
the corruption of modern marriages," the editor would have
scented some preachment and said, "Well, give him two sticks."
But instead she came into the office exclaiming, "Gee, I've
got a hot one! That fool muck-raker tore up his marriage
certificate before my eyes! He says that married women are
sold like horses and he's sorry he's married to his wife!" So
the city editor exclaimed, "Holy Smoke!"—seeing a story
he could telegraph to the main offices in New York and
Chicago, thus attracting to himself the attention of the heads
of the Hearst machine.

For you must understand that while the city editor of the
"San Francisco Examiner" will be getting three or four
thousand dollars a year, above him are big positions of
responsibility and power—Arthur Brisbane, getting ninety or

a hundred thousand, Ihmsen, Carvalho, von Hamm and the rest, getting thirty or forty thousand. If you are to be lifted into those higher regions, you must show one thing and one thing only; it is called "a nose for news," and it means a nose for the millions of pennies which come pouring into the Hearst coffers every day. From top to bottom every human being in the vast Hearst machine, man, woman and office-boy, has every nerve and sinew stretched to the task of bringing in that flood of pennies; each is fighting for a tiny bit of prestige, a tiny addition to his personal share of the flood. And always, of course, from top to bottom the thing to be considered is the million-headed public—what will tickle its fancies, what particular words printed in large red and black letters will cause it to pay out each day the greatest possible number of pennies.

In conflict with such motives, considerations of honor, truth and justice count for absolutely nothing. The men and women who turn out the Hearst newspapers were willing, not merely to destroy my reputation, they have been willing again and again to drive perfectly innocent men and women to ruin and suicide, in order that the copper flood may continue to pour in. They have been willing by deliberate and shameful lies, made out of whole cloth, to stir nations to enmity and drive them to murderous war. Mr. Hearst's newspaper machine telegraphed that vile misrepresentation of me all the way round the world; it telegraphed my repudiation of it nowhere, and I was helpless in the matter. Millions of people were caused to think of me as a vulgar and fatuous person—and some of them were permitted to denounce me in Mr. Hearst's own papers! The following contribution by the Rev. Charles H. Parkhurst, a sensational clergyman of New York, was featured in the "New York Evening Journal" with large headlines and a portrait of the reverend physiognomy:

> Upton Sinclair seems to be a person so profusely developed on the animal side that marriage is not able to be conceived of by him as being other than a mere matter of commerce between two parties of opposite sexes, and sex simply a principle that starts and stops at the level of the physical without ever mounting up into the region of intellect and spirit.
>
> A pig will contemplate even a garden of flowers with a pig's eye, and instead of arranging those flowers into a bouquet will bore into them with his snout.

Mr. Sinclair's doctrine is that of free love, and matrimony a physical luxury and an evanescent convenience.

This comes dangerously near to companioning him with the cattle and makes the marriage relation an elegant reproduction of the nuptials of the pasture.

Also I quote a few scattered sentences from a long editorial in the "Commercial-Appeal" of Memphis, Tennessee, an extremely conservative family newspaper, widely read throughout the South:

A few years ago a young man by the name of Upton Sinclair wrote a novel about Packingtown. We do not recall the name of the book; but it should have been entitled "The Slaughterhouse." It was just about the most nauseating novel that has ever been written by an American. It was a compound of blood and filth and slaughter, commingled with vice and shame. It was the kind of a book to be handled with a pair of tongs . . . . But recently Mr. Sinclair has aired his views upon matrimony, and what he has to say is simply shocking to decency. . . . . It is hard for any decent person to understand such an attitude. If there is any one thing that distinguishes man from cats and dogs and other animals it is matrimony. . . . . If Upton Sinclair's offensive philosophy should be embraced, it would mean the absolute destruction of family life. . . . . The Sinclair philosophy is the philosophy of lust and animalism and it could only emanate from a diseased and perverted mind.

I have quoted the above because there is a "human interest" story connected with it, which will perhaps bring home to you the harm which dishonest journalism does. For something like thirty years the "Memphis Commercial-Appeal" has been read by the honorable and high-minded old Southern gentleman who is now my father-in-law. Like all good Americans, this gentleman believes what he reads in his morning paper; like most busy Americans, he gets the greater part of his ideas about the world outside from his morning paper. He read this editorial, and got a certain impression of Upton Sinclair; and so you may imagine his feelings when, two or three years later, he learned that his favorite daughter intended to marry the possessor of this "diseased and perverted mind." He took the beautiful oil painting of his favorite daughter which hangs in his drawing-room, and turned it to the wall. And that may bring a smile to you, but it brought no smile to the parties concerned; for in the South, you must understand, it is the custom for daughters to be devotedly attached to their fathers, and also to be devotedly obedient to their fathers. If you had seen the tears I saw, you would know that this old gentleman's daughter was not an exception to the rule.

And since we have started the subject, perhaps I might complete the "human interest" story by stating that after all the tears had been shed and the marriage was a couple of years in the past, I went down to visit this old Southern gentleman. It was a queer introduction; because the old gentleman was horribly embarrassed, and I, being impersonal and used to being called bad names, had no idea of it. After we had chatted for an hour or two I retired, and the daughter said: "Well, Papa, what do you think of him?"

The old gentleman is quaintly shy and reticent, and had probably never made an apology in his life before. He did it all in one sentence: "I see I overspoke myself."

CHAPTER XVII

"GAMING" ON THE SABBATH

I moved myself and family to the little single-tax colony at Arden, Delaware, and spent a winter living in tents. The newspapers of Philadelphia and Wilmington used Arden as the newspapers of New York had used Helicon Hall—for purposes of comic relief. For the most part it was not especially harmful publicity; it had to do with pageants and mediaeval costumes and tennis tournaments and singing festivals. But always there was ridicule, even though mild; and this was not a just light in which to place a group of people who had a serious and useful message to convey. I noticed that in their Arden stories the newspapers carefully refrained from giving any hint of what the single tax meant, or of why single taxers went to live in a colony. What got publicity was the fact that one of the Arden boys built himself a screened sleeping-place up in the branches of a big tree. "Arden Residents Roost in Tree-Tops"! ran the headlines. I wasn't roosting in tree-tops myself, but the newspapers wanted pictures for this full-page story, and my picture happened to be on hand, so in it went.

I was writing a book, and trying to keep well, and doing my honest best to keep out of the "limelight"; but the fates were in a mood of special waggery, it appeared, and came and dragged me out of my hiding-place.

Close upon the edge of Arden there dwelt an Anarchist philosopher, a shoemaker hermit, whose greatest pleasure in life was to rise in public meetings and in the presence of young girls explain his ideas on the physiology of sex. The little Economic Club of Arden invited him to shut up, and when he claimed the privileges of "free speech," the club excluded him from its meetings, and when he persisted in coming, had him arrested. It happened that the members of this Economic Club were also members of the base-ball team, and they played a game on Sunday morning; so the Anarchist shoemaker repaired to Wilmington and swore out warrants, on the ground of their having violated an ancient statute, dating back to 1793, forbidding "gaming" on the Sabbath. It happened that I did not belong to the Economic Club, and had had nothing to do with the trouble; but I had played tennis that Sabbath morning, so the Anarchist shoe-maker included me in his warrants. He told me afterwards that he knew I would add publicity and "spice" to the adventure.

So behold us, eleven young men summoned to the office of a Wilmington Justice of the Peace one evening, and finding the street packed solid for a block, and people even climbing up telegraph poles and lamp-posts to look in at the window and watch the proceedings. I am accused of seeking notoriety, but on this occasion at least I may be acquitted of the charge. A constable had appeared at my home and interrupted my literary labors, with a notice to appear in this public spectacle, under penalty of dire displeasure of the law!

The members of the Arden Athletic Association appointed me their spokesman, and for an hour or two I labored to persuade the local magistrate that "gaming" meant gambling and not playing tennis and baseball. But the magistrate insisted that there was another statute against gambling, and he had no option but to find us guilty, and to fine us the sum of four dollars and costs, which amounted to a total of one hundred and thirty-two dollars. A large part of this would go to the magistrate and the constable, and we suspected that this was the basis of his decision; therefore we declined to pay our fines, and accepted the alternative of a jail-sentence. The limit under the law was twenty-four hours. We received eighteen, it being mercifully provided that our sentences should begin forthwith—at nine o'clock in the evening. We invited the constable to an ice-cream parlor, and served part of our sentence there, and another part of it taking a trolley-ride to the Newcastle County Workhouse. We sang songs on the way, and the motorman remarked that we were the happiest bunch of convicts he had ever taken to the institution.

This is a book on Journalism, and not on prison-reform, so I will be brief. We spent the night in cells which were swarming with vermin and had filthy, stinking toilets; we were served food which was unfit for animals, and we spent seven or eight hours working on a rock-pile under the charge of men, some of whom were brutal and dishonest. This was the state prison of Delaware, as well as the county workhouse, and it held three or four hundred men, white and black, some twenty of them serving life-sentences, working in a clothing-factory under a sweatshop contractor. The prison had been recently built, and was advertised as a model one, yet there was no exercise-court or spot where men serving life-sentences could get a glimpse of the sunlight or a breath of fresh air!

When we came out from the jail we were met by twenty-two newspaper reporters and three camera-men, and everything we had to say took the front page, top of column. Incidentally, I got a curious revelation. For years I had written poetry, and had never been able to get it published; but now I found that by the simple device of writing it in jail, I could get it on the front page of every newspaper in Philadelphia and New York! The poem was "The Menagerie," which you may find in "The Cry for Justice," if you are interested. I had lain on the floor of my cell all night, listening to the sounds which echoed through the long steel corridors. I quote two lines:

> And then in sudden stillness mark the sound—
> Some beast that rasps his vermin-haunted hide.

When my cell-mate, Berkeley Tobey, read those lines, he remarked: "That's me!" To which I answered: "Tobey, that's you!"

What we told about conditions in that jail made an uproar in Delaware. There was still more uproar because the Anarchist shoemaker was threatening to have us arrested every Sunday, if the Economic Club continued to exclude him from its meetings; and we made investigation and discovered that members of the Wilmington Country Club, including the Attorney General of the State and the Chief Justice of the Supreme Court, were accustomed to play golf on Sunday. We served notice that we would employ detectives and have them all arrested and sent to the Newcastle County Workhouse every Monday, so that they might discover what it meant to be confined in a place with no exercise-court and no chance for a glimpse of sunlight or breath of fresh air. The magistrates of Wilmington held a private conference and decided that they would issue no more warrants upon the charge of "gaming on the Sabbath." Also the prison commissioners of Newcastle County held a meeting and decided that they had been intending all along to add an exercise-court to the prison.

Here was a case where I got publicity from the newspapers; yet the reader will note, I do not show much gratitude. This story took the front page, not because the newspapers cared anything about conditions in the Newcastle County Workhouse, but solely because the story was funny. Van Valkenburg, publisher of the "Philadelphia North American," told a friend of mine that it was the funniest newspaper story he remembered in his entire experience. And of course the facts about the jail conditions were an inseparable part of the fun. What "made" the story was precisely this—that eleven clean and well-educated and refined young idealists were taken and shut up all night in steel cells, were put in prison clothes and set to work on a stone-pile. The fact that the cells were alive with lice could not be omitted, if you were to appreciate the joke on a well-known charity-worker of Philadelphia, now advertising manager of the "New Republic," who figured in a poem as "some beast that rasps his vermin-haunted hide." The fact that the food served in the jail was vile was necessary to set off the joke that the author of "The Jungle" had made a bolt for an ice-cream parlor as soon as he was released. And so on.

I look back upon my life of nearly twenty years of muckraking, and am able to put my finger on exactly one concrete benefit that I have brought to mankind. Twenty or more men who are serving life-sentences in the Newcastle County Workhouse owe it to me that they get every now and then a glimpse of the sunlight and a breath of fresh air! These men know that they owe it to me, and I have the thought of their gratitude to warm my heart when I am tempted by "the blues." One of our eleven Sabbath "gamesters," Donald Stephens, became in war-time a conscientious objector, and was sentenced to the Newcastle County Workhouse in real earnest. He was recently released, and wrote me about his experiences; I quote:

You will be pleased to learn that the short visit we Ardenites paid that institution some years back and the publicity you gave to conditions then led to social improvements—chief of which was the building of an outside recreation yard. Some of the old-timers expressed heartfelt appreciation for the good work you did.

In view of this can you blame me if I am pursued by the thought of how much we could do to remedy social evils, if only we had an honest and disinterested press? Also, can you blame me if I stored away in my mind for future reference the fact that when it is necessary to get some important news into the papers, I can manage it by getting myself sent to jail? This is a discovery which is made, sooner or later, by all social reformers; and so going to jail becomes a popular diversion and an honorable public service.

CHAPTER XVIII

AN ESSENTIAL MONOGAMIST

The adventure of Sabbath "gaming" served as a curtain raiser to the great tragedy of my life. I pause on the brink of this tragedy, hesitating to take the plunge, even in memory; hesitating for the reader's sake as much as for my own. I ask myself, "Will anybody endure to read a detailed statement of the grievances of one man, at a time when so many millions of men are suffering?" Again, reader, let me beg you to believe that I am not writing this book to defend myself. Amid the terrific events that are going on in the world at this hour, I would not take ten minutes of my time for such a purpose.

I am telling this story in defense of a cause. It was not I, but the cause, that was maimed and tortured through these years, and any other man in my place would have met my experience. The matter at issue in this book is not the character of Upton Sinclair, but the character of the machinery upon which you rely every day of your life for news of the world about you. If that machinery can be used deliberately and systematically to lie about Upton Sinclair, it can be used to disorganize the people's movement throughout the world, and to set back the coming of Social Justice.

I grope in my mind for a simile to make clear how I feel about this book, how I would have you feel. Say to yourself that Upton Sinclair is a guinea-pig—surely a sufficiently unpretentious creature! It would be entirely preposterous of a guinea-pig to expect that a book should be written about him, or that a research-laboratory should devote its attention to him. But the scientist reaches into a pen full of guinea-pigs, and catches up one by the neck, and makes him the subject of an experiment—removes his thyroid gland, let us say, or gives him an injection of a serum. So suddenly it becomes of the utmost consequence what happens to this guinea-pig. Trained experts take his temperature every ten minutes; they keep a chart of his pulse, they watch his respiration, they analyze his excretions; and nobody thinks this preposterous—on the contrary, every man of science understands that the condition of this guinea-pig may be of greater moment to mankind than the fall of an empire.

So it is that I am giving this story; giving everything—because that is what science requires. In the case of the great tragedy of my life, my divorce scandal, I confront the ordeal with as much shrinking as ever any guinea-pig exhibited. During all the time of this affair, I refused again and again, in spite of great provocation, to say a public word in my own defense; nor have I ever told the story, except to a few intimate friends. The prospect of having to bring it up again was the cause of my putting off writing this book for several years.

Obviously, the story must be told. It is generally believed that there was something in the affair discreditable to me, and if now I pass it over, my critics will say: "Ah, yes! He is quite willing to play the game of frankness, so long as the cards run his way; but when his luck changes, then suddenly he gets 'cold feet,' and retires from the game!" Anyone can see that will not do; I must either tell this story, or I must leave the book unwritten. Having decided that it is my duty to write the book, I proceed to the story. I shall tell just as little as I have to tell, in order to make clear the part played by the newspapers. More especially, I shall do my best to spare the feelings of my former wife and her family. My former wife has remarried, and neither her maiden name nor her present name is anybody's concern in this book.

In Ellen Key's "Love and Marriage" occurs a passage explaining that while monogamy is probably the best marital arrangement for the majority of people, there are some individuals so constituted that monogamy is unsatisfactory to them; they find that the fulfillment of their nature requires that they should have more than one love at one time. When my former wife came upon that passage, she brought it to me in triumph. Here was the thesis upon which she had been arguing for many years, and here was a woman, recognized as a great teacher, who believed as she did. I do no unkindness to my former wife in making this statement, because she was accustomed to quote the passage to every one she met, and she defended it in published writings.

Now, I have a respect for Ellen Key's personality, and

for many of her ideas. I admit that she may know more about the nature of woman than I do, and may be correct in her statements as to the love-needs and the love-rights of some women. All I could say was that I found the idea offensive, and I would part company with anyone who acted upon it. What men and women might agree to do in some far-off blissful future I did not attempt to say, but for the present we lived in a world in which venereal disease was an unforgetable menace, and on this account if no other, one had the right to demand marital fidelity. I argued this question through long years, and my former wife found my arguments tiresome and oppressive. To the newspapers she described me as "an essential monogamist," a phrase which gave great glee to the "Tenderloin" loungers and the newspaper wits who serve them. Just how these wits reconciled the phrase with the charge that I was a "free-lover," I can not explain, nor have the wits explained it.

Now ordinarily, when Americans find that they are hopelessly disagreed upon such a question, they proceed to establish a residence in Reno or Texas. Etiquette requires that the man should pay all the expenses, and also that he should bear the odium involved. In one of Bernard Shaw's plays he explains that the English law requires not merely infidelity, but cruelty in the presence of witnesses, and therefore the convention has come to be that the man and woman shall repair to the garden, and there in the presence of the gardener the husband shall knock his wife into a flower-bed. I remember some years ago Mr. Booth Tarkington stepped off a steamer from Europe and was informed by reporters that his wife was suing him for divorce, alleging cruelty; he was asked for a comment, and replied, graciously: "When one's wife accuses one of cruelty, no gentleman would think of making a reply."

I was prepared to play my part as a gentleman according to this standard, and several times I made the necessary practical arrangements; but each time the other party changed her mind. She pleaded that the world attached a certain stigma to "a divorced woman"; therefore, it was cruel and unkind for a man to insist upon having a divorce. I might at least allow her the protection of my name. To this argument I was weak enough to yield.

I had endured for some eight years this kind of domestic

precariousness; a maelstrom in which a man's physical, mental, and moral integrity are subtly and bewilderingly tossed and buffeted and maimed. But finally I came upon certain facts which decided me to put an end to it. It happened in midsummer, when my lawyer was in the country, and in my haste to consult him I made the greatest blunder of my life. I sent a telegram inquiring whether a letter of admission from the other party was evidence in a divorce-suit in New York State; and to this telegram I signed my name.

I have since been told that it is a regular custom of the "yellow" journals, in places where the "smart set" or other people of prominence gather, to maintain relations with telegraph-clerks. When telegrams containing news or hints of news are filed, the clerk furnishes a copy to the newspaper, and is paid according to the importance of the "tip." Three or four hours after I filed that telegram, I was called to the telephone by the "New York American," which told me they had information that I was bringing suit for divorce. I was astounded, for I had not mentioned the matter to a soul. At first I denied the fact, but they said their information was positive, and they would publish the story. So it was a choice between having a false story or a true story made known, and I replied, "I will prepare a statement and send it to you some time this evening." I prepared the briefest possible statement, to the effect that my wife had left me with another man, and had written to that effect, and that I was preparing to bring suit. The last paragraph read:

I make this statement because I have just learned that word of my intention has reached one newspaper, and I would rather the real facts were printed than anybody's conjectures. I have nothing to add to this statement and I respectfully ask to be spared requests for interviews.

I sent this statement, and next morning the "American" published it on the front page, with my picture, and a picture of my former wife, and a picture of a boy which was not our boy, but a "fake." I quote a few lines:

SINCLAIR ACCUSES HIS WIFE

Upton Sinclair, the author and social colonizer, in a surprising statement last night announced his intention to bring suit for divorce. . . . .

The action of Mr. Sinclair in giving out such a statement, or bringing suit for divorce from his wife, will be a great surprise to his friends and co-workers. . . . .

You will note the phrasing of this, so carefully calculated to make me odious—a man who rushed to the newspapers with an attack upon his wife! And then followed several paragraphs from that old and false San Francisco interview on marriage, to the effect that women are bought in marriage as dogs and horses are bought. How singular that a man who held such ideas should object to marital infidelity!

I am not going into detail concerning the horrors of the next few weeks. Suffice it to say that the herd had me down and proceeded to trample on my face. My personality, my affairs, my opinions and my every-day actions became the subject of discourse and speculation upon the front pages of the New York papers. My mother's apartment, where I was living, was besieged by reporters, and when I refused to see them, it made no difference—they went away and wrote what they thought I might have said. The other party to the case was interviewed to the extent of pages—I mean literally pages. Gelett Burgess, who passes for a man of letters, and was one of the founders of the Author's League of America, wrote a full-page burlesque of the tragedy, which was published with illustrations in the "New York American." Mr. Burgess told a friend of mine some time afterwards that he had done it because he needed the money, but he was ashamed of having done it. It is not my wish to spare him any of this shame; therefore I reproduce the headlines of his elegant composition:

Why Hungry Mrs. Upton Sinclair Went Home to Mamma.
Gelett Burgess Discusses the Failure of Poetry à la carte as an Appetite Satisfier, and the Triumph of a Meal Ticket over Free but Famished Love.

Also I ought not to fail to mention one of the editors of "Life," who went to see my former wife in company with a fat little pig of a publisher, his pockets stuffed with bills, which were offered the lady to write a scandal-story of her life with me!

The opinions of the newspaper commentators on the scandal varied from day to day. The generally accepted explanation was that I had married an innocent young girl and taught her "free love" doctrines, and then, when she practised these doctrines, I kicked her out of my home. But some of the newspapers found the matter worse than that. The "Chicago Evening Post" gave an elaborate analysis of my

character and motives. It said it would be possible to forgive
me if what I had done was "the jealous rage of a male brute
infuriated past reason"; but the awful truth was plain—I had
done this deed as "publicity work" for the second volume of
"Love's Pilgrimage"!

The idea that there lived on earth a human being who
could have enjoyed the experience I was then undergoing
was one which would not have occurred to me; however,
the fact that this newspaper writer could conceive it indicated
that there was at least one such person living. I have since
heard that certain actors and actresses have increased their
fame and incomes by being many times divorced and remarried.
But with authors it does not work out that way. Mitchell
Kennerley, publisher of "Love's Pilgrimage," had been selling
a thousand copies a week of this book, and after the divorce-
scandal he did not sell a hundred copies in six months!

I felt in those terrible days precisely like a hunted animal
which seeks refuge in a hole, and is tormented with sharp
sticks and smoke and boiling water. Under the law it had
been necessary for me to obtain certain evidence. I had taken
steps to obtain it, and this became a source of mystery as
thrilling as a detective-story. For days men followed me
every step I took; my mail was tampered with continually,
and likewise the mail of my friends. I ran away into the
country to hide, I even changed my name for a while, but
that did no good—I was found out. Up to this time I had
never had a grey hair in my head, but I found many after
these months, and have them still.

Among the mass of newspaper items I note one that
seems trifling, yet is curiously significant. There appeared in
the "New York Times" a telegraphic dispatch from Wilmington, Delaware, to the effect that I was being sued by a store-
keeper in New Jersey for thirty-eight dollars worth of fertilizer. Stop and think a minute how many men in America
are sued every day for bills which they refuse to pay, and
how seldom does the "New York Times" hunt out such news
by telegraph! Often I have tried to get radical news into
the "Times," and heard the editors plead space limitations;
yet they found room for a dispatch about my being sued for
thirty-eight dollars!

Five years before this I had owned a little farm, and had
left it in charge of a man who contracted bills in my name.

I had paid all the bills which were properly rendered; but after four years had passed, and I had sold the farm and wiped the matter off my books, I received for the first time a bill for thirty-eight dollars worth of fertilizer. Naturally I refused to pay this bill; so I was sued—and the "New York Times," having me down and desiring to trample further on my face, obtained the news and published it in connection with my divorce-scandal.

Nor was that all. The day after this item was published, there appeared in the "New York World" a column of humor about me, one part of which I quote. Please take the trouble to read it carefully, because it illustrates a significant point.

The following statement, with several long-hand corrections, was received by the "World" yesterday:

"With regard to the report that I am being sued for thirty-eight dollars worth of fertilizer I might mention that I am being sued for something I never purchased or received. The dealer has admitted in writing that he did not send me the bill until four years after the alleged purchase. I like to get my bills a little sooner than that.

Upton Sinclair.

"Please put the above in the form of an interview."

Now this was funny, was it not? It was a complete exposition of an ass; reading it, you would be perfectly sure you were dealing with an ass——unless possibly with a crook. The "Chicago Evening Post" took the latter view. It quoted the tell-tale sentence with the comment: "Other papers fell for 'Interviews,' but it was evidently one of the 'World's' busy days, when not even a cub-reporter could be spared for re-write." On the basis of this, the "Post" went on to expose me as a cold and calculating notoriety-hunter.

Now what is the truth about the statement in the "New York World"? Here it is:

Three times in the course of that day the "World" had sent a reporter to seek me out. Would I not say something about the report of my intention to file my suit in Delaware instead of in New York? Would I not say something about the fact that a man had called up the "New York World" on the telephone, and announced himself as the co-respondent in my divorce case, on his way to have a fist-fight with me? Finally, the third time, would I not at least say something about this suit for thirty-eight dollars worth of fertilizer?

I saw no reason why I should not state the facts in this

last matter, so I said to the reporter: "I will not give an interview, because I have been misquoted so many times, and am sick of it. But I will write out what I have to say, and you can make an interview of that, provided you do not change it. I have to look up the dates of the fertilizer bill, and I'll send what I have to say by a messenger." This was agreed to, and I wrote out the statement. Having been previously made to appear as seeking publicity, I wanted to be particularly careful in this case, so to remind the reporter of his promise, I added: "Put the above in the form of an interview."

I have often written those words in sending copy to newspapers. For example, they wire asking for an expression of opinion, and in replying, I remind them that they made the first move, not I. They perfectly understand the meaning of the request, "Put the above in the form of an interview," and do not commit a breach of confidence except for a definite purpose, to make some person odious. In this particular case it was no oversight, no lack of a "cub-reporter"; it was the deliberate act of malice of the "World" reporter, abetted by the editors who passed the copy. I know that my statement reached the right reporter, because the rest of the article contained things which he had said to me in the course of his calls. I have gone into such minute detail about this episode, because it shows so perfectly how these corrupt and greedy newspapers have you at their mercy. They do whatever they please to you, and you are helpless. If for any reason, good or bad, you make them angry, they trample you like a vicious stallion. Or perhaps you seem funny to them, and then they amuse themselves with you, about as a wanton child who picks a butterfly to pieces.

CHAPTER XIX

IN THE LION'S DEN

To understand the rest of this episode, you must know something about the divorce laws of New York, and about divorce procedure. The code of the State, which was framed by a combination of Puritan bigotry with Roman Catholic obscurantism, requires infidelity legally proven. The defendant cannot confess, and neither party to the suit can testify against the other; moreover, if it appears that both have desired the divorce or consented to the divorce, there is "collusion" and the divorce is not granted. These laws are administered by judges who are almost invariably corrupt, many of them in addition being under the spell of Catholic superstition, considering that they have decreased the period of their sojourn in purgatory when they succeed in twisting the law or the evidence so as to balk some person's desire to be free from marital disharmony.

Into this jungle of ravening beasts and poisonous serpents I now walked, unarmed and unprotected—having made the mistake of employing a lawyer who was a sensitive and honorable gentleman. The Court appointed a referee to hear the case, and before this referee I appeared with my counsel and my witnesses; also there appeared the counsel for the other party, as required by law, and a solemn farce was played. The referee had got the case as a morsel of graft from the infamous Tammany machine; whether he was malicious or merely ignorant, I do not know, but he was evidently possessed with curiosity concerning the notorious scandal, and questioned me concerning my attitude toward the matters in evidence— how I had regarded them and what I had done about them My attorney objected that under the law I was not permitted to testify concerning my wife's conduct, but the referee insisted that I should answer his questions, and for fear of angering him, and possibly exciting his suspicions, I answered.

Under the law it was provided that all this testimony should be secret, the property of the Court. My attorney and the attorney for the other party demanded of the referee

and of the clerk of the Court that the law should be obeyed.
But when the referee's report was handed in, a full account
of it and of the testimony was published in every newspaper
in New York. When inquiry was made by my attorney,
it developed that twenty-six different clerks had had access
to those papers, and it was not possible to determine which
one of the twenty-six had accepted a bribe from the newspapers. Suffice it to say that the whole obscene story was
spread before the world. I say "obscene"—it was that of
necessity, you understand; the New York State divorce law
requires it to be that, literally. The law requires that the
witnesses must have seen something tending to prove a
physical act of infidelity; and if they shrink from going
into detail, the referee compels them to go into detail—and
then the details are served as delicious tidbits by the "yellow"
journals.

I waited a month or two in suspense and shame, until at
last the august judge handed down his decision. The referee
had erred in questioning me as to the other party's actions
and my attitude thereto; therefore the referee's recommen-
dations were not accepted, and another referee must be appointed and the solemn farce must be gone through with a
second time. I observed with bewildered interest that the
erring referee was not compelled to return to me the money
which the law had compelled me to turn over to him as his
share of the "swag." I must pay another referee and a new
set of court costs, and must wait several months longer
for my peace of soul and self-respect to be restored to me.

The second referee was appointed and the farce was
played again. This time the referee would make no mistake,
he would ask me no questions; he was a business-like gentleman, and put the job through in short order. He turned in
his report, with the recommendation that my petition should
be granted; and again the newspapers got the story—only
now, of course, it was a stale story, the public was sick of
the very name of me.

Again I waited in an agony of suspense, until a Roman
Catholic judge handed down his august decision. It appeared that the evidence in the case was defective. The
other party had been identified by means of photographs,
and this was not admissible. Both attorneys in the case
and the referee declared that there were innumerable prec-

edents for photographs having been admitted, but the Roman
Catholic judge said no. Also he said that there was some
indication of "collusion"; I had behaved too humanely towards
the other party in the domestic conflict. Apparently it was
my legal duty to behave like Othello, or to do what the relatives
of Héloïse did to Abélard.

I understood, of course, what the decision meant; the
Roman Catholic judge had got his opportunity to step upon
the nose of a notorious Socialist, and he had taken it. My
lawyer urged me to appeal the case, but I remembered a
talk I had had with James B. Dill three or four years previously. Dill was the highest paid corporation-lawyer in
America, having been paid a million dollars for organizing
the Steel Trust. Before he died, he was judge of the highest
court of New Jersey, and I had spent long evenings at his
home listening to his anecdotes. I recalled one remark: "There
are twenty-two judges of the Appellate Court in New York
State, and only three of them are honest. To each of the
other nineteen I can say, I know whose man you are; I
know who paid you and just how he paid you. And not
one of them would be able to deny my statements." Reflecting on this, I decided that I would not spend any more
of my hard-earned money in appealing—more especially as
by so doing I stood to lose what little privacy the law had
preserved to me; the law required that in the event of an
appeal I must pay to have the evidence in the case printed,
and made public property forever! I had received a letter
from my friend Dr. Frederik van Eeden, the Dutch poet and
novelist, assuring me that he lived in a civilized country,
where divorce was granted upon admission of infidelity, without evidence being given. So I set out for Holland; and in
establishing my residence I did not have to resort to any
technicalities. I really intended to spend the rest of my life
in Europe; it seemed to me that I could not bear the sight
of America again.

My earning power had, of course, been entirely destroyed;
no one would read my books, no one would publish what I
wrote. As Mitchell Kennerley said to me: "If people can
read about you for one cent, they are not going to pay a
dollar and a half to do it." Also, my health seemed permanently undermined; I did not think I was going to live, and
I did not very much care. But I established my residence

in Holland and obtained my divorce, quietly, and without scandal. I wish to pay tribute to the kindest and most friendly people I have ever met—the Dutch. When I came to them, sick with grief, they did not probe into my shame; they invited me to their drawing-rooms for discussions of literature and art, and with tact and sweetness they let me warm my shivering heart at their firesides. Their newspapers treated me as a man of letters—an entirely new experience to me. They sent men of culture and understanding to ask my opinions, and they published these opinions correctly and with dignity. When I filed my divorce-suit they published nothing. When the decree was granted, they published three or four lines about it in the columns given to court proceedings, a bare statement of the names and dates, as required by law. And even when I proposed to rid my home of fleas by means of cyanogen gas, they did not spread the fact on the front pages of their newspapers, making it a "comic relief" story for the vacuous-minded crowd.

There were many men in Holland, as in England and Germany and Italy and France, who hated and feared my Socialist ideas. I made no secret of my ideas; I spoke on public platforms abroad, as I had spoken at home. When reporters for the great Tory newspapers of England came to interview me, I told them of the war that was coming with Germany, and how bitterly England would repent her lack of education and modern efficiency, and her failure to feed and house her workers as human beings. These opinions were hateful to the British Tories, and they attacked me; but they did not attack the author of the opinions, by making him into a public scarecrow and publishing scandals about his private life. This, as my Dutch chemist would have said, is "a characteristically American procedure"!

CHAPTER XX

THE STORY OF A LYNCHING

The first American I visited in Europe was George D. Herron, then living in Florence, the home of his favorite poet, Dante. Dante had been exiled from Florence by the oligarchy which ruled that city, and in exactly the same way Herron had been exiled from America by America's oligarchy, the capitalist press. I had known him for ten years, and had witnessed his martyrdom at first hand. The story is told in full in some pages of "Love's Pilgrimage," but I must sketch it here, where I am dealing with the subject of marriage and divorce, and the attitude of our Journalism thereto. As it happens, the story is timely, for Herron has again been brought into the public eye, and the capitalist press has dragged out the old skeleton and rattled its dry bones before the world.

George D. Herron had been a clergyman, a professor of Christian morals in a Middle Western college. He had been married as a boy and was wretchedly unhappy. I am not free to discuss that early marriage; suffice it to say that when he told me the story, the tears came into his eyes. He had become a Socialist, and had set out to preach the cause of the poor and oppressed from one end of America to the other. Among his converts was an elderly rich woman, Mrs. Rand, whose fortune came from railroad and lumber interests in the Middle West. And now Herron came to love the daughter of Mrs. Rand. Being a clergyman, he had no idea of divorcing his wife, and the discovery that he loved another woman only added to his misery. His health gave way under the strain, but he held out—until finally his wife brought suit for divorce, alleging desertion.

Herron had founded a Christian Socialist organization, and was one of the most popular radical orators in the country. He was a dangerous man to the "interests," and here was the chance to destroy him. A perfect storm of obloquy and abuse overwhelmed him. He was a "free lover," they declared, a proof of the claim that all Socialists believed and practised "free love." The Rev. Newell Dwight Hillis refused to shake hands with him, turning his back upon him on a public platform: Newell Dwight Hillis, whose greed for money led him into a series of disgusting scandals, and forced him finally to bow his head with shame and confess his financial sins before his congregation! The Rev. Thomas Dixon wrote a novel, "The One Woman," in which he portrayed Herron as a sort of human gorilla: Dixon, dealer in pulpit-slang, who has since turned to the movies as a means of glorifying race-hatred and militarism, and pouring out his venom upon all that is humane and generous in life.

I have many friends who were present at the marriage of George D. Herron and Carrie Rand. They were married by a Congregational clergyman, William Thurston Brown, and I have seen the marriage certificate. Yet all over this country, and in fact all over the world, the newspapers portrayed the ceremony as a "free love wedding," no real marriage, but just a say-so to be terminated at pleasure. The most horrible tales were told, the most horrible pictures were published—of Herron, and of his first wife, and of his "soul mate" and his "soul mate's" mother.

I saw that the strain of the thing was killing Herron, and persuaded him to go abroad to live and do his writing. Three or four years later old Mrs. Rand died, leaving a part of her money to found the Rand School; Herron and his wife came home to bury her, and again the storm broke out. He had purchased a farm at Metuchen, New Jersey, intending to live there; a reporter came, representing that the "Cosmopolitan Magazine" wished to publish a series of articles about the wives of distinguished American writers. On this pretext the reporter obtained a photograph of a painting which Herron had had made of his wife and baby, and a week later there appeared in the magazine section of the "New York Sunday American" a horrible scare story about the "free love colony" which Herron was founding in the midst of an exclusive residential suburb of New Jersey. There was a picture of the free love wife and the free love baby, and of Herron standing upon a ladder, tacking upon a wall his repudiation of the institution of marriage. The headlines ran:

ELEVEN MILLION DOLLARS TO PROMOTE THIS DOCTRINE
How the Vast Fortune of the Late Mrs. Rand, Who Gave Prof.
Herron's Deserted Wife $60,000 to Divorce Him, is Being Used in
an Amazing Warfare on Marriage and Religion Under the Leader-
ship of Herron and Mrs. Rand's Daughter.

This story went all over the country, and recently when
Herron was named by President Wilson as one of the delegates
to confer with the Russian Soviets, the story was rehashed in
our newspapers, and made the subject of indignant protest
by religious bodies. Having visited this Metuchen home and
seen the whole story in the making, I am in a position to
state that the Metuchen "free love colony" was entirely a
product of the obscene minds of the editors of the "Sunday
Yellows." What is the moral character of these "yellow"
editors you may judge from the fact that, soon after this,
one of the editors of the "Sunday World" was arrested by
Anthony Comstock and sent to jail for a year or two, for
having in his possession several thousand obscene photographs
which he used in the corrupting of boys. In such minds
the Metuchen story was born; and seventeen years later its
foul carcass is exhumed by the "Churchman," organ of "the
Church of Good Society" in New York, and made the basis
of a vicious sneer at President Wilson. I quote:

In dealing with Russian liberals, it may be necessary to select
as mediators men who share their political ideas. It is not necessary
to choose men who share their moral practices. We read that the
Presbyterian Union of Newark has adopted resolutions protesting
against the appointment of George D. Herron as a representative of
the United States to confer with the Bolsheviks. The resolution
condemns Herron as a man who has flagrantly violated the laws
of God and man, and they call upon President Wilson to revoke his
appointment. They go into past history and assert that Mr. Herron
endeavored at one time to establish a free love colony at Metuchen,
New Jersey.
Time wasted! We warn the Newark protestants. Mr. Herron's
appointment will not be revoked. What is the marriage vow among
the makers of millenniums?

And lest you think this is merely *odium theologicum*, I give
an example of the comment of the laity, from "Harvey's
Weekly":

Why not make Herron the Turkish Mandatory? Herron's matrimonial views are broad and comprehensive. His poultry-yard standard
of morals might possibly be a little looser than the Turkish, but
he would doubtless conform himself in theory and practice to the
narrower Turkish matrimonial prejudices.

I wonder which is the more disagreeable phenomenon, sexual license or venal hypocrisy. It is a question I face when I read denunciations of the morals of radicals in capitalist newspapers. I have known men and women in a score of different worlds; I have talked with them and compared their sexual ethics, and I know that the newspaper people cannot afford to throw stones at the rest.

There are causes for this, of course. Their work is irregular and exhausting; they squeeze out the juices from their nerve-centers, they work under high pressure, in furious competition. Such men are apt to make immoderate use of tobacco and alcohol, and to take their pleasure where they find it. But this applies only to the rank and file in the newspaper world, to reporters and penny-a-liners; it does not apply to the big men at the top. These men have ease and security, and surely we might expect them to conform to the moral laws which they lay down for the rest of mankind!

I have in mind a certain editor. In this book where I am sparing no one, I should perhaps give his name; but I yield to human weakness, having been a guest at his home. Suffice it to say that this editor is one of America's very greatest, one to whom the masses of Americans look every day for enlightenment. This man wrote and published a most atrocious editorial concerning Herron's sexual morals. And what was his own sexual life at the time?

When the "Jungle" was published, this editor wrote to me that he had a friend who wished very much to meet me. I accepted, and went to dinner in a beautiful apartment in New York, luxuriously furnished, where I met a charming and cultured lady whom I will call Mrs. Smith. There were two lovely children, and there was Mr. Smith, a quiet, rather insignificant gentleman. I spent an enjoyable evening, and went away with no suspicion of anything unusual in the Smith family. But afterwards, when I mentioned the matter to others who knew this editor, I learned that the editor was the father of the children, and that Mr. Smith was maintained in luxury as a blind to cover the situation. I could hardly believe my ears; but I found that everybody who knew this editor intimately knew all about it, and that the editor made no secret of it among his friends. Later on, I came to know a certain brilliant and beautiful young suffrage leader, since deceased, who told me how she had exercised the privilege of the modern emancipated young woman, and had asked this editor to marry her. His answer was that he was very sorry, but he was not free, Mrs. Smith having given him to understand that if ever he left her, she would kill herself.

Here again we face the New York State law, forced upon the public by the Roman Catholic Church, making the grounds of divorce infidelity plus a scandal. Driven by the terror of scandal, men have been led by thousands and tens of thousands to make arrangements such as I have here described. Believing as I do that this divorce-law is an abomination, a product of vicious priest-craft, I hesitate before I blame these men; but no one need hesitate to blame them when, knowing what the law is, and what they themselves have been driven to, they publicly spit upon and trample the face of a modern prophet like George D. Herron.

And lest you think this case exceptional, I will give you another. There is a newspaper in New York, a pillar of capitalist respectability, the very corner-stone of the temple of bourgeois authority. This paper, of course, denounced Herron in unmeasured terms; recently it took up the attack again, in its solemn and ponderous manner rebuking the President for his lack of understanding of the moral sentiments of the American people. This great newspaper is owned and published by a Hebrew gentleman, intimately connected with the great financial interests of New York. He is one of the most respectable Hebrew gentlemen imaginable. And what are his sexual habits?

I know a lady, one of America's popular novelists. She is a charming lady, but without a trace of that appearance and manner which in the world is called "fast"; on the contrary, she is one of the women you know to be straightforward and self-respecting, the kind you would choose for your sister. She came to New York, young and inexperienced, desirous of earning a living. Naturally, she thought first of this great publisher, whom she had known socially in her home city. She went to him and told him that she had made something of a success at writing, and she wanted to write for the great metropolitan paper. He answered that he would be delighted, and arrangements were made. They were alone in the office, and she stood by his desk to shake hands with him in

parting, and he pulled her over and took her on his knee;
whereupon she boxed his ears and walked out of the office,
and never did any writing for the great metropolitan paper.

The above anecdote is, of course, hearsay so far as I am
concerned. I was not in the publisher's office, and I did not
see him take the lady-novelist on his knee; but my wife and
I knew this lady-novelist well, and she had no possible motive
for telling us a falsehood. The story came up casually in the
course of conversation, and was told spontaneously, and with
humor; for the lady takes life cheerfully, and had got over
being angry with the publisher—satisfied, I suppose, with
having boxed his ears so thoroughly. I wrote to her, to make
sure I had got matters straight, and in reply she asked me
not to use the story, even without her name. I quote:

> You know, of course, that I should be glad to do, at once and
> freely, anything I could to be helpful in your affairs. I have thought
> it over and it stands about like this in my mind. I am living a life
> that has its own aims—a thing apart from public attack and defense.
> If I had determined to make public—after all these years—any
> offense —— was guilty of toward me, my own feeling is clear that
> I should do it myself, openly and for reasons that seemed to me
> compelling. . . . . So leave me out of this matter, my dear Upton.

And so I confront a problem of conscience, or at any rate
of etiquette. Have I the right to tell this story, even without
giving names? I owe a certain loyalty to this friend; but
then, I think of the great publisher, and the manifold falsehoods I have known him to feed to the public. I think of
the prestige of such men, their solemn hypocrisy, their ponderous respectability. After weighing the matter, I am risking a friendship and telling the story. I hope that in the course
of time the lady will realize my point of view, and forgive me.

A different kind of problem confronts me with another
story, which I heard three or four years ago, just after it
happened. I had this book in mind at the time, and I said
to myself: "I'll name that man, and take the consequences."
But meantime, alas, the man has died; and now I ask myself:
"Can I tell this story about a dead man, a man who cannot
face me and compel me to take the consequences?" I think
of the man's life-long prostitution of truth, his infinite betrayal of the public interest, and I harden my heart, and
write the story, naming him. But then I weaken, and ask

advice. I ask women, and they say: "Name him!" I ask men, and they say: "You cannot tell such a story about a dead man!" Which is right?

Everything that the profit-system could do for one of its darlings had been done for this man. Millions of books, millions of magazinelets went out bearing his name; wealth, power, prominence, applause—all these things he had; his life was one long triumph—and one long treason to public welfare. And what was the man's private life? What use did he make of his fame, and more especially of his wealth?

The story was told to me by a woman-writer—not the one I have just referred to, but as different from her as one woman can be from another: a vivid and dashing creature, especially constructed both in body and mind for the confounding of the male. This lady was standing on a corner of Fifth Avenue, waiting for the stage, when a man stepped up beside her, and said out of the corner of his mouth, "I'll give you five dollars if you come with me." The lady made no response, and again the voice said, "I'll give you ten dollars if you come with me." Again there was no response, and the voice said, "I'll give you twenty-five dollars if you come with me." The stage arrived, and the auction was interrupted. But it happened that evening that the lady was invited to a dinner-party, to meet a great literary celebrity, a darling of the profit-system—and behold, it was the man who had bid for her on the street! "Mr. —— and I have met before," said the lady, icily; and, as she writes me, "this paralyzed him."

I ask this lady if I may tell the story. She answers: "Go the limit!" So here, at least, my conscience is at ease!

CHAPTER XXI

JOURNALISM AND BURGLARY

I was obliged to return to America to give testimony concerning an automobile accident of which I had been a witness. I had been sitting in the rear seat of a friend's car, which was proceeding at a very moderate rate of speed along a down-town street, when a fruit-peddler leaped out from behino an ice-wagon. He had a bunch of bananas in his hand and was looking up toward a woman in a window; he was not two feet ahead of the car when he sprang in front of it, and was struck before those in the car could move a finger. The account in the news column of the "New York Times" made clear that I had been merely a passenger, in another man's car, yet the "Times" found space on its editorial page for a letter from some correspondent, sneering at me as a Socialist who rode down poor men in automobiles!

During my return to America I remarried. The ceremony took place in Virginia, at the home of relatives of my wife's family, and I was interested to observe that the "Times," which had pursued me so continually, printed a perfectly respectful account of the wedding, with no editorial sneers. I was not puzzled by this, for I observed that the "Times" had taken the trouble to telegraph to Mississippi, to make inquiries concerning the lady I was marrying, and the report from their correspondent stated that the bride's father was "one of the wealthiest men in this section, and controls large banking interests." How many, many times I have observed the great organ of American plutocracy thus awed into decency by wealth! When Frank Walsh, as chairman of the United States Commission on Industrial Relations, made a radical speech in New York, the "Times" telegraphed to Kansas City and learned that Walsh was a lawyer earning an income of fifty thousand dollars a year. It was comical to observe the struggle between its desire to lambast a man who had made a radical speech, and its cringing before a man who was earning fifty thousand dollars a year!

In the same way, I have observed the attitude of the New

York newspapers toward my friend, J. G. Phelps Stokes, a Socialist who is reputed to be a millionaire, and who belongs to one of the oldest families in New York "society." So it makes no difference what he says or does, you never see a disrespectful word about him in a New York newspaper. On one occasion, I remember, he and his wife made Socialist speeches from a fire-escape in the tenement-district of New York—and even that was treated respectfully! Upton Sinclair, who is not reputed to be a millionaire, gave a perfectly decorous lecture on Socialism, at the request of his fellow passengers on an ocean-liner—and when he landed in New York he read in the "Evening World" that he had delivered a "tirade." I might add that the above remarks are not to be taken as in any manner derogatory to Stokes, who is in no possible way to blame for the fact that the newspapers spare him the treatment they give to other American Socialists, including Mrs. Stokes.

At this time ten or twenty thousand silk-workers in Paterson, New Jersey, went on strike, affording the usual spectacle —a horde of ill-paid, half-starved wage slaves being bludgeoned into submission by policemen's clubs, backed by propaganda of lying newspapers. The silk-mill owners of Paterson of course owned the city government, and were using the police-force to prevent meetings of the strikers; but it happened that the near-by village of Haledon had a Socialist mayor, and there was no way to keep the strikers from walking there for open air mass-meetings. There was clamor for the State troops to prevent such gatherings, and the newspapers were called on to make them into near-riots. My wife and I would go out to the place and attend a perfectly orderly gathering, addressed by such men as Ernest Poole and Hutchins Hapgood, and then we would come back to New York and buy a copy of the "Evening Telegram" and read all across the front page scare-headlines about riots, dynamite and assassination. I have before me a clipping from the "New York World," of Monday, May 19, 1913. *"Paterson's Fiercest Fight Feared Today,"* runs the headline.

On this same date my old friend the "New York Times" achieved a little masterpiece of subtle knavery. I quote:

UPTON SINCLAIR IS HEARD

After Mohl came another newcomer so far as Paterson is concerned—Upton Sinclair.

"I just simply could not stand it any longer," said Sinclair, "and I let my books go and came here to congratulate you. Yours is the finest exhibition of solidarity ever seen in the Eastern States."

Sinclair stated that the strikers had the police at their mercy, but added that perhaps they did not realize it.

This, please understand, was part of a campaign to make the general public regard the Paterson silk-workers as anarchists and desperadoes. "The strikers have the police at their mercy," says Sinclair; and what conclusion does the reader draw from these words? Obviously, Sinclair is advising the strikers to grab up clubs and brick-bats and overwhelm the police. You would have drawn that conclusion, would you not? Perhaps maybe you are one of the readers of the "Times," and *did* draw that conclusion! As it happens, when I read that item, I took the trouble to jot down what I acually did say, and to preserve the record along with the clipping. I quote:

You fellows go out on the picket-line and the police fall upon you with clubs, they ride you down with their horses, they raid your offices, and suppress your papers and throw your leaders into jail, and you think you are helpless. You don't realize that you have the police at your mercy. All those policemen are appointed by the city government; they get their orders from the city government and every year or two you go to the ballot-box and say whether you like what they have been doing. In other words, you vote for Republican or Democratic politicians, instead of electing Socialists to office, and having a city government that will give you your lawful rights.

To get the full significance of the above, you must realize that this was an I. W. W. strike; I went out to a meeting conducted by Bill Haywood and Carlo Tresca and Elizabeth Gurley Flynn, and was permitted to preach a doctrine of political action which these leaders despised. I, who have all my life urged upon the workers of America the futility of the strike alone, and the necessity of political action, went out and said my say in the midst of a campaign of "direct action"; and see how much understanding I got from the great metropolitan newspapers for my defense of political methods! One year later, after the Colorado coal-strike, the little urchins in the village of Croton-on-Hudson where I lived used to follow me on the street and shout: "I won't work!" I used to reflect that our great organs of publicity, the "New

York Times" and "World" and "Herald" and "Tribune" and
"Sun," stood upon precisely the same level of intelligence as
these little village urchins.

At this time the newspapers were trying to obtain from
me a photograph of the lady who went with me to strike-
meetings, in spite of the fact that her father was "one of
the wealthiest men in this section, and controls large banking
interests." They didn't get the photograph, so they were in
desperate straits. A reporter for a Philadelphia newspaper
—I have the clipping, but unfortunately not the name of
the paper—went to Arden to look me up, and was told by
my friend Donald Stephens that I was not there. The homes
in Arden are scattered about through the woods, and life
is informal; I had locked the doors of my house, but the
windows were not fastened. I am not in a position to prove
that the reporter for a Philadelphia newspaper burglarized
my house and stole a picture of my wife. I cannot state
positively that a course in house-breaking is a part of the
training of newspaper reporters in the City of Brotherly Love.
All I can state is the following set of facts:

1. In my desk in the house there lay a kodak-picture
of my wife and myself and my wife's younger sister.

2. This copy was the only one in existence, having been
taken by my sister-in-law in an out-of-the-way place, and
developed by a photographer who knew nothing about us.

3. Upon my return to Arden, this picture was discovered
to be missing from my desk.

4. This missing picture was published in a Philadelphia
newspaper.

CHAPTER XXII

A MILLIONAIRE AND AN AUTHOR

The thesis of this book is that our newspapers do not represent public interests, but private interests; they do not represent humanity, but property; they value a man, not because he is great, or good, or wise, or useful, but because he is wealthy, or of service to vested wealth. And suppose that you wished to make a test of this thesis, a test of the most rigid scientific character—what would you do? You would put up two men, one representing property, the other representing humanity. You would endeavor rigidly to exclude all other factors; you would find one man who represented property to the exclusion of humanity, and you would find another man who represented humanity to the exclusion of property. You would put these two men before the public, having them do the same thing, so far as humanly possible, and then you would keep a record of the newspaper results. These results would give you mathematically, in column-inches, the relative importance to each newspaper of the man of property and the man of humanity. Such an exact, scientific test I have now to record.

I introduce the two persons. First, the man of humanity: At the time the test was made, in December, 1913, he was thirty-five years of age; he was known everywhere throughout the United States, and was, with the possible exception of Jack London, the most widely known of living American writers throughout the world. At the time of the test he did not own more than a couple of hundred dollars.

Second, the man of property. He was at this time twenty-two years of age, and had done four things which had been widely heralded: First, he was born. Second, he decided to conduct some experiments in farming. Third, he decided to marry a young lady of his acquaintance. Fourth, he inherited sixty-five million dollars. Three of these things are not at all unusual; many a farmer's boy has done them, and has not had the distinction of seeing the newspapers devote columns of space to them. But the other thing is quite unique; since the beginning of American history, no other person has ever inherited sixty-five million dollars. So it may be asserted beyond dispute that this young man's reputation depended upon property, and nothing but property; he was the perfect specimen which the sociological scientist would require for his test—the man of property pur sang.

And now for the action of the two men. It appears that the "New York Times," a great organ of world-capitalism, in its efforts to camouflage its true functions, had resorted to the ancient device of charity, used by the Christian Church ever since it sold out to the Emperor Constantine. Early in December of each year the "Times" publishes a list which it calls "One Hundred Neediest Cases," and collects money for these hundred families in distress. The "Times" never goes into the question of the social system which produces these harrowing cases, nor does it allow anyone else to go into this question; what it does is to present the hundred victims of the system with enough money to preserve them until the following December, so that they may again enter into competition for mention in the list, and have their miseries exploited by the "Times."

In addition to this, the "Times" publishes every Sunday an illustrated supplement of pictures to entertain its variety of readers; and it happened that on the Sunday when it published the "Hundred Neediest Cases" it published also a photograph of a "recreation building" which young Mr. Vincent Astor was erecting on his country estate at a cost of one million dollars. This building was for the use of Astor and his friends; it had no place for the public. It was devoted to tennis and swimming and gymnastics; it had no place for literature, music, art, science, or religion—it was a typical product of the private property régime. So the man who represented humanity sat himself down and wrote a "Christmas letter" to the millionaire, in substance asking him how he could enjoy his Christmas, how he could be content to play in a million-dollar "recreation-building," when he had before him such positive evidence that millions of his fellow-beings were starving. This letter was picturesque, interesting and well-written; as news it was in every way "live."

So came the first test. This "Christmas letter" to Vincent Astor was offered to every newspaper in New York City on the same date, addressed "City Editor," special delivery. It

was sent to both morning and afternoon papers. And how
many published it? Just one—the New York "Call"—the
Socialist paper. No other paper in New York, morning or
afternoon, printed a line of it, or referred to it in any way.
It was offered to every big news agency in the country. And
how many handled it? Not one. Outside of New York it
was published in the "Appeal to Reason," and in one Chicago
paper which happened to be edited by a personal friend of
the author's. So here you have the first verdict of the capitalist journalism of New York City; a letter written by a man
of humanity represents a total news-value of precisely 0.

There the matter might have rested, the test might never
have been completed, but for the fact that the millionaire disagreed with the judgment of his newspaper editors; he thought
the letter of the author was important, and he answered it.

How this came to happen I have no idea. Maybe the
millionaire's conscience was touched; maybe he had ambition
to be something else than a man of property pur sang. Maybe
he himself wrote the answer; maybe some shrewd family
lawyer wrote it; maybe his secretary or some other employe
wrote it—all I know is that two or three weeks later the
millionaire wrote to the author, and at the same time gave
his letter to the newspapers.

The author's letter had been, of course, an attack upon
capitalism. The millionaire's was a defense of it. And so
came the second test. Every New York newspaper was offered an opportunity to publish the millionaire's letter to the
author. And how many availed themselves of the opportunity?
Every one, absolutely every one! Every one published the
letter, and published it *entire!* Most of them put it on the
front page, with the millionaire's picture; some of them added
columns of interviews about it, and editorials discussing it.
The New York newspapers' idea of the news-value of a man of
property was precisely one hundred per cent!

The above would have been sufficient for any sociological
scientist; but, as it happened, the test was carried one stage
farther yet. The author was not entirely overwhelmed by
the evidence of his unimportance as compared with a millionaire; he was a Socialist, and Socialists are notoriously hard
to squelch. He wrote a second letter to the millionaire, answering the millionaire's arguments; and again he offered it to
every paper and to every news agency in New York—the

same ones that had spread out the millionaire's arguments in full. And how many printed it? How many printed the whole of it? Just one—the "Call," the Socialist paper. How many printed parts of it? And how large were these parts? Let us see.

The author's first letter measured in newspaper columns sixty-three inches; the millionaire's reply measured nineteen, and the author's reply to that measured sixty-one. If it be objected that the author was claiming more than his fair share, it should be pointed out that the author was attacking an established institution, something one cannot do in a few sentences. On the other hand, the most foolish person can reply, "I don't agree with you"—and claim the virtue of brevity. Also, be it noted that the question here is not what the author *claimed*, but what he *got*. Here is a table showing what he got, in column inches, from the leading morning papers of New York:

	Author	Millionaire	Author
Times	0	19	0
Herald	0	19	0
Press	0	19	0
Tribune	0	19	0
American	0	19	2
World	0	19	2¼
Sun	0	19	4½
Call	63	19	61

Let it be noted that the above takes no account of headlines, which were all big for the millionaire and small for the author; it does not include editorials, interviews and photographs, nor does it reckon the advantage of first-page position.

In order to make the significance of the figures quite clear, let them be reduced to percentages. Each paper had 124 author-inches offered to it, and 19 millionaire-inches. To begin with the "Times": this paper printed all the millionaire inches—also a few extra which it hunted up for itself; it printed none at all of the author-inches. Hence we see that, to put it mathematically, the "Times" considers an author absolutely *nothing* in comparison with a millionaire. Exactly the same is true of the "Herald," the "Press," and the "Tribune." The "World" printed 100 per cent of possible millionaire-inches and less than 2 per cent of possible author-inches, thus giving the millionaire more than fifty times the advantage. Similarly, the "American" favored him sixty to one. The "Call" placed the two on a par—that is to say, the "Call" printed the *news*.

I conclude the account of this little episode by quoting a passage from the published "Memoirs" of a wise old Chinese gentleman, Li-Hung-Chang, who happened to be a man of humanity as well as of property:

A poor man is ever at a disadvantage in matters of public concern. When he rises to speak, or writes a letter to his superiors, they ask: "Who is this fellow that offers advice?" And when it is known that he is without coin they spit their hands at him, and use his letters in the cooks' fires. But if it be a man of wealth who would speak, or write, or denounce, even though he have the brain of a yearling dromedary, or a spine as crooked and unseemly, the whole city listens to his words and declares them wise.

CHAPTER XXIII

THE "HEART WIFE"

The next story has to do with the phenomenon known as "Hearst Journalism." It is a most extraordinary story; in its sensational elements it discounts the most lurid detective yarn, it discounts anything which is published in the Hearst newspapers themselves. At fii t the reader may find it beyond belief; if so, let him bear in mind that the story was published in full in the "New York Call" for August 9, 1914, and that no one of the parties named brought a libel suit, nor made so much as a peep concerning the charges. I may fairly assert that this story of "Hearst Journalism" is one which Mr. Hearst and his editors themselves admit to be true.

William Randolph Hearst has been at various times a candidate for high office in America, and has been able to exert much influence on the course of the Democratic party— in New York, in Illinois, and even throughout the nation. What are the Hearst newspapers? How are they made? And what is the character of the men who make them? These questions seem to me of sufficient importance to be worth answering in detail.

In order to make matters clear from the outset, let me point out to the reader that, for once, I am not dealing with a grievance of my own. Throughout this whole affair my purpose was to get some money from a Hearst newspaper, but I was not trying to get this money for myself; I was trying to get it for a destitute and distracted woman. All parties concerned knew that and knew it beyond dispute. The wrong was done, not to me, but to a destitute and distracted woman, and so I can present to the reader a case in which he can not possibly attribute an ulterior motive to me.

The story began at Christmas, 1913. In the New York papers there appeared one day an account of the death of a lawyer named Couch, in the little town of Monticello, N. Y. This man was nearly 60 years old, a cripple and eccentric, who lived most of the time in his little office in the village, going once a week to the home upon the hill where lived his wife and family. The news of his death in the middle of the night was brought to a physician by a strange, terrified woman, who was afterwards missing, but next day was discovered by Mr. Couch's widow and daughter, cowering in an inner portion of his office, which had been partitioned off to make a separate room.

Investigation was made, and an extraordinary set of circumstances disclosed. The man and woman had been lovers for fifteen years, and for the last three years the woman had spent her entire time in this walled-off room, never going outside, never even daring to go near the window in the daytime. This sacrifice she had made for the sake of the old man, because she had been necessary to his life, and there was no other way of keeping secret a situation which would have ruined him.

The story seemed to make a deep impression upon the public, at least if one could judge from the newspapers. There were long accounts from Monticello day by day. The woman was described as grief-stricken, terrified by her sudden confrontation with the world. She was taken to the county jail and kept there until after the dead man's funeral. No charges were brought against her, but she remained in jail because she had nowhere else to go, and because her condition was so pitiful that the authorities delayed to turn her out. She was helpless, friendless, with but one idea, a longing for death. She was besieged by newspaper reporters, vaudeville impresarios and moving picture makers, to all of whom she denied herself, refusing to make capital of her grief. She was described as a person of refinement and education, and everything she said bore out this view of her character. She was, apparently, a woman of mature mind, who had deliberately sacrificed everything else in life in order to care for an unhappy old man whom she loved, and whom she could not marry because of the rigid New York divorce law.

One morning the papers stated that the relatives of this "hidden woman" refused to offer a home to her. My wife wrote to her, offering to help her, provided this could be done without any publicity; but time passed without a reply. My wife was only three or four weeks out of the hospital after an operation for an injury to the spine. We had made plans to spend the winter in Bermuda, to give her an opportunity to recuperate, and our steamer was to sail at midnight on Monday. On Sunday morning, while I was away from home, my wife was called on the phone by Miss Branch, who announced that she had left the Sullivan County jail, and was at the ferry in New York, with no idea what to do—except to leap off into the river. My wife told her to take a cab and come to our home, and sent word to me what she had done.

Not to drag out the story too much, I will say briefly that Miss Branch proved to be a woman of refinement, and also of remarkable mind. She has read widely and thought for herself, and I have in my possession a number of her earlier manuscripts which show, not merely that she can write, but that she has worked out for herself a point of view and an attitude to life. She was one of the most pitiful and tragic figures it has ever been our fate to encounter, and the twenty-four hours which we spent in trying to give her comfort and the strength to face life again will not soon be forgotten by either of us.

We interested some friends, Dr. and Mrs. James P. Warbasse, in the case, and they very generously offered to place Miss Branch in a sanitarium. Before she left she implored me to make a correction of certain misstatements about her which had appeared in the papers. She was deeply grieved because of the shame she had brought upon her brother and his family, and she thought their sufferings might be partly relieved if they and others read the truth about her character and motives.

At this time, it should be understood, Miss Branch was the newspaper mystery of the hour. She had vanished from Monticello, and on Monday morning the newspapers had nothing on the case but their own inventions. I sought the advice of a friend, J. O'Hara Cosgrave, a well known editor, who suggested that the story ought to be worth money. "As you say that Miss Branch is penniless, why not let one of the papers buy it and pay the money to her? The 'Evening Journal' has been playing the story up on the front page every day. Sell it to them."

I said, "You can't sell a newspaper a tip without first telling them what the story is—and can you trust them?"

He answered, "I personally know Van Hamm, managing editor of the 'Evening Journal,' and if you will make it a personal matter with him, you can trust him."

"Are you sure?" I asked.

"Absolutely," he replied.

I talked the matter over with my wife, who was much opposed to the suggestion, refusing to believe that any Hearst man could be trusted. They would betray me, and use my name, and we should be in for disagreeable publicity. Moreover, Miss Branch would never get the money, unless I got a contract in writing. I answered that there was no time to get it in writing. It was then about one o'clock in the afternoon, and the matter would have to be arranged over the phone at once, if it were to be of any use to an evening paper. So finally my wife consented to the attempt being made, upon the definite understanding that she was to stand beside me at the telephone and hear what I said, and that I was to repeat every word the party at the other end of the wire said, in such a way that both he and she would hear the repetition. In this way she would be a witness to the conversation.

And now, as everything depends upon the question of what was said, let me state in advance that this conversation was written down from the memory of both of us a few hours afterward, and that we are prepared, if necessary, to make affidavit that every word of it was spoken, not once, but several times; that the various points covered in it were repeated so frequently and explicitly that the party at the other end of the wire once or twice showed himself annoyed at the delays. The conversation was as follows:

"Is this Mr. Van Hamm, managing editor of the 'Evening Journal'? Mr. Van Hamm, I have called you up because Jack Cosgrave has told me that you are a man who can be trusted. I wish to ask you if you will give me your word of honor to deal fairly with me in a certain matter. I have some information to offer you which will make a big story. I am offering to sell it for a price, and I wish it to be distinctly understood, in advance, beyond any possible question, that you may have this story if you are willing to pay the price. If you don't want to pay the price, I have your word of honor that you will not in any manner whatever use any syllable of what I tell you."

This was repeated and agreed to, and then I told him what I had. "I am not at liberty to tell you where Miss Branch is at present," I said. "I am offering you a story, and a statement which she desires me to give out for her. The price for it is three hundred dollars fcr **Miss Branch.** I don't want the money myself—I won't even handle it. Is the price agreeable to you?"

The answer was, "Yes, I will send a man up at once."

I said, "It is distinctly understood that you are to publish nothing whatever about this matter unless the sum of three hundred dollars is paid to Miss Branch?"

"Yes. Where is she, so that I can pay the money to her?"

"I will give you the name of a man who knows where she is. This man will take the money and will bring you her receipt. I wish to give you the name of this man in confidence, for he does not wish his name brought into the case in any way."

The answer was: "Put the name of the man in a sealed envelope and give it to the reporter, who will give it to me. I will personally see that the money is sent to him, and then will forget his name."

"Very well," I replied, and added, "I have written a thousand-word article discussing the case. I will give you this article along with the rest of the information. But you must not print either this article or a single word about this matter unless you pay three hundred dollars to Miss Branch. You understand that distinctly?"

He replied, "I understand. A man will be up to see you in half an hour."

Fifteen minutes after the conversation there came a telephone-call; a voice, sharp and determined, at the other end of the wire, "Is Miss Branch there?" My wife was answering the phone and she beckoned to me. We stared at each other, uncertain what to answer or what to think.

"Miss Branch?" said my wife. "No! Certainly Miss Branch is not here."

"Then where is she?" came the next question, imperative and urgent.

" I do not know," said my wife. "Who are you?"

"I have been sent by Sheriff Kinnie, of Sullivan County Jail, who has an important message to be delivered to Miss Branch at once."

Said I (taking the phone): "Have you credentials from Sheriff Kinnie?"

"No," was the reply, "I have not."

"Then," I said, "you cannot see Miss Branch."

"But," said the voice, "I must see her at once. It is really very important."

"Come here and see me," I said.

"No," was the answer, "I cannot. Please tell me where Miss Branch is. It is a matter of the utmost urgency to Miss Branch herself."

This went on for several minutes, and, finally, having made sure he could get nothing further, the man at the other end of the wire made an appointment to see me at 5:30 P. M.

As soon as I hung up the receiver my wife said: "That is a newspaper reporter. Some other paper knows about her."

But how could this be? Miss Branch had assured us that she had not mentioned our names to any one, nor shown the letter we had written to her; that no one in Monticello had the remotest idea where she was going, not even the kind sheriff; that no one had boarded the train at her station. She had been most careful, because my wife in her letter had laid such stress upon her distaste for publicity.

Of course, if other papers had the story of her having come to us, then Miss Branch would not get the money from Mr. Van Hamm. I had sold an exclusive story, and it would be said that I had not delivered the goods. I at once telephoned to Mr. Van Hamm to tell him of this incident, but I was told that he was out, and I left word for him to call me up the minute he returned.

His reporter arrived, Mr. Thorpe by name. I will say for Mr. Thorpe that I think he tried to be decent all through this ugly matter. I detected in him before it was over the manner of a man who has been sent to do a job he does not like. I explained to him that I had just had a call from a man I suspected to be a reporter, and therefore I would not give him the story until I had had another talk with Mr. Van Hamm and explained the circumstances to him. So Mr. Thorpe sat for awhile in conversation with me. My wife came out and talked to him—much to my surprise, for she has a dread of reporters. Soon, however, I discovered that it was my wife who was doing the interviewing. She called me out of the room and said: "That telephone call was from the 'Journal' office."

"How do you know?" I asked.

"From everything this young man says, and from his manner. 'I've tried to make him answer me, whether Mr.

Van Hamm could have been responsible for that telephone-
call, and he evaded the question."

"But," I said, "what object could they have?"

"They may have been trying to probe you. They have
believed that Miss Branch is still with us. This man is trying
to find out right now, for he cranes his neck and peers every
time I open a door."

I did not think this could be, but I was more than ever
determined to have another talk with Mr. Van Hamm. However, this gentleman continued to be mysteriously absent. I
will sum up this aspect of the matter by saying that he continued to be "expected every few minutes" at his office and at
his home until 12 o'clock that night. I made not less than
twenty efforts to get him, but he would not even let me
hear his voice.

As I still refused to give up my story, Mr. Thorpe was
suddenly seized with a desire for cigarettes, and went out to
purchase some. I am not in a position to say that he called
up the office, and turned in what information he had been
able to get in the course of our conversation. I will only
say that such information appeared an hour or two later in
the columns of the "Evening Journal."

Mr. Thorpe returned, and still Mr. Van Hamm was mysteriously missing. At last I got tired of waiting, and I gave
Mr. Thorpe the interview and the article, and also a letter
addressed to Mr. Van Hamm, in which I explicitly repeated
the specifications of my telephone conversation with him. I
read it to Mr. Thorpe and my wife.

It was then time for the mysterious stranger to appear,
but needless to say, he did not keep his appointment. I will
conclude this aspect of the story by quoting the following letter
from Sheriff Frank Kinnie, of Sullivan County, N. Y.

Your favor relative to Miss Branch received this morning and
wish to state that the statement is a falsehood absolutely, as I had no
idea whatever as to Miss Branch's whereabouts, and if you meet Miss
Branch she will tell you that no one here in her confidence knew
where she was going. I trust a kind Providence will protect and
care for her.

To continue: I had that evening to attend a reception
given to the delegates of the Intercollegiate Socialist Society,
at the home of a friend of mine who conducts a boarding
school for young ladies. Little dreaming what an avalanche

I was to bring down upon the head of this unfortunate friend,
I left word at the office that Mr. Van Hamm was to call me at
this school at 8 o'clock that evening.

My wife and I then proceeded to pack our belongings for
the steamer—the first opportunity we had had in all this
excitement. The superintendent of the apartment-house came
to us to ask if we could leave an hour earlier than we had
intended, as there were two gentlemen who had rented it and
wanted to move in immediately. My wife said: "Surely no
one can move into an apartment in the state of disorder in
which we are leaving this!"

"It seems strange," was the reply, "but that is what they
want to do. They do not want to wait to have it put in order.
They are waiting, and they want to come in the minute you
leave."

If I had been dealing with Hearst newspapers for a sufficiently long time, I would have understood in advance the
significance of this phenomenon. As it was, I simply pitied
the two unfortunate young men, who would have to spend
the night in the midst of the chaotic mass of torn manuscripts
and scraps of letters and envelopes which littered the floor.
Later on I was glad that I had married a lawyer's daughter—
when my wife informed me she had gone over this trash
and burned every scrap of paper relating to Miss Branch and
her affairs!

I went to the reception, and at about 8 o'clock in the
evening the "Journal" called me up—"Mr. Williams" on the
wire—to say that Mr. Van Hamm had considered my article
and regretted to say that he could not use it. The information
that I had offered him was not considered worth the sum of
three hundred dollars. I asked what it was worth, and was
told twenty-five dollars. I said, "That won't do. I will offer
it somewhere else." I demanded the right to speak to Mr. Van
Hamm himself on the subject, but was told that he was "out."
I was obliged to content myself with impressing upon "Mr.
Williams" the fact that not a syllable that I had confided to
Mr. Van Hamm was to be used by the "Journal." "Mr.
Williams" solemnly assured me that my demand would be complied with—and this in face of the fact that the last edition
of the "Evening Journal," containing the whole story, was then
in the "Journal" wagons, being distributed over the city! I
called up a friend of mine on the "World" to offer him the

story, and the reader will need a vivid imagination to get an idea of my emotions when this friend exclaimed, "Why, that story has already been used by the 'Journal'!"

"That is impossible!" I exclaimed.

He answered, "I have a copy of it upon my desk."

It was not until I was going on board the steamer that I got a copy of the "final extra" of the "New York Evening Journal," the issue of Monday, December 29, 1913. At the top of the front page, in red letters more than one-half inch high, appeared the caption:

"JOURNAL FINDS MISS BRANCH HERE"

with two index hands to point out this wonderful news to the reader. A good portion of the remainder of the front page was occupied by an article with these headings:

HEART-WIFE IS IN NEW YORK

Found Here by Journal.

"Miss Branch Traced to Well-Known Writer's Home After Secret Flight.

Adelaide M. Branch, for three years the heart-wife of Melvin H. Couch, former District Attorney of Sullivan County, is today in New York City. She is secluded at the home of a well-known sociologist and writer who has interested himself in her case and has offered her a home, at least until she can make definite plans for the future.

Miss Branch was traced to her hiding place in this city by the "Evening Journal." The former "love slave" of Couch told the sociologist that she wished to be absolutely quiet and undisturbed. So for the present it is not possible to give her address.

And so continued a long article, which contained practically everything of what I gave to Mr. Thorpe, sometimes even using the very phrases which I had used in the presence of my wife.

I will not trouble the reader with a description of the state of mind we were in when our steamer set out for Bermuda. I will simply give a brief summary of what else occurred in this incredible affair:

First, someone got, or pretended to get, from the hall-boy at the apartment where I had been staying, an elaborate and entirely fictitious account of how Miss Branch had arrived, and how she had swooned and my wife had caught her in her arms, and how some other people had come and carried her away in an automobile. This account was published in full.

Then the records of my telephone-calls were consulted, and
every person whom I had called up in my last two days in
the apartment was hounded. My poor mother was driven
nearly to desperation. In our telephone-call list was found
the name of Dr. Warbasse, who had taken Miss Branch away,
and Dr. Warbasse later received a wireless message from
Bermuda, as follows:

"Give Branch story to papers."

Shortly afterward the doctor was called up by the "Evening
Journal," and was told that the "Journal" had received a wireless message from me, instructing them to call on him for information concerning Miss Branch. I quote from Dr. Warbasse's letter to me:

> I believed the only way they could have learned of my connection
> with the case was from you, and accordingly gave them a short state-
> ment of the facts, but withheld the location of Miss Branch. They
> published very distorted versions of what little I gave them. They
> were particularly solicitous for her whereabouts. A few days later
> I had another wireless from you, asking me to send you Branch's
> address. By this time I had grown suspicious, and sent you my
> address instead. I am now wondering whether the wireless messages
> were from you or were newspaper fakery. If the latter is the case,
> it was well done, believe me, and does great credit to the unscrupu-
> lousness of the press.

Needless to say, I had sent no such message. What is
more significant, I did not receive the message which Dr.
Warbasse sent to me, giving me his address! Is the "Evening
Journal" able to intercept cablegrams? I don't know; but
soon after my arrival in Bermuda I received a letter from my
friend who conducts the school for young ladies, scolding me
for the terrible trouble into which I had got her. The "Journal,"
she said, had become convinced that Miss Branch was hidden
in the school, and it was only by desperate efforts that she had
kept this highly sensational rumor from going out to the
world. I thought, of course, that I was to blame for my
thoughtlessness in having given her telephone number to the
"Evening Journal" on the eve of my departure from New
York, and I wrote abjectly apologizing for this. What was
my consternation to receive a letter assuring me that this was
not what had angered her, but the fact that I had been so
foolish as to send her a wireless message, instructing her to
give the story of Miss Branch to the paper, and had wired
the "Journal" to call upon her for the information!

Mr. Arthur Brisbane is the man whom I had always understood to be the editor in charge of the "Evening Journal." I
wrote him asking him to investigate this affair; and I sent
a registered copy of the letter to Mr. Hearst, who, I assumed,
would be jealous for the journalistic honor of his papers.
I pointed out the fact that on the Monday afternoon in question
every newspaper in New York had had the story that Miss
Branch was going West to see a brother of hers. In all
editions of the "Evening Journal," except the final edition,
the following statement had appeared:

> Heart-wife flees to asylum. Miss Branch is in hiding in a sani-
> tarium within ten miles of Monticello. As soon as she recovers her
> strength she will probably join her brother.

I said that I wished to know what Mr. Van Hamm had
to say, as to how the "Journal" had got the information it
published in its final edition. If it was an independent tip,
who gave that tip? And if the telephone-call alleged to be
from the Sheriff had come from any other paper than the
"Journal," why had not that paper used the story?

Mr. Brisbane replied that he was now in Chicago, and had
no longer anything to do with the "New York Evening
Journal," but that the matter would undoubtedly be investigated by Mr. Hearst.

A friend of mine, an old newspaper man, wrote me à propos
of this: "Don't imagine for one minute that anything will
be done about it; don't imagine but that Van Hamm is Hearst.
Hearst knows exactly what Van Hamm does, and if Van
Hamm failed to do it, he would lose his job." This sounded
somewhat cynical, but it seemed to be borne out by Mr.
Hearst's course. He chose to veil himself in Olympian silence.
I wrote him a second courteous letter, to the effect that unless
I heard from him and received some explanation, I would be
compelled to assume that he intended to make the actions of
his subordinates his own. He has not replied to that letter,
so I presume that I am justified in the assumption. And this
man wishes to be United States Senator from New York!

Several years ago he desired to be Governor, and there resulted such a tempest of public wrath, such a chorus of exposure and denunciation, that he was overwhelmed; if he had
not had a very tough skin he would have fled from political
life forever. Unquestionably a deal of this denunciation came

from vested interests which he had frightened by his radicalism; but, on the other hand, it betrayed a note of personal loathing that was unmistakable. I marvelled at it at the time; but now I think I understand it.

The story of Miss Branch is forgotten, but other stories are filling the Hearst papers day by day. Are they all got with the same disregard for every consideration of decency, for all the rules which control the dealings of civilized men with one another? Get clear the meaning of this story of mine—the reason for all this lying, sneaking, forging of cablegrams, bribing of hall-boys, violation of honor and good faith. Was it to get a story? No—the "Journal" had the story offered to it on a silver tray! The reason for all the knavery was to avoid the payment of three hundred dollars to a destitute and distracted woman—that, and that alone! And if such be Hearst's attitude to his pocket-book, if such be the methods of his newspaper-machine where his pocket-book is concerned, there must be thousands and tens of thousands of people in New York—politicians, journalists, authors, businessmen—who have run into that machine as I did, and been knocked bruised and bloody into the ditch. When Mr. Hearst runs for office, all these men jump into the arena and get their revenge!

CHAPTER XXIV

THE MOURNING PICKETS

I had a book to write that winter, and my wife's health to think about. We had got as far from the newspapers as we knew how—a little cottage in one of the remotest parts of the Bermuda Islands, with sand-dunes and coral-crags all about us, and a sweep of the Southern ocean in front. There we lived for several months, and thought we were safe. I never went anywhere, except to play tennis—so surely I ought to have been safe! But I wasn't.

All at once my clipping-bureau began sending me articles from newspapers all over the United States. I was starting a ranch for the training of incorrigible boys in Nevada! First, I was in Chicago for an assortment of boys; I wanted the very wildest and most blood-thirsty that could be found; I had picked out several young criminals who had been given up by reformatories. Then, a little later, I was out in Nevada, starting this "Last Chance Ranch," with a score or two of boys. And then one of the boys ran away; he complained that I fed him on vegetarian food, and he couldn't stand it. As it happened, I had not been a vegetarian for a long time; also, as it happened, I was in Bermuda instead of Nevada; but what did that matter to the newspapers? Before long I found myself riding on horseback across the desert, chasing this runaway boy, John Fargo. I had been riding for three days and had nothing in my saddle-bags but peanuts and canned beans.

And there I was left. To this day I don't know what happened to me; whether I caught "John Fargo," or what become of my "Last Chance Ranch." Is there a phantom Upton Sinclair, still chasing "John Fargo" over the Nevada desert, and living on peanuts and canned beans?

It may have been, of course, that there was some one impersonating me. A friend of mine, a school-teacher, told me the other day that one of her pupils had assured her quite solemnly that he knew me well; I was a cripple, and went about in a wheel-chair. Also, I was told by a waiter in a

142

Los Angeles hotel that a bald-headed man had reserved a table in my name, and given an elaborate dinner, and that the hotel staff had thought they were dining me. I am wondering what would have happened in the newspapers if that bald-headed man had drunk too much champagne, and had thrown a bottle through one of the dining-room mirrors?

I came back to America, and made an investigation of the Colorado coal-strike, and so began one of the most sensational episodes of my life. It is a long story, but I shall tell it in full, because it is not a personal story, but a story of eleven thousand miners with their wives and children, living in slavery in lonely mountain fortresses, making a desperate fight for the rights of human beings, and crushed back into their slave-pens by all the agencies of capitalist repression.

I had been to Colorado, and knew intimately the conditions. Now the strike was on, and the miners and their families living in tent-colonies had been raided, beaten, shot up by gun-men. Finally a couple of machine-guns had been turned loose on them, their tent-colony at Ludlow had been burned, and three women and fourteen children had been suffocated to death. I sat in Carnegie Hall, New York City, amid an audience of three thousand people, and listened to an account of these conditions by eye-witnesses; next morning I opened the newspapers, and found an account in the "New York Call," a Socialist paper, and two inches in the "New York World"—and not a line in any other New York paper!

I talked over the problem with my wife, and we agreed that something must be done to break this conspiracy of silence. I had trustworthy information to the effect that young Rockefeller was in charge of what was going on in Colorado, though he was vigorously denying it at this time, and continued to deny it until the Walsh commission published his letters and telegrams to his representatives in Denver. Evidently, therefore, Mr. Rockefeller was the shining mark at which we must aim. It happened that one of the speakers at the Carnegie Hall meeting had been Mrs. Laura G. Cannon, whose husband was an organizer for the United Mine Workers, and had been thrown into jail by the militia and kept there without warrant or charge for a considerable time. So we called on Mrs. Cannon to go with us to the offices of Mr. Rockefeller.

We were received by a polite secretary, to whom we delivered a carefully phrased letter, asking Mr. Rockefeller to meet Mrs. Cannon, and hear at first hand what she had personally witnessed of the strike. We were invited to come back an hour later for our reply, and we came, and were informed that Mr. Rockefeller would not see us. So we presented a second letter, prepared in advance, to the effect that if he persisted in his refusal to see us, we should consider ourselves obligated to indict him for murder before the bar of public opinion. To this letter the polite secretary informed us, not quite so politely, there was "no answer."

What was to be done now? I had learned by experience that it would be necessary to do something sensational. An indignation meeting in Carnegie Hall, attended by three thousand people, was not enough. At first I thought that I would go to young Mr. Rockefeller's office and watch for him in the hall, and give him a horse-whipping. But this would have been hard on me, because I am constitutionally opposed to violence, and I did not think Mr. Rockefeller worth such a sacrifice of my feelings. What I wanted was something that would be picturesque and dramatic, but would not involve violence; and finally I hit on the idea of inviting a group of people to put bands of crepe around their arms, and to walk up and down in front of 26 Broadway in dead silence, to symbolize our grief for the dead women and children of Ludlow. I called a group of radicals to discuss the project; also I called the newspaper reporters.

Picketing, except in labor strikes, was a new thing at that time, though the suffragists have since made it familiar. The novelty of the thing, plus the fact that it was being done by a group of well-known people, furnished that element of sensation which is necessary if radical news is to be forced into the papers. A dozen reporters attended our meeting at the Liberal Club, and next morning the newspapers reported the proceedings in full.

So at ten o'clock, when I repaired to 26 Broadway, I found a great crowd of curious people who had read of the matter; also, a number of reporters and camera-men. The reporters swarmed about me and besought me for interviews, but according to agreement I refused to speak a word, and began simply to walk up and down on the sidewalk. I was joined by three ladies who had been present at the meeting of the night before, one of them Elizabeth Freeman, a well-known suffragette. A number of others had promised to come, but apparently had thought better of it in the cold light of the morning after. However, the deficit was made up by a lady, a stranger to us all, who had read about the matter that morning, and had hastily made herself a white flag with a bleeding heart, and now stood on the steps of 26 Broadway, shrieking my name at the top of her voice. It had been agreed that the "mourning pickets" were all to preserve silence, and to make no demonstration except the band of crepe agreed upon. But alas, we had no control over the actions of this strange lady!

Of course there were a number of policemen on hand, and very soon they informed me that I must stop walking up and down. I explained politely that I had made inquiry and ascertained that I was breaking no law in walking on the sidewalk in silence; therefore I didn't intend to stop. So I was placed under arrest, and likewise the four ladies. We were taken to the station-house, where I found myself confronting the sergeant at the desk, and surrounded by a dozen reporters with note-books. The sergeant was considerate, and let me tell the entire story of the Colorado coal-strike, and what I thought about it; the pencils of the reporters flew, and a couple of hours later, when the first edition of the afternoon newspapers made their appearance on the street, every one of them had three or four columns of what I had said. Such a little thing, you see! You just have to get yourself arrested, and instantly the concrete-walls turn into news-channels!

There is one detail to be recorded about this particular action of the news-channels. The United Press, which is a liberal organization, sent out a perfectly truthful account of what had happened. The Associated Press, which is a reactionary organization, sent out a false account, stating that my wife had been arrested. My wife, knowing how this report would shock her family and friends in the South, sent a special delivery letter to the Associated Press calling their attention to the error, but the Associated Press did not correct the error, nor did it reply to this letter. My wife's mother, an old-fashioned Southern lady, took the first train out of Mississippi, to rescue her child from jail and from disgrace; but by the time the good lady reached New York, she was so ill with grief and shame that if her child had really been in

10

jail she could have rendered but little assistance. All she could do was to inform her that even though she was not in jail, her father had disinherited her after reading his morning paper. My wife was informed by lawyers that she was in position to collect large damages from the Associated Press, and from every newspaper which had printed the false report. Some thirty suits were filed, but my wife's health did not permit her to go on with them.

We were taken to the Tombs prison, where the ladies sang the Marseillaise, and I wrote a poem entitled "The Marseillaise in the Tombs," and again found it possible to have my poetry published in the New York newspapers! The magistrate who tried us was an agreeable little gentleman, who allowed us to talk without limit—the talk all being taken down by the reporters. The charge against us read "using threatening, abusive and insulting behavior." The witnesses were the policemen, who testified that my conduct had been "that of a perfect gentleman." Nevertheless we were found guilty, and fined three dollars, and refused to pay the fine, and went back to the Tombs.

The newspapers tore me to pieces for my "clownish conduct," but I managed to keep cheerful, because I saw that they were publishing the news about the Colorado coal-strike, which before they had banned from their columns. The "New York World," for example, published a sneering editorial entitled, "Pink-tea Martyrdom." "No genuine desire to effect a reform actuates them, but only morbid craving for notoriety." But at the same time the "World" sent a special correspondent to the coal-fields, and during the entire time of our demonstration and for a couple of weeks thereafter they published every day from half a column to a column of news about the strike.

I spent two days and part of a third in the Tombs. Every day the reporters came to see me, and I gave interviews and wrote special articles—all the news about Colorado I could get hold of. And every day there was a crowd of ten thousand people in front of Twenty-six Broadway, and young Rockefeller fled to his home in the country, and "Standard Oil," for the first time in its history, issued public statements in defense of its crimes.

My wife had taken up the demonstration after my arrest, and I was amused to observe that the police did not arrest

her, nor did the newspapers ridicule her. Was it because
she was a woman? No, for I have seen the police beat and
club women doing picket-duty—working-women, you understand. I have seen the newspapers lie about working-women
on picket-duty; in the course of this Colorado campaign I saw
them print the vilest and most cowardly slanders about the
wives of some strikers who went to Washington to make
appeal to President Wilson. No, it was not because my wife
was a woman; it was because she was a "lady." It was
because in the files of the New York newspapers there reposed
a clipping recording the fact that her father was "one of the
wealthiest men in this section and controls large banking
interests."

Please pardon these personalities, for they are essential to
the thesis of this book—that American Journalism is a class
institution, serving the rich and spurning the poor. It happens
that M. C. S. is conspicuously and inescapably what is called
a "lady"; she not merely looks the part, she acts it and speaks
it in those subtle details that count most. All her young ladyhood she spent as what is known in the South as a "belle";
incidentally, of course, as an ungodly little snob. She has
got over that; but in case of an emergency like our Broadway
affair, she naturally used every weapon she had. Against the
New York reporters and the New York police department
she used the weapon of snobbery—and it worked.

In the South, you see, a "lady" takes for granted the slave-
psychology in those she regards as her "social inferiors." Not
merely does she expect immediate obedience from all members
of the colored race; she feels the same way about policemen
in uniform—it would never occur to her to think of a police-
man as anything but a servant, prepared to behave as such.
I assured her that she might not find this the case with the
husky sons of St. Patrick who lord it over the New York
crowds. But M. C. S. answered that she would see.

Far be it from me to know to what extent she did these
things deliberately; my advice in such matters is not sought,
and I am allowed to see the results only. What I saw in
this case—or rather learned about later—was that M. C. S.
arrived in front of 26 Broadway an hour late, clad in supple
and exquisite white broadcloth, military cape and all; and
that on sight of this costume the New York City police department collapsed.

For two weeks the "lady" from the far South marshalled the demonstration, walking side by side with eminent poets from California, and half-starved Russian Jews from the East side slums, and gigantic lumber-jacks from the Oregon forests. If those Russian Jews and Oregon lumber-jacks had tried such a stunt on Broadway by themselves, they would have had their scalps split open in the first five minutes. But the lady in the white military cape was there—never speaking, but looking firmly ahead; and so for two weeks the New York police department devoted itself to keeping everybody else off the sidewalks in front of 26 Broadway, so that our "free silence" advocates might have room to walk up and down undisturbed. They even had mounted policemen to clear lanes in the street, so that the cars might get through; and when some one hired thugs to try to pick quarrels with us and cause a disturbance, the police actually drove the thugs away. I feel quite certain that this was the first time in New York City's history that thugs employed by a great corporation to terrorize strike-pickets had met with opposition from the police.

And lest you think that M. C. S. is still a snob, and got a sense of triumph from all this, I ought to add the humiliating truth—that each day after going through with her ordeal, she would come home at night and cry! She would talk quietly and firmly to the reporters who came to our apartment; but after they had gone, she would be in a nervous fever of rage, because we had had to do such a "stunt," in order to get the truth into the rotten newspapers.

Ladies in the South are, of course, not accustomed to having their husbands in jail; so on the third day M. C. S. collected all our most respectable-looking "mourners," Leonard Abbott, George Sterling, Frank Shay and Mr. and Mrs. Ryan Walker, and put them on duty. Then she betook herself to the Criminal Courts Building, where she caused much embarrassment to several gentlemen in high station. The District-Attorney told her what to do, and helped her to make out the necessary papers; then she set out to find the judge. But the Criminal Courts Building is confusing to strangers; there is a central balcony, and all four sides of it look exactly alike, and M. C. S. got lost. She stopped a gentleman coming out of a court-room, and asked where she could find Justice So-and-so. "He is in room seventeen," was the answer. "But I can't find room seventeen," said M. C. S. "Please show me." "What do you wish with Justice So-and-so?" inquired the gentleman, politely. "Why," said M. C. S., "some imbecile of a judge has sent my husband to jail." "Madam," said the gentleman—still politely, "I am the judge."

She found Justice So-and-so. His court was in session and he could not be interrupted. But in the South, you understand, anything from a court to a fire-engine will stop to pick up a lady's handkerchief. And moreover, the father of M. C. S. is a judge, so she knows about them. She walked down the aisle and addressed his honor with her quietest smile, and —the court proceedings halted while the necessary papers were signed, and a Socialist muck-raker was released from jail.

The reason for this step was our desire to test in the higher courts the question whether a man whose conduct had been "that of a perfect gentleman" could properly be found guilty of "using threatening, abusive and insulting behavior." In order to appeal the case it was necessary to pay the fine under protest, so I paid one dollar, and came out on the last day—to behold the crowd of ten thousand people, and the mounted policemen, and the moving-picture operators in the windows of nearby office-buildings. And so, day after day, we were enabled to give information about the Colorado coal-strike to a group of reporters for the New York papers!

Several of these reporters were men of conscience. One, Isaac Russell of the "Times," became our friend, and day after day he would tell us of his struggles in the "Times" office, and how nearly every word favorable to myself or to the strikers was blue-penciled from his story. So during this Broadway demonstration, and the affair in Tarrytown which followed it, we lived, as it were, on the inside of the "Times" office, and watched the process of strangling the news. We have seen the tears come into Russell's eyes as he told about what was done. And on top of it all, Mr. Adolph Ochs gave a banquet to the "Times" staff, to celebrate some anniversary of the paper, and got up and made a speech to them—a speech to Isaac Russell!—telling what a wonderful institution he had made out of the "Times," and how it stood consecrated to the public welfare and the service of the truth!

P. S.—Isaac Russell reads the above, and corrects one serious error. He writes in emphatic capitals:

"WE REPORTERS PAID FOR THAT DINNER!"

CHAPTER XXV

THE CASE OF THE "A. P."

It must be understood that at this time the Colorado coal-strike had been going on for six or seven months. Most of the tent-colonies had been broken up, and the miners were being slowly starved into submission. To one who comes into close touch with such a situation and realizes its human meanings, it becomes an intolerable nightmare, a slow murder committed in a buried dungeon. My mail was full of letters from the miners and their leaders, and I went out to Colorado to see what else could be done to reach the consciences of the American people. I arrived in Denver at a time when the first public fury over the Ludlow massacre had spent itself, and silence had once more been clamped down upon the newspapers. I spoke at a mass meeting in the State capitol, attended by one or two thousand people, and when I called on the audience to pledge itself never to permit the prostituted State militia to go back into the coal districts, I think every person in the legislative chamber raised his hand and took the pledge. Yet not a line about my speech was published in any Denver newspaper next morning, and needless to say, not a line was sent out by the Associated Press.

The Associated Press was playing here precisely the same part it had played with the "condemned meat industry;" that is, it was a concrete wall. I have now to tell about a thorough test of this leading agency of capitalist repression. I consider the incident the most important which this book contains, and therefore I shall tell it in detail. By far the greater part of the news which the American people absorb about the outside world comes through the Associated Press, and the news they get is, of course, the raw material of their thought. If the news is colored or doctored, then public opinion is betrayed and the national life is corrupted at its source. There is no more important question to be considered by the American people than the question, Is the Associated Press fair? Does it transmit the news?

Some time previous to the Colorado coal-strike I had

attended a dinner of the Socialist Press Club, at which the question of dishonest newspapers was debated, and one of the speakers was Mr. Fabian Franklin, then editor of the "Evening Post," an amiable old gentleman who quite naïvely referred to the Associated Press as he would have referred to the Holy Trinity. He told of some radical friend of his who had pointed out that the Associated Press had circulated the news of a defeat of the Initiative and Referendum in Oregon, and subsequently, when the Initiative and Referendum had been victorious, had failed to report the victory. "Just think of it!" said this amiable old gentleman. "My radical friend actually believed that the Associated Press would have some motive in suppressing news about the success of the Initiative and Referendum in Oregon!"

I was called upon to answer this argument. I quote from an account of the discussion in the "New York Call":

> Sinclair was saying that when the fusion of capitalism beat Seidel (Socialist) in Milwaukee, the wires were full of it, but when Duncan (Socialist) beat a fusion in Butte, the press was as silent as the tomb. Franklin said that it was merely that Butte had no news value, while Milwaukee, "Schlitz beer—everybody wants to know about Milwaukee."

Incidentally I might mention in passing that this amiable old gentleman, Mr. Fabian Franklin, who thinks that the Associated Press would be incapable of suppressing news about a triumph of the Initiative and Referendum, and that it would naturally send out political news about Milwaukee because Schlitz beer is made in Milwaukee, has just recently been selected by a group of reactionaries to conduct a weekly organ of safety and sanity, "The Review." The reader will be able from the above anecdote to form an idea of the intellectual status of Mr. Franklin, and the likelihood of his having anything worth while to say to the American people in this greatest crisis of history!

Shortly afterwards came the case of the "Masses," which published a cartoon representing the president of the Associated Press as pouring a bottle labeled "Poison" into a reservoir entitled "Public Opinion." The Associated Press caused the arrest of Max Eastman and Art Young on a charge of criminal libel. They knew that by starting such a proceeding they would gain an opportunity of propaganda, and of this they hastened to make use. They issued an elaborate statement attacking the "Masses" and defending their own attitude toward the news, which statement was published in practically every paper in New York. I remember particularly that our organ of civic virtue, the "New York Evening Post," published it in full. It included this sort of "dope":

If these young men had investigated before they spoke, they would never have said what they did; for if there is a clean thing in the United States it is the Associated Press. The personnel of the service is made up as a whole of newspaper men of the finest type; throughout the profession employment in its service is regarded as an evidence of character and reliability. No general policy of suppression or distortion could be carried on without the knowledge and indeed the active connivance of these men, stationed at strategic points all over the world. Aside from that, the Associated Press has the active competition of several other aggressive press associations and thousands of special correspondents, and any laxity or deliberate failure on its part would be exposed instantly to its members, who would be quick to resent and punish any such procedure. These members, some nine hundred in number, represent every shade of political and economic opinion, and it is absurd to suppose that a general policy of distortion or suppression could be carried on without immediate exposure.

The editors of the "Masses," of course, proceeded to collect evidence, and the Associated Press must have realized very quickly that they were in for serious trouble. They caused a subservient district attorney to bring another indictment, charging libel against the individual who had been portrayed in the cartoon: the purpose of the change being that they hoped to exclude from the trial all evidence against the Associated Press as an organization, and to force the "Masses" to prove that this one individual had had personal knowledge of each instance of news suppression and perversion.

Gilbert E. Roe, who was preparing the case for the "Masses," asked me to tell him of my experiences with the Associated Press, and in talking the matter over he explained what would be required to constitute legal evidence of the suppression of news. I had no such legal evidence in the case of the "condemned meat industry," because I had not kept copies of my letters to the Associated Press, and I had not kept the clippings of what they actually did send out on the story. I promised Mr. Roe that the next time I went to the bat with the "A. P.," I would take pains to get proper evidence; and now in Denver I came suddenly upon my opportunity. I got real legal evidence, and the Associated Press knows that I got it, and I have been told that because of this they will never again dare to bring radicals into court, or to defend the thesis that they handle the news impartially. In my challenge I deliberately repeated the words for use of which the "Masses" editors were indicted, as follows:

> I now, over my own signature and as a deliberate challenge, charge that the Associated Press has poisoned the news of the Colorado situation at its source. Will the owners and managers of the Associated Press take up this challenge and make an attempt to send me to prison? I am waiting, gentlemen, for your answer.

This was published May 30, 1914, and I am still waiting. I made every effort, both public and private, to get this answer. I besieged the Associated Press and also the Associated Press newspapers, but no answer could be had, so I think I may fairly say that the Associated Press admitted its guilt in this case. The story, first published in the "Appeal to Reason," was written within a few hours of the events narrated, and gave all the documents. With the addition of a few explanations, made necessary by the lapse of time, the story is given unchanged in the next two chapters. It is a long story; but it will repay study, for there are few narratives of recent events which take you quite so far into the "inside," or reveal quite so clearly how Politics, Journalism, and Big Business work hand in hand for the hoodwinking of the public and the plundering of labor. I urge the reader to follow the narrative carefully, for every detail is necessary to the proper comprehension of the plot.

CHAPTER XXVI

A GOVERNOR AND HIS LIE

The crux of the struggle in Denver during these critical months was the State militia. This militia had been called out and sent to the strike-field because of violence deliberately and systematically committed by the armed thugs of the Baldwin-Felts Detective Agency. There were one or two thousand of these thugs in the field, and they had beaten up the strikers and their wives, and turned machine-guns upon their tent-colonies. The militia had come, supposedly to restore law and order, but the militia authorities had proceeded to recruit new companies from among these detectives and thugs. This was systematically denied by the newspapers, not merely in Colorado, but all over the country; later on, however, the State legislature forced the production of the roster of the militia, and it appeared that of one single company, newly recruited, one hundred and nineteen members out of one hundred and twenty-two had been employes of the strike-breaking agencies, and had continued on the pay-rolls of the coal-companies while serving in the State militia! They had been armed by the State, clothed in the uniform of the State, covered by the flag of the State—and turned loose to commit the very crimes they were supposed to be preventing! The culmination of this perversion of government had been the Ludlow Massacre, which drove the miners to frenzy. There had been a miniature revolution in Colorado; armed working-men had taken possession of the coal-country, and the helpless State government had appealed to the Federal authorities to send in Federal troops.

The Federal troops had come, and the miners had loyally obeyed them. From the hour that the first regulars appeared, no shot was fired in the whole region. The Federal authorities preserved law and order, and meantime the State legislature was called to deal with the situation. This State legislature was composed of hand-picked machine politicians, and all its orders were given from the offices of the Colorado Fuel &

Iron Company. Senator Van Tilborg, machine-leader, personally declared to me his opinion that all the State needed
was "three hundred men who could shoot straight and quick."
The State authorities meant to find these three hundred men;
they passed a bill appropriating a million dollars for military
purposes, and another bill providing for the disarming of
all people in the State who were not in the service of the corporations.

The strike at this time had continued for seven months, and
the strikers were in their tent-colonies, sullenly awaiting de-
velopments. The program of the corporations was to strengthen
the State militia, then have it take charge and maintain itself
by machine-guns. The attitude of the general public to this
proposition may be gathered from the mass-meeting in the
State capitol, where one or two thousand people raised their
hands and pledged themselves that they would never permit
the prostituted militia to go back to the mines.

So stood the situation on Saturday, May 16, 1914, the
day the State legislature was scheduled to adjourn. President
Wilson, who had sent in the Federal troops reluctantly, was
waiting in Washington to see what measures the State authorities would take to put an end to the prevailing civil war. By
Saturday morning he had come to realize that no adequate
measures were being taken, and he sent from Washington a
telegram to Governor Ammons of Colorado:

> Am disturbed to hear of the probability of the adjournment of
> your legislature, and feel bound to remind you that my constitutional
> obligations with regard to the maintenance of order in Colorado are
> not to be indefinitely continued by the inaction of the State legislature.
> The Federal forces are there only until the State of Colorado has
> time and opportunity to resume complete sovereignty and control in
> the matter. I cannot conceive that the State is willing to forego her
> sovereignty, or to throw herself entirely upon the government of the
> United States, and I am quite clear that she has no constitutional
> right to do so when it is within the power of her legislature to take
> effective action.

And now begins a story of political crookedness, the like
of which had never come under my personal observation. I
had been in Denver four days, and had opportunity to meet a
score of people who knew the situation intimately, and who
were able to put me on the "inside." So I can invite you
into the Governor's private office at eleven o'clock on Saturday

morning, when the above telegram from President Wilson arrived. First, let me describe this Governor, as I wrote about him in the "Denver Express":

> I went yesterday afternoon to see your Governor. I wish to be very careful what I say of him. He is apparently a kindly man; in intellectual caliber fitted for the duties of a Sunday-School superintendent in a small village. He is one of the most pitiful figures it has ever been my fate to encounter. He pleaded with me that he was a ranchman, a workingman, that he was ignorant about such matters as mines. When I pointed out to him that, according to government figures, there were twelve times as many miners killed and injured by accidents in the southern Colorado fields as elsewhere, his only answer was that he had heard some vague statement to the effect that conditions were different in other places. He pleaded tearfully that he had brought upon himself the hatred of everyone, he admitted that he was utterly bewildered, and had no idea what to do in this crisis. His every word made evident his utter ignorance of the economic forces which have produced this frightful situation. He cried out for some solution; yet, every time that I sought to suggest a solution, and to pin him down to a "yes" or a "no" upon a certain course of action, he lost control of himself and cried out that I was trying to make him "express an opinion." He, the Governor of the State, had no business to have opinions about such a dispute!

It is no accident, of course, that a man of this type comes to be governor of a State like Colorado. The corporations deliberately select such men because they wish to be let alone, and they prefer men who are too weak to interfere with them, even if they wish to interfere. So now at eleven o'clock on Saturday morning this poor pitiful Governor sends for his advisors—the leaders of the hand-picked machine majority in the State legislature. What is to be done? If the President's telegram is sent to the legislature, it may refuse to adjourn, and insist upon considering the President's demand. Therefore, at all hazards, the telegram must be suppressed. Also, it must be sent to the coal-operators in the city, in order that they may consult and tell the Governor what reply to make to the President. All the newspaper men in Denver knew the names of the two men who took the message about to the operators. It was considered by the operators for three or four hours, and a reply drafted and sent; and meantime desperate efforts were made by the machine leaders to obtain the adjournment of the legislature. The reply drafted by the operators and sent by the Governor was as follows:

Hon. Woodrow Wilson, President of the United States, Washington:

    I regret exceedingly that you have been misinformed. The legislature has just passed an act, which I have approved, providing for a bond issue of one million dollars for the purpose of paying the indebtedness which has been incurred and which may be incurred in suppressing insurrection and defending the State. As soon as these bonds can be issued, these funds will be available and this State can and will control the situation. This is the only constitutional method of raising funds in immediate future. In addition to this act the legislature has enacted a law permitting the Governor to close saloons in time of disorder, and also a law prohibiting the carrying and disposition of firearms in time of disorder. Moreover, a committee on mediation on the present strike has been provided for and appointed.

    Now the heart of our story is this last sentence in the Governor's telegram: this "committee on mediation on the present strike." If such a committee had been appointed, the legislature might fairly claim to have done its best to settle the strife. But *had* such a committee been appointed? It had *not*. The coal-operators, confused by the President's sudden action, had caused their poor Governor to telegraph the President a lie; and now all their agencies of repression were brought to bear to keep the truth, not merely from the President, but from the whole country.

    First of all, it must be kept from the State legislature itself! A senator tried to have the President's telegram and the Governor's answer read in the senate, but by parliamentary juggling this was prevented. All debate was forbidden; but a Democratic woman senator, Helen Ring Robinson, succeeded in getting in a few words of protest, under the guise of an "explanation" of her vote. Senator Robinson read the last sentence of the Governor's answer: "Moreover a committee on mediation on the present strike has been provided for and appointed." Said Senator Robinson: "I know of no such committee which has been appointed by this assembly."

    Lieutenant-Governor Fitzgarald replied that the resolution providing for the "strike investigating committee" provided for mediation.

    "But," protested Senator Robinson, "I can't find a sentence in that resolution that mentions 'mediation.' I can't see a word on 'mediation' in the resolutions."

    "Whereupon" (I am quoting the account from the "Rocky Mountain News" of May 17th), "Senator A. N. Parrish, conservative Republican, objected that the motion was not debatable. Further discussion was shut off, the motion to read the President's telegram was laid on the table, and the senate adjourned."

Now on that critical Saturday evening it happened that I was a guest at the home of the late Chief Justice Steele of Colorado, and there I met Senator Robinson. She asked me if I could not do something to make this matter clear to the country. Could I, for example, find out if the Associated Press had gotten the point straight? With the Senator sitting by my side I called the Associated Press on the 'phone and spoke with Mr. A. C. Rowsey, its night-editor in charge in Denver. I told Mr. Rowsey that I was in consultation with an opposition Senator, and that my attention had been called to this point, which I endeavored to explain.

Mr. Rowsey laughed good naturedly at my effort to enlighten his great institution. He informed me that they had trained men up at the capitol watching every point of the procedure, and that they had got the story quite correct. I endeavored to make the precise point about the phrase "mediation"; but not having any copy of the proceedings before me, and being really unable to believe that Senator Robinson could be correct in attributing such an open falsehood to the Governor of the State, I permitted Mr. Rowsey to back me down, and hung up the receiver feeling that I had made a fool of myself.

But later that evening I went to the office of the "Rocky Mountain News," where I was able to see a copy of the official record in the case, the House Journal of the proceedings of May 15, 1914. The measure was contained on pages 7, 8, and 9, and on page 47 there was an amendment. I read the bill and amendment, line by line, and I did not find in it the word "mediation." The measure provided as follows:

Resolved, That a joint committee of six members, three selected by the senate and three by the house, said members to be selected by the body of each house shall be appointed and directed to confer and advise with the Governor and other executive officers of the State to the end that the legislative department may render all assistance in its power to the executive department in the enforcement of law and the maintenance of order, and to consider ways and means of restoring and maintaining peace and good order throughout the State; and to investigate and make report at the next session of the legislature upon the following matters and subjects:

The bill then goes on to outline an elaborate series of

matters for investigation—whether the coal companies have
obeyed the laws; what wages they have paid; the terms of
the mining leases; the employment of gunmen; what efforts
have been made to settle the strike, etc. The amendment
provides for further inquiry into the names of strike leaders,
their nationality, etc., and the causes of violence. These subjects were, of course, enough to occupy a committee for many
months. There was nowhere in the bill anything suggested
about settling the present strike. On the contrary, the express
task of the committee was said to be "to generally investigate
all matters connected with said strike; that remedial legislation
may be enacted *at the next General Assembly* which will tend
to prevent *a recurrence of insurrection and public disorder."*

Now, do not think that I am juggling words over the
question of the precise meaning of the above bill. The distinction between the bill which had actually been passed, and
the bill which the Governor told President Wilson had been
passed, was vital and fundamental. Here was a desperate
struggle, the class-war in literal truth, involving the two
greatest forces in modern society. The whole State was torn
apart over it, and if anybody were going to "mediate" and
"settle" it, the whole State wished to know it, and must have
known it. At the time that this investigation bill was passed,
it was an investigation bill and nothing else, and this was understood by everyone who had anything to do with it. The
measure was regarded as of so little importance that the
"Rocky Mountain News" of the day after its passage did not
even refer to it. It was one more "committee to investigate,"
and the State was sick of such. By actual count there had
been more than *sixty* such committees appointed already—one
of them a committee from Congress, which had taken testimony
filling ten volumes! It was perfectly understood by everyone
that the purpose of this new legislative committee was to
collect a lot of facts prejudicial to the strikers. Its members
were all machine politicians of the very worst type. The idea
of such a committee attempting to "mediate," or to "settle the
strike," would have been regarded as a joke by the whole
State; but no one had any such idea. It was not until Governor
Ammons and his advisors found themselves "in a hole," that
they hit upon the scheme of calling this a "committee on
mediation."

Also, let us get clear the purpose of this trickery. The purpose was to keep the President of the United States from intervening to force a compromise, as he was threatening to do. The legislature was to be adjourned, and the President was to find himself in a position where he would have to keep the Federal troops in the field and do the work of repression which the prostituted State militia of Colorado could no longer do. Such was the plan—and I might add that it was carried out completely.

Next morning, by consulting with other members of the legislature, and with several lawyers in Denver, I made quite certain of the facts. Also I made certain that the Associated Press had sent out no hint of these facts. The Associated Press had sent merely the President's telegram and the Governor's answer. Presumably, therefore, the President had swallowed the Governor's lie. Beyond question the country had swallowed it. It seemed to me that here was an occasion for an honest man to make his voice heard; so I sent a telegram to President Wilson, as follows:

President Woodrow Wilson, Washington, D. C.:

As one in position to observe from inside the events in this capital, I respectfully call your attention to the lack of fairness of Governor Ammons in withholding your telegram from the legislature for four hours while efforts were made to adjourn. All newspaper men know that during that time your telegram was in the hands of all coal-operators in this city, and they know the men who took it to them. Furthermore, they know that Governor Ammons' telegram to you contains a falsehood. The word "mediation" did not appear in the measure referred to, which provides for investigation only. There has been a ten-volume investigation already. Governor Ammons declared to me personally that he means to return the militia to the strike-fields. Twenty independent investigators, reporters, lawyers, relief-workers assure me result will be civil war on a scale never before known in American labor dispute. Miners by thousands pledged to die rather than submit to more government by gunmen.

UPTON SINCLAIR.

I took this telegram on Sunday evening to the editor of the "Rocky Mountain News." He said, "It is a splendid telegram; it covers the case." I said, "Will you publish it?" He answered, "I will." I said, "Will the Associated Press get it from the News?" He answered, "It will." It might be well to finish this part of the matter by stating that on the next evening I had a conversation with Mr. Rowsey, in charge of the Associated Press, as follows: "Did you get my telegram from the 'News'?" "We did." "You did not send it out, I believe?" "We did not."

The "Rocky Mountain News" had been for many years a hide-bound corporation newspaper, but at this moment the owner of the paper had, so I was told, some kind of a personal quarrel with the coal operators. At any rate, he had placed in charge a young Chicago newspaper man, Wm. L. Chenery, with orders to publish the truth. That the "News" was not favoring me personally will be clearly seen from the fact that on Tuesday morning it published a ferocious attack upon me by Gov. Ammons, and refused to publish a word of what I offered in reply. Nevertheless, on Monday morning the "News" published a two-column editorial headed: "To the Patriots of Colorado." Says the "News": "Not one word about mediation is contained in the entire resolution. The committee is given no power to mediate. They may investigate, examine and report, and that is all." And elsewhere the editorial says: "A committee on mediation has not been provided for; and none has been appointed. Think of the inutterable weakness of such conduct! Think of its stupidity!"

Such was the voice of unprejudiced opinion in the city of Denver on the subject of the Governor's telegram. And what did the country hear about the controversy? Not a word! The Associated Press had all facts. It came to the "News" office and got everything the "News" had; and it sent out not one word! On the contrary, the Associated Press did its best to persuade the country that the President was pleased with Ammons' reply. It sent out the following:

Washington, May 16.—President Wilson expressed satisfaction with the situation after he received Governor Ammons' reply late tonight. It was said by officials in close touch with the President that Wilson was greatly pleased with what had been done after he had been informed by Governor Ammons of the work of the Colorado legislature, and that he hoped the State would assume control of the situation in the near future so the Federal troops might be withdrawn.

That this was an Associated Press invention, made to help out the poor Governor, was made clear the next morning by the "News," whose own correspondent wired the following:

Washington, May 17.—At the White House it was stated that nothing had been given out which would justify the statement printed in some of the morning papers that the President is entirely satisfied with the telegram received yesterday from Governor Ammons.

I was by this time thoroughly wrought up over the situation, determined that the country should somehow hear the truth. I besieged the offices of the Denver newspapers; as a result the "Denver Post," on Monday afternoon, published on its front page, with a heading in large red letters, an interview with Governor Ammons, in which that worthy denounced me as an "itinerant investigator," also as a "prevaricator." The Governor's defense on the point at issue was this:

> In regard to Sinclair's declaration that the word "mediation" did not appear in the resolution appointing a committee to investigate the strike, Ammons explained:
> "Probably that particular word does not occur, but a reading of the resolution will show that it gives the legislative committee power 'to assist in settling the strike.' If that isn't mediation I'd like to know the true meaning of the word."

I felt pretty sick when I read that interview; I thought the Governor must "have" me for sure! With sinking heart I went and procured a copy of the House Journal, to see if I could possibly have overlooked such a phrase as "to assist in settling the strike." I read over line by line the three pages of the bill, and the one page of amendment; and, behold, there was no such phrase: "to assist in settling the strike." There was nothing in any way remotely suggesting it! On the contrary, there was the explicit statement of the purposes of the committee *"to generally investigate all matters connected with said strike; that remedial legislation may be enacted* AT THE NEXT GENERAL ASSEMBLY *which will tend to prevent* A RECURRENCE OF INSURRECTION AND PUBLIC DISORDER."

The Governor had lied again!

So then I wrote the Governor a letter. I said:

> You have relied upon the fact that the man in the street has not access to the volume of the House Journal, and will accept your statements upon their face. This, of course, puts me at a cruel disadvantage, for you are a prominent official and I am only an "itinerant investigator." But I propose, if possible, to compel you to face this issue. I will name two friends as a committee to represent me to settle this question at issue. I request you to name two friends. I request you to point out to them in the measure in question the word "mediation" or the phrase "to assist in settling the strike." Your two friends will then bring it to my two friends, who, seeing the phrase in print in the House Journal, will be obliged to admit that I am wrong. You have objected to my presence in the State, upon the ground that I am meddling in the affairs of the people of Colorado. Very well, sir, I hereby offer you a simple way to rid the State of my presence.

I hereby agree that if your two friends can point out to my two friends the word or phrase in question, I will quit the borders of your State within twenty-four hours and never return to it. Upon your acceptance of this proposition, I shall name my two friends.

This letter was mailed to the Governor on Monday night; also copies were mailed to the newspapers. At ten o'clock Tuesday morning, while dictating my article for the "Appeal to Reason," I called up Mr. F. G. Bonfils, editor in charge and one of the owners of the "Denver Post." The following conversation occurred:

"Good morning, Mr. Bonfils; this is Upton Sinclair. Did you receive the copy of the letter which I mailed to Governor Ammons last night?"

"I did."

"May I ask if you intend to publish it?"

"I do not."

"May I ask what is your reason for refusing?"

"The reason is that things have been stirred up enough, we think. The people in this city want peace."

"Does it seem to you that this is fair journalism?"

"Now, listen, my boy, don't try to argue with me; you have had plenty of room to spread your ideas in our paper."

"You are entirely mistaken, Mr. Bonfils. You have not reported a single speech that I made in this town. You did not even print my telegram to President Wilson. But you print the Governor's answer to it."

"Well, now, we don't want to stir up this question any further. We think this State is very much in need of peace. We are not looking for trouble. If we printed your answer to the Governor, we should have to print the Governor's answer to you. And so it would go on indefinitely, and we don't want people calling each other names in our paper."

"If that is the case, why did you print the Governor's attack upon me?"

"Now, listen, kid, don't get excited."

"I was never less excited in my life, Mr. Bonfils. I am simply asking politely for an explanation."

"Well, now, we don't care to argue this question with you."

"You have called me a liar in your paper, and refuse me an opportunity to defend myself? Is that correct?"

"Yes; it's correct."

"Well, then I simply wish to tell you this one further thing.

I am at present in a stenographer's office dictating an account of this conversation for a publication which has a circulation of five hundred thousand ——"

"I don't care if it has a circulation of five hundred million."

"Then you are willing for this conversation to be reported as expressing the attitude of the 'Post'?"

"Say, Bill, we have been attacked so often by fellows like you, and we have got so prosperous on it, that we don't care anything about it."

"Very well, then; good morning."

The above conversation was recorded in the following way. The stenographer sat by my side at the telephone, and took down every word that I said. Immediately afterwards this was read off to me, and I filled in Mr. Bonfils' answers. As it happens that I have a good memory for words, I can state that the above is for practical purposes a stenographic record of the conversation. And later on I went out and bought an early edition of the "Post," and found the man had "carried over" the Governor's attack, a reprint from the day before! And then, walking down the street, I came to the building of the "Post," and looked up and saw—oh, masterpiece of humor! —an inscription graven all the way across the stone front of the building:

JUSTICE, WHEN EXPELLED FROM OTHER HABITA-TIONS, MAKE THIS THY DWELLING-PLACE.

CHAPTER XXVII

THE ASSOCIATED PRESS AT THE BAR

Let us return to Monday evening, and to our main theme, the Associated Press. I saw here my long-awaited chance to put this organization on record. I believed, and still believe, that this was a perfect case of news-suppression. Here was the closest approach yet made to social revolution in America; here was the class-war, naked and undisguised—on the one side the lives of thirty or forty thousand wage-slaves, on the other side a hundred million dollars of invested capital, controlling the government of an entire state, and using this control to suppress every legal and constitutional right of American citizens, and to drive them to armed revolt. To this conspiracy the Associated Press had lent itself; it was being used, precisely as the Baldwin-Felts Detective Agency, precisely as the puppets of the State government. The directors and managers of the Associated Press were as directly responsible for the subsequent starvation of these thousands of Colorado mine-slaves as if they had taken them and strangled them with their naked fingers. If it had been such individual crimes of strangling, all society would have agreed on the need of publicity. I have made it my task in life to force the same kind of publicity for the economic crimes of predatory social classes. I considered now that the time for action had come, and as my final test of the "A. P." I prepared a second telegram to President Wilson, as follows:

President Woodrow Wilson, Washington, D. C.:

In interview tonight, Governor Ammons brands me as prevaricator for my statement to you that commission of mediation was not provided. He now admits the word "mediation" does not appear, but insists that the phrase "to assist in settling the strike" is equivalent. No such phrase occurs. I urgently request you to get the full text of this resolution and realize what it means that the Governor of this State is wilfully and deliberately endeavoring to deceive you and the public in this crisis.

Wishing to make quite certain in this vital matter, I took the trouble to write out my plan of action, and took it to a personal friend, a leading newspaper editor in Denver. He said, "Don't do it." I asked, "Why not?" The answer was,

"It will make you so many powerful enemies that you will be unable to do anything more to send out news." I answered that I had never been able to do anything with the Associated Press—it was always and invariably closed to what I had to say, and only mentioned me when it had something considered discreditable, such as my being sent to jail. My friend answered, "Well, if you can stand being hated and suppressed for the balance of your life, go ahead."

I could stand that. So I took the volume of the House Journal and a copy of my telegram to President Wilson, and went down to the office of the Associated Press in the Ernest & Cranmer Building, and saw Mr. A. C. Rowsey, with whom I had talked over the phone the night before. He was very pleasant and friendly; and I wish to state that the attitude manifested by the Associated Press in this test case was in no way due to any personal difficulty or ill feeling. Mr. Rowsey showed himself a gracious host, and I never had a more pleasant interview with anyone.

I showed him the House Journal, and he read the four pages with interest. He read my telegram to the President, and then stated that they would refuse to carry it, as they had refused to carry the one they had got from the "News" on the previous day. His explanation was that it was the policy of the Associated Press "to avoid controversy." If they once got started they would never know where to stop.

I said, "But Mr. Rowsey, this controversy is the most important item of news on the Colorado situation tonight. I have here put before you indisputable documentary evidence that Governor Ammons has lied to President Wilson; and surely the public would want to know that fact. Surely the public has at least a right to know of the charge, and to make up its own mind as to its truth or falsity." Mr. Rowsey's answer was, "Our wire from Colorado is very much crowded these days, and this controversy does not seem to us to be news." I said, "Very well, Mr. Rowsey; will you now permit me to hand to you this letter, which I have drafted to serve as a record of the circumstances."

He took the letter and read as follows:

Denver, Colo., May 18, 1914.

CORRESPONDENT ASSOCIATED PRESS,
    Denver, Colorado.
Dear Sir:
    Yesterday I sent President Wilson a telegram, which I believed

and still believe was of vital public importance. A copy of this telegram was put into your hands last night by the "Rocky Mountain News" and was refused by you. I now offer you a second telegram, bearing upon this subject. At the same time I offer for your inspection a copy of the House Journal in order that you may verify the truth of the statements contained in my telegram to President Wilson. I shall first, in a personal interview, politely request you to send this telegram over your wires. If you refuse to do so, I shall—in order to put you upon record—place this letter in your hands and request you to sign the statement below. If you refuse to sign it, I shall understand that you refuse to send out this telegram over your wires, and I shall proceed to send it to the papers myself, and I shall subsequently take steps to make these circumstances known to the public.

Respectfully,

Upton Sinclair.

Mr. Upton Sinclair, City:

Dear Sir:—The undersigned, correspondent of the Associated Press in Denver, agrees to send your telegram to President Wilson over its wires tonight.

....

Mr. Rowsey read this letter and handed it back to me, with the smiling remark: "I see you are getting a good story." I thanked him, and left. I went down-stairs to the telegraph-office and sent a copy of my telegram to President Wilson to a selection of newspapers all over the country. They were as follows: New York "Times," "World," "Herald," "Sun" and "Call"; Chicago "Examiner" and "Tribune"; Philadelphia "North American" and "Press"; Baltimore "Sun"; Washington "Times"; Boston "Herald" and "Journal"; Topeka "Journal"; Kansas City "Star"; Milwaukee "Journal"; Atlanta "Georgian"; New Orleans "Times-Democrat"; Omaha "News"; Pittsburg "Post."

Now, I submit that here is a definite test of the service of the Associated Press. Is it sending out all the material which its papers want? Is it suppressing anything which its papers would be glad to publish if they could get it? Let the reader observe that these newspapers are not merely radical and progressive ones; they include some of the staunchest stand-pat papers in the country, the New York "Times" and "Herald," for example. They are all save two or three of them Associated Press papers. To make the test automatic I sent the telegrams "collect." The editors had the right to read the message, and if they did not want it, to refuse to pay for it, having it sent back to me for collection. Out of the twenty papers, how many took this step? Only five! The other fifteen took the story that the Associated Press refused to send out. This is a remarkable showing, considering the fact that I sent the telegram late in the evening, and too late for most of the Eastern papers. It should be pointed out that a newspaper editor is far less disposed to print a dispatch which comes from an unauthorized person. My charge was a startling one, and an editor would naturally doubt it. He would say, "If it is true, why doesn't the Associated Press send it?" Mr. Rowsey, in Denver, had the House Journal before him; but the city editors of newspapers all over the country did not have this advantage, and would naturally be disposed to rely upon Mr. Rowsey.

It might be worth while to add that the claims made in my two telegrams to President Wilson were fully vindicated by subsequent events. The committee of six machine legislators, appointed to collect material discreditable to the strikers and their leaders, proceeded to vindicate the Governor and redeem his reputation by going through a pretense of "mediation"; but the public paid so little attention to the farce that it petered out in two or three days. The strike lasted for another seven months, and all that time the Federal troops remained in the field—the very thing which President Wilson had declared himself determined to avoid, and which the coal-operators had been determined to force upon him!

P. S. to ninth edition: In a debate concerning "The Brass Check," conducted in the columns of the "New York Globe" with Professor James Melvin Lee, director of the Department of Journalism of New York University, the latter brought forward the discovery that in the printed version of the proceedings of the Colorado legislature, the word "Mediation" appears in the *caption* of the bill. I investigated, and learned that this printed volume is regularly prepared three or four months subsequent to the adjournment of the legislature. The caption had been obviously put over the bill as a device to protect the Governor. The word mediation does not appear in the *text* of the bill. No caption had appeared in the House Journal as printed while I was in Denver.

CHAPTER XXVIII

THE ASSOCIATED PRESS AND ITS NEWSPAPERS

I am giving a great deal of space in a small book to this one test of the Associated Press. I think that the subject is an important one, and that the documents in the case should be available to students. In the present chapter I give the reaction of the press of America to this particular test. If the reader is not interested in such details, he may skip this chapter.

I have talked over this case with many lawyers, and shown them the documents, and asked: "Is there any legal flaw in them?" They have never been able to point out one. Also I have talked the case over with journalists—some of the most eminent of capitalist journalists, as I shall presently narrate, and have asked them to point out a flaw. They have pointed out what they think is a flaw—that in presenting to the Associated Press my telegram to President Wilson, I was asking the Associated Press to give publicity to my name and personality, and the Associated Press might have been justified in refusing the request.

I answer that there were many ways in which the "A. P." could have handled this matter without mentioning my name: a fact which I plainly pointed out to Mr. Rowsey. The first time I spoke to him—over the telephone—I was speaking, not for myself, but for Senator Robinson. She, a duly elected representative of the people of Colorado, speaking in their legislature, had nailed the Governor's lie, and it was Mr. Rowsey's unquestionable duty to report her words. It was only when I realized how completely the "A. P." was in the hands of the coal-operators that I "butted in" on the matter at all. And when my telegram was refused by Mr. Rowsey, I was careful to point out to him that there were other ways he might handle this news. He might give the story as coming from Senator Robinson; he might send extracts from the editorial of the "Rocky Mountain News"; he might send a dispatch saying, "It is generally reported in Denver," or "Protests are being made in Denver." All this I made clear, and he in return made clear why he did not do so. Anyone who had been present at our long and partly humorous interview would have perceived that this was no error in judgment of an individual employe of the "A. P.," but a definite policy of the great machine. Mr. Rowsey went so far as to say to me that he was a Socialist, in sympathy with my point of view, and that he personally would have been willing to send out a straight story.

In exactly the same way, when I took this story to various newspapers and magazines, I tried to suppress my own personality. I said to the editors: "If you are not willing to discuss the grievance of Upton Sinclair, then make an investigation of your own. Send a representative to Denver and interview Senator Robinson and write about the efforts of a progressive woman senator for fair play in this strike. Take the telegrams which passed between the President and the Governor of Colorado, take the pretenses of the fake mediation commission and the false reports of the Associated Press about it, and write the story without mentioning my name." But all such suggestions were in vain. There was no capitalist magazine or newspaper in the United States that would take up the conduct of the Associated Press in the Colorado strike.

In one of its published statements in the "New York Evening Post," the Associated Press had explained its stern attitude toward the editors of the "Masses":

The Associated Press is not prosecuting the case in any vengeful spirit, but is fighting for a public vindication. For several years the association has sat silent under accusations of this kind, reflecting upon the integrity of the service and the personal honor of its responsible officers, because the charges were made either on the floor of Congress, where no redress is possible, or by persons who were careful or lucky in avoiding the legal limitations of civil or criminal libel. In several cases the persons making the charges retracted them absolutely. At last they have a case involving libel per se, and they purpose to avail themselves of the opportunity to present to the public the facts regarding the service.

This, you perceive, is dignified and impressive; dignity and impressiveness are virtues permissible to great capitalist institutions. But now make note: my challenge to the Associated Press, published in the "Appeal to Reason," repeated the identical words for which the editors of the "Masses" had been arrested; and I sent a copy to all the leading officers of the Associated Press; I afterwards saw a letter, signed by Melville E. Stone, general manager of the Associated Press, acknowledging that he had seen it. Here surely was a charge "involving libel per se," and one which I had taken pains to make as emphatic, as unconditional, as damaging as possible. It was a public challenge, appearing on the front page of a newspaper whose circulation for that week was five hundred and forty-eight thousand and forty. Yet the Associated Press did not take up the challenge; it swallowed the insult.

Not only that, but every newspaper having the Associated Press service did the same; some nine hundred newspapers throughout the United States sat in silence and let this challenge pass unanswered. I had the "Appeal to Reason" send a marked copy of this issue to every one of the nine hundred Associated Press papers, and I wrote to my clipping-bureau, asking them to watch especially for mention of the matter. This clipping-bureau is the best in the country, and seldom misses anything of importance. It could not find me a single mention of my challenge to the Associated Press.

I next selected a list of forty of the leading papers of the country, including the twenty to which I had sent the telegram from Denver. I sent them a marked copy of the article, with a letter addressed to the managing editor, pointing out what my challenge meant—that I had publicly indicted the source from which this paper got the news which it gave to the public. Would the paper defend the integrity of its news? Would it force the Associated Press to explain this incident. Three papers replied to my letter. I shall deal with them a little later. The other thirty-seven papers left my letter unanswered. And let it be noted that this included all the papers which make the greatest pose of dignity and honor, such as the "Boston Evening Transcript," the "Springfield Republican," the "New York Times," the "Philadelphia Public Ledger," the "Baltimore Sun," the "Chicago Tribune," the "Louisville Courier-Journal," the "Memphis Commercial-Appeal," the "Atlanta Constitution." Also, I tried the magazines. One week after the publication of my challenge to the Associated Press there had appeared in "Collier's Weekly" a leading editorial entitled "In Justice to the A. P.":

The officers and members of the Associated Press have been kept busy lately repelling attacks upon that organization. In so far as they are defending themselves from the charge of wilful distortion of the news, we sympathize with them. Six or seven years ago we printed a series of articles which dealt with the general subject of "tainted news," and from time to time since then we have pointed out examples of this insidious practice. During this time not less than a score of persons have come to us with alleged examples of tampering with the news on the part of the Associated Press. All of these cases we looked into with care and pains, and many of the same were investigated by other publications and persons. We have never found a case that justified us in publishing the details or in making any charge of wilful distortion against the Associated Press.

I wrote now to "Collier's Weekly." They had investigated a score of cases, here was one more. Would they agree to investigate this, and to publish the facts? To this challenge "Collier's Weekly" made no response. "Collier's Weekly" did not investigate, and it never published a line about the matter. Then I wrote to the editors of the "Outlook," the extremely pious instrument of the "clerical camouflage." In its issue of May 30, 1914, the "Outlook" had published two articles dealing with the Associated Press. I now wrote and invited it to take up this case, and the "Outlook" did not reply. Also I wrote "The Independent," which was once a liberal paper, and it too refused any publicity.

To return to the three newspapers which answered my letter: Mr. Frederick S. Forbes, acting managing editor of the "Philadelphia North American," replied that his paper had "frequently had occasion to criticize the news distributing agencies of the country," and would investigate my story. That was the last I ever heard from the matter. When I wrote to remind the "Philadelphia North American," they did not answer. In the course of a year I wrote several times, but they did not answer.

And then the "New York World." The "World" had published a challenge, defying anyone to point out where it had failed to print important news. I now took this case of the Associated Press to the "World," and the "World" answered that having published my telegram to the President from Denver, the "World" had published the news! The fact that the "World" had got this telegram from me instead of from the Associated Press—that was not news! The fact that I had published a challenge, deliberately repeating the words of the "Masses" editors, and that the Associated Press and all its newspapers had passed my challenge by—that was not news, in the judgment of the "World"!

The third paper which replied to me was the "New York Evening Post"; the only one which took up the matter in what I considered the proper spirit. Mr. John P. Gavit, managing editor of the "Evening Post," wrote as follows:

Your letter of recent date, together with the exhibit embodied in the first page of the "Appeal to Reason" for May 30th, is hereby acknowledged. I have undertaken an investigation of the matter which will take considerable time and I am writing now only to prevent your having the mistaken impression that your communication is to be ignored. I attach for your information copy of a self-explanatory letter which I have addressed to Mr. Melville E. Stone, General Manager of The Associated Press.

Dear Mr. Stone:

I hand you herewith copy of the letter which we have received from Mr. Upton Sinclair, together with a page from the "Appeal to Reason" published at Girard, Kansas, under date of May 30th, 1914. I have been out of town, which fact will explain my delay in taking this matter up with you.

I am perfectly aware of Mr. Sinclair's reputation among newspaper men as an insatiable hunter of personal publicity; but it seems to me that his telegram to President Wilson, making specific allegations in connection with a matter of the utmost public consequence at a critical time, ought to have been transmitted by the Associated Press men at Denver. Of course, it is perfectly absurd for any Associated Press man to say that it is the policy of the Associated Press "to avoid controversy"; that theory of the service is long out of date, and two-thirds of its news reports relate to controversies in one way or another. I have not examined the reports of the matters to which Mr. Sinclair refers, but on its face his article certainly creates a prima facie of suppression of important facts regarding the situation at Denver. At the time to which he refers, I realize that the Denver correspondent was in a very difficult position in all this business, but in this case I think he made a palpable mistake.

It is evidently necessary under the circumstances that the "Evening Post" should deal with this subject, and I shall be glad to have at your early convenience any statement which you will be willing to have published over your signature. I personally believe that this should include some explanation from the Denver correspondent as to his reason for refusing to mention Sinclair's telegram to the President; though, of course, that is a matter entirely within your discretion.

Yours very truly,
John P. Gavit,
Managing Editor.

The above letter was perfectly satisfactory to me. It did not trouble me what either Mr. Gavit or Mr. Stone thought about my reputation among newspaper men. All that I was concerned about, all that I have ever been concerned about, was that the truth about social injustice should be made public.

Mr. Gavit sent me a copy of Mr. Stone's reply, promising to make an immediate investigation of the matter and report. I felt so sure of the outcome that I ventured to make an announcement in the "Appeal," June 20, 1914, to the effect that the "A. P." was to be "smoked out," it was to be compelled to answer my charges.

But alas for my hopes of fair play, my faith in the organ of arm-chair respectability! Time passed, and I wrote to Mr. Gavit, again reminding him of his promises, and in reply he asked me to call to see him. I called, and found myself up against the concrete wall. Mr. Gavit was as polite as I could have requested; all that he failed in was action. He would not tell me the result of the investigation which Mr. Stone had made, or had promised to make. He would not tell me anything, except that the case was a subtle and difficult one to judge, and that he could not see his way to take it up. I quoted to him his letter to Mr. Stone, "It is evidently necessary under the circumstances that the 'Evening Post' should deal with this subject"; Mr. Gavit was uncomfortable and embarrassed, but he would not make good his words, nor would he publish in the "Evening Post" the facts about my challenge to the Associated Press. He never published a line about it, and on the basis of the facts above stated, I believe that I can claim to have proven positively that the "New York Evening Post" is not what it pretends to be, a newspaper serving the public interest.

I make the same claim concerning the "New York Times." The "Times" did not answer my letter, it did not pay any attention to me; but it happens that I read the "Times," and know some of its editors, so I went after it again and again. I will quote from the last of my letters, so that the reader may see how desperately I tried to get something done:

New York City, June 15, 1914.

EDITOR, THE NEW YORK TIMES:

    Some time ago I wrote you a letter with regard to charges I had made against the Associated Press. I asked you to consider these charges and lay them before your readers, and give them an opportunity to decide of their truth. Not hearing from you, I wrote a second time, to ask you to do me the courtesy to let me know your intentions in the matter. Still not hearing from you, I assume that it is your intention to treat my communication with contempt. I want to call your attention to the fact that in writing to you I am making a test of the sense of honor of your publication. I am putting you on record, and I shall find means to make your attitude known to the public. You are an Associated Press newspaper, and your honor is definitely bound up with that of the organization which serves you. You sell Associated Press news to the public. If the Associated Press news is false news, you are selling false news to the public, and you are refusing the public any opportunity to judge a most serious, a carefully documented charge that this news is false. It is true that you published my telegram to the President in one edition of your paper. But it is also true that you published it only because I sent it to you. The Associated Press did not send it to you. And I cannot always be in Colorado, and cannot always make it my business to supply you with antidotes to the poison which you are getting from the Associated Press. Only today, for example, you are, through the agency of the Associated Press, responsible for suppressing an important piece of news from Colorado: that is to say, the fact that Judge Lindsey has issued a statement defending himself, and especially the women who went with him, against the charges which have been made against them by the "interests" in Colorado. The "New York World" gave that letter a column, from its special correspondent. The "New York Call," having the Laffan Service, also had some account of the letter. You, having the Associated Press service, have not a word about it. And this is a vital and most important piece of news.

I then went on to tell about the "Evening Post" and its promise to investigate. I said:

The "Times" is involved in the matter in exactly the same way, and to exactly the same extent as the "Evening Post." The "Times" published the officially inspired defense of the Associated Press in exactly the same way as the "Evening Post." I believe that it is up to you to explain the reasons for your silence in this matter. I believe that if you maintain silence, I shall be justified in declaring to all the world that you have shown yourself in this matter a newspaper without a high sense of honor, and false to the motto which you carry, "All the News that's Fit to Print." I assure you that I shall make this charge against you on many occasions in future. You may think that the five hundred thousand a week circulation of the "Appeal to Reason" is a factor which you can afford to neglect, but I believe that in the course of time you will realize that you were mistaken in permitting me to place you on record in this matter.

So ends the story of my test of the Associated Press and its newspapers. In the second part of this book, which deals with causes, I shall return to the subject, and show exactly why these things happen: Why the "New York Times" is without honor where the Associated Press is concerned, and just how many thousands of dollars it would have cost the "New York Evening Post" if its managing editor had carried out his bold promise to me.

CHAPTER XXIX

THE SCANDAL-BUREAU

There is one other incident which must be told before I finish with the subject of Denver, its criminal government and prostitute newspapers. I had been in Denver before, also I had read Ben Lindsey's "The Beast"; so I knew, before I arrived, what I might expect to encounter. Standing in the Pennsylvania station, bidding my wife farewell, I said: "Let me give you this warning; whatever you read about me, don't worry. If there is any scandal, pay no attention to it, for that is the way they fight in Denver."

And when I reached my destination, I had cause to be glad of my forethought. John Reed, who had just come up from the coal-country, told me of the vile slanders which had been invented and circulated concerning the women of the coal-fields who had been active in defense of their cause. The scandal-mongers had not even spared a poor, half-crazed Italian woman, whose three babies had been burned to death in the holocaust at Ludlow! Louis Tikas, a young Greek idealist, a graduate of the University of Athens, who had been trying to uplift his people and had been foully murdered by corporation thugs, they blackguarded as a "brothel hanger-on" before his corpse was under ground! John Reed himself they had got involved with a charming young widow in Denver; he had met her twice at dinner-parties! (In passing, to show you how far Colorado had progressed toward civil war, I might mention that this lady, upon learning what had been done to the strikers, sent to the East and purchased two machine-guns and hid them in her cellar, ready to be shipped to the strike-field for use by the strikers in case the militia attempted to return.)

Every Socialist and magazine-writer, even every writer for conservative publications, was taken in hand upon his arrival in Denver, and fitted out with a scandal. So far as I know, the only one who escaped was Harvey O'Higgins—and this because he took the precaution to bring his wife along. I had not brought my wife; also I was a "divorced man," and an

easy victim. There was a young Jewish girl, a probation-
officer in Judge Lindsey's court, whom I was so indiscreet as
to treat to a sandwich in a dairy lunch-room; that was sufficient for the scandal-bureau, which had to hustle in these
crowded days. I recollect a funny scene in the home of James
Randolph Walker, where several of these "affinities" learned
for the first time to whom they had been assigned. We had a
merry time over it; but meanwhile, at the meetings of the Law
and Order League, and other places where the ladies of "good
society" in Denver gathered to abuse the strikers, all these
scandals were solemnly taken for granted, and quoted as
evidence of the depravity of "foreign agitators" and the radicals who abetted them!

For myself, let me explain that during my three weeks in
Denver I kept two stenographers busy all day; I wrote a score
of articles, I sent hundreds of telegrams and letters—working
under terrific pressure, hardly taking time to eat. My wife
was back in New York, risking her frail health in the midst
of public uproar, and with reason to fear that she might be
assaulted by thugs at any moment. Every thought I had to
spare was for her, all my loyalty was for her; yet "good
society" in Denver was imagining me involved in a dirty
intrigue! In several intrigues—such a Bluebeard I am! I
had been in the city perhaps a week, when a young lady came
to me and spoke as follows:

"Mr. Sinclair, I represent the 'Denver Post.' We have a
rumor concerning you about which I wish to ask you."

"What is it?"

"We understand that you are about to move from your
hotel."

"I have no such intention. Who told you that?"

"Well, I hope you will not take offense; I will tell you the
report, just as it was given to me."

"Very well, go ahead."

I am sorry I cannot remember the exact words of the rig-
marole; it was five years ago, and I have had more important
things to remember. Suffice it to say that it was a new scandal—not the Jewish probation-officer; I had uttered a mysterious and portentous sentence, expressive of my guilty fear;
if my wife were to learn why I had left the hotel, "it would
be all over." I looked the young lady from the "Denver Post"
in the eye and answered: "Standing in the Pennsylvania

12

station, bidding my wife farewell, I said to her: 'Let me give you one warning; whatever you may read about me, don't worry. If there is any scandal, pay no attention to it, for that is the way they fight in Denver.'" And so the young lady from the "Denver Post" went away, and did not publish that awful "rumor."

There are people who live upright and straightforward lives, and concerning whom no breath of scandal is ever whispered; such people are apt to think that all anyone has to do to avoid scandal is to lead upright and straightforward lives as they do. They see some man who keeps dubious company, and is given to "smart" conversation; concerning such a man an evil report is readily believed; and they conclude that if any man is a victim of scandal, he must be such a man as that. But how if a scandal were deliberately started, concerning a person who had done nothing whatever to deserve it? My wife tells of a woman in her home town who would destroy the reputation of a young girl by the lifting of an eyebrow, the gesture of a fan in a ballroom. She would do this, sometimes from pure malice, sometimes from jealousy for her daughter. You can understand that among sophisticated people such practices might become a subtle art; and how if it were to occur to great "interests," threatened in their power, to hire such arts? Let me assure you that this thing is done all over the United States; it is done all over the world, where there is privilege defending itself against social protest.

There was a certain labor leader in America, who was winning a great strike. It was sought to bribe him in vain, and finally a woman was sent after him, a woman experienced in seduction, and she lured this man into a hotel room, and at one o'clock in the morning the door was broken down, and the labor leader was confronted with a newspaper story, ready to be put on the press in a few minutes. This man had a wife and children, and had to choose between them and the strike; he called off the strike, and the union went to pieces. This anecdote was told to me, not by a Socialist, not by a labor agitator, but by a well-known United States official, a prominent Catholic.

I cite this to show the lengths to which Big Business will go in order to have its way. In San Francisco they raised a million dollar fund, and with the help of their newspapers set to work deliberately to railroad five perfectly innocent labor-men to the gallows. In Lawrence, Massachusetts, the great Woolen Trust planted dynamite in the homes of strike-breakers, and with the help of their newspapers sought to fasten this crime upon the union; only by an accident were these conspirators exposed, and all but the rich one brought to justice. Do you think that "interests" which would undertake such elaborate plots would stop at inventing and circulating scandal about their enemies?

Most certainly they did this in Denver. I was assured by Judge Lindsey, and by James Randolph Walker, at that time chairman of Denver's reform organization, that the corporations of that city had a regular bureau for such work. The head of it was a woman doctor, provided with a large subsidy, numerous agents, and a regular card catalogue of her victims. When someone was to be ruined, she would invent a story which fitted as far as possible with the victim's character and habits; and then some scheme would be devised to enable the newspapers to print the story without danger of libel suits.

There are a hundred ways by which this can be done; watch "Town Topics" in New York, or "Town Talk" and the "Wasp" in San Francisco, and you will see. The victim will be asked if there is dissension between him and his wife; when he denies it, there will be an item to the effect that he denies it—the item being so worded as to cause people to smile knowingly. I know a radical whose wife nearly died of appendicitis; while she was still bed-ridden, she was taken to a sanatorium by her mother and her family physician, a man old enough to be her grandfather. The day after she left, her husband was called upon to "deny" a report that his wife "had eloped with a Jew."

Or perhaps maybe a report will be brought to the man that somebody else has made charges against him; he is naturally indignant, and when he is asked if he will bring a libel suit, he answers that he will think about it; so the newspaper has a story that the man is thinking about bringing a libel suit. Or someone will be hired to slander him to his face, and when he knocks the slanderer down, the newspaper will have a story of a public disturbance, so worded as to put the victim in the wrong, and at the same time to make known the slander.

In extreme cases they will go as far as they did with Judge Lindsey—hiring perjured affidavits, and getting up a fake reform organization to give them authority. Lindsey, you understand, has made his life-work the founding of a children's court, which shall work by love and not by terror. Love of children—ah, yes, all scandal-bureaus know what that means! So they had a collection of affidavits accusing Lindsey of sodomy. They brought the charges while he was in the East; a reporter went to the Denver hotel where his young bride was staying, and when she refused to see the reporter, or to hear the charges against her husband, the reporter stood in the hallway and shouted the charges to her through the transom, and then went away and wrote up an interview!

Or perhaps the Scandal-Bureau will maintain for its foul purposes a special publication which is libel-proof; one of those "fly-by-night" sheets, whose editor-in-charge is an office-boy, and whose worldly possessions are a telephone address and three pieces of furniture. This was a part of their scheme in Denver. The publication was called—oh, most delicious allurement!—"Polly Pry"! I don't know if it is still published, but I saw copies of it during the coal-strike, and it was full of the cruelest libels concerning everybody who stood for the strikers.

I remember one full-page story about "Mother Jones," a white-haired old woman of eighty-two years, who was being held in jail without warrant or charge for several months, because she persisted in coming back to the strike-field every time she was deported. And what do you think they said about "Mother Jones"? In her early years she had been the keeper of a house of prostitution! They went into the most elaborate detail about it; they gave the names of people who knew about it, they gave the address of the house—and then they had their "kept" congressman, a man by the name of Kindel, to read this number of "Polly Pry" into the "Congressional Record"! So, of course, it was "privileged"; all the "kept" newspapers all over the state of Colorado and elsewhere might quote the story without danger of punishment! They might quote it, not from "Polly Pry," but from the "Congressional Record"!!

I took the trouble to ask "Mother Jones" about this story. It appears that in those early days she was a sewing woman; she earned a precarious living, and felt herself justified in working for anyone who would pay her. She did some sewing for a girl of the streets, and this girl died of tuberculosis, and the Catholic church refused her a burial service, and

"Mother Jones" wrote to a newspaper to protest against this action—her first appearance in public life, her first utterance of radicalism. And this had been remembered all these years, it was brought up against her in one labor struggle after another; only they made her the "madame" of the house where the poor girl of the streets had lived!

We who sympathize with the cause of labor grow used to such things, and do not care for ourselves. What hurts us is this—that in a time of crisis, when the need of labor is so great, our influence with the public is destroyed by these slanderers. The average law-abiding and credulous citizen has no remotest idea of the existence of such machinery for influencing his mind. He takes the truth of these stories for granted, and concludes that a cause which is represented by such advocates can have no claim upon him. While I was in Denver, the "Law and Order League" held several meetings in the parlors of the great hotels. I offered to address these ladies, and I know that if I had been permitted to do so, I could have opened the eyes of some of them. But the league voted against it, and I have no doubt that this vote was because of the Scandal Bureau and its work. Instead of hearing me, the league heard a clergyman, the Rev. Pingree, who declared that if he could have his way he would blow up all the strikers' homes with dynamite! After that I always referred to this organization as the "Law and Murder League."

But the crowning achievement of the Scandal-Bureau was still to come. In the effort to induce President Wilson to intervene in the strike, I had evolved what I thought was a wonderful idea—that Judge Lindsey and his wife should escort three of the miners' wives to Washington to tell their story to the President. It took days and nights of diplomacy, for Lindsey had an election campaign ahead of him, and his wife was in delicate health; but the emergency was extreme, and at last "our little Ben," as the children called him, made up his mind to the sacrifice. The party set out, and spoke at large meetings in Chicago and New York, and interviewed the President in Washington, and afforded the Associated Press another opportunity to display its complete subservience to the Colorado Fuel and Iron Company.

And meantime, in Denver, the newspapers were pouring out an incessant stream of invective upon Lindsey. The Scandal-Bureau revived the old yarn, that he was "the insane son of insane parents." (I knew his mother, an excellent old lady, as sane as I am.) On every stage of this journey Lindsey was accompanied by his young wife, to whom he had been married only a few months; nevertheless, it was plainly stated in the Colorado papers, and generally believed by Denver "society," that the three strikers' wives constituted part of a harem. If only you could have seen them—three pathetic, bedraggled poor women, two of them in deep mourning! And when Mrs. Lindsey, owing to the strain of the journey, suffered a miscarriage, and had to be carried from the train to a hospital in Chicago, several Colorado newspapers reported that this was owing to mistreatment by her husband! At a meeting of the Denver Real Estate Exchange, it was proposed to appoint a committee to "spit on Lindsey's shoes" when he returned; and this was the kind of news that was thought worth forwarding out of Denver!

I write to Judge Lindsey, so that you may have these incredible incidents upon his authority, not upon mine. He confirms every statement I have made. He tells of a woman detective, employed by the Scandal-Bureau—

> The Lewis woman circulated the story that my wife came out of a house of prostitution, and that her mother was a "madame"; and the corporations paid the woman for it. There is no doubt about this, and it can be proved.

Judge Lindsey goes on to narrate the extraordinary circumstances under which these proofs became available. One of the members of the State legislature, a man named Howland, was caught receiving a bribe in the legislature. He had introduced a "strike bill" against the Tobacco Trust, and a messenger-boy had handed him an envelope of money, said to be from an agent of the Tobacco Trust. In order to save this man Howland, the head of the Scandal-Bureau, Dr. Mary Elizabeth Bates, came forward and testified before the legislative committee that she had sent this money to Howland in order to pay detectives to "get Lindsey." Says Lindsey in his letter to me:

> Mind you, *she testified* to her part in the infamy, and was backed up by some of our rich citizens, feeling that she was quite safe from prosecution—as she was. But Howland was found guilty of perjury in this case, having sworn that the money came for an entirely different purpose. Because of the general belief of the legislators that the whole thing was part of a frame-up against me, and the fear that it

would lead to the truth being told about the fight against me, they came to a compromise in the case against Howland, which was merely to expel him from the legislature for perjury. He never was tried for perjury or conspiracy to ruin me and my court work, as was undoubtedly his plan.

And how stands the matter today? Let Lindsey tell it in his own words:

During the war I was absolutely outlawed from every opportunity to be of any patriotic service here by the privilege and special interest crowd who control all patriotism, especially in the food and other administrations. When I returned from France I was permitted to speak for the Liberty Loan, but the chairman of the meeting told me that one of Boss Evans' old tools had threatened to "read him out of the Republican party" for daring to let me take part in that patriotic celebration. Fourteen bills for the protection of women and children were killed in the last legislature through the open statement of certain members of the legislature who were tools of the Interests that: "If Lindsey has anything to do with it, swat it." All this you will understand is my heritage of hate because of the part my wife and I took in that strike, and against big crooks generally when they have time and again tried to rob our city. Since "The Beast and the Jungle" stories, and my part in the Colorado coal-strike, it has been almost impossible for me to speak before such assemblies as High Schools, Woman's Clubs, Mothers' Congresses and the like. As one woman said to me frankly. "Mrs. So-and-so's husband is a big contributor to our club, and if we permitted you to appear on the program she would be highly indignant and withdraw her support." I am sure you will understand just exactly what the influence is, and how insidiously it works.

As I read the page-proofs of this book, the great coal strike comes, and the miners in the Southern Colorado field are out again, and Federal troops are guarding the mines. But this time it is not necessary for the Scandal Bureau and the Associated Press to muzzle the strikers and their sympathizers. This time the job has been done by the Federal court injunction!

CHAPTER XXX

THE CONCRETE WALL

I returned to New York, and at a meeting in Berkeley Hall I told the story of conditions in Colorado. I did not get myself arrested, however, so the New York newspapers printed only a few words of what I said, and the Associated Press sent out nothing. It was again the concrete wall, impenetrable, insurmountable: on one side I, with my facts about the outrages upon the miners; and on the other side the public—as far out of reach as if it had been in the moon.

The greatest atrocity of the strike was the fact, previously set forth, that the state militia in the coal-fields had been recruited from strike-breakers and Baldwin-Felts gunmen. The facts had been refused, even to the state legislature; until finally the legislature appointed a committee to wait upon the militia general and not leave his office until they got the roster of the guard. So it was disclosed that in Company A of the state guard there had been one hundred and twenty-two members, and all but three of them coal-company employes, receiving the pay of coal-companies while they wore the uniform and carried the flag of the state!

It was an incredible prostitution of government; and what did the newspapers do with the story? What did the Associated Press do with it? I was unable to find the story in a single newspaper, outside of Denver. I brought the full-page story clipped from the "Rocky Mountain News" to New York with me, and tried the big New York dailies, and could not get one of them to publish it.

The "Chicago Tribune" had published in full a letter of mine to John D. Rockefeller, Jr., setting forth these facts in detail. Also the "Tribune" had published a very fair and just editorial, headed: "All the Truth," from which I quote:

Facts are charged by Mr. Sinclair—and others, it must be said—which, if true, are a disgrace to the men responsible and to the community in which they existed. To ascertain the truth and to deal with the situation are duties which must be performed. . . . . Let us have the facts about this terrible industrial tragedy, and all the facts. Let us know the guilty and all the guilty.

Three days later the "Chicago Tribune" took up my definite charges concerning the guard. It said:

> If, as he asserts, the Adjutant General's report shows any such abuse of the guard, the situation calls for prompt rebuke and effective action, if such action is possible under our laws. . . . . We suggest the National Guard take cognizance of the above allegations of Sinclair, and if they are substantiated by the Adjutant General of Colorado that the guard publicly protest against the abuse.

Five days after that the "Chicago Tribune" published a letter from P. A. Wieting of Denver, as follows:

> Referring to your editorial "Abusing the Guard," in your issue of June 5. If Upton Sinclair said that the official records of Adjutant General Chase showed that an overwhelming majority of the Colorado militia were mine guards and other employes of the coal companies, he deliberately lied. Mr. Chase's records showed nothing of the sort, and could not; for the statement is absolutely false and absurd. The National Guard of Colorado is made up like in other states, of young business and professional men, students, farmer boys and the like, and includes the sons of many of our best families.
>
> It is surprising that a paper of the standing of the "Tribune" should accept offhand such a preposterous charge against a great state made by a professional muckraker. If you still entertain the slightest belief in Sinclair's foolish charge, any banker, any reputable business man, any college president in Colorado will tell you, as I do, that the man who made the statement quoted lied and knew that he lied.

Now here was a direct issue of fact. If P. A. Wieting were a real person, living in Denver, Colorado, and if he read a morning newspaper, he must have read the "Rocky Mountain News," because that was the only morning newspaper published in Denver. And on the entire front page of the "Rocky Mountain News" had been published the roster of Company A of the Colorado state militia, as given to the press by a committee of the state legislature, also a report of this committee of the legislature, giving all the facts as to these members of Company A, the capacity in which one hundred and nineteen out of one hundred and twenty-two of them were employed by the coal-operators or the Baldwin-Felts Detective Agency, and the wages they were paid by these concerns. The evidence was as complete and as authoritative as it was possible for evidence to be; and therefore, when P. A. Wieting wrote this letter to the "Chicago Tribune," deliberately accusing me of deliberate lying, he was deliberately lying himself.

I thought, of course, that the "Tribune," having taken a brave stand and called for the truth, really wanted the truth,

and would push the controversy to the end. Therefore I sent
to the "Tribune" by registered mail a copy of the "Rocky
Mountain News," containing the facts, and I looked to see
this full-page report transferred to a page of the "Chicago
Tribune." Or I looked to have the "Tribune" have some
representative in Denver look up the facts, as it might so easily
have done. Instead of that, I saw not one line about the matter. What strings had been pulled in the "Tribune" office, I
don't happen to know. All I know is that I wrote several
times, protesting, and that no attention was paid to my letters.
Now, while I am preparing this book, I write to the "Tribune,"
lest by any chance the "Tribune" published something in some
edition which I missed, and which my clipping bureau missed;
but the "Tribune" leaves my letter unanswered!

Also I write to Denver to find out about P. A. Wieting—
if he is a real person. I find that he is assistant cashier of the
Colorado Fuel & Iron Co., Mr. Rockefeller's concern which
broke the strike!

All this time, you must understand, the "kept" writers on
the other side of the concrete wall were having their will with
the public. Arthur Brisbane, for example, whose editorial
against the strikers was submitted to Mr. Rockefeller by Mr.
Rockefeller's press agent as a proof of the press agent's skill!
And Elbert Hubbard of East Aurora—you will find a special
chapter in this book devoted to the "Fra," and in it you may
read how he sought to sell out the Colorado strikers. And the
Rev. Newell Dwight Hillis, a clerical gentleman whom we have
seen spurning George D. Herron in public, and apologizing in
tears before his congregation because his greed for money had
led him into a mess of lawsuits. This clerical gentleman
preached a sermon, in which he referred to our Broadway
"pickets" as "a lot of silly people," and incidentally told some
score of lies about the strikers. Somebody, name unknown,
was circulating this sermon in expensive pamphlet form by the
hundreds of thousands of copies; so George Creel wrote to
Hillis—but in vain. If you are near a library, look up Creel's
"Open Letter" in "Harper's Weekly," May 29, 1915, and see
how many lies a greedy preacher can pack into one sermon.
I also wrote to the reverend gentleman, and succeeded in
getting a reply from him. I quote my final letter, which covers
the case, I think:

Rev. Newell Dwight Hillis,
  Brooklyn, New York.
My Dear Sir:
  I have your letter and note that you are going West to Colorado, and that if you can find any errors in your sermon you will correct them. I would say that definite and specific errors are pointed out in George Creel's letters; errors that you would not have to go to Colorado to find out about. They are proven in the sworn testimony given before the Congressional Investigation Committee and before the hearings of the Commission on Industrial Relations. While you can, of course, not recollect who gave you this or that detail of information, you must certainly know from what source you took the definite false statements of figures and facts to which Mr. Creel calls your attention. Moreover, the most important questions in both Mr. Creel's letter and mine, you have entirely ignored. I wish to ask you, before you go West, will you answer the following specific questions?
  Who is circulating and paying for the expensive pamphlet form of your sermon?
  Second, did this party obtain your permission to circulate it in this form?
  Third, did you receive any payment for permitting this circulation?
  Fourth, if, after investigation of Mr. Creel's points in Colorado you find that you were wrong and he was right, will you compel the party who is circulating this pamphlet to give to your corrections the same amount of circulation?
  I have, of course no right to insist that you should answer any of these questions. I will merely say that by failing to answer them, and answer them promptly and explicitly, you will leave your name open to exceedingly grave suspicions.

This letter remained unanswered; yet such utter lack of concern about his good name has not injured the pastor of Plymouth Church, Brooklyn, with the great organs of capitalist opinion! Only recently "McClure's Magazine" has selected him for its prize anti-Bolshevik liar. Please make a mental note of him, for reference when we come to the anti-Bolshevik liars and their lies.

It was still our hope that President Wilson could be persuaded to interfere in the strike and force the Rockefellers to some compromise. It being the way of public officials to move only in response to public clamor, we were driven to keep on butting our heads against the concrete wall. Our "mourning picket" demonstration had gathered about us a group of young radicals, who could not endure to see the effort die down and the strangling of the strike completed. Every day one would come to us with some new idea. One group wished to go up to Rockefeller's home on Madison Avenue, and walk up and down in front of it. We objected to this, because we were

not attacking **Mr. Rockefeller** personally, we were attacking
his business policy, and his office seemed the proper place.
Nevertheless, one boy ventured up on Madison Avenue, and
was promptly arrested and sent to jail for sixty days.

There was another group which wished to visit Tarrytown,
where young Rockefeller had retired to the seclusion of his
country home, with a high iron fence all around it, and iron
gates, and a score or two of armed guards patrolling day and
night. This group tried to hold a street meeting in the village
of Tarrytown, and were arrested. So I was driven into a
campaign on behalf of free speech. I have told in Chapter
XII of my experience with the "Tarrytown News"; I have
now to tell of my experience with the "New York Herald."
It is one of the few of my newspaper adventures from the
contemplation of which I derive satisfaction.

I had several sessions with the board of trustees of the
village of Tarrytown. They were courteous, and permitted
me to argue the issue of free speech—which I did courteously.
I brought to them a charming letter from Georg Brandes,
then a visitor in New York. They held a public session,
addressed by Leonard Abbott, Theodore Schroeder, and
myself, and in the course of my talk I pointed out that the
result of repression of free speech was violence. In England,
where the radicals were allowed to gather in Hyde Park and
say what they chose, crimes of political violence were practically unknown. On the other hand, in America, where it
was customary for the police to arrest radicals and club and
jail them, such crimes were common. Only the other day the
newspapers had told of the assassination of the chief of police
of Spokane, where the I. W. W. had been prevented from
speaking.

There were a dozen newspaper reporters present at this
hearing, and accounts of it appeared in the New York papers
next morning. The "Herald" stated that I had threatened the
trustees of Tarrytown with violence in case they refused my
request. I quote from the "Herald's" narrative:

Suddenly Frank R. Pierson, president of the village, leaped to his
feet and said:
"We shall not be intimidated by threats. We will hear no more
of this kind of argument. For one, I was willing to listen to what
these people had to say and to hear them fairly and honestly, but when
they come here with threats of death, of assassination and of mob rule,
I will not hear them further."

Now, concerning this account there is only one thing to be said: it was absolute fiction. I have never met a more agreeable gentleman than Mr. Pierson, president of the Tarrytown village board; he voted my way on every occasion, and from first to last we never exchanged a word that was not cordial. On reading this account I at once went to see him, and ascertained that both he and the other trustees considered the report to be false and inexcusable. I then sent a letter to the "Herald" informing them that they had libeled me, and threatening them with a suit. They sent a reporter to see me, and I explained to this reporter the basis of my complaint, and next morning the "Herald" published my letter of complaint, together with an article reiterating its statement, and quoting three of the trustees as supporting its statement. I quote the "Herald" reporter's words:

> I saw Frank R. Pierson, president of the village, and asked his opinion of the correctness of the account published in the "Herald." Mr. Pierson carefully read the article and then said:
> "Mr. Sinclair certainly made the remarks attributed to him in the 'Herald,' if I heard aright, and I did jump up and declare that we should not be intimidated by threats. Mr. Sinclair may not have intended to make a threat, but the inference was plain. The 'Herald' did not misquote either Mr. Sinclair or me."

And concerning the above interview also there is only one thing to be said; it was absolute fiction. I went to see Mr. Pierson again, and he assured me that he had given no such interview, and would appear in court and testify accordingly. Another of the trustees wrote me that the "Herald" interview with him was a "fake," and so I put the matter into the hands of my attorneys, and a libel-suit was filed against the "New York Herald." It dragged for a year or two, and I came to California and dismissed the matter from my mind. When the time came for the suit to come to trial, I was unwilling to take the trip to New York, and asked my lawyers to have the matter dropped. You may imagine my consternation when I received a letter from them, telling me that they had been negotiating with the attorneys for the "Herald," and had succeeded in settling the case upon the basis of a payment of twenty-five hundred dollars damages! Never, if I live to be as old as Methuselah, shall I spend money that will bring me more satisfaction than that twenty-five hundred dollars!

Throughout these Tarrytown adventures, which lasted several weeks, each newspaper had one reporter who followed the story day by day, and two or three of these men became friendly to me. Isaac Russell, reporter for the "Times," invited me to lunch in a restaurant in Tarrytown, with a couple of other men. I explained that I was ill and not eating anything, but would sit and chat with them. As they were finishing, there came in the reporter for the "World," who, as it happened, had been drunk during most of the time. Next morning there appeared in the "World" a particularly nasty account of the day's events, in which it was described how I had come to Tarrytown with four women in my train, had had lunch with several reporters, and had permitted them to pay the bill. I took the trouble to go down to the office of the "World" and see Mr. Frank Cobb, managing editor; explaining to him that I had come alone to Tarrytown, had spoken to no woman in Tarrytown, and had eaten no lunch in Tarrytown. Mr. Cobb admitted that I had a grievance, and by way of recompense allowed me to dictate a column interview about the meaning of the free speech fight in Tarrytown; incidentally he took the drunken reporter off the assignment. From the other reporters I got the "inside" story of what had happened, and it throws an amusing light upon newspaper ethics. The drunken reporter had lost out in the contest with me, not because he had been drunk, nor because he had lied about a radical, but because he had implied in his article that a reporter was a social inferior! Was not a reporter privileged to invite an author to lunch, and to pay for the lunch if he saw fit?

CHAPTER XXXI

MAKING BOMB-MAKERS

It had been agreed by the trustees of Tarrytown that while we might not tell about the Ludlow massacre at a street-meeting, we might tell about it at a meeting in a theatre or hall. I set out to find a theatre or hall, but there was no theatre or hall that could be rented for that purpose. I then went up on the heights, where the Rockefellers live, and appealed to the sense of fair play of Mr. Rockefeller's neighbors. This is the Pocantico hills country, a line of magnificent estates and palatial homes, of which you see pictures in the "Sunday supplements." You might have thought it poor territory for radical propaganda; nevertheless, I was able to persuade one of the residents, Mrs. Charles J. Gould, to allow the use of her open-air theatre for a meeting in defense of free speech. Imagine, if you can, the excitement of the New York newspapers, when they learned that there was to be an I. W. W. meeting—so they called it—in an open-air theatre on a millionaire estate almost next door to the Rockefellers!

We held the meeting, attended by some three hundred people of the town, rich and poor, including a number of laborers from young Mr. Rockefeller's estate. John W. Brown, organizer of the United Mine-workers, told the story of the strike, and we moved a resolution that it was the sense of the meeting that Mr. Rockefeller's treatment of his strikers had been such that we called upon the President of the United States to confiscate his mines. We discussed that resolution for a couple of hours, and we carried it *unanimously!* But alas, it happened that Adolf Wolff, an Anarchist sculptor and poet, got up and delivered a tirade, abusing me for having pleaded for free speech with the trustees of Tarrytown. "We shouldn't plead, we should take!" declared Comrade Wolff. A lady from the South got up and sang negro-songs to pacify the tumultuous meeting, and so the newspapers could make a joke of the whole affair—which they did.

In their last public session with us, the trustees of the

village had admitted that there could be no interference with a meeting held upon the strip of property through which ran the city aqueduct—this property being under State control. So now the radicals whose friends were in jail wanted to hold a meeting on this aqueduct property. They asked me to come, but I happened to be ill. Leonard Abbott went with them, also a boy named Arthur Caron, whose story I must briefly tell. Caron had been one of the finest lads who had joined our Broadway demonstrations. He was a French-Canadian, whose wife and baby had starved to death during the Lawrence strike. He had come to New York and taken part in the unemployed demonstration of the previous winter, and the police had arrested him and beaten him in his cell, breaking his nose and one ear-drum. He was a non-resistant, he told us, and had been one of the most useful in helping us to keep our demonstration peaceable. Now he went, at my suggestion, to avail himself of the public assurance given by the Tarrytown trustees, that a meeting on the aqueduct would not be interfered with.

But, as it happened, the "Tarrytown News" was carrying on a furious war against the village trustees, because of their halfway-decent treatment of the "agitators"; the "News" wanted us all exterminated, and it called on the "law-abiding" citizens of the village to assemble at the aqueduct and stop that meeting. So the speakers were met by a mob of rich men and chauffeurs, who tooted horns and howled at them, threw rotten vegetables and sand and stones into their faces, filling their eyes and mouth with filth and streaming blood. Running through the village toward the railroad-station, the little group was ridden down by mounted members of the aqueduct police-force, who pursued them even on board the train, and clubbed them over the heads when they sought refuge in the seats. These incidents were described to me by several indignant newspaper reporters, including my friend Isaac Russell, of the "Times." But the "Times" cut out from Russell's story the incident of the clubbing on the train.

Here was another call for protest; but by this time the Sinclair family had reached the point of exhaustion. My wife had been a semi-invalid at the beginning of the affair, and was now near to nervous breakdown. We had spent every dollar we owned, and a great many that we did not own; so we were forced to retire, and let the Tarrytown rowdies and their rowdy newspapers have their way. We remained in New York for a couple of weeks to straighten our affairs; and on the very day we had planned to leave for the country, the telephone rang, and my wife answered, and a voice said: "This is the 100th St. Police Station. Do you know a man named Arthur Caron?"

Yes, my wife knew Arthur Caron. "What about him?" she asked, and the voice answered: "We found your name in a notebook in his pocket. Will you come to the station and identify his body?"

There had been, it appeared, an explosion in a tenement-house on Third Avenue. At first the police thought it was a gas-explosion, but soon the truth became known; Arthur Caron and two or three of his friends had been making bombs with the intention of blowing up the Rockefellers. There had been a premature explosion, which had blown out several stories of the tenement, and killed the three lads.

It was interesting to observe the conduct of the New York newspapers during this affair. It made, of course, a tremendous excitement. Bombs are news; they are heard all the way around the world. But the outrages which have caused the bombs are not news, and no one ever refers to them. No one makes clear that these outrages will continue to cause bombs, so long as the human soul remains what it is.

Now the New York newspapers knew perfectly well that our Broadway demonstration, our "Free Silence League," as they had dubbed it, had been a peaceable demonstration. They knew that at the opening meeting, at which the plan was discussed, I had declared that I desired the co-operation only of those who would pledge their word to me personally that they would offer no resistance, no matter what was done to them; that they would not even speak a word, nor argue with anyone, they would do nothing but walk up and down. At our first meeting Frederick Sumner Boyd, an I. W. W. leader, repudiated my ideas, and called upon the meeting to organize itself to raise money and send arms to the coal-strikers. I replied that if any wished to organize such a group, it was his right, but I had called this meeting for the purpose of organizing one kind of demonstration, and I thought that those who wished to organize some other kind of demonstration should utilize one of the other rooms of the Liberal Club; whereupon

Boyd and about half the audience withdrew. All this had been
fully reported in the New York papers, and was known to
everyone.

Also it was known to the Rockefellers that at the headquarters of our Colorado Committee I personally obtained the
pledge of every man and woman, before I allowed them to
join us, that they would conform to the rule laid down. I
say this was known to the Rockefellers, because they had spies
among us; I knew perfectly well who those spies were, and
allowed one of them to think he was my friend. From first to
last I had nothing to hide, and for that reason I had nothing
to fear, and this was as well known to the newspapers as it
was to the police who were probing the explosion. Except
for the first telephone call, which had come from a desk-ser-
geant who knew nothing about the matter whatever, the police
did not trouble us, nor even question us; yet day by day, while
that sensation was before the public, the whole effort of the
New York newspapers was concentrated upon making it appear
that Upton Sinclair was in some way connected with the bomb-
plot. Day after day there would be circumstantial accounts
of how the police and the coroner and other officials were
preparing to summon my wife and myself, and to subject us
to a "rigid examination" concerning Arthur Caron and the
other victims of the explosion. We would call up the police
and the coroner and other officials, and inform them that we
were perfectly willing to be questioned, but that we knew nothing but what we had told the public; to which the police and
the coroner and the other officials would reply: "We have no
wish to question you; that's just newspaper talk." All
officials understand what "newspaper talk" means; but the
public doesn't understand, and so what the public carried away
from this affair was the general impression that my wife and
I were dangerous characters. We were too cunning to get
caught, of course; but we incited obscure and half-educated
young people to make bombs and set them off, and then we
washed our hands of them and left them to their fate.

There is one final story which ought to be told in connection with these "mourning pickets." You may recall that I
had appealed against the decision of Police-magistrate Sims,
to the effect that one whose conduct had been "that of a perfect
gentleman" might properly be found guilty of "using threatening, abusive and insulting behavior." I had told the story of

this court-decision at a public meeting in the State capitol in Denver, and again at a dinner of the Progressive Party workers in Chicago—saying: "I don't know whom the magistrate supposed I had threatened, abused and insulted—unless perhaps it were John D. Rockefeller, Junior!" The audience had laughed appreciatively; they thought that was a funny joke; I, too, thought it was a funny joke. But now—can you believe it?—Justice Crain of the Court of General Sessions handed down his august decision, which had cost me several hundred dollars in lawyer's fees and court costs to obtain; and this Daniel come to judgment upheld the decision of Police-magistrate Sims, and gave his reasons therefor—and lo, his reasons were my funny joke! Seventeen thousand, five hundred dollars per year the people of New York State pay to Justice Crain of the Court of General Sessions, for handing down such august decisions; and forever and ever, so long as capitalist civilization endures, that particular august decision will be printed on expensive paper, and bound in expensive sheepskin, and treasured in the libraries of learned jurists. Such a wonder of a decision deserves to be read, as well as preserved in law-books; so I will quote it here, as follows:

No citizen has a right to rebuke another citizen by subjecting him to ridicule or insult.

The defendant intended by his conduct in the presence of others to rebuke the conduct of Mr. Rockefeller. His action was in the language of the statute, abusive or insulting; abusive because it is derogatory to the one whose conduct is referred to, and the insult lies in part in the subject matter of the rebuke and in part in the publicity of the infliction.

Now let me put to you this problem. The "New York Herald" had published a cartoon, in which I was portrayed as a hideous monster with a filthy muck-rake; and now suppose that I had appealed to Justice Crain of the Court of General Sessions, complaining that James Gordon Bennett had "rebuked a citizen" by "subjecting him to ridicule or insult"—do you think that Justice Crain would have sent Bennett to jail? And do you think that the newspapers would have printed the decision with solemn and respectful comment, praising it as a proper rebuke to a disturber of public order?

I close the story of this long Colorado struggle with a benediction sent to me all the way across the continent: the "Los Angeles Times," July 9th, 1914:

It develops that Upton Sinclair only served two of his three days' sentence, after all. He was on a hunger strike, and after he had gone unfed for two days, his wife came and paid the rest of his fine and forced him out of jail. Wait till they have been married a little longer, and perhaps she will let him serve three years if he wants to do it.

I enquire among friends and learn that the general impression is that I declared a "hunger-strike," and couldn't stick it out, and let my wife come to my rescue. Again the newspapers! The truth is that I was as comfortable as any man ought to ask to be in jail; I had a cell to myself, and it was clean, and near a window, and I was allowed to have my mail, and all the books I wanted, and visitors at reasonable hours. But I wanted to appeal from that stupid decision; and in order to appeal, the lawyers explained, I must have something to appeal *for*. I couldn't appeal for the time I spent in jail, for no court could restore that to me. I had to pay some money— one dollar at the least; and having paid this, I had to come out, whether I would or no. So the newspapers had a chance to report that Upton Sinclair, who had written a book telling how he had fasted for ten or twelve days, had been unable to stick out a three-day "hunger-strike"!

CHAPTER XXXII

THE ROOF-GARDEN OF THE WORLD

After these strenuous adventures I retired to private life to recuperate. I edited "The Cry for Justice," and then, finding that I was still haunted by the Colorado situation, I wrote "King Coal." Meantime I had moved to Southern California, seeking an open-air life. I have been here four years, and alas, I have had a new set of experiences with newspapers. As preliminary to them, there must be given a brief account of this "Roof-garden of the World."

It exists because of climate. There are, of course, ranchmen who raise fruits and vegetables, and there are servants and chauffeurs and house-builders and plumbers, but the main industry of Southern California is climate. Everybody is consuming climate, and in addition to this, nearly everybody is trying to sell climate to "come-ons" from the East. The country has been settled by retired elderly people, whose health has broken down, and who have come here to live on their incomes. They have no organic connection with one another; each is an individual, desiring to live his own little life, and to be protected in his own little privileges. The community is thus a parasite upon the great industrial centres of other parts of America. It is smug and self-satisfied, making the sacredness of property the first and last article of its creed. It has a vast number of churches of innumerable sects, and takes their aged dogmas with deadly seriousness; its social life is display, its intellectual life is "boosting," and its politics are run by Chambers of Commerce and Real Estate Exchanges.

There are, of course, a great number of ladies in Southern California with nothing to do. They have culture clubs, which pay celebrities to come and entertain them, and next to marrying a millionairess, this is the easiest way to get your living in Southern California. They will pay you as much as a hundred dollars for a lecture, and such an opportunity is naturally not to be sneezed at by a strike-agitator in debt. I had been living quietly for a year or so, working on "King Coal," when I was invited to meet at luncheon one of the officials of the ultra-exclusive Friday Morning Club of Los Angeles. I was duly inspected and adjudged presentable, and received an invitation to set forth my intellectual wares before the club assemblage.

Now, this was an important opportunity, as my friends pointed out. There are many such clubs in Los Angeles, and scores of others in the leisure-class towns round about. This first lecture was a test, and if I "made good," I would receive more invitations, and might be able to live quietly and do my writing. The ladies who came to hear Upton Sinclair would, of course, come expecting to be shocked. If I didn't shock them at all, my lecture would be a failure; I must be judicious, and shock them just exactly enough, so that they would come for more shocks. I am fortunate in having a wife who understands the psychology of ladies, and who undertook to groom me for this new role of leisure-class lecturer.

In the first place, there was the question of clothes. "You haven't had a new suit in four or five years," said my wife.

"How about the one I bought in England?"

"That heavy woolen suit? If you wore that on a summer day, the perspiration would stream down your face!"

"Well," I ventured, "mightn't they think it proper for a Socialist to wear old clothes? Mightn't I be pathetic——"

Said M. C. S. "They don't want anybody around who is not well dressed. It's depressing. You must have a new suit."

"But— we just haven't the money to spare."

"You can get a Palm Beach suit for ten dollars."

"Isn't that rather festive? I never wore anything like it."

"Idiot! Papa wears them all the time."

Now "papa," you must understand, is—well, what "papa" does is the standard. So it was arranged that I should go into Los Angeles an hour or two earlier in the morning, and provide myself with a Palm Beach suit and pair of white shoes for two dollars. "They will be made of paper," said my wife, "but you won't have far to walk, and they'll do for other lectures."

M. C. S. does not go with me on these adventures, having not been well since the Colorado excitement. She stays at home and mends socks and writes sonnets, while I administer shocks to the leisure-class ladies. Her last injunction was a hair-cut. "The day of long-haired geniuses is past. Promise me you'll have your hair cut."

I promise, and I get the Palm Beach suit and the shoes,

and then look for a barber. It is ten or eleven months before
America's entry into the war, but the "preparedness" enthu-
siasts are having some kind of celebration in Los Angeles,
and the streets are a mass of red and white bunting; I walk a
long distance, and find half a dozen places with red and white
ribbons wound about poles, but they are not barber-shops. At
last, however, I find one, just in the nick of time, and at ten
o'clock sharp I present myself, all freshly groomed, to the
charming ladies of the club, and am escorted onto the platform.

My theme is "The Voice of the Ages," and I bring with
me a copy of "The Cry for Justice," and read passages from
eminent ancient authors, startling my hearers by the revelation
that Plato and Euripides and Isaiah and Jesus and Confucius
and Dante and Martin Luther and George Washington were
all members of the I. W. W. of their time. I read them Isaiah
on "Ladies of Fashion"—all save one obscene sentence, which
could not be uttered before modern ladies. I give them just
exactly the proper number of thrills, mixed with the proper
number of smiles, and they bombard me with questions for an
hour, and we have a most enjoyable time.

But one tragedy befalls. I am quoting Frederick the Great
on the subject of Militarism, and am moved to mention the
fact that Los Angeles is now in a military mood. "I promised
my wife I would get a hair-cut before I came here, but I
almost missed it, because there were so many red and white
decorations on the streets that I couldn't find a barber-shop."
The instant the words were out of my mouth, I realized that
I had, as the boys say, "spilled the beans." Driving home with
a friend who is a member of the club, she told me what a
success the lecture had been, and I replied: "Ah, no, you are
mistaken! I ruined everything!"

"How?" asked my friend.

"Didn't you hear me confuse the American flag with a
barber-pole?"

"Nonsense!" said my friend. "They all laughed."

"May be so," said I. "But wait until you see the papers
tomorrow morning!"

And sure enough, it was as I said! Next morning the
"Los Angeles Times" published an account of the lecture, in
which I was portrayed as a dandified creature who had
appeared before the ladies decked in tennis flannels. Having
since met Alma Whitaker, the woman who wrote this account,

I dare stake my life that she knows perfectly well the difference between a Palm Beach suit and tennis flannels; but she wanted to make me hateful, and that was such a little lie! She went on to tell about my lecture, in which I had sneered at Jesus, and compared the American flag to a barber-pole! My audience had been highly indignant, according to her account, and one eminent lady had left the room in disgust.

And so next morning there was an editorial in the "Times," of which I will quote about half. You will be struck by its peculiar style, and may be interested to know that it was written by General Otis himself, being a fair sample of the vitriol which every day for thirty years he poured out upon everything enlightened in California:

UPTON SINCLAIR'S RAVINGS

Many people believe that the prattlings of an anarchistic Upton Sinclair before a woman's club are unworthy of serious attention; but the fact that the hall of the Friday Morning Club was filled to overflowing at his programme, and that the great majority of them sat throughout the entire lecture, would seem to prove that such illogical ravings have at least some power to impress. Some few women have been found courageous enough to voice their indignation that the club rostrum should be used for such ungodly purposes.

It is depressing to find a great number of intelligent women, well able to think for themselves, lending time and ear to a piffling collection of more-or-less brilliant quotations upholding anarchy, destruction, lawlessness, revolution, from the lips of an effeminate young man with a fatuous smile, a weak chin and a sloping forehead, talking in a false treble, and accusing them of leading selfish, self-indulgent lives. It would be laughable if it were not a little disconcerting. These women, who are doing such earnest work for their city, who, indeed, rank among the best intellect of the city, who have deeds rather than words to their credit—it seems incredible that they should be prepared to lend encouragement to such unintelligent, witless, anarchistic outpourings.

While slyly veiling his false doctrines as quotations from "intelligent ancient peasants," and the prophet Isaiah, and the Greek classics, Upton Sinclair nevertheless makes no secret of his sympathy with dynamiters and murderers, and considers it an example of exquisite wit to speak of Jesus Christ with patronizing irreverence. His sense of humor also demanded that he belittle the flag of the United States, and, after pretending to confuse it with a barber's pole scoff at the great national wave of emotion for the country's righteous defense and honor.

An assembly of men of the same standing as the women of the Friday Morning Club could never be induced to listen to such insults to their creed and their country without violent protest. Never before an audience of red-blooded men could Upton Sinclair have voiced his weak, pernicious, vicious doctrines. His naïve, fatuous smile alone

would have aroused their ire before he opened his vainglorious mouth.
Let the fact remain that this slim, beflanneled example of perverted masculinity could and did get several hundred women to listen
to him.

Now, as a matter of fact, it happened that I had given a
far more radical lecture at the monthly dinner of the University Club, where three hundred men of Los Angeles had
heard me with every evidence of cordial interest. The secretary of the club had told me that it was the only occasion he
could remember when none of the diners had withdrawn to
play chess until after the speaking was finished. But I had,
of course, no way to make known this fact to the readers of
the "Times," nor even the true sentiments of the ladies of the
Friday Morning Club. It happened that my friend George
Sterling spoke at the club the following week, and I went with
him and was asked to speak at the luncheon. I referred play-
fully to what the "Times" had said about me, and was
astonished at the ovation I received. The women rose from
their seats to let me know that they appreciated the insult to
them involved in the "Times" editorial. It is the same thing
that I have noted everywhere, whenever I refer to the subject
of our newspapers. The American people thoroughly despise
and hate their newspapers; yet they seem to have no idea what
to do about it, and take it for granted that they must go on
reading falsehoods for the balance of their days!

CHAPTER XXXIII

A FOUNTAIN OF POISON

I have lived in Southern California four years, and it is literally a fact that I have yet to meet a single person who does not despise and hate his "Times." This paper, founded by Harrison Gray Otis, one of the most corrupt and most violent old men that ever appeared in American public life, has continued for thirty years to rave at every conceivable social reform, with complete disregard for truth, and with abusiveness which seems almost insane. To one who understands our present economic condition, the volcano of social hate which is smouldering under the surface of our society, it would seem better to turn loose a hundred thousand mad dogs in the streets of Los Angeles, than to send out a hundred thousand copies of the "Times" every day.

You cannot live in Southern California and stand for any sort of liberal ideas without encountering the wrath of this paper. And when you have once done this, it pursues you with personal vindictiveness; no occasion is too small for it to lay hold of, nor does it ever forget you, no matter how many years may pass. My friend Rob Wagner writes me an amusing story about the feud between Otis and the city of Santa Barbara, a millionaire colony about a hundred miles from Los Angeles:

When the big fleet came around here some years ago I was director-generaling a very snappy flower festival at Santa Barbara, and as the "Times" played up all the bar-room brawls the sailors got into and belittled my pretty show, I got hold of the local correspondent and says: "Mac, why are you crabbing the show and featuring the rough stuff?" "Well the truth is, Bob, my pay depends upon the kind of stuff I send. A rotten story is good for columns, against a few paragraphs of the birds and the flowers. You know the General has towns as well as individuals on his index, and Santa Barbara is one of them. The General once owned the Santa Barbara 'Press,' and with his usual cave-man methods got in bad with the villagers, and they bumped him socially so hard that he finally left in great heat and swore vengeance, which he practices to this day. This has been going on for years."

Now the old "General" is gone, but his "index" still stands.

The song should read: "Old Otis' body lies a-moulderin' in the grave, but his soul goes cursing on!" It goes on cursing, not merely movements of social reform and those who advocate them; it goes on cursing Santa Barbara! Soon after we came to Pasadena there was an earthquake shock, sufficiently severe to cause us to run out of our house. You understand, of course, that earthquakes are damaging to real-estate values; therefore there was no report of an earthquake in any Los Angeles paper next day—save that the "Times" reported an earthquake in Santa Barbara! A year or two later this happened again—and again it was an earthquake in Santa Barbara.

Also, Rob Wagner tells me of his own amusing experience with the "Times." I quote:

> During the Harriman campaign I deserted my class, kicked in and had Socialist meetings at my studio, and even enjoyed the degradation of offering hospice to Ben Reitman and Emma Goldman the night after they were run out of San Diego. So the General paid me the amazing compliment of putting me on his index, and gave orders that my name should not appear thereafter in his art columns. Anthony Anderson proved it to me by slipping in a harmless little notice of a portrait exhibit I was holding, which got the blue pencil. So you see that even an artist who might help the town in its very ingrowing aestheticism got the General's axe if the General didn't like his politics!

It happens, curiously enough, that I have met socially half a dozen members of the "Times" staff. They are cynical worldlings, doing a work which they despise, and doing it because they believe that life is a matter of "dog eat dog." I met the lady, Alma Whitaker, who had written the account of my Friday Morning Club lecture. She had enjoyed the lecture, she said, but afterwards had gone to the managing editor and inquired how I was to be handled; she took it for granted that I would understand this, and would regard it tolerantly. I explained to her the embarrassments of an author in relation to an unpaid grocer's bill. As a result of what she had written about me, I had not been invited by any other woman's club in Southern California!

Also I met one of the high editors of the "Times," an important personage whom they feature. Talking about the question of journalistic integrity, he said: "Sinclair, it has been so long since I have written anything that I believed that I don't think I would know the sensation."

My answer was: "I have been writing on public questions

for twenty years, and I can say that I have never written a
single word that I did not believe."

I have had much to say about the Associated Press in the
course of this book. I need say only one thing about it in
Southern California—that its headquarters are in the editorial
rooms of the "Los Angeles Times." A good part of what
goes on the Associated Press wire is first strained through the
"Times" sieve; and so I can inform Mr. Fabian Franklin,
formerly of the "New York Evening Post" and now of the
"Review," that his sacred divinity, the Associated Press, has
established here in Southern California a system which makes
it impossible that any news favorable to the radical cause
should get onto the Associated Press wires, and that everything dealing with the radical movement in Southern California which goes over the Associated Press wires should be
not merely false, but violently and maliciously false. For
example a prominent criminal lawyer in Los Angeles is blown
up by a bomb, and the report goes out to the country that the
police authorities believe that this was the work of "radicals."
But next day the police authorities state officially that they
have no such belief; and a couple of days later the crime is
proven to have had a purely personal motive.

I have myself tested out, not once but several score of
times, the system of the concrete wall and the news channel
as it works here in Los Angeles. For example, when I read
that Russia had a Socialist premier by the name of Kerensky,
and that he did not know what to do with the Tsar and his
family, I wrote to him a letter suggesting "An Island of
Kings"—one of the Catalina Islands, off Los Angeles, as a
place where the dethroned sovereigns of Europe might be
interned, under the guardianship of the United States government. This, you perceive, was a "boost" to Southern California; it conveyed to the outside world the information that
Southern California has a wonderful out-door climate, and
beautiful islands with wild goats running over them, and deep
sea fishing off the shores. I offered this story to the "Los
Angeles Times," and they grabbed it, and it went out at once
over the Associated Press wires.

Then, again, America went into the war, and I found
myself compelled to revise the conclusions of a life-time, and
to give my support to a war. I debated the issue at a gathering of Socialists; and here again was news which world-

capitalism desired to have circulated, here was a well-known Socialist turning to the capitalist side! The "Times" printed the story and the "A. P." sent it out. In order to make the record clear, I quote from the "Times":

UPTON SINCLAIR FAVORS WAR

Has a Complete Reversal of Former Ideas.

Publicly Announces Views in Crown City.

Holds World's Democracy Is in Danger.

Pasadena, Feb. 19.—After preaching vehemently against war for twenty years, Upton Sinclair, the Socialist writer, has joined hands with Mars. The propagandist's exit from the ranks of the peace-at-any-price Socialists was made unexpectedly and dramatically yesterday afternoon at a mass meeting at the Pasadena High School. Sinclair's announcement of his change of heart came after an address by Prof. I. W. Howeth of the University of California on the history and causes of war. In the open forum, which followed the addresses, Sinclair was the storm center in a discussion in which his stand was criticized by the Socialists and other peace advocates and applauded by others in favor of supporting the stand taken by President Wilson.

And then followed long extracts from my speech. As sent out by the Associated Press it was so garbled that I will ask the reader to read four paragraphs of the "Times" account. My reasons for asking this will appear later:

"My one interest in the world is democratic self-government. I have fought for this at every sacrifice of personal advantage for twenty years. I consider that all modern governments are evil, based upon injustice, but I am bound to recognize that there are degrees in this evil. The test is whether the government leaves the people free to agitate against it. This the British government to a great extent has done; so has the French; the German has not.

"For us to permit the Prussian ruling class to beat England to her knees by the methods of general piracy that have been adopted is to put democracy in peril of its life, and to make certain an age of military preparation in the United States, Canada and Australia.

"If we go into the war the thing to do is to decide in advance the terms, and let these be such as to unite all the democratic forces of the world behind us. We do not want Germany beaten to her knees and territories given to her enemies. We do not want to underwrite the program of Russia in Constantinople. We want to remove these points of contention from the arena.

"We want to heal up the ancient wounds. We want to teach all rulers and all peoples that civilization will permit no one to gain territory by war. We want to inter-nationalize the Dardanelles, Alsace-Lorraine, Belgium, Poland, and to say that we, all the world, will fight to put down any state which at any time attempts to invade them."

Again, on the first anniversary of the Russian revolution,

before a mass meeting of the Russian Revolutionary Society of Los Angeles, I defended the idea that Russia must stand by the Allies until the Kaiser was overthrown. The "Times" gave two columns to this story, with big headlines. I quote the opening paragraphs, with apologies for the "Times'" atrocious English:

TOSSES WRENCH INTO RED RUSSIAN MACHINE
Invited Speaker Gives the Bolshevik Adherents Talk on Patriotism.

Upton Sinclair threw a monkey-wrench of facts of American manufacture into a mass meeting of Socialists and near-Socialists at the Labor Temple yesterday, that after cheers and tears for the Bolsheviki, their red riot of revolution, pledges of support of Lenine and his associates, and a notable evasion of facts for the sake of indulgence in rhetorical idealism, wound up by adopting a resolution for home rule in Ireland.

"So long as the United States government is behind the small nations and for justice in the world, every Socialist and every revolutionist should be behind the American government," Sinclair told more than five hundred men and women, ranging in their sympathies from pale pacifism and yellow disloyalty up, amid hisses and cheers.

Mr. Sinclair's speech, while not unexpected by the committee in charge of the arrangements, was not in keeping with the spirit of the meeting and threw a damp blanket on the more radical element that had gathered to pass resolutions and cheer the social revolution and the economic disintegration of the Russian Empire.

The Sinclair speech, which bristled with loyal and patriotic utterances, was sandwiched between an address by Michael Bey, secretary to Prof. Lomonosoff of the Russian Mission, and the address of Paul Jordan Smith.

Such was my stand during the war, as set forth in the news columns of the "Times." But when the Kaiser was overthrown, and I saw America's war for democracy being turned into a war to put down the first proletarian government in history, I went back into the radical camp—and what happened then? What happened was that instantly the news channels became a concrete wall! If you know anything about my going back into the radical camp, and the reasons therefor, you know it from the radical press, and not from the capitalist press. Since the day when I announced the change, the Associated Press has sent out *not one word* about my point of view or my utterances; while the "Los Angeles Times" goes farther yet—the "Times" deliberately blinks the fact that I once "tossed a wrench into the red Russian machine," and embarks on a campaign to make the public believe that I was disloyal during the war! You may find this beyond believing; but I shall prove it to you. And so far successful has it been that recently a high school principal in Los Angeles, addressing the pupils of her school, referred to me as a "notorious disloyalist and traitor"!

There are, of course, libel laws in California, so the "Times" dares not come out fairly and squarely with the statement that I was disloyal during the war. What it does is to scan my every word and action, and report them with subtly chosen phrases which expose me to suspicion, without making definite charges. Surely you must admit that such calculated and systematic treachery on the part of an enormously rich and powerful newspaper is of public importance. You will expect me to prove my charge. Very well, here are two cases. Case one:

While I stood by the war, I didn't stand by the Espionage act, and when some of my friends were arrested as pacifists, and stood in danger of ten or twenty years in jail, I went to the authorities and interceded, and succeeded in having the cases settled on the basis of a plea of guilty and the payment of fines. The "Times" knew what I was doing, and was foaming at the mouth about it, so I was told by several of its staff; but it dared not say anything, because I had won both the Federal judge and the prosecuting authorities to my way of thinking.

The deputy United States attorney, Mr. Palmer, happened to be a Southerner, a type of man I understand, and I got to know him during these negotiations. Later on I went to see him and said: "Mr. Palmer, I am writing a story, 'Jimmie Higgins,' which I want to publish serially in my magazine. It is a story of a Socialist in war-time, and its purpose is to win the Socialists to the idea of supporting the war. But I am in this dilemma. If I am going to show a man converted from opposition to the war, I first have to show how he felt when he was opposing it; I have to make him a real character, I have to make his arguments real arguments—which is a difficult thing to do in war-time. I would not want anybody to misunderstand my purpose and point of view; so I wonder if you would read the manuscript, and tell me if there is anything in it that might be open to misunderstanding."

Mr. Palmer's answer was that he was forbidden to give official opinions on anything before publication, but he would be very glad to give me a personal, unofficial opinion. I answered that I would regard this as a favor, and Mr. Palmer read the manuscript. No doubt he spoke about it to others, and the "Times" must have heard of the matter. Some months later appeared the following paragraph on the editorial page of the "Times":

Upton Sinclair has stuck his fingers in the Tom Mooney mess. Sinclair has dropped his pen that for some time has been engaged in preparing the manuscript of a book whose loyalty had to be passed on by the United States District-Attorney, and is therefore in a position to sympathize with those who might run afoul of the law.

Now, note the subtle treachery of this phrasing. The loyalty of my manuscript "had to" be passed on. Practically everybody who read that paragraph would understand from it that the government had taken some action in the matter, had placed me under compulsion to submit the manuscript. Nobody would get the impression that the compulsion in the matter was the compulsion of my own conscience and judgment, my wish to make sure that my piece of fiction was not open to misunderstanding. Needless to say, the "Times" didn't mention the fact that Mr. Palmer, having read the manuscript, wrote cordially to assure me that there was no possibility of its being misunderstood, and no need of any changes being made.

Case two—and still more significant:

It happened a year or more ago that I had to undergo an operation for appendicitis. I requested the authorities at the hospital not to give out news about this operation, because I do not care to have purely personal matters exploited in the papers. Thus it was a couple of weeks later, after I was out of the hospital, before anything was known about my operation. A friend of mine called me on the phone to ask if I would meet the Pasadena correspondent of the "Times," Robert Harwood, a decent young fellow who was trying to learn to write. I said that I could not meet him at that time, because I had just come out of the hospital. My friend explained these circumstances to Harwood, and Harwood sent in a news item, which appeared next morning under the headline: *"Anarchist Writer in Hospital."*

Now, of course, the editors of the "Times" know perfectly well that I am not an Anarchist. When they call me an Anarchist, they do it merely to hurt me. When in war-time they add the words: "Sinclair is still under surveillance," they mean, of course, that their readers shall derive the impression that the "Anarchist writer" is under surveillance by the Department of Justice; but if I should sue them for libel, they would plead that they meant I was under surveillance by a surgeon!

A couple of weeks later I met young Harwood, and he made an embarrassed apology for the item, explaining that he had turned in to the "Times" a perfectly decent and straight mention of my operation; the article had been rewritten in the "Times" office, and the false headline put on by the managing editor of the paper. The manuscript of the copy that Harwood had turned in had been read in advance by another man who was present at the dinner, Ralph Bayes, formerly city editor of the "Los Angeles Record," so there were two witnesses to the facts.

To call a man an Anarchist at this time was to place him in obloquy and in physical danger. Both Harwood and Bayes were willing to testify to the facts, and I considered the possibility of suing the "Times." I consulted a lawyer who knows Los Angeles conditions intimately, and he said: "If you expect to win this suit, you will have to be prepared to spend many thousands of dollars investigating with detectives the records and opinions of every prospective talesman. The 'Times' will do that—does it regularly in damage-suits. If you don't do it, you will find yourself confronting a jury of Roman Catholics and political crooks. In any case you will have a jury which has no remotest idea of any difference between a Socialist and an Anarchist, so the utmost you could possibly get would be six cents."

A few days later young Harwood came to see me again. He was anxious for me to bring suit, because he was sick of his job. There was a strike of the Pacific Electric Railway employes in Los Angeles. The city, you understand, is celebrated as an "open shop" town, and the "Times" is the propaganda organ of the forces of repression.

"Mr. Sinclair," said Harwood, "I was at the car-barns here in Pasadena all evening yesterday, and not a single car came in. I wrote the facts in my story, and the 'Times' altered it, reporting that the cars had run on schedule every ten minutes."

This is the regular practice of the "Times." All its accounts of strikes are hate-stories, entirely disregarding the facts; all its accounts of political events and conditions, local, state, or national, are class-propaganda. It will write its own

14

views of political conditions in Washington, and label it "Exclusive Dispatch." It will take the dispatches which come through the Associated Press, and put hate head-lines over them—and sometimes it is so overpowered by hate that the head-lines do not fit the context! Thus I read a large head-line, "STOKES WOMAN SENT TO PRISON"; and when I read the dispatch under the head-line I discover, quite plainly stated, that the "Stokes woman" is *not* sent to prison! Again, the Western Union Telegraph Company defies the United States Government, refusing to accept the decision of the War Labor Board. This is placed under the head-line: "TELE-GRAPH COMPANY DEFIES UNION LABOR." A few days later comes the news that the telegraphers' union is threatening to strike because of the company's attitude. This bears the title: "TELEGRAPHERS' UNION DEFIES GOVERNMENT."

Needless to say, a newspaper which thus lies in the interest of privilege is deeply and reverently religious. Every Monday the "Times" prints a couple of pages of extracts from sermons, and now and then its editorial page breaks into a spiritual ecstasy of its own. I clipped one sample during the war—two columns, twelve point leaded, with caps here and there: *"The One Tremendous Thought."*

And what is this thought which overwhelms the "Times"? The thought "that in this war the world is to be made safe, not so much for democracy, as for men's souls." This war, "sinister, cruel, bloody and bestial though it be," has placed our soldier-boys under the care of religion. "Upon the Protestant soldiers are the sleepless eyes of the Young Men's Christian Association. Around our Catholic soldiers are the faithful arms of the Knights of Columbus." Christianity had been weakening before "the noisy school of the sciences"; but—

Now cometh the war! And behold, a professedly Christian world that had been slipping away from belief in THE GREAT MIRACLE OF THE AGES, now swings back to the old belief again. The Chris-tian world is more truly Christian.
This then is the striking fact of the war.
And this is the one tremendous thought.

And from this overpowering sublimity, take a jump to the news columns, in which the "Times" reports family scandals in minute detail. Observe the chaste refinement of its head-lines—this pious organ of sanctity!

RACY CHARGES MADE BY RICH

Says Wife Sneaked Paramour Into Room to Beat Him.
She Avers He Made Love to Widow in a Flat.
Sensational Accusations in Wealthy Man's Fight.

Also the "Times" has deep convictions on the subject of Economics. I quote about half of one editorial:

MY LADY POVERTY

There is many a thing in this world much dreaded by us that we have no need to dread. We often regard as a foe that which is really a friend. And how many times we think of as being ugly that which is indeed beautiful.

Perverted thus as we are in our natures, how unwelcome at the door of life is the presence of poverty. Next to sickness and disease we dread to be poor. And yet poverty is not a curse but a blessing.

Have you ever dwelt upon the sweet dignity and the beauty with which St. Francis of Assisi clothed poverty? "My Lady Poverty" he called it, giving to his rags and his hunger a personality, and taking that personality into his heart.

And richly did his Lady Poverty reward Francis for his devotion and his love. She cast out the dross from his nature, made life unspeakably sweet and joyous for him, endeared him to the world forever and immortalized him as few men have ever been immortalized. . . . .

It must be that you will have thought often, too, of old blind Homer who begged his way from door to door in the old times of Greece. He was the master singer. He was the greatest, by far, of all the poets that sung before him or that since have sung. Not Sappho, nor Shakespeare, nor Tasso, nor Longfellow nor any one of all that palm-crowned company was the peer of old blind Homer begging his way from door to door.

Now, had not My Lady Poverty claimed Homer as a lover, had he been rich, with a palace to live in and servants to wait upon him, there would have been no Odyssey, no Iliad.

It was My Lady Poverty that lured Schiller to his garret and the crust that was there; it was she who wove her fingers in Goldsmith's hair when he wandered through Erin playing for pennies on his flute.

So, if some day, there shall be some among us who will wake to find the Lady Poverty standing at the door, think not that fate will then have served us ill. Fling back the creaking hinges and let her in. Make room for her gracious presence in the wide guest chambers of your heart.

This, you perceive, is exquisitely written and deeply felt. In order to appreciate fully its passionate and consecrated sincerity you need to be informed that the newspaper which features it boasts a profit of something like a million dollars a year; this income being derived from the publication of the filthiest patent medicine advertisements, of pages upon pages of news about moving-picture rubbish, real estate speculations, oil stocks, gold mines, every kind of swindling—all paid for.

I shall have much to say in later chapters about the "Times" fortune and the way it was made. For the moment I give one anecdote, to round out my picture.

My authority is a gentleman who a few years ago was managing editor of the "Los Angeles Herald." The "Herald" was then a morning paper, a rival of the "Times," and was controlled and practically owned by the Farmers' & Merchants' National Bank of Los Angeles. The president of this institution is the biggest banker on the coast, and was engaged, with the connivance of the newspapers, in unloading upon the city for two and a half million dollars a water company which was practically worthless. It was found that the "Herald" was not paying, and the banker decided to reduce the price from five cents to two cents. But Otis of the "Times" got wind of it, and notified the banker that if he lowered the price of the "Herald," the "Times" would at once open up on the water company swindle. "Oh, very well, General," replied the banker. "If that's the way you feel about it, we'll forget it." So the price of the "Herald" stayed up, and the paper lost money, and finally Otis bought it for a song, ran it for a while in pretended rivalry to the "Times," and then sold it at a profit, upon condition that it be made an evening paper, so that it should not interfere with the "Times."

Reading this, you will not be surprised to learn that the particular page upon which appeared the rhapsody to "My Lady Poverty" bears the name of the particular "Times" editor who told me: "It has been so long since I have written anything that I believe, that I don't think I would know the sensation!"

CHAPTER XXXIV

THE DAILY CAT-AND-DOG FIGHT

There are other newspapers published in this "Roof-garden of the World." There is the Hearst newspaper, the "Los Angeles Examiner," which publishes the editorials of Arthur Brisbane, and follows, somewhat haltingly, the Hearst propaganda for government ownership. But so far as its local policy is concerned, it is entirely commercial, its fervors are for the local industry of "boosting." It has an especially annoying habit of disguising its advertisements so as to trap you into reading them as news. You will be informed in head-lines of a notable event in local history, and when you read, you learn that Johnnie Jones, of 2249 S. Peanut Street, sold all his chickens within two hours by using "Examiner Want Ads." Again, you read a headline about an aviator just returned from France, and what you learn about him is that Jones & Co. have put out twenty thousand pictures of him in twenty thousand boxes of "Frizzlies." "This confection is especially delicious," says our naïve "Examiner." And now, as I write, some editor has an inspiration, and day after day I am confronted with an illustrated article: *"Aspirants to Shapely Limbs Title.* Who owns the most beautiful limbs on the stage? Look them over."

Later on I shall tell of the "Examiner's" treatment of various radicals. For the present I am dealing with personal experiences, so I relate that in the spring of 1919 I was invited to speak at a mass-meeting of the Jews of Los Angeles, in protest against the pogroms in Poland. The other speakers at this meeting expressed indignation at these pogroms; I endeavored to explain them. The French bankers, who now rule the continent of Europe, are engaged in setting up a substitute for the Russian Tsardom on the east of Germany; and this new Polish empire is using the Jews as a scapegoat, precisely as the Russian Tsardom did. Referring to President Wilson, I said: "I have supported him through the war, and I am not one of those who are denouncing him now. I think he has made a pitiful failure in Europe, but I understand that failure; it is due in part to the fact that the American people do not realize what is going on in Europe, and do not make clear their determination that American money shall not be poured out in support of reaction and imperialism."

Such was the substance of my argument. Next day the "Los Angeles Times" did not mention it; while the "Los Angeles Examiner" reported it with outraged indignation, under the scare head-line: "SINCLAIR ATTACKS WILSON." In this form it was telegraphed all over the country. The amusing feature of the story is that the "Examiner" itself was at this time attacking Wilson most venomously—both on its editorial page and in its Washington dispatches. But it did not want my aid; it would not permit a Socialist to "attack" the President of the United States!

In various cities there are various standards prevailing for the conduct of newspapers in their rivalries with one another. In New York the rule is that they never praise one another, and only denounce one another in extreme cases. One thing they absolutely never do is to mention one another's libel suits. But here in Los Angeles the rivalry between the "Times" and "Examiner" is a daily cat-and-dog fight. Not merely do they spread each other's libel suits over the front page; they charge each other with numerous crimes, they call names and make faces like two ill-mannered children. And they keep this up, day after day, for weeks, so that it is impossible to get the news of world-events in Southern California without having their greeds and spites thrust upon you.

One day you read in the "Times" that the "Examiner" is dressing up agents as soldiers, and circulating slanders against the "Times." Next day there begins in the "Examiner" a series of cartoons of Harry Andrews, managing editor of the "Times," representing him in grotesque and disgusting positions. Next day you read in the "Times" that William Bayard Hale, a former correspondent of the "Examiner," is charged with having taken German money. Next day you read in the "Examiner" that Harry Carr, assistant managing editor of the "Times," has been shown to have had his travelling expenses in Germany paid by the German government; also that Willard Huntington Wright, former literary editor of the "Times," is accused of having taken German money. Next day you read in the "Examiner" that the mayor of Los Angeles has been indicted upon a charge of taking bribe-money from negro brothel-keepers, and that his chief confederate is Horace Karr, former political editor of the "Times." Next day you read in the "Times" about this same Horace Karr—only he isn't a former political editor of the "Times," he is a former reporter for the "Examiner"! This particular civic scandal is spread over a page of both papers for a month, the "Examiner" playing it up, the "Times" playing it down, both of them telling patent falsehoods, and both of them continuing, day after day, to describe Horace Karr as a former employe of the other!

One of the funniest instances of this rivalry occurred recently upon the death of Mrs. Phoebe Hearst, mother of William Randolph Hearst, owner of the "Examiner." I made a study of the "Examiner" and the "Times" next morning. The "Examiner" gave three columns on the first page and five columns on the third page to accounts of Mrs. Hearst and her virtues. There were two pictures, one a picture of Mrs. Hearst, occupying fifty-eight square inches, and the other a picture of "the family of William Randolph Hearst visiting their grandmother," this occupying forty square inches.

The "Times," of course, was not so much interested in Mrs. Hearst. It gave her only the amount of space which it would give to any California millionaire who died—that is, two columns. The picture of Mrs. Hearst occupied only twenty-four square inches, and the contrast with the picture in the "Examiner" was most diverting. The picture in the "Examiner" showed a magnificent and stately lady, some duchess by Gainsborough. How the picture in the "Times" originated I do not know, but it appeared as if the editor of the "Times" had said to his artist: "Find me a picture of the ugliest old woman you have on file; or better yet, get me a picture of a grim old man with a double chin, and draw me a woman's bonnet on top of him, and a woman's dress over his shoulders, and label it 'Mrs. Phoebe Apperson Hearst'."

Also there are three afternoon papers in Los Angeles—all three sensational, all three commercial, with hardly the pretense of a public policy. There was brought to my attention the case of Raoul Palma, a young Mexican Socialist of an especially fine type, who had earned the enmity of the Los Angeles police by persisting in speaking on the Plaza. They had brought against him a charge of murder, as perfect a case of "frame-up" as I ever saw. I spent much time investigating the case, which failed for lack of evidence when brought before a jury. But the city editors and managing editors of the Los Angeles newspapers, to whom I took the evidence of this "frame-up," were not moved to any fervors. I was able to get one or two small items published, but I was not able to find a spark of human feeling, nor yet an ideal of public welfare in the management of the journals upon which I called. But suppose that I had gone to them with the news that I was about to build a new million dollar hotel in Los Angeles; or that I had purchased the Catalina Islands, and was about to develop them for tourists; or that I was about to start an airplane service up the coast!

Quite recently a great rubber concern has started a six million dollar factory in Los Angeles; and such ecstasies as seize our papers! Columns and columns, day after day; pictures of the wondrous structure, and of the president of the company—I think I have had the features of this pudgy little person thrust upon me not less than a dozen times! And his ideas—not merely about the rubber business and the commercial prospects of Southern California, but about the League of Nations, and the "Plumb plan" and labor unions and strikes and Bolshevism!

On the other hand, there is a movement now under way to organize the actors in the motion-picture industry in Southern California; and how much space does this get from the Los Angeles newspapers? On August 18, 1919, there was held in the Hollywood Hotel a mass meeting of members of the theatrical profession, to inform them concerning the meaning of the actors' strike in New York, and to solicit donations for the strikers. Not a line about this meeting in any Los Angeles paper! And not a line about the strike of the moving picture workers which came soon afterwards!

Now, as I finish this book, the office of the "Dugout," a returned soldiers' paper, is raided by the Federal authorities. The editor, Sydney R. Flowers, served three years as a volunteer in the Canadian army, was twice wounded, and once gassed. He joined a veterans' organization in Los Angeles, but found it was being courted by the Merchants' and Manufacturers' Association as a strike-breaking agency; so he rebelled, and started a rival organization, and now the "M. and M." plotters have persuaded the government to raid his rooms and break up his propaganda. It happened that I myself was present, and saw the raid, and half a dozen witnesses can testify to the condition in which the offices were left. At my instance the "Examiner" sent a photographer and took a flashlight of the scene; but then it suppressed the picture! As for the "Times," it quite solemnly informs its readers that the war veterans wrecked their own offices, in order to have a ground of complaint against the government! It repeats this, in circumstantial detail, two days in succession!

This is a somber tale I am telling, so let us not miss the few laughs that belong. Some time ago I had a call from a young lady reporter for the "Los Angeles Record." She was a very young lady indeed—just out of school, I should say—and she explained that Max Eastman had given an interview on the subject of "free love," and would I please to give an interview on the subject of "free love." In reply I explained to this young lady that as a result of previous painful experiences I had made an iron-clad rule on the subject of the sex-question. I would not trust any newspaper reporter, not even the most amiable, to interpret my views on that delicate subject.

The young lady argued and pleaded. She did her very charming best to get me to give her a hint of my opinion of Max Eastman's opinion of "free love." But I have become a wise bird—having had my wing-feathers shot out so many times; I gave no hint, either of my own opinions or of my opinions of Max Eastman's opinions.

Finally the young lady said: "Do you ever write on the subject, Mr. Sinclair?"

I answered: "Sometimes I do. When I write, I choose my own words and say what I mean, and then I am willing to stand by it."

"Well," said the young lady, "will you write an article on 'free love' for the 'Record'?"

"Certainly I will," said I—"if the 'Record' will pay my price."

"What is your price?"

"Ten cents a word."

The young lady looked troubled. "I don't know if the 'Record' could pay that," said she, "but this is my position—I will explain frankly, and hope you won't mind. I've just started to be a newspaper woman, and I'm very anxious to make good. I don't have to earn my living, because my parents have money. What I want to do is to have a career.

If I go back to the 'Record' and report that I failed to get an interview, I won't keep this job. So won't you please write an article for me, and let me pay for it at the rate of ten cents a word?"

You may share a smile over this queer situation. I pleaded embarrassment, I argued with the young lady that I couldn't possibly take her money. But she argued back, very charmingly; she would be heart-broken if I did not consent. So at last I said: "All right, I will write you an article. How many words do you want?"

The young lady meditated; she figured for a while on the back of her note-book; and finally she said: "I think I'd like fifty words, please."

Really, I explained, I couldn't express my views on such a complicated subject in the limits of a night letter; so the young lady raised her bid to a hundred words. In the end we had to break off negotiations, and she went away disappointed. I was told afterwards by friends that she published an article in the "Record," describing this interview, and having an amusing time with me; so presumably her job was saved. I didn't see her article, for the "Record" is an evening paper, and publishes half a dozen editions, no two alike, and the only way you can find out what it says about you is to stand on the street-corner for six or eight hours, and catch each fleeting edition as it fleets.

I have come to the end of my own experiences. I read the manuscript and the proofs, over and over, as I have to do, and a guilty feeling haunts me. Will the radical movement consider that I have forced upon it a ventilation of my own egotisms, in the guise of a work on Journalism? I cannot be sure; but at least I can say this: Have patience, and read the second part of the book, in which you will find little about myself, and a great deal about other people, to whom you owe your trust and affection; also a mass of facts about your Journalism, without reference to anybody's personality.

PART II
THE EXPLANATION

CHAPTER XXXV

THE CAUSES OF THINGS

I studied Latin for five years in college, and from this study brought away a dozen Latin verses. One of them is from Virgil: "Happy he who has learned to know the causes of things." The words have stayed in my mind, summing up the purpose of my intellectual life: Not to rest content with observing phenomena, but to know what they mean, how they have come to be, how they may be guided and developed, or, if evil, may be counteracted. I would not have taken the trouble to write a book to say to the reader: I have been persecuted for twenty years by prostitute Journalism. The thing I am interested in saying is: The prostitution of Journalism is due to such and such factors, and may be remedied by such and such changes.

Here is one of the five continents of the world, perhaps the richest of the five in natural resources. As far back as history, anthropology, and even zoology can trace, these natural resources have been the object of competitive struggle. For the past four hundred years this struggle has been ordained by the laws and sanctified by the religions of man. "Each for himself," we say, and, "the devil take the hindmost." "Dog eat dog," we say. "Do others or they will do you," we say. "Business is business," we say. "Get the stuff," we say. "Money talks," we say. "The Almighty Dollar," we say. So, by a thousand native witticisms, we Americans make clear our attitude toward the natural resources of our continent.

As a result of four centuries of this attitude, ordained by law and sanctified by religion, it has come about that at this beginning of the twentieth century the massed control of the wealth of America lies in the hands of perhaps a score of powerful individuals. We in America speak of steel kings and coal barons, of lords of wheat and lumber and oil and railroads, and think perhaps that we are using metaphors; but the simple fact is that the men to whom we refer occupy in the world of industry precisely the same position and fill precisely the same roles as were filled in the political world by King Louis, who said, "I am the State."

This power of concentrated wealth which rules America is known by many names. It is "Wall Street," it is "Big Business," it is "the Trusts." It is the "System" of Lincoln Steffens, the "Invisible Government" of Woodrow Wilson, the "Empire of Business" of Andrew Carnegie, the "Plutocracy" of the populists. It has been made the theme of so much stump-oratory that in cultured circles it is considered good form to speak of it in quotation marks, with a playful and skeptical implication; but the simple fact is that this power has controlled American public life since the civil war, and is greater at this hour than ever before in our history.

The one difference between the Empire of Business and the Empire of Louis is that the former exists side by side with a political democracy. To keep this political democracy subservient to its ends, the industrial autocracy maintains and subsidizes two rival political machines, and every now and then stages an elaborate sham-battle, contributing millions of dollars to the campaign funds of both sides, burning thousands of tons of red fire, pouring out millions of reams of paper propaganda and billions of words of speeches. The people take interest in this sham-battle—but all sensible men understand that whichever way the contest is decided, business will continue to be business, and money will continue to talk.

So we are in position to understand the facts presented in this book. Journalism is one of the devices whereby industrial autocracy keeps its control over political democracy; it is the day-by-day, between-elections propaganda, whereby the minds of the people are kept in a state of acquiescence, so that when the crisis of an election comes, they go to the polls and cast their ballots for either one of the two candidates of their exploiters. Not hyperbolically and contemptuously, but literally and with scientific precision, we define Journalism in America as the business and practice of presenting the news of the day in the interest of economic privilege.

A modern newspaper is an enormously expensive institution. The day is past when a country printer could set up a hand-press and print news about the wedding of the village blacksmith's daughter and the lawn-party of the Christian Endeavor Society, and so make his way as a journalist. Now-a-days people want the last hour's news from the battle-field or the council-hall. If they do not get it in the local paper, they get it in the "extras" from the big cities, which are thrown off the fast express-trains. The franchise which entitles a paper to this news from all over the world is very costly; in most cities and towns it is an iron-clad monopoly. You cannot afford to pay for this service, and to print this news, unless you have a large circulation, and for that you need complicated and costly presses, a big building, a highly trained staff. Incidentally you will find yourself running an advertising agency and a public employment service; you will find yourself giving picnics for news-boys, investigating conditions in the county-hospital, raising subscription funds for a monument to Our Heroes in France. In other words, you will be an enormous and complex institution, fighting day and night for the attention of the public, pitting your composite brain against other composite brains in the struggle to draw in the pennies of the populace.

Incidentally, of course, you are an institution running under the capitalist system. You are employing hundreds, perhaps thousands of men, women and children. You are paying them under the iron law of wages, working them under the rule of "the devil take the hindmost." You have foremen and managers and directors, precisely as if you were a steel-mill or a coal-mine; also you have policemen and detectives, judges and courts and jailers, soldiers with machine-guns and sailors with battleships to protect you and your interests—precisely as does the rest of the predatory system of which you are a part.

And, of course, you have the capitalist psychology; you have it complete and vivid—you being the livest part of that system. You know what is going on hour by hour; you are more class-conscious, more alert to the meaning of events than anyone else in the capitalist community. You know what you want from your wage-slaves, and you see that they "deliver the goods." You know what you are furnishing to your advertisers, and your terms are "net cash." You know where you get your money, your "credit"; so you know "Who's Who" in America, you know whom to praise and whom to hate and fear.

There are perhaps a dozen newspapers in America which have been built up by slow stages out of the pennies of workingmen, and which exist to assert the rights of workingmen. The ones I happen to know are the "New York Call," the

"Jewish Daily Forwards," the "Milwaukee Leader," the "Seattle Union Record," the "Butte Daily Bulletin." It should be understood that in future discussions I except such newspapers from what I say about American Journalism. This reservation being made, I assert there is no daily newspaper in America which does not represent and serve vested wealth, and which has not for its ultimate aim the protection of economic privilege.

I am trying in this book to state the exact facts. I do not expect to please contemporary Journalism, but I expect to produce a book which the student of the future will recognize as just. So let me explain that I realize fully the differences between newspapers. Some are dishonest, and some are more dishonest; some are capitalistic, and some are more capitalistic. But great as are the differences between them, and clever as are the pretenses of some of them, there is no one which does not serve vested wealth, which has not for its ultimate aim the protection of economic privilege. The great stream of capitalist prosperity may flow irregularly, it may have eddies and counter-currents, stagnant places which deceive you for a while; but if you study this great stream long enough, you find that it all moves in one direction, and that everything upon its surface moves with it. A capitalist newspaper may espouse this cause or that, it may make this pretense or that, but sooner or later you realize that a capitalist newspaper lives by the capitalist system, it fights for that system, and in the nature of the case cannot do otherwise. Some one has said that to talk of regulating capital is to talk of moralizing a tiger; I would say that to expect justice and truth-telling of a capitalist newspaper is to expect asceticism at a cannibal feast.

It would be instructive to take the leading newspapers of America and classify them according to the nature of their financial control, showing precisely how and where this control shapes the policy of the paper. There will be certain immediate financial interests—the great family which owns the paper, the great bank which holds its bonds, the important local trade which furnishes its advertising. Concerning these people you observe that no impolite word is ever spoken, and the début parties given to the young ladies of these families are reported in detail. On the other hand, if there are interests aggressively hostile to the great family, the great bank, the important local trade, you observe that here the newspaper becomes suddenly and unexpectedly altruistic. It will be in favor of public ownership of the gas-works; it will be in favor of more rigid control of state banks; whatever its policy may be, you will, if you sit at the dinner-tables of the rich in that city, have revealed to you the financial interests which lie behind that unexpected altruism.

In the days of the ancient régime, nations went to war because someone made a slighting remark about the king's mistress; and in our present Empire of Business you find exactly the same thing happening. I know of a newspaper which is still living upon the reputation it made by defending the strikers in a great labor struggle. The paper had never defended strikers before, it has never defended strikers since; but on this occasion it happened that the president of the corporation involved in the strike had remarked at a dinner-party that the owner of the newspaper was living with an opera-singer.

Some ten years ago I remember that the city of Chicago was torn wide open by a teamsters' strike. Brickbats were flying, mobs were swarming in the streets, militiamen were stabbing people with bayonets. Some time afterwards there was an investigation, and it transpired that a certain labor-leader, Sam Parks by name, had been paid five or ten thousand dollars by a great mail-order house to call a strike on a rival mail-order house. And in precisely this way great newspapers quarrel, and the public has no idea what it means. I have heard a leading Hearst editor tell, quite simply and as a matter of course, how Mr. Hearst would come into the office at twelve o'clock at night and turn the batteries of the "New York American" and "Journal" upon the business and politics of August Belmont, because Mr. Belmont had slighted Mr. Hearst, or Mr. Hearst's wife—I forget which—at a dinner-party. One year you would see Mr. Hearst printing a cartoon every day, showing "Charlie" Murphy, boss of Tammany Hall, in convict's stripes; next year Mr. Hearst would make a deal with Tammany—and the other newspapers of New York would be showing Mr. Hearst in convict's stripes!

Or come to the other side of the continent, and consider the "San Francisco Chronicle," owned by "Mike" de Young.

Here is a picture of Mr. de Young, drawn by one of his wage-slaves, a man who for many years has helped to run his profit-machine:

He uses much perfume, and is extremely conceited. He is author of the remark that no reporter is worth more than twenty dollars a week, or ever will be. He is a secret laugh-producer because of his inordinate love for the camera spotlight. Strangely enough, his likeness is seldom to be found in any paper except his own; the "Chronicle's" camera men have standing instructions at public gatherings to pay as little attention to other men as possible and to concentrate on de Young. On his own paper everybody is Jones or Smith except himself. He must always be referred to as Mr. de Young. Owner of much valuable real estate near Golden Gate park, he made a vigorous fight to have the Panama-Pacific Exposition located in the park, hoping thereby to increase the value of his holdings. Defeated, he turned his wrath on the exposition officials, and denounces them at every opportunity. Mention of President C. C. Moore of the Exposition Company is forbidden in the columns of the "Chronicle."

There are differences, of course, in the moral character of men. There are some men who do not take part in large-scale real-estate intrigues, and some who do not live with opera-singers; there are capitalists who pay their debts, and regard their word of honor as their bond. And there have been newspapers owned by such men, and conducted according to such principles. You could not buy the editorial support of the "Springfield Republican" or the "Baltimore Sun"; you could not buy the advertising space of these papers for the cheaper and more obvious kinds of fraud. But ask yourself this question: Is there a newspaper in America which will print news unfavorable to department-stores? If the girl-slaves of the local department-store go on strike, will the newspaper maintain their right to picket? Will it even print the truth about what they do and say?

Some years ago a one-time teacher of mine was killed by falling down the elevator-shaft of a New York department-store. I noted that my newspaper did not give the name of the department-store. As a matter of curiosity, I bought all the newspapers, and discovered that none of them gave the name of the department-store. It was not absolutely essential, of course; my one-time teacher was just as dead as if the name of the store had been given. But suppose the accident had taken place at the People's House, owned by the Socialists—would all the newspapers of New York have withheld the name of the place?

In New York City one of the Gimbel brothers, owners of a Philadelphia department store, was arrested, charged with sodomy, and he cut his throat. Not a single newspaper in Philadelphia gave this news! This was in the days before Gimbel Brothers had a store in New York, therefore it occurred to the "New York Evening Journal" that here was an opportunity to build up circulation in a new field. Large quantities of the paper were snipped to Philadelphia, and the police of Philadelphia stopped the newsboys on the streets and took away the papers and the Philadelphia papers said nothing about it!

And this department-store interest supervises not only the news columns, but the editorial columns. Some years ago one of the girl-slaves of a New York department-store committed suicide, leaving behind her a note to the effect that she could not stand twenty cent dinners any longer. The "New York World," which collects several thousand dollars every day from department-stores, judged it necessary to deal with this incident. "The World," you understand, is a "democratic" paper, a "liberal" paper, an "independent" paper, a paper of "the people." Said the "World":

> There are some people who make too large a demand upon fortune. Fixing their eyes upon the standards of living flaunted by the rich, they measure their requirements by their desires. Such persons are easily affected by outside influences, and perhaps in this case the recent discussions, more often silly than wise, concerning the relation of wages to vice, may have made the girl more susceptible than usual to the depressing effects of cheap dinners.

And do you think that is a solitary instance, the result of a temporary editorial aberration? No, it is typical of the capitalistic mind, which is so frugal that it extracts profit even from the suicide of its victims. Some years ago an old man committed suicide because his few shares of express-stock lost their value. The "New York Times" was opposing parcel-post, because the big express-companies were a prominent part of the city's political and financial machine; the "New York Times" presented this item of news as a suicide caused by the parcel-post!

CHAPTER XXXVI

THE EMPIRE OF BUSINESS

Let the reader not misunderstand my thesis. I do not claim that there exists in America one thoroughly organized and completely conscious business government. What we have is a number of groups, struggling for power; and sometimes these groups fall out with one another, and make war upon one another, and then we see a modern application of the ancient adage, "When thieves fall out, honest men come into their own." If, for example, you had studied the press of New York City at the time of the life insurance exposures, you would certainly have concluded that this press was serving the public interest. As it happens, I followed that drama of life insurance with the one man in America who had most to do with it, the late James B. Dill. Judge Dill ran a publicity bureau in New York for several months, and handed out the greater part of this scandal to the newspaper reporters. He told me precisely how he was doing it, and precisely why he was doing it, and I knew that this whole affair, which shook the nation to its depths, was simply the Morgan and Ryan interests taking away the control of life insurance money from irresponsible people like "Jimmy" Hyde, and bringing it under the control of people who were responsible—that is, responsible to Morgan and Ryan. The whole campaign was conducted for that purpose; the newspapers of New York all understood that it was conducted for that purpose, and when that purpose was accomplished, the legislative investigations and the newspaper clamor stopped almost over-night.

And all through this terrific uproar I noticed one curious thing—there was never in any single newspaper or magazine or speech dealing with the question the faintest hint of the one intelligent solution of the problem—that is, government insurance. I made several efforts to get something on the subject into the New York papers; I gave interviews—I have forgotten now to what papers, but I know that these interviews never got by the blue pencil. It took the emergency of war-time to force government insurance—and now the lobby of the private insurance companies is busy in Washington, trying to scuttle government insurance, as government telegraphs and telephones, government railroads, government shipping, government employment agencies, have all one by one been scuttled.

The thieves fall out; and also new thieves are continually trying to break into the "ring." There is always an enormous temptation presented by our peculiar newspaper situation; our Journalism is maintaining a vacuum, with incessant pressure on the outside. The people want the news; the people clamor for the news; and there is always a mass of vitally important news withheld. The Socialist papers are publishing scraps of it, orators are turning it into wild rumor on ten thousand soap-boxes; if only the people could get it in a newspaper or a magazine, what fortunes they would pay! And of course there are wide-awake men in the world of Journalism who know this: what more natural than that one of them should now and then yield to the temptation to get rich by telling the truth?

The whole history of the American magazine-world is summed up in that formula. Some fifteen years ago our magazine publishers made the discovery of this unworked gold-mine; "McClure's," "Success," "Everybody's," "The American," "Hampton's," "Pearson's," the "Metropolitan," even the staid and dignified "Century" jumped in to work this mine. Their circulations began to go up—a hundred thousand increase a month was not unknown in those days of popular delirium. Magazine publication became what it had never before been in American history, and what it has never been since—a competitive industry, instead of a camouflaged propaganda. Is it not a complete vindication of my thesis, that in a couple of years half a dozen magazines were able to build up half a million circulation, by no other means whatever than telling what the newspapers were refusing to tell? And is it not a proof of the pitiful helplessness of the public, that they still go on reading these same magazines, in spite of the fact that they have been bought up by "the interests," and are filled with what one of their "kept" editors described to me, in a voice of unutterable loathing, as: "Slush for the women!"

For, of course, the industrial autocracy very quickly awakened to the peril of these "muck-raking" magazines, and set to work to put out the fire. Some magazines were offered millions, and sold out. Those that refused to sell out had their advertising trimmed down, their bank-loans called, their stockholders intimidated—until finally, in one way or another, they consented to "be good."

"Success" refused to "be good"; it persisted in exposing Cannonism, and maintaining a "People's Lobby" in Washington; so "Success" was put out of business. The "National Post" adopted a radical policy, and it was put out of business; likewise "Human Life," edited by Alfred Henry Lewis; likewise the "Twentieth Century Magazine," edited by B. O. Flower; likewise the "Times Magazine"—a monthly having nothing to do with the "New York Times," but edited by a young man of means who naïvely supposed that he would be allowed to tell the truth to the people of New York. "Pearson's" of the old régime was brought to ruin, and it survives in its new form by the defiant genius of one man, Frank Harris. "Harper's Weekly" started out bravely, with Norman Hapgood as editor, and Charles R. Crane as "angel"; for two or three years it fought the advertising boycott, and then it died.

In the "Profits of Religion" I told in detail the story of how "Hampton's Magazine" was put out of business. I did not intend to repeat this story, but it happens that I have just met my old friend Ben Hampton again, and have gathered fresh details. I will let him tell his own story:

Never in the history of magazine-publishing was there such a great success in such a short time as that of "Hampton's." This is not my conversation. It is simply the records of the American News Company. We had, I think, 425,000 circulation, and we broke all records for the same length of time. No other magazine ever succeeded with an investment as small as ours. When they took the magazine away from me I think we had nearly thirty thousand dollars a month advertising.

But it is a peculiarity of magazines that when they grow too fast they lose money for a time. You have contracted for a year to publish advertisements, based on a circulation of a hundred thousand copies. If, three months later you have four hundred thousand circulation, you are giving four times as much as you were paid for; also, you have to have four times as much paper and press-work, for which you do not get returns until three months later. Hampton put in all his fortune and his wife's, and then he started selling stock to his readers. He had just got by the difficult place; his printing-company and the bank which owned the printing-company had audited his books, and the bank-auditor had certified that in the first four months of 1911 the magazine "had earned a profit of not less than three thousand and not more than seven thousand dollars per month."

Yet they put "Hampton's Magazine" out of business! Hampton had started Charles Edward Russell's articles exposing the "New Haven" swindle—two or three years before the truth broke out, you understand. An agent from the "New Haven" came to inform him that if he started this publication, he would be put out of business. I now learn for the first time the name of this agent—Sylvester J. Baxter. Readers of the "Profits of Religion" will give a start of recognition: the same gentleman who contributed that wonderful boost of the "New Haven" to the "Outlook," organ of the Clerical Camouflage! And the "Outlook" pretended not to know that this was an official boost of the "New Haven," and to have been astonished when the "New Haven" ordered a big edition of this issue!

Let Ben Hampton tell the rest of the story:

A nice young man got a job in our accounting department. He was one of the finest fellows we had ever had around. He was willing to work days and nights, and he did work days and nights, and one night when he was working, he took a copy of our list of stockholders. Of course, we did not find this out for months. In the meantime, a man and a woman, working separately, visited all our stockholders they could reach and told them I was robbing the Company. They said I had a large estate in the Adirondacks and a home in the Fifth Avenue district of New York City. At that time Mrs. Hampton and I were having a time to buy clothing for the children. We were drawing almost no salary from the magazine, and we had put all our money in the undertaking. In fact, we were near the line of desperation, we were so hard up.

Something like twenty brokers on the Wall Street curb began to advertise our five dollars par stock at four dollars, down to three dollars a share. We sent to them and offered to buy the stock and were never able to buy one share. One of the brokers afterwards admitted to us that they had none of the stock, and that they were paid to do the advertising.

All these methods, of course, created confusion in the minds of our stockholders, and practically killed our efforts to raise thirty thousand dollars, which was the insignificant sum of money needed to pay off our paper bill. We were entitled to a line of credit of three hundred thousand dollars at the paper makers. We owed the paper maker, I think, about forty thousand dollars and he notified us arbitrarily on a Monday that we would have to pay the bill Wednesday, or he would decline to furnish paper for the current edition, which was then on the press.

When I saw trouble coming I got together a committee of my stockholders in New York City, and a group of about a dozen men endorsed three notes of ten thousand dollars each. The net worth of these dozen men was over two million dollars. We took the notes to one bank in New York City. The bank accepted them. We checked against them, and got money on them, and the next day were notified we would have to take the notes out of the bank.

Of course you say this is an illegal proceeding, and can't be done. I assure you it was done. We were thrown out of that bank, after the bank had accepted our paper, and after we had checked against it. The manager of the bank told me that he was powerless—that the "down-town" folks had thrown us out. Several other banks that had loaned me money for ten years told me that they could not do anything for me now—that I was in bad "down-town."

One banker who flatly said he would loan us money whether Morgan's crowd wanted him to or not, was put out of business himself within a few months. This man's name is Earle. He was then running the Nassau Bank. I do not know whether Earle would tell his story or not, but the way the Morgan crowd drove him out of the banking business was one of the coldest-blooded things I ever heard of. They punished him for trying to accept perfectly good banking-paper to help me out of my crisis.

The foregoing facts are dictated hurriedly but there are some points in them that I believe you will want. Of course you know the finish of the properties. Within ten days after the thing began to close in on me, I had to turn my affairs over to the lawyers, and then a group of people appeared who were said to be the "International Correspondence" group of Scranton, Pa. They brought in letters from bankers, etc., showing they were very reputable and high-classed, and I had the choice of going into the hands of the receiver, or letting them take the property. They paid me just money enough so I could get my stock out of hock. The rest of the money they were to pay me was evidenced by a contract. I turned the contract over to my attorneys for protection of my preferred stockholders. Within a few weeks' time we became convinced that the fellows who had taken over the property intended to loot it. The bookkeeper told me they took one hundred and seventy-five thousand dollars out of the property in a few months, and took the books down to the East River and threw them off the bridge.

The result of it all was that I worked with the United States Government and had the crowd indicted. In time we brought them to trial. The trial lasted four or five weeks. We literally could not prove anything. We did prove that "Hampton's Magazine" was a valuable piece of property and that it was making money, but we could not prove that the fellows who got it were crooks. All the records were destroyed. The result was, the judge threw the case out of court, after it had been in court for four or five weeks, and we never got back any of the money. Of course, the property in the meantime had been ruined.

I have told about several of the magazines which consented to "be good." I have shown the pitiful plight of the "American," and the miserable piffle they are publishing. And what is the meaning of it? The meaning was given in an item published in the "New York Press" early in 1911, when the "American Magazine" was taken over by the Crowell Publishing Company. The "Press" stated that this concern was controlled by Thomas W. Lamont, of J. P. Morgan and Company, and declared "The 'American' will do no more muckraking." In answer, the "American" in its next issue made a statement, haughtily announcing that the same editors, John S. Phillips, Ray Stannard Baker, Ida Tarbell and Finley Peter Dunne were remaining in charge, and that "the policy of the magazine will be unchanged." To a discussion of this, my own language is inadequate; I have to employ the vocabulary of my son, a student in high school: "The poor boobs!" Four years these editors stuck it out, and then they quit, and a couple of young fellows who had been their office-clerks are now the "editors" of the "American Magazine"—which boasts a million circulation, and fifty-eight thousand lines of advertisements per month! Now, as I write, I learn that this Crowell Publishing Company has purchased "Collier's," and we shall see the same thing happening to our "National Weekly"!

In the same tragic way, my old friend Ridgway, who published the "Condemned Meat Industry," is out of "Everybody's," and a new and wholly "tame" staff is in charge, acceptable to the Butterick Publishing Co. In the same way S. S. McClure was turned out of his magazine, which once published Ida Tarbell's exposure of Standard Oil, and now publishes the solemn futilities of Cleveland Moffett, and anti-Socialist propaganda by the unspeakable Newell Dwight Hillis. It happened the other day that I was glancing over a back number of "McClure's," and my eye was caught by the opening instalment of a serial, announced in this style:

At last! A great new novel by the author of "The Broad Highway." "BELTANE THE STRONG," by JEFFREY FARNOL, who also wrote "The Amateur Gentleman" and "The Money-Moon." This is no ordinary story. Many novelists would have written three books, some six, in the time Jeffrey Farnol has given to this tremendous love-tale of Beltane and Lady Helen. The result is the finest thing of its kind "McClure's" has ever printed—by all means the novel of the year.

And opposite this a full-page pink and purple illustration

of a misty, mystical girl in a thrilling state of semi-nudity, with this quotation:

> Breathless and as one entranced he gazed upon her: saw how her long hair glowed a wondrous red 'neath the kisses of the dying sun; saw how her purpled gown, belted at the slender waist, clung about the beauties of her shapely body; saw how the little shoe peeped forth from the perfumed mystery of its folds—and so stood speechless, bound by the spell of her beauty.

"The perfumed mystery of its folds!" Such is the perfumed garbage now being fed to the American public in the name of Sam McClure!

Or take the "Metropolitan," which a few years ago announced itself as a Socialist magazine. We were all tremendously thrilled by the idea that the money of Harry Payne Whitney was to be used to bring about Social Justice in America; but then we saw the "Metropolitan" suppress its exposé of Rasputin at behest of the embassy of the late Tsar; now we see it turning over its editorial columns to Gen. Leonard Wood, to be used in a propaganda for universal military training! In this greatest crisis of history, the people's cause is left without a single champion in our popular magazines. There are only the Socialist papers, and two or three radical weeklies of limited circulation; the rest is Barbarism.

In every newspaper-office in America the same struggle between the business-office and the news-department is going on all the time. The business of getting the news involves "hustle," and young brains are constantly being brought in, and these young brains have to be taught the discipline of special privilege, and sometimes they never entirely submit. They have powerful arguments on their side. "You want circulation, don't you? What's the use of a paper without circulation? And how can you get circulation if you let the fellow around the corner have this 'scoop'?" So the owner of the paper has to get busy and make a gentleman's agreement with the other papers to suppress the news; and sometimes it turns out that the other fellow isn't a gentleman, and there is a row, and the live young "hustlers" get their way for a while, and the public gets a bit of the news.

Various stages of this struggle are exemplified by different newspapers, or by the same newspaper at different times. You may see a staid old family organ—say the "New

York Tribune," owned by a rich capitalist, Whitelaw Reid, who publishes it as a side issue to gratify his vanity, taking his pay in the form of an ambassadorship. The circulation of such a paper will go steadily down. But then perhaps the old man will die, and his sons will take charge, and his sons won't feel like paying out twenty or thirty thousand dollars a month, and will get a "live newspaper man" to "put life into" the paper; or perhaps they will sell out to people who have less money, and will be tempted to give the public a little of what it wants.

The fundamental thing that the public wants is, of course, enough to eat. Modern society is complex, and there are thousands of public issues clamoring for newspaper attention, but in the final analysis all these questions boil down to one question—why is the cost of living going up faster than wages and salaries? So the spectre of "radicalism" haunts every newspaper office. The young publisher who wants to make money, the "live newspaper man" who wants to make a reputation, find themselves at every hour tempted to attack some form of privilege and exploitation.

So come "crusades." The kind of crusade which the newspaper undertakes will depend upon the character of circulation for which it is bidding. If the paper sells for three cents, and is read by bankers and elderly maiden aunts, the newspaper will print the sermons of some clergyman who is exposing the horrors of the red-light district, or it will call on the district attorney to begin prosecuting the loan-sharks who are robbing the poor, or it will start a free ice fund for babies in the tenements. Any cause will do, provided the victims are plunderers of a shady character—that is, small plunderers.

Or perhaps the newspaper is a popular organ. It sells at a low price to the common people. In that case it may go to extremes of radicalism; it may clamor for government ownership, and attack big public service corporations in a way that seems entirely independent and fearless. You say: "Surely this is honest journalism," and you acquire the habit of reading that newspaper. But then gradually you see the campaign die down, the great cause forgotten. The plundering of the public goes right on, the only thing that has been changed is that you, who used to be a reader of the "World," are now a reader of the "Journal"; and that is the change which the "Journal" had in mind from the outset. You will see the

"Journal" tabulating the amount of advertising it publishes each week or each month, and boasting that it is greater than the "World" publishes; and maybe you feel proud about that, you like to be in the boat with the best fishermen—even though you are there as a fish.

Anyone who is familiar with the newspaper-world can think of a score of publications to which the above statement would apply. There exists a chain of one-cent evening papers scattered over the country, the Scripps papers, catering to working-class audiences. They were founded by a real radical and friend of the people, E. W. Scripps, and for a decade or two were the main resource of the workers in many localities. Now E. W. Scripps is a sick man, out of the game, and his eldest son, who runs the papers, is a young business man, interested in the business management of a great property; so in one city after another you see the Scripps papers "toned-down." They espouse the cause of strikers no longer. The other day I was staggered to find them dragging out that shop-worn old bugaboo, the nationalization of women in Russia! In the Seattle strike the Scripps paper, the "Star," "scabbed" on the strike, and its editorial attitude won it the name, the "Shooting Star."

Or take the "New York World." This paper was built up by one crusade after another; it was the people's friend for a generation. Today it is a property worth several million dollars, living on its reputation. It still makes, of course, the old pretenses of "democracy," but when it comes to a real issue, it is an organ of bitter and savage reaction, it is edited by the telegraph and railroad securities in which the Pulitzer fortune is invested. The "New York World's" opinion of the "Plumb plan" is that of a Russian grand duke discussing Bolshevism.

Or the Hearst papers. They too have been made out of the pennies of the masses; they too have lured the masses by rainbows of many-colored hopes. They still ask for government ownership—when they happen to think of it; but they lie remorselessly about radicals, and exclude the word Socialism from their columns, except when some Socialist is sent to jail. They support Sinn Fein and twist the lion's tail, because it brings in the Irish-Catholic pennies; but the one revolution in which their heart is really engaged is the one which is to make Hearst's Mexican acres into American acres.

CHAPTER XXXVII

THE DREGS OF THE CUP

I would call the reader's attention to the fact that in this book I am dealing with our standard magazines and newspapers, the ones which are considered respectable, which all ladies and gentlemen accept as they accept the doctor's pills and the clergyman's sermons, the Bible and the multiplication table and Marian Harland's cook-book. I have not made my case easy by dwelling on the cultural content of the "mail order" and "household" publications, of which there are scores with a circulation of a million or more; or of the agricultural papers of the country, whose total circulation amounts to tens of millions. How I could freeze your blood if I were to summarize the contents of the "Ladies' World," the "Gentlewoman," the "Household Guest," "Home Life," the "Household," "Comfort," the "Home Friend," "Mother's Magazine," "Everyday Life," the "People's Popular Monthly," the "Clover Leaf" weeklies and the "Boyce" weeklies, the "Saturday Blade" and the "Chicago Ledger"! If I were to tell about the various "Family Story Papers," which are left in area-ways for servants! Or the "fashion-papers," the "Butterick Trio," with close to two millions, the "Woman's World," with two millions, and "Vogue," the "Delineator," the "Parisienne," the "Ladies' Pictorial," "Needlecraft" with their half million or more. Or the "fast" papers, which cultivate a taste for perfumed smut—and which I will not advertise by naming! Or the papers of the sporting and racing and gambling worlds, down to the "Police Gazette," with its "leg-shows" and illustrated murders!

Also the local papers, the small dailies, the weeklies and semi-monthlies and monthlies by the thousands and tens of thousands! If you wish to get a complete picture of American Journalism, you must take these into account; you must descend from the heights of metropolitan dignity into the filthiest swamps of provincial ignorance and venality. Hardly a week passes that someone does not send me a copy of some country paper which calls for the stringing-up of Socialists to

lamp-posts, and denounces highly educated Bolshevik leaders
in editorials with half a dozen grammatical errors to the
column.

And if you go to the small town in Pennsylvania or
Arkansas or Colorado, or wherever this paper is published, you
find a country editor on the level of intelligence of the local
horse-doctors of Englewood, New Jersey, and Tarrytown,
New York, whose proceedings I have described in this book.
Frequently you find this editor hanging on by his eye-teeth,
with a mortgage at the local bank, carried because of favors
he does to the local money-power. You find him getting a
regular monthly income from the copper-interests or the coal-
interests or the lumber-interests, whatever happens to be
dominant in that locality. You find him heavily subsidized
at election-time by the two political machines of these great
interests. His paper is used to print the speeches of the candidates of these interests, and five or ten or fifty thousand copies
of this particular issue are paid for by these interests and
distributed at meetings. Campaign circulars and other literature are printed in the printing-office of this newspaper, and
of course the public advertising appears in its columns—a graft
which is found in every state and county of the Union, and is
a means by which hundreds of millions of dollars are paid
as a disguised subsidy by the interests which run our two-party
political system.

Our great metropolitan newspapers take a fine tone of
dignity, they stand for the welfare of the general public, they
are above all considerations of greed. But the conditions
under which these small-town newspapers are published do
not permit them to pretend to such austerity, or even to conceive of it. They are quite frankly "out for the stuff"—as
everybody else they know is "out for the stuff." For example,
the "Tarrytown News," which jumped on me with its cloven
hoofs, declaring that my home had been raided as a "free
love" place. This "Tarrytown News" explained quite honestly
why it was opposed to allowing agitators to come to Tarrytown
and denounce the Rockefellers. And why was it? Because the
Rockefellers stood for religion and the home, the Constitution
and the Star-Spangled Banner and the Declaration of Independence? No, not at all; it was because the Rockefellers
carried a pay-roll in Tarrytown of thirty thousand dollars a
month!

The average country or small-town editor is an entirely ignorant man; the world of culture is a sealed book to him. His idea of literature is the "Saturday Evening Post"—only as a rule he doesn't have time to read it. His idea of art is a lithograph of the President and Vice-President with a stand of flags. His idea of music is "Onward, Christian Soldiers," and "Columbia the Gem of the Ocean." He has an idea what is good for his readers; "optimism" and "boost," "cheer-up" stuff, "mother, home and heaven" stuff, "sob" stuff, "slush for the women." He has no money to pay writers, of course; he doesn't even set type, except for local news. He gets his "filler" in the form of "boiler-plate," sent practically free from Washington and New York—this matter containing fiction, poetry, "special stories," novelty and gossip of the sort his readers find entertaining. What difference does it make if sandwiched in between this reading matter is the poison propaganda of the Merchants' and Manufacturers' Association, of the tariff-lobbyists, the railroad-lobbyists, the liquor-lobbyists, the whole machine of capitalist graft and greed?

Several years ago I had a brilliant and wonderful idea. I was finishing "King Coal," and thought that I had an excellent serial, timely, and full of swift incident. I ascertained that there were seventeen thousand weekly newspapers in America; surely among this number must be a few hundred which would like to give their readers the truth about labor conditions in a basic American industry! I would build up a little syndicate of my own, I would market my future books, and perhaps those of other writers! I prepared a circular, outlining the plan, and offering the entire serial for some nominal sum, ten or fifteen dollars, plus the cost of the plates from which the printing would be done. I prepared a sample sheet, containing the first half-dozen chapters of "King Coal"; you may consult the volume and satisfy yourself as to whether they are interesting chapters. I sent out the offer to thousands of weeklies, and waited for replies. How many do you think I got? I didn't keep a record, but you could have counted them on your fingers, without your thumbs!

No, the editors of country and small-town newspapers are not giving their readers the truth about labor conditions in basic American industries. They know, as the phrase is, "which side their bread is buttered on," and they keep that side up with care. I have said that there are fortunes to be made by giving the news to the people; I must qualify the statement by explaining that it must be done on a large scale, and you must have capital to keep you going until you reach the people who can understand you. If you try it on a small scale, and without capital, you are crushed before you get your head out of the mud. And you know that, and govern yourself accordingly. The other day I had a call from the editor of a small newspaper, out here in this broad free West, about which you read in romances. The editor explained that he hadn't dared to write and order my books; he couldn't afford to let a check, payable to me, go through his bank; he called personally, and would carry the books home in his trunk!

Also this chapter would be incomplete without mention of the swarm of "house organs," published by big industrial concerns for the edification of their employes. According to the "New York Times" (Oct. 26, 1919), there are three hundred and seventy-five such publications in America, many with circulations running into thousands. During the war seventy-three were started in the shipyard industry alone. "During the past spring and summer they multiplied like bacteria." And the "Times" tells admiringly of the subtle arts whereby slave-labor is cajoled and idealized: "saying it in ragtime . . . . jazz variations to the vast delight of its reading public . . . . a Diamond Dick sort of tale . . . . the story has punch . . . . all as intimate as the small town weekly" . . . . and so on through columns of poison prescriptions. They trap the poor devils in their homes:

The woman's page is one of the most carefully thought out departments, on the theory that the influence of the family is counted on to sway the man from radicalism. Fully half of this group of publications is sent to the man's home by mail, to give the wife first innings. In this particular magazine the woman's page is fairly crawling with babies. . . . .

You hardly notice the propaganda even when you're looking for it with a microscope, but it is there. It is in the weave and the woof, rather than in the conspicuous pattern. You find it in similes, "like soap in the home of a Bolshevik. Some novelty!" The agitator is taken down from the dignity of his soapbox throne and flippantly advised to bathe.

CHAPTER XXXVIII

OWNING THE PRESS

The methods by which the "Empire of Business" maintains its control over Journalism are four: First, ownership of the papers; second, ownership of the owners; third, advertising subsidies; and fourth, direct bribery. By these methods there exists in America a control of news and of current comment more absolute than any monopoly in any other industry. This statement may sound extreme, but if you will think about it you will realize that in the very nature of the case it must be true. It does not destroy the steel trust if there are a few independent steel-makers, it does not destroy the money trust if there are a few independent men of wealth, but it does destroy the news trust if there is a single independent newspaper to let the cat out of the bag.

The extent to which outright ownership of newspapers and magazines has been acquired by our financial autocracy would cause astonishment if it were set forth in figures. One could take a map of America and a paint-brush, and make large smudges of color, representing journalistic ownership of whole districts, sometimes of whole states, by special interests. The Upper Peninsula of Michigan would be swept with a yellow smudge—that is copper. The whole state of Montana would be the same, and the greater part of Arizona. A black smudge for Southern Colorado, and another in the Northern part—that is coal. A gray smudge in Western Pennsylvania, and another in Illinois—that is steel. A green smudge in Wisconsin, and another in Oregon and Washington—that is lumber. A white smudge in North Dakota and Minnesota— that is the milling trust, backed by the railroads and the banks. A dirty smudge in central California, representing "Southern Pacific" and "United Railways," now reinforced by "M. and M."

Ten years ago there was a terrific reform campaign in San Francisco, and the reformers started a little weekly called the "Liberator." I quote from one issue:

Many San Francisco weekly papers were bought up with cash payments, coming principally from the offices of the "United Railroads." But this did not seem to satisfy the plans of the defense, and suddenly the Calkins Syndicate developed into a concern of astonishing magnitude. From the publisher of obscure weeklies and dailies, it established a modern publishing plant, and took over much of the printing of the "Sunset Magazine," which contract alone brought the Calkins outfit several thousand dollars a month. The "Sacramento Union" and the "Fresno Herald" were purchased, and a bid made for the "San Francisco Post." The syndicate failed to get the "Post." The "San Francisco Globe" was started instead. Whatever money could do in the newspaper line, Calkins for a few months did. Newspaper men knew, of course, that the losses were enormous. The questions were, "Who is filling the sack? How long will the sack last?"

This particular syndicate failed, but others, working in secret and with more subtlety, have succeeded. The Calkins syndicate had its exact counterpart in Montana; or rather two counterparts, for Senator Clark and Marcus Daly, copper kings, were carrying on a feud, and each purchased or established a string of newspapers to slander the other. Now the gigantic "Anaconda" has swallowed them both, and there are only two newspapers in Montana which are not owned or controlled by "copper." One of these is owned by a politician who, I am assured, serves the "interests" without hire; and the other is the "Butte Daily Bulletin," Socialist, whose editor goes in hourly peril of his life. In Oklahoma nearly everything is "Standard Oil"; and at the other end of the continent is the New York "Outlook," one of whose important stockholders was discovered to be James Stillman, of the National City Bank of New York—Standard Oil!

I have given elsewhere a picture of conditions in Los Angeles. In San Diego are two papers owned by the sugar-king, and one paper of the Scripps group. In San Francisco are two Hearst papers, the "Examiner" and the "Call"; the "Chronicle," owned by "Mike" de Young, whom I have portrayed; and the "Bulletin" whose assorted knaveries will soon be set forth in detail. Also there is a monthly, the "Sunset," formerly owned by the Southern Pacific, and now serving the anti-union campaign of the "M. and M."—the Merchants' and Manufacturers' Association which has raised a million dollar slush fund; also a weekly, popularly known as "the Rich Man's Door-mat," and a number of gossip-weeklies and "kept" political sheets. The "Labor Digest" has recently gone over with startling suddenness to the cause of capital, reversing itself absolutely on the Mooney case. The publisher, a veteran labor union official, recently informed an applicant for the job of editor that he was "running the paper to make money." The applicant said that he favored the Plumb plan; so there was "nothing doing."

Moving on up the coast, there is the "Portland Oregonian," owned by the estate of a huge-scale lumber operator, one of the richest men in the Northwest. An employe of this paper writes to me:

> He was so public-spirited and free-handed that the appraisal of the estate showed that he had invested to the extent of five dollars in war savings stamps and in only five thousand dollars worth of war bonds, and that under direct compulsion, so it was revealed, of his fellow-citizens. The "Oregonian" is born of corporate power, conceived for corporate purposes, and exists to do the corporate bidding, avowedly so.

Also there is the "Portland Telegram," owned by the two sons of a timber magnate, who obtained most of his lands by the popular "dummy entry" system. The same informant, who once worked for this paper, writes me of these owners:

> Neither has ever had to do a stroke of work in his life, and the attitude of both toward the man on the payroll is the most typically snobbish I have ever encountered. The younger brother directs the paper, although he could not earn fifteen dollars a week salary in any department if he were put on his own. The paper consequently is so wobbly in its policies and practices that it rapidly is becoming a joke.

In this vicinity is a third paper, owned by a politician of whom friends tell me that he has in past times taken the popular side, but now is old, and has got himself a business manager. A friend who knows this young man describes him:

> "Energetic, cold as steel, a typical corporation, business, money man, who is wiping the paper clean of every trace of democracy."

And then, moving farther North to Seattle, there is the "Times," an enormously valuable property, built up with the financial assistance of the Hill interests and the Great Northern Railroad—which, I believe, made more money out of a small investment than any other enterprise in America. The "Times" is paying five per cent dividends on six million dollars, and so naturally believes in the profit system. Also there is the "Star," a Scripps paper—the "Shooting Star," which was willing to lose thirty-five thousand readers in order to smash the Seattle strike. And finally there is the "Post-Intelligencer," which was purchased in the interest of James J. Hill and the Great Northern Railroad, and placed one hundred and seventy thousand dollars worth of its bonds in the hands of these interests. The paper was taken over, says my informant, by "the notorious Jacob Furth interests of Seattle. Furth was head of the Seattle transportation lines and the Seattle National Bank, and was the village pawnbroker. The paper had gradually gotten more and more into debt to the banks, and its present ownership arose out of that fact."

Such is the newspaper plight of the Pacific coast! And now come to the Atlantic coast, and take one of our great centers of culture; take the Hub of the Universe, take Boston. The newspaper plight of Boston is beyond telling. There is the "Evening Transcript," owned by an extremely wealthy and reactionary family, serving every wealthy and reactionary interest, and incidentally taking advertising bribes, as I shall presently show. There is the "Boston American," owned by Hearst, and the "Boston Daily Advertiser," also owned by Hearst. The latter is the oldest newspaper in Boston, and a year ago its circulation was cut down to a thousand copies, its publication being continued merely in order that Hearst may retain its Associated Press franchise. There is the "Boston Globe," and its evening edition, controlled, I am informed, by Standard Oil. There is the "Boston Herald," and its evening edition, the "Traveler," owned by the Plant and United Shoe Machinery interests, with ex-Senator Crane, one of the leading reactionaries of New England, holding the balance of power. There is the "Post," not in debt, but whose owner is described to me by one who knows him as "a sick man, who like all men who have accumulated a great deal of wealth, is inclined to be conservative and fearful of change."

Finally, there is the "Christian Science Monitor," owned and run by a group of wealthy metaphysicians, who teach that Poverty is a Delusion of Mortal Mind, and that Hunger can be relieved by Thinking. I make it a practice when a public emergency arises, and I have something to say which I think is important, to send it to leading newspapers by telegraph collect. Sometimes the newspapers publish it, nearly always they accept it and pay for it—because they judge there is a possibility of their getting something important by this method.

The "Christian Science Monitor" stands alone among American newspapers in that it wrote me not to send it telegrams, because there was no chance of its caring to print what I might have to say!

Or take Cincinnati, where I happen to have friends on the "inside." There is the "Cincinnati Inquirer" and "Post," owned by the estate of McLean, who made thirty million dollars out of street railway and gas franchises, obtained by bribery. This estate also owns the "Washington Post," whose knaveries I shall tell about later on. And there is the "Times-Star," owned by Charles P. Taft, brother of our ex-president. "Charlie" Taft married twenty million dollars, and bought a newspaper, and started out as a valiant reformer, and everybody in Cincinnati thought how lovely that a fine, clean, young millionaire was going in for civic reform. But at the very outset he trod on the toes of Boss Cox, and Boss Cox showed how he could injure the Taft fortune; whereupon "Charlie" made a deal with the boss, and since then his paper has been the leading champion of civic corruption.

In most big cities you find papers owned by big local "trusts," and one or two others belonging to a "trust" of newspapers, a publishing-system like that of Calkins or Capper or Munsey or Scripps or Hearst. For the rule that the big fish swallow the little ones applies in the newspaper world as elsewhere. The publisher of a big newspaper comes upon a chance to buy a small newspaper in a neighboring city, and presently he finds himself with a chain of newspapers. Then he learns of a magazine that is "on the rocks," and it occurs to him that a magazine can help his newspapers, or vice versa. So you find Munsey, a self-confessed stock-gambler, with three magazines and several newspapers; the Hearst machine with a dozen newspapers, also "Hearst's Magazine," the "Cosmopolitan," and four other periodicals. Every month in the Hearst newspapers you read editorials which are disguised advertisements of these magazines.

Also it has been discovered that magazines can combine to their financial advantage. The agents who come to your home and pester the life out of you for subscriptions find that they can get more of your money by offering clubbing-rates for a group of magazines: a farm paper, another paper with "slush for the women," a third paper with slush for the whole family—such as I have quoted from the "American" and

"McClure's." So you see a vast commercial machine building itself up. There is Street and Smith, with no less than eight magazines, all of them having enormous circulations, and devoted exclusively to trash. There is the Butterick Company, with seven; "Vanity Fair" and the Crowell Company, with four each; the Curtis Company, "Munsey's," the "Atlantic," the "World's Work," the "Smart Set," the "Red Book"—each with three. In England we have seen great chains of publications built up in connection with the selling of cocoa and soap; in America we see them built up in connection with the selling of dress-patterns, as with the Buttericks; with the boosting of moving pictures, as formerly done by "McClure's"; with grocery-stores and stock-manipulation, as "Munsey's"; with the selling of subscription-books, as "Collier's," or dictionaries, as the "Literary Digest." Or perhaps it will be a magazine run by a book-publisher, as a means of advertising and reviewing his own books; and if you investigate, you find that the book-publisher in turn is owned by some great financial interest, which sees that he publishes commercial stuff and rejects all new ideas. This process of centralization has continued in England until now Lord Northcliffe owns fifty or sixty magazines and newspapers of all varieties.

Northcliffe had a personal quarrel with Lloyd George, and that part of British "Big Business" which makes its profits out of the Lloyd George policies felt the need of more publicity, and went into the market and bought the "Chronicle" for several million dollars. When the masters of industry pay such sums for a newspaper, they buy not merely the building and the presses and the name; they buy what they call the "good-will"—that is, they buy *you*. And they proceed to change your whole psychology—everything that you believe about life. You might object to it, if you knew; but they do their work so subtly that you never guess what is happening to you!

By way of illustration, let me tell you the amusing story of one American newspaper which was thus bought in the open market. Some years ago there was a Standard Oil magnate, H. M. Flagler, who took a fancy to the state of Florida, and entertained himself by developing it into a leisure-class resort. He owned all the railroads, and a great chain of hotels, and also, as a matter of course, the State legislature. He had the misfortune to have an insane wife, and the laws of Florida did not permit him to divorce this wife, so he caused to be introduced and passed a bill permitting divorce on grounds of insanity. But, being a moral citizen, who believed in the sanctity of marriage for everybody but himself, Mr. Flagler allowed this law to stand only long enough for him to get his divorce. He then had his legislature repeal the law, so that no one might be corrupted by his evil example.

He married another woman, and shortly afterwards left her a widow with a hundred million dollars. Needless to say, such widows are not left very long to mourn; Mrs. Flagler espoused a certain Judge Bingham, a leading citizen of Kentucky. A pre-nuptial contract barred him from inheriting her estate; nevertheless she managed, eight months after their wedding, and six weeks before her death, to present to him a trifling matter of five million dollars. Then she died, and he, being lonely, and in possession of spare cash, looked around for something to play with. He decided to play with *you*—that is, with a newspaper!

There was an old newspaper in Louisville, the "Courier-Journal," which had been made by the genius of Col. Henry Watterson, a picturesque old-style Democrat, a radical of the Jeffersonian type, who stormed with vivid and diverting ferocity at the "robber barons" of Wall Street. The paper had got into financial difficulties, owing to family quarrels of the owners, and Judge Bingham bought it, with its evening edition, the "Louisville Times," for something over a million dollars. Col. Watterson was to stay as "Editor Emeritus"; that is, he was to be a figure-head, to blind the public to the sinister realities of modern capitalism. But modern capitalism is too greedy and too ruthless a force for the old-style gentleman of the South; Col. Watterson could not stand the editorial policy of his new owner, so he quit, and today the "Courier-Journal" challenges the "Los Angeles Times" as an organ of venomous reaction. I quote one sample of its editorials—the subject being that especially infamous variety of pervert known as the "Christian Socialist clergyman." Behold him!—

Some person who has never worked in his life—except his tongue—and yet talks to his "congregation" about problems of workingmen. This rogue is sometimes an elocutionary shyster who rambles about the downtrodden—meaning his prosperous followers and, of course, himself—the expected revolution, the rights of the pee-pul, and so on. What he desires to do is to heroize himself, to appear to his pee-pul as a courageous leader against oppression; which is to say, against the law and the Government which protect this people in the possession of their homes, automobiles and liberties.

Col. Watterson resigned. But as a rule the professional journalist pockets his Brass Check, and delivers the goods to his master in the silence and secrecy of the journalistic brothel. A professional journalist may be defined as a man who holds himself ready at a day's notice to adjust his opinions to the pocket-book of a new owner. I have heard Arthur Brisbane remark that the "New York Times" was sold on several occasions, and on each occasion its "editor" was sold with it. Yet when you read this "editor's" preachments, they are all so solemn and dignified, high-sounding and moral—you would never dream but that you were reading actual opinions of a man!

Quite recently we saw the "New York Evening Post" put up on the journalistic bargain-counter. I have told how the "Evening Post" treated me at various times, so you will see that the paper was hardly to be classified as "radical." But during the war it became treasonable to the gigantic trading corporation which calls itself the British Government; it persisted in this stubborn course, even when it knew that J. P. Morgan & Company were selling billions of British bonds, and handling all the purchases of the British Government in America. When the Bolsheviki gave out the secret treaties of the Allies, the "Evening Post" was the one non-Socialist newspaper in America which published them in full. So it was evident that something must be done, and done quickly, about the "Evening Post."

The paper was in financial difficulties, because of the constantly increasing cost of material and wages. Its owner gave an option to his associates, with the pledge on their part that they would not take the paper to "Wall Street"; then, three weeks later, the paper was sold to Thomas W. Lamont, of the firm of J. P. Morgan & Company; the owner being kept in ignorance of the name of the purchaser. So now the "New York Evening Post" looks upon the peace treaty, and finds it "a voice from heaven." "A voice from heaven" commanding the French to grab the Saar Valley, and the Japs to seize Shantung! "A voice from heaven" commanding the workers of Russia to pay the bad debts of the Tsar—and to pay them through the banking-house of J. P. Morgan & Company!

And if you do not care to get your opinions from the gigantic trading-corporation which calls itself the British government, you may read the "New York Evening Mail," which was bought with the money of the German government! Or you may read the "New York Evening Sun," which was bought by Frank A. Munsey, with part of the million dollars which he boasted of having made out of your troubles in the 1907 panic. If you do not like papers which are bought and sold, you may read the "New York Evening Telegram," which has remained the property of the Bennett estate, and is working for the pocket-book of the Bennett estate, forty-one editions every week. In the morning, you may read the "Herald," which is working for the same estate. If you get tired of the point of view of that estate, you may try the estate of Whitelaw Reid, capitalist, or of Joseph Pulitzer, invested in railroads and telegraphs, or of Searles, of the Sugar Trust. Or, if you prefer living men, you may give up your mind to the keeping of Adolph Ochs, of the Traction gang, or of William Rockefeller of Standard Oil, or of William Randolph Hearst of Eternal Infamy. This concludes the list of choices that are open to you in New York—unless you are willing to read a Socialist paper, the "New York Call"; and of course you cannot get the "Call" all the time, because sometimes the police bar it from the stands, and sometimes the soldier-boys raid its offices and throw the editors out of the windows, and sometimes the Postmaster-General bars it from the mails, and at all times he refuses it second class entry. So if I wish to get it out here in California, I have to pay two and one half times as much as I pay for the papers of the Searles estate and the Pulitzer estate and the Hearst estate and the Bennett estate and the Reid estate.

CHAPTER XXXIX

THE WAR-MAKERS

What is the moral tone in the offices of these great "kept" institutions? The best description I know of the inside of such a newspaper is found in an article, "The Blue Pencil," by Maxwell Anderson, published in the "New Republic" for December 14, 1918. It is very evident that Mr. Anderson has worked in the office of some newspaper; he doesn't give names, but his text indicates that the city is San Francisco. The name of the imaginary owner is H. N. De Smith, and if you are familiar with San Francisco affairs, you don't have to be a wizard to make your guess.

Mr. Anderson portrays one after another of the staff of the paper: the managing editor, the assistant managing editor, the city editor, the copy reader, the reporter, the dramatic critic, the artist, the designer, the copy boy. Every one of these persons is a slave with a chain about his neck; everyone of them clearly understands that his function in life is to subserve the glory of his owner.

They think unkindly of Hank De Smith; they speak derisively of his park, his policies, and the amount he is supposed to drink up in a day. But they obey him. Pasted before each man is a typed schedule of prejudice, known technically as the son-of-a-bitch list, and consisting of the names of men who must be given no free publicity. Here all prominent radicals and the business men who have refused to advertise in the paper are lumped in an eternal obloquy of silence.

"Refer to Dealer
"Any copy containing name of:
.............., ..., ..., ...,
"Names Not to Appear in Headlines:
.............., ..., ...
"Use Title of 'Mr.'
"Only in connection with H. N. De Smith."

What smouldering envies or balked ambitions may lie behind this absurd catalogue they do not know. But when this same De Smith buys a block of charity stock, as a matter of course they run headlines across the second title page to inform the city of it.

"Praise Hank, from whom all blessings flow," the tall and heavy Texan sneers gravely.

And here is the assistant managing editor; I have interviewed such a managing editor as this, not once, but fifty times; and not only in San Francisco, but in a score of other American cities:

> He is acute and politic, as you discover when first you hear him call up Henry N. De Smith to ask for a decision. Such action is very seldom necessary. The assistant managing editor knows the owner's prejudices and failings by long association. He is versed in a most essential knowledge of what may be printed in the paper, and what it would be dangerous for the public to know. Under his care comes the immense problem of general policy, the direction of opinion in the city in the paths most favorable to his master's fame and fortune. Nothing unpleasing to friend or advertiser must by any chance appear. It means nothing to him that given such conditions, advertising becomes a kind of legitimate blackmail, for his mind is not attuned to delicate moral vibrations.

Such is San Francisco; and lest you think that is prejudice, or an anomaly, come to Chicago and have a glimpse of the insides of the "Chronicle," given in a book of confessions, "The Career of a Journalist," by William Salisbury:

> It was no easy matter, either, to be Copy Reader on the "Chronicle." In addition to the average Copy Reader's immense fund of knowledge, one had to know almost by heart the names of the sixteen corporations in which owner Walsh was interested, such as banks and street railways and gas and contracting companies. He had to know, too, the names of the prominent men Mr. Walsh liked or disliked, so as to treat them accordingly. A mistake in such things would much more quickly bring a telephone order from Mr. Walsh's banking offices for changes in the staff than any other error.

It may seem an extreme statement; but I doubt if there is a newspaper-office in America in which such things as this do not happen. There may be newspapers whose owners sternly refrain from using them as a means of personal glorification; there may be newspapers which do not give special attention to the owner's after-dinner speeches, and to the social events that go on in the owner's home. But is there any paper which does not show consideration for the associates and intimate friends of the owner? It happened to me once to be sitting in a hotel-room with a millionaire who was under arrest and liable to serve ten years in jail. This man's relatives were among the rulers of the city, and I heard him go to the telephone and call up his relatives, and advise them how to approach the newspapers, and precisely what instructions to give; next morning I saw those instructions followed by the newspapers. Has any man ever held an executive position on a newspaper in America without witnessing incidents of this sort? The testimony available is not merely that of radicals and "muck-rakers." Here is a most conservative editor, Hamilton Holt, in his book, "Commercialism and Journalism," mentioning "a certain daily whose editor recently told me that there was on his desk a list three feet long of prominent people whose names were not to be mentioned in his paper."

Is there any newspaper which does not show consideration for the business interests of its owners? Come to Los Angeles, which I happen to know especially well, because I live only twelve miles away from it. It calls itself the "City of the Angels"; I have taken the liberty of changing the name to the "City of the Black Angels." This city gets its water-supply from distant mountains, and its great financial interests owned vast tracts of land between the city and the sources of supply. There were four newspapers, all in a state of most ferocious rivalry; but all of them owned some of this land, and all of them united in the campaign for an aqueduct. For years they kept the population terrified by pictures of failing water-supply; people say they had the water run out of the reservoirs, and the city parks allowed to dry up! So they got their aqueduct, and land that had cost forty dollars an acre became worth a thousand dollars. A single individual cleared a million dollars by this deal.

I have given in this book a fairly thorough account of the "Los Angeles Times," the perfect illustration of a great newspaper conducted in the financial interest of one man. The personality of that man infected it so powerfully that the infection has persisted after the man is dead. I have never heard anybody in Los Angeles maintain that the "Times" is an honest newspaper, or a newspaper which serves the public interest; but I have heard them say that Otis was "sincere according to his lights," that "you always knew where to find him." I have heard this said by several different men, and it is extraordinary testimony to the extent to which newspaper knavery can be successful.

No, you didn't "always know where to find Otis"; for many years it was a toss-up where you would find him, for Otis had two offices in Los Angeles. One was the office of the "Times," a "Republican" newspaper, maintaining ferociously the "open-shop" policy—so ferociously that some outraged labor leaders blew it up with a dynamite-bomb. But at the same time Otis owned secretly another Los Angeles newspaper, the "Herald"; and the "Herald" was an "independent" newspaper, a "Democratic" newspaper, a "closed-shop" newspaper! So here was Otis handing out one kind of dope to the Los Angeles public with one hand, and handing out the opposite kind of dope to the Los Angeles public with the other hand—and taking in money from the Los Angeles public with both hands. When you read my statement that "Big Business stages a sham-battle every now and then, to make the people think they are controlling the government," you smiled, no doubt—taking it for the exuberance of a radical. But what better proof could you have of a sham-battle, than to find the same man fighting furiously on both sides?

And how comes it that the public of Los Angeles is ignorant of this extraordinary situation? Why, simply that when the news came out, there was no Los Angeles newspaper that would feature it; the newspapers were in on some "deal," and the only place the story could be exploited was in "La Follette's," in Wisconsin! It was told there by Frank E. Wolfe, formerly managing editor of the "Herald," the man who took the orders of Otis and carried them out.

Some thirty years ago my friend Gaylord Wilshire started in Los Angeles a publication called the "Nationalist," advocating the ideas of Edward Bellamy. This paper was printed at the office of the "Los Angeles Express," and one day, walking down the street, Wilshire met General Otis.

"I see you people have got a weekly paper," said the General.

"Yes," said Wilshire.

"Well, now, the 'Times' has a new and modern printing-plant. We would like very much to do that work for you. Suppose you give us a trial."

"Well, General, it's all right so far as I am concerned, because I don't mind such things; but some of my associates consider that you don't treat our ideas fairly in the 'Times'."

"Oh, now, now, you don't mind a thing like that! Surely, now, you ought to understand a joke!"

"Well, as I say, I don't mind, but some of my associates take it seriously."

"Well, I'll show you about that. We'll fix that up very easily."

So the General went off, and next day there appeared in the "Times" an editorial speaking very cordially of the Edward Bellamy brand of social idealism. And thereafter for two or three weeks, the "Times" spoke pleasantly of the Edward Bellamy brand of social idealism, and it faithfully reported the meetings of the Nationalists. But the "Nationalist" did not change its printing-plant, and so the General got tired of waiting, and shifted back to his old method of sneering and abuse. This, you understand, for a job-printing contract worth fifty, or perhaps a hundred dollars, a week!

By methods such as these Otis grew wealthy, and later on he purchased six hundred and fifty thousand acres of land in Northern Mexico. When the Diaz régime was overthrown, Otis had trouble in getting his cattle out, so he wanted a counter-revolution in Mexico, and for years the whole policy of his paper has been directed to bringing on intervention and conquest of that country. At one time the Federal authorities indicted Harry Chandler, son-in-law of Otis, and his successor in control of the "Times," for conspiracy to ship arms into Mexico. Mr. Chandler was acquitted. If you will turn back to page 209 of this book, you will find a statement by a prominent Los Angeles lawyer as to jury trials in the "City of the Black Angels."

Mr. Hearst also owns enormous stretches of land in Mexico, and Mr. Hearst also understands that if Mexico were conquered and annexed by the United States, the value of his lands would be increased many times over. Therefore for fifteen years the Hearst newspapers have been used as a means of forcing war with Mexico. Mr. Hearst admits and is proud of the fact that it was he who made the Spanish-American war. He sent Frederick Remington to Cuba to make pictures of the war, and Remington was afraid there wasn't going to be any war, and so cabled Mr. Hearst. Mr. Hearst answered: "You make the pictures and I'll make the war."

That was in 1897 or 1898. I was a boy just out of college, and fell victim to this modern kind of "war-making." I was

walking on the street, and heard news-boys shouting an extra,
and saw these words, printed across the front page of the
"New York Evening Journal":

W A R

D E C L A R E D !

So I parted with one of my hard-earned pennies, and read:

W A R

may be

D E C L A R E D

soon

But did that bit of knavery keep me from buying the Hearst
newspapers forever after? It did not. I am an American,
and can no more resist sensational headlines printed in a newspaper than a donkey can resist a field of fat clover. So I still
take a Hearst newspaper, the "Los Angeles Examiner," and
watch Mr. Hearst prepare my mind for the bloody process of
annexing millions of Hearst acres to my country. Both the
Hearst paper and the Otis paper print elaborate accounts of
how the government is preparing to invade Mexico. There
are details of diplomatic negotiations and of military preparations, stories elaborate, complete, and apparently entirely
authentic. Once in a while the State Department issues a
formal denial that it has any such intentions, or is making any
such preparations; the "Times" and "Examiner" print these
denials—and then go on blandly printing their stories! I am
left to wonder which is lying, the American government or the
American press.

You know the part which the newspapers of Europe took
in the making of the late war, the "last" war, as we were told.
It was stated that munition interests subsidized the "reptile
press" of Germany, using it to foment hatred of France;
while at the same time they subsidized some of the leading
Chauvinist newspapers of France, to publish denunciations
and threats against Germany, so that the new war appropria-
tions might be forced through the Reichstag. Karl Lieb-
knecht exposed the Krupp activities, and the ruling caste of
the country never forgave him, and in the crisis of the late
rebellion they found their chance to pay him back.

Among the secret documents made public by the Bolsheviki
were some letters from the Russian Minister to France,

informing his home government of negotiations whereby
Russia was to be allowed to seize Constantinople. He told
how the French newspapers might be used, and pointed out
how Italy did this while she was grabbing Tripoli:

> It is of the highest importance to see to it that we have a good
> press here. . . . . As an example of how useful it is to have money to
> offer the press . . . . I know how Tittoni has worked up the leading
> French papers most thoroughly and with the most open hand. The
> result is now manifest to all.

We read about such infamies in Europe, and shudder at
them, and congratulate ourselves that our "sweet land of
liberty" is more clean. But put yourself in the place of an
educated Mexican, and see how it appears to him. American
financial promoters bring their wealth to Mexico, and buy the
Mexican government, and obtain ownership of the most
valuable land and oil and minerals of the country. · The
Mexican people overthrow this corrupt government, and
attempt to tax these legally stolen properties; but the foreign
governments say that these properties may not be taxed, and
the newspapers owned and published by these foreign interests
carry on for years an elaborate campaign of slanders against
Mexico, to the end that the American people may make war
upon the Mexican people and exploit them. And this is done,
not merely by the Otis paper and the Hearst papers, which
all thinking people know to be corrupt; it is done by papers
like the "New York Times" and "Tribune" and "Chicago
Tribune," which are considered to be entirely respectable. As
I write, the correspondent of the "New York Tribune" in
Mexico, L. J. de Bekker, resigns, and states as his reason that
his dispatches were suppressed or cut in the "Tribune" office.

And of course, in a campaign of this sort they count upon
the cordial help of the Associated Press. Says the "Heraldo
de Mexico," August 15, 1919: "We see that the Associated
Press lies with frequency." And you do not have to take this
solely on the word of a Mexican newspaper. The Mexican
minister of foreign relations gives out a letter from the vice-
president of the Mexican Northwestern Railroad, whose offices
are in Toronto, Canada: "I see that the Associated Press
mentions with frequency, in its reports, the name of our company." He goes on to explain that the Associated Press has
stated that his company complains of the confiscation of lands,

whereas these reports are wholly false; his company has had no difficulty whatever with the Mexican government. He says: "It is intolerable that our name should be used." And also the Associated Press sends out a circumstantial story of the alleged withdrawal of the Canadian Pearson's from business in Mexico. The vice-president of this company issues a point-blank denial that he has had any difficulty with the Mexican government. Says Mr. de Bekker, protesting to the assistant manager of the Associated Press: "It is a most marked example of the A. P.'s unfairness. And it is a fair presumption that the A. P. will not carry this denial."

The Mexicans are a backward people, and we complain that there are bandits among them. But which is worse, the spontaneous violence of a primitive people, or the organized and systematic treachery of a highly developed people? You have a child; and suppose that, instead of loving this child, understanding and helping it, you do nothing but scold at it, menace it, and tell falsehoods about it—would you be surprised if the child now and then kicked your shins?

POSTSCRIPT TO THE 8TH EDITION:

In the fall of 1920 Big Business is trying to force a war for the destruction of Soviet Russia, camouflaged as a war for the defense of Poland. Therefore Poland is the pet of the Associated Press and its newspapers, and all news injurious to Poland is barred. The British government conducted an official investigation into the massacres of Jews by the Polish government. The Associated Press said nothing about the report of this British commission. When the Jews of New York brought pressure upon the Associated Press, it at last consented to send an account of the report—which account was directly opposite to the facts! It quoted the report as saying that there had been no massacres. When efforts were made to persuade the "New York Times" to publish the truth, the "New York Times" refused—and this in spite of the fact that the "Times" is owned by a Jew, and is the principal organ of propaganda of the rich Jews in New York. The editor of the "Day," a Jewish paper in New York, was obliged to insert a paid advertisement in the "New York Times" in order to get the facts told.

CHAPTER XL

OWNING THE OWNERS

The second of the methods by which our Journalism is controlled is by far the most important of all the four. I do not mean merely that the owners are owned by mortgages, and such crude financial ties. They are owned by ambition, by pressure upon their families, by club associations, by gentlemen's agreements, by the thousand subtle understandings which make the solidarity of the capitalist class. I have written elsewhere of labor-leaders, otherwise incorruptible, who have accepted "the dress-suit bribe." These same bribes are passed in the business-world, and are the biggest bribes of all. When you have your shoes shined, you pay the bootblack ten cents; but can you figure what you are paid for having your shoes shined? When you buy a new suit of clothes, you pay the dealer, say, one hundred dollars; but can you figure what you are paid for being immaculately dressed, for having just the right kind of tie, just the right kind of accent, just the right manner of asserting your own importance and securing your own place at the banquet-table of Big Business?

If you are the publisher of a great newspaper or magazine, you belong to the ruling-class of your community. You are invited to a place of prominence on all public occasions; your voice is heard whenever you choose to lift it. You may become a senator like Medill McCormick or Capper of Kansas, who owns eight newspapers and six magazines; a cabinet-member like Daniels, or an ambassador like Whitelaw Reid or Walter Page. You will float upon a wave of prosperity, and in this prosperity all your family will share; your sons will have careers open to them, your wife and your daughters will move in the "best society." All this, of course, provided that you stand in with the powers that be, and play the game according to their rules. If by any chance you interfere with them, if you break their rules, then instantly in a thousand forms you feel the pressure of their displeasure. You are "cut" at the clubs, your sons and daughters are not invited

to parties—you find your domestic happiness has become
dependent upon your converting the whole family to your
strange new revolutionary whim! And what if your youngest
daughter does not share your enthusiasm for the "great
unwashed"? What if your wife takes the side of her darling?

It is such hidden forces as this which account for much
of the snobbery in American newspapers; the fact that in
every department and in every feature they favor the rich and
powerful, and reveal themselves as priests of the cult of
Mammon. I have watched the great metropolitan dailies, and
those in many smaller cities and towns; I have yet to see an
American newspaper which does not hold money for its god,
and the local masters of money for demi-gods at the least.
The interests of these Olympian beings, their sports, their
social doings, their political opinions, their comings and goings,
are assumed by the newspapers to be the object of the absorbed
interest of every American who knows how to read.

On every page and in every column of every page the
American newspaper preaches the lesson: "Get money, and
all things else shall be added unto you—especially newspaper
attention." When Mr. John P. Gavit, managing editor of the
"New York Evening Post," wrote to Mr. Melville E. Stone,
general manager of the Associated Press, that I had a reputation "as an insatiable hunter of personal publicity," what
Mr. Gavit meant was that I was accustomed to demand and
obtain more space in newspapers than the amount of my
worldly possessions entitled me to. Some years ago my wife
went for a visit to her home in the far South, after the unusual
adventure of marrying a Socialist; she met one of her girl-
hood friends, who exclaimed:

"My, but your husband must be a rich man!"

"My husband is a poor man," said M. C. S.

Whereat the girl-friend laughed at her. "I know better,"
said she.

"But it's true," said M. C. S. "He has no money at all;
he never had any."

"Well," said the other, skeptically, "then what are the
papers all the time talking about him for?"

A large part of what is called "conservatism" in our
Journalism is this instinctive reverence for wealth, as deeply
rooted in every American as respect for a duke in an English
butler. So the average American newspaper editor is a horse

that stands without hitching, and travels without a whip. But emergencies arise, a fork in the road, a sudden turn, a race with another vehicle; and then a driver is needed—and perhaps also a whip! I showed you Mr. Ochs pulling the "Metropolis" story off the front page of the "New York Times" at one o'clock in the morning. Every Hearst editor has stories to tell of one-o'clock-in-the-morning visits from the owner, resulting in the whole policy of the paper being shifted. And where the owner is owned, maybe somebody will call *him* up and lay down the law; maybe an agent will be set to keep watch over his doings, and to become the real master of his paper. I could name more than one famous editor and publisher who has been thus turned out of his job, and remains nothing but a name.

For great "interests" have a way of being wide-awake even at the late hour when the forms of newspapers close; they have a way of knowing what they want, and of getting it. "I am a great clamorer for dividends," testified old Rockefeller; and imagine, if you can, a publishing enterprise controlled by old Rockefeller—how closely the policy of that enterprise would be attended to! Imagine, if you can, one controlled by Pierpont Morgan!

It happens that I can tell you about one of these latter. The story has to do with one of the most famous publishing-houses in America, a house which is a national institution, known to every literate person—the ancient house of "Harper's," which now has the misfortune to have an eight hundred thousand dollar mortgage reposing in the vaults of J. P. Morgan & Company. Would you think me absurd if I should state that the publishing-business of Harper & Bros. is managed to the minutest detail by this mortgage?

First, recall to mind "The Money-changers," a novel dealing with the causes of the 1907 panic. The "villain" of this novel is a certain "Dan Waterman," a great financier who dominates the life of Wall Street, and who in his relations to women is an old wild boar. The veil of fiction was thin, and was meant to be. Every one who knew the great Metropolis of Mammon would recognize Pierpont Morgan, the elder, and would know that the picture was true both in detail and in spirit. Naturally old "J. P." himself would be furious, and his hired partisans would be looking for a chance to punish his assailant.

Very well. Five years passed, and I was editing an anthology of revolutionary literature. I was quoting authors from Homer to H. G. Wells, several hundred in all, and as part of the routine of the job, I addressed a long list of authors and publishing-houses, requesting permission to quote brief extracts from copyrighted books, due credit of course to be given. Such quotations are a valuable advertisement for any book, the more valuable because they are permanent; the request is a matter of form, and its granting a matter of course. It proved to be such in the case of all publishing-houses both in America and in England—all save one, the house of the eight hundred thousand dollar mortgage! This house informed me that no book of mine might contain a line from any book published by them. My reputation was such that I would injure the value of any book which I quoted!

I am interested in this capitalistic world, and try to find out as much about it as I can. So I took the trouble to visit the dingy old building in Franklin Square, and to interview the up-to-date gentleman who had rendered this unexpected decision. He was perfectly polite, and I was the same. I pointed out to him that some of the authors—"his" authors— were personal friends of mine, and that they themselves desired to be quoted in my anthology. Mr. Charles Rann Kennedy, for example, was a Socialist. Mr. William Dean Howells was one of Harper's own editors; he was in that very office, and I had in my hand a letter from him, giving cordial consent to the publication of two passages from "A Traveller from Altruria"! Also Mr. H. G. Wells, an English Socialist, who had honored me with his friendship, had published "When the Sleeper Wakes" through "Harper's," and now requested that I be permitted to quote from this book in my anthology. Also Mark Twain had honored me with his friendship; he had visited my home in Bermuda, and had expressed appreciation of my writings. He was no longer where I could consult him in the matter, but I offered evidence to Messrs. Harper & Bros. proving that he had not regarded me as a social outcast. But no matter; the decision stood.

I took the question to the authors themselves, and I am sorry to have to record that neither Mr. William Dean Howells nor Mr. Charles Rann Kennedy cared to support a fellow-Socialist in this controversy with a great capitalist publishing-house. So it comes about that you will not find Mr. Kennedy or Mr. Howells quoted in "The Cry for Justice"; but you will find "When the Sleeper Wakes" quoted, the reason being that Mr. Wells did stand by me. Mr. Wells lives farther away, and is not so deeply influenced by an eight hundred thousand dollar mortgage in the vaults of a Wall Street banking-house!

The point of this story is the petty nature of the vengeance of this mortgage, the trouble it took, the minute detail into which it was willing to go. The moral for you is just this: that when you pick up your morning or evening newspaper, and think you are reading the news of the world, what you are really reading is a propaganda which has been selected, revised, and doctored by some power which has a financial interest in you; and which, for the protecting of that financial interest, has been willing to take trouble, and to go into the most minute detail!

You will miss the point of this book if you fail to get clear that the perversion of news and the betrayal of public opinion is no haphazard and accidental thing; for twenty-five years—that is, since the day of Mark Hanna—it has been a thing deliberately planned and systematically carried out, a science and a technique. High-priced experts devote their lives to it, they sit in counsel with the masters of industry, and report on the condition of the public mind, and determine precisely how this shall be presented and how that shall be suppressed. They create a public psychology, a force in the grip of which you, their victim, are as helpless as a moth in the glare of an arc-light. And what is the purpose of it all? One thing, and one only—that the wage-slaves of America shall continue to believe in and support the system whereby their bones are picked bare and thrown upon the scrap-heap of the profit-system.

P. S. to ninth edition: There have been changes on the staff of Harper & Bros., and I am pleased to record that the decision against me has been rescinded, and you will find the quotations in the new edition of "The Cry for Justice."

CHAPTER XLI

THE OWNER IN POLITICS

What counts with newspapers, as everywhere else in the business world, is not so much the bulk of the wealth as its activity. Wealth which is invested in government bonds and farm-mortgages is asleep, and will stay asleep until the profit system itself is threatened. On the other hand, one or two hundred thousand dollars which happens to be in the hands of new men, trying to break into the game, may be exercising an influence out of all proportion to its amount. Such wealth may be bidding for a new franchise. It will come to the newspaper publisher and offer him stock; or it will point out to him that if the franchise is granted, certain real estate that he holds will be increased in value; or it will offer to help nominate him for mayor; or it will point out to him that his rival newspaper is enlisted on the other side, and is looking for some unrighteous graft. The story of every newspaper is a story of such a game of power-politics incessantly going on. No newspaper can exist without taking part in it, because every newspaper wields influence, and every newspaper must cast its decision on every issue that arises. Every paper is expected to have its candidates for political office; every paper is expected to have its political policies, and inevitably in our system these candidates and these policies are a screen behind which great financial interests move to their ends.

For example, here is the "Denver Post," as portrayed by Judge Lindsey, founder of the children's court. Lindsey is telling in his book, "The Beast," how one of the political machines sought to use him as a candidate for Governor:

A few days later the "Post" endorsed me editorially as a candidate for Governor, and there was a flurry in the corporation camp. The paper was no more than on the streets before Mr. Field (telephone magnate) . . . . . made a frantic effort to have the edition stopped and the paper's support reconsidered. But the "Post" had just lost in a fight with Evans (gas magnate) about a public franchise deal, and the proprietors were eager for revenge. Their newspaper rivalry with Senator Patterson made them ambitious to defeat him as leader of the reform Democrats, by forcing my nomination in spite of him. I found myself in the storm-centre of a small political cyclone.

You may recall Mr. Bonfils, one of the owners of the "Denver Post," who "jollied" me over the telephone during the time of the Colorado coal-strike. Now hear Judge Lindsey:

> When this latter ticket was named I found it largely composed of Speer corporation Democrats. Mr. Fred G. Bonfils, one of the proprietors of the "Denver Post" (which was still supporting me), assured me that Speer and his city organization would aid me if I would agree to lend my name to this ticket.
>
> In short, the corporations being sure of Adams (the opposition candidate), now wished to make sure of me by tying me to the candidacy of a lot of corporation tools who would never allow us to obtain a reform law. I refused to lend my name to any such business, and I lost thereby the support of the "Post" and the Speer Democrats.

And then, of course, Judge Lindsey was marked for destruction by the "Post." He tells how a false news dispatch reported him as saying in a public lecture in the East that the copper king of the state ought to be hanged. The Denver Chamber of Commerce passed a resolution declaring Lindsey "an enemy of the state." Says Lindsey: "The 'Denver Post' followed the resolution with a demand that I be driven from town, and stirred up all possible enmity against me as a 'defamer' of my state."

Or take San Francisco. Here is Fremont Older, for twenty-five years managing editor of the "Bulletin," telling the story of his life. I shall have more to say about Older later on; for the present, take one incident from his book. Older, leading a terrific reform campaign, is after the "man higher up," and decides that the highest of all is Herrin, head of the law department of the Southern Pacific Railroad. "Herrin is the man behind the corruption of our whole state. Herrin is the man who has broken down the morals of thousands of our young men, debauched our cities and our towns and our villages, corrupted our legislatures and courts." But it appears that Crothers, owner of the "Bulletin," has been taking money from Herrin in times past.

> Crothers became very nervous about it and suggested several times to me that he didn't want Herrin attacked. I felt then that he feared Herrin would expose the Wells money paid the paper, but in spite of that power which Herrin held over us, I continued to go on with the campaign against him.
>
> Frequently Crothers would go into the printing office and look

over the headlines himself, and if he discovered Herrin's name, would insist on its being lifted out of the paper, but even with this interference I managed to keep up the fight.

Finally, he told me flatly that he wanted the attacks on Herrin stopped, the criticism of Herrin to cease. I replied frankly that it was impossible for me to do that, that the entire reportorial force was under full headway in the fight, and they were writing, all of them, from the angle of the paper's policy as it appeared to them, and I could not go to each man and tell him that he must not criticise Herrin.

"I can't do it, Mr. Crothers, because I am ashamed for you. If it's to be done, you'll have to do it yourself. I can not."

He did not have the courage to do it, and it was never done. However, all the time our opponents were trying to reach into the office. They succeeded in getting the business manager at that time to undertake to break me down, but I resisted all his efforts. The fight became more burdensome, because it extended into the very building in which I worked.

The political campaign waxed warmer, and Crothers demanded that Older should support Herrin's candidate; but Older refused.

He replied that he owned the "Bulletin," and that it would support whomever he chose. I grew very angry and excited and replied, "Yes, what you say is perfectly true. You do own the 'Bulletin,' but you don't own me, and I won't stand for Crocker."

I walked out of the room, very angry, determined never to return. I went to my wife and told her that I was through with the "Bulletin." She wanted to know the reason and I told her that Crothers had gone back to his old methods. He was determined to get behind the candidate who represented the men we had been fighting, and I could not bring myself to continue in my position.

Or take St. Paul, Minnesota. Here is the grain country, entirely possessed by the milling interests, with their allied railroads and banks. Until the Farmer's Nonpartisan movement arose, the politics and journalism of Minnesota were exclusively in the hands of these interests. In the "Nonpartisan Leader" for May 27, June 3 and June 10, 1918, appeared a series of articles by Walter W. Liggett, formerly exchange editor of the "St. Paul Pioneer Press" and its evening edition, the "St. Paul Dispatch." Mr. Liggett made a great number of damaging charges against these newspapers, and in order to make sure of the facts, I address their managing editor, inquiring if he has ever published any denial of the charges, or if he cares to deny them to me. His answer is:

We never made any reply at all to them. . . . . Nor do I care,

as you suggest, to make any denial to you personally. It seems to me
the record of the "Dispatch" and the "Pioneer Press" is the important
thing, and this is open to anybody who cares to read our files.

The letter concludes by warning me of the risk I shall run
if I reprint "the assertions of a dismissed employe." I reply
to the writer, Mr. H. R. Galt, managing editor of the "Dispatch" and the "Pioneer Press," that his letter is unsatisfactory. The strong point about Mr. Liggett's three articles
is that they are based upon precisely the thing Mr. Galt
invites—a study of the files of the newspapers. Mr. Liggett
states that certain things are found in these files. I offer to
send Mr. Galt copies of the articles, which he says he does not
possess; I again invite him to point out to me in detail which
of Mr. Liggett's charges are false. I also ask him why, if
the charges are false, he did not take Mr. Liggett up at the
time, and inflict upon him the legal penalties with which he
threatens me. I suggest that any jury of Americans will display curiosity about that point. To which Mr. Galt replies:

> I shall be content to advise you again, as I did in my previous
> letter, that the articles upon which you have apparently based your
> verdict are untruthful in every particular in which they reflect upon
> the "Dispatch" and "Pioneer Press," and that in republishing them
> or any part of them, or in repeating any statements reflecting on these
> newspapers which may be contained in them, you will not only be pub-
> lishing falsehoods, but having been advised in advance that they are
> falsehoods, you will publish them maliciously.
>
> Now pray proceed with your indictment of American Journalism
> as reported by Mr. Liggett, and do not worry yourself about the
> curiosity of any jury so far as we are concerned. At the proper time
> we shall be abundantly able to satisfy any curiosity on this point.

Now, when a man comes at me making a face like that, I
have but one impulse in my soul—that is, to jump into a pair
of seven-league boots, and turn and skedaddle as hard as I
know how to the other side of the world and hide in a coal-bin.
I am not joking; that is really the way I feel. There is nothing in the world I dread so much as a personal wrangle, and
these fierce and haughty and powerful men throw me into a
tremble of terror. The things I enjoy in this world are my
books and my garden, and rather than go into a jury-room,
and wrangle with fierce and haughty and powerful men, I
would have my eye-teeth pulled out. But then I think, as I
have thought many times in my life before, of the millions of

pitiful wage-slaves who are exploited by these fierce and haughty and powerful men. I think of the millions of honest and true Americans who swallow the poison that is fed to them by our capitalist newspapers; and so I clench my hands and bite my lips together and turn on the fierce and haughty and powerful men with a yell of rage. Then a strange and startling, an almost incredible thing happens—the fierce and haughty and powerful men jump into *their* seven-league boots, and turn and skedaddle to the other side of the world and hide in a coal-bin!

Why is this? Is it because I am an especially terrifying person, with an especially terrifying face? No; it is simply because, in these contests, I have always taken one precaution at the outset—I have made certain of having the truth on my side. I have cast in my lot with the truth; whereas these fierce and haughty and powerful men with whom I enter the lists of combat have made all their success out of falsehood, and fear truth as they fear nothing else on God's earth.

Before I go to the bat with Mr. Galt, managing editor of the "St. Paul Dispatch" and "Pioneer Press," I will point out one important fact about my life, as follows:

In the course of my twenty years career as an assailant of special privilege, I have attacked pretty nearly every important interest in America. The statements I have made, if false, would have been enough to deprive me of a thousand times all the property I ever owned, and to have sent me to prison for a thousand times a normal man's life. I have been called a liar on many occasions, needless to say; but never once in all these twenty years has one of my enemies ventured to bring me into a court of law, and to submit the issue between us to a jury of American citizens. Several times they have come near to doing it. I was told, by a lawyer who was present at the event, that there was a conference, lasting three days and a good part of three nights, between Mr. J. Ogden Armour and his lawyers, in which Mr. Armour insisted upon having me arrested for criminal libel, and his lawyers insisted that he could not "stand the gaff." As you have seen in this book, Mr. William E. Corey threatened to sue me for libel; I am informed that young Mr. Rockefeller desired ardently to do it, and Madame Tingley, the "Purple Mother" of Theosophy, actually sent her lawyers after me for my jests about her in

"The Profits of Religion." But, if Mr. H. R. Galt actually files a suit against me, he will be the first of our captains of privilege who has ventured that far.

Now, to return to the "St. Paul Dispatch" and "Pioneer Press": I have not made a detailed study of the files of these papers, but I have made a study of the Nonpartisan League movement and its "Nonpartisan Leader," also I have made a study of Mr. Walter W. Liggett, formerly exchange editor of the "Dispatch" and the "Pioneer Press." Mr. Liggett assures me that every statement he makes can be abundantly proven from the files of the papers, and I believe Mr. Liggett. Accordingly I take the risk of summarizing the statements which Mr. Liggett published concerning these two papers, and which these two papers allowed to pass unchallenged. My guess is that Mr. H. R. Galt will do one of two things: either he will do what Mr. Ogden Armour did, and what Mr. Corey did, and what Mr. Rockefeller did, and what Madame Tingley did—that is, nothing. Or else he will do what the Associated Press did in the case of the "Masses"—he will file a suit, or ask for an indictment, and thus get occasion to publish in his papers a high-sounding and dignified statement of his own righteousness; he will put me to the expense of employing lawyers and making a thorough study of his files; and then, when the case comes up, he will drop it, and say not one word about it in his papers!

Now, what is it that Mr. Liggett has to say? His statements are briefly as follows:

The "St. Paul Dispatch" and "Pioneer Press" were financed and put on their feet by a street-car magnate, and for twenty years, from a generous and pure emotion of gratitude, have supported this street-car magnate in all his doings; hiding his tax-dodging and his franchise grafting, ridiculing and misrepresenting his employes when they go on strike. The papers could probably not be purchased for a million dollars, yet they pay taxes on less than fifty-seven thousand dollars. Until quite recently they were charging the city an illegal price for the publication of city advertisements, and only quit when an independent citizen forced an exposure. They have defended the Hill railroad interests systematically; they have suppressed news of public agitation against the packers and the millers, and have editorially defended these and other profiteers. After borrowing three hundred thousand dollars from the Capital Trust and Savings Company, they did their best to start a run on the St. Paul municipal bank, and only failed because their false statements were promptly exposed. They have lied systematically about the farmers' movement, and have refused to publish corrections, even in the form of paid advertisements. They were ultra-patriotic, and urged all employers to continue their employes' wages while the latter were in the army; but they themselves failed to follow this advice!

And now come, Mr. Galt, and explain to a jury of American citizens how it happened that these articles, "untruthful in every particular in which they reflect upon the 'Dispatch' and the 'Pioneer Press'," were allowed by you to be published in a paper having two hundred thousand circulation in Minnesota and adjoining states, and were left unanswered and unchallenged by you for a period of fifteen months!

The Nonpartisan League is an issue, not only in Minnesota and North Dakota, but all over the country where the interests are in terror of a farmers' revolt. And so the whole power of the kept press is enlisted to malign it. The League is doing business through the Scandinavian-American Bank of Fargo, and the enemies of the League raid this institution, with the help of subservient public officials, and throw it into the hands of a receiver. From one end of the country to the other goes the story of crooked banking by the farmers' party, and is featured by the capitalist press. The "New York Times" has several detailed dispatches, also solemn editorials. A week or two later the Supreme Court of the State denounces the proceedings as a conspiracy, declares the bank sound, and orders its return to the owners. The "Times" gives this—not one line! Or take the "Kansas City Star," a most completely respectable organ, which features the smash-up of the bank, and reports the restoration in a tiny item, giving the name of the bank, but not mentioning it as the League bank—understanding perfectly well that ninety-nine out of a hundred readers will not make the connection, and will not know that the League has been vindicated!

And then, a few days later, the American Bar Association issues a denunciation of the League, declaring it is "pure Socialism," and Socialism means the "nationalization of women." The "Chicago Tribune" gets out a big headline:

"SOCIALISTS HOPE TO COMMUNIZE U. S. GIRLS, CLAIM."

The "Chicago Tribune" is in politics you see; and like Richard Croker, it is working for its own pocket all the time. Let us hear William Marion Reedy, a journalist of forty years' training:

In Chicago there is the case of two great newspapers, one of them Republican and the other Independent, which have been found clearly guilty of robbery of the school children of that city. Through the connivance of a school board, one of the members of which was an attorney for one of these newspapers, the land occupied by both these journals, in the very heart of the business center of Chicago, was leased to these great institutions for the moulding of public opinion, on a basis of a site-value absolutely absurd and ridiculous, and upon terms very much lower than those granted on·similar lands to other lease-holders in the same neighborhood. This favor exacted of a public body, and at public expense was given solely through fear of attack by, or desire to stand well with the publications in question. When there came into power in the school board, under Mayor Dunne, a number of men who could not be reached by political or other interests, and these men attempted to set aside the outrageous lease in question, both these papers began a crusade against the honesty and intelligence of the school board, and developed the campaign into one for the election of a mayor who would oust these school board members who tried to win back the property for the school children. They rallied to their support all the corrupt and vicious element of the Chicago slums, likewise the forces that could be controlled by the street railways and other public service corporations, elected the mayor, and turned the honest members of the school board out of office. They have since been reinstated, but not until the corporation Mayor had appointed a sufficient number of "safe and sane" friends of the powers that be, to block any effort that might be made by the honest members to secure from these great publications a just compensation for the use of the land belonging to the public schools of Illinois and Chicago.

Reedy omits to give us the names of these two Chicago newspapers. As I am dealing with names in this book, I state that one of them is the most "respectable" of all Chicago's newspapers, the "Tribune," which carries on its front page the legend: "The World's Greatest Newspaper." The other is the most "liberal" of all Chicago's newspapers, the "Daily News," owned by Victor F. Lawson, who is generally cited as the one among the fifteen directors of the Associated Press who has any trace of progressive sympathy.

P. S. to ninth edition: Seven years later, and I have not yet heard from Mr. Galt.

CHAPTER XLII

OWNING THE ASSOCIATED PRESS

When it comes to the Associated Press, the clearest statement I have read was made by Charles Edward Russell in "Pearson's Magazine," April, 1914. Says Russell:

About nine hundred daily newspapers in the United States, comprising the great majority of the journals of influence and circulation, receive and print the news dispatches of the Associated Press.

This means that concerning any event of importance an identical dispatch is printed about fifteen million times and may be read by thirty million persons.

According to the construction and wording of that dispatch, so will be the impression these thirty million persons will receive, and the opinion they will form and pass along to others.

Here is the most tremendous engine for Power that ever existed in this world. If you can conceive all that Power ever wielded by the great autocrats of history, by the Alexanders, Caesars, Tamburlaines, Kubla Khans and Napoleons, to be massed together into one vast unit of Power, even this would be less than the Power now wielded by the Associated Press.

Thought is the ultimate force in the world and here you have an engine that causes thirty million minds to have the same thought at the same moment, and nothing on earth can equal the force thus generated.

Well-informed men know that the great Controlling Interests have secured most of the other sources and engines of Power. They own or control most of the newspapers, most of the magazines, most of the pulpits, all of the politicians and most of the public men.

We are asked to believe that they do not own or control the Associated Press, by far the most desirable and potent of these engines. We are asked to believe that the character and wording of the dispatches upon which depends so much public opinion is never influenced in behalf of the Controlling Interests. We are asked to believe that Interests that have absorbed all other such agencies for their benefit have overlooked this, the most useful and valuable of all. We are even asked to believe that, although the Associated Press is a mutual concern, owned by the newspapers, and although these newspapers that own it are in turn owned by the Controlling Interests, the Controlling Interests do not own, control or influence the Associated Press, which goes its immaculate way, furnishing impartial and unbiased news to the partial and biased journals that own it.

That is to say that when you buy a house you do not buy its foundations.

The point about the Associated Press upon which it lays greatest stress, and which it never fails to bring forward in defending itself, is that it is a "mutual" corporation; it is owned and controlled by the many hundreds of newspapers which use its services. In La Follette's magazine during the year 1909 there appeared a series of articles on the Associated Press by William Kittle. Mr. Kittle showed, taking the figures of the year 1909, that the seven hundred newspapers which then used the service had less than one-seventh of the voting control of the organization. The rest of the votes were cast on bonds which had been sold to certain of the members. These bonds represented a voting-strength of four thousand, eight hundred and ninety as against seven hundred and seventy-five votes of the member newspapers. The total of fifty-six hundred and sixty-five votes elected the board of directors, and this board, having power to issue new bonds at any time, could keep its control absolute. Could anyone imagine a smoother scheme for holding a corporation in bondage? And then fancy Melville E. Stone coming before the public and making this statement concerning his organization:

It is purely mutual in its character, and in this respect is unique. All of the other news-supplying agencies of the world are proprietary concerns. It issues no stock, makes no profit, and declares no dividend. It does not sell news to any one. It is a clearing-house for the interchange of news among its members only.

I wrote to Mr. Stone, explaining that I was discussing his organization in my book, and wished to be scrupulously fair in every statement I made; would Mr. Stone tell me the present status of these bonds and their votes? Mr. Stone delayed for some time to answer, and when he did so, explained the delay:

First, because I have been taking a vacation, and have had no leisure to think of you, and second, because in the slight reading I have given to your publications, I was led to believe that any failure to acquaint yourself with the facts of a matter would in no wise embarrass you in presenting your case.

My answer was that, curiously enough, this was precisely the impression I had formed of Mr. Stone's organization; the only difference being that whereas he admitted having given only a slight reading to my publications, I had had intimate first-hand experience with his organization over a period of fifteen or twenty years.

However, Mr. Stone consented to give me a list of the present bond-holders; also his explanation of the matter:

In the organization of the Associated Press in 1900 it was necessary to provide a certain sum to buy fixtures, etc., and certain first mortgage bonds were issued and sold to the members, the proceeds being applied in the way indicated. The Charter authorized an issuance of $150,000. But this sum was found to be unnecessary. The actual issue was $131,425. This has since been reduced by redemption in certain cases so that today there is outstanding $113,125. Under the law of New York, holders of first mortgage bonds are entitled to vote for Directors in proportion to their holdings. They have no right to vote upon bonds on any other matter in the conduct of the business.

Many times, in the course of my experiences as a muck-raker, I have had great captains of privilege endeavor to impose upon my intelligence; but I cannot recall having ever been offered so childish a pretext as I am here offered by Mr. Stone. I am asked to believe that in the nineteen years of its history, this enormous concern has been able to pay off less than twenty thousand dollars of the debt incurred for its office furniture! I am asked to believe that these bond-holders have votes because the law requires them to have votes; and that never once has it occurred to the shrewd gentlemen who manage the Associated Press that by the simple device of remaining in debt for their office furniture, they can keep their organization permanently and irrevocably in the control of the big reactionary newspapers of the country!

Will Irwin, writing in "Harper's Weekly" five years ago, speaks of the "ring of old, Tory, forty-one vote papers in control" of the Associated Press. It appears that the bonds of the organization are for twenty-five dollars each, and when the association was formed, the big insiders each took one thousand dollars worth—giving them forty votes, with one additional vote as member.

I look down the list which Mr. Stone sends me, and I see that these "forty-one vote papers" include all of the biggest reactionary sheets in America. One after another I look for those which I have pilloried in this book—they are all here! The "Los Angeles Times" is here, and de Young's "San Francisco Chronicle," and the "San Francisco Bulletin," of the itching palm, and the "San Francisco Examiner," which sent out my Shredded Wheat story, and the "Sacramento Union," which was sold to the Calkins syndicate. Here is the "Pueblo Chieftain," which circulated the foul slanders about Judge

18

Lindsey and the miners' wives. Here is the "Baltimore News" of Munsey, the stock-gambler. Here is the "Washington Post," which, as I shall narrate, had a typewritten copy of a speech by Albert Williams, and deliberately made up false quotations. Here is the "Chicago Tribune," which slandered Henry Ford, and the "Chicago Daily News," which, with the "Tribune," robs the Chicago school-children. Here is the "Cincinnati Times-Star," which set out to fight Boss Cox, and didn't. Here is the "Boston Herald," which, I shall show you, refused President Wilson's speech as an advertisement, and the "Boston Traveller," which lied about my magazine. Here is the "Kansas City Star," which hounded Mrs. Stokes to jail, and the "St. Paul Dispatch," whose misdeeds I have just listed. Here is the "Oil City Derrick," owned by Standard Oil, and the "Seattle Post-Intelligencer," whose bonds were found in the vaults of the Great Northern Railroad. Here is the "Portland Oregonian," which exists for large-scale capital, and the "Milwaukee Sentinel," owned by Pfister, who owns most of Milwaukee. Here is the "New York Herald," which suppressed my Packingtown story, and paid me damages for the Tarrytown libel. Here is the "New York Evening Post," which failed to expose the Associated Press, and the "New York World," which favors twenty-cent meals for department-store girls; here is the "New York Tribune," which lied about the Socialist state legislators, and the "New York Times," which has lied about me so many times that I can't count them.

Such are the newspapers which control the Associated Press: a "stand-pat" machine, precisely like the Aldrich machine which once controlled the United States Senate, and the Cannon machine which once controlled the House. Mr. Stone does his best to persuade me that in the maintenance of this control the bonds have not played any part. He writes:

Since the organization, over one hundred elections of directors have taken place. In one case only, I believe, was the result different from what it would have been if no votes had been cast upon the bonds.

And here again Mr. Stone is treating me as a child. Of the total bonds the big insiders control nine-tenths. Of the total number of votes cast at elections, they control five-sixths. A successful rebellion is thus obviously impossible; and the penalty of an unsuccessful rebellion, as I shall presently show, is annihilation; yet Mr. Stone feels virtuous because nobody rebels! Let Mr. Stone pay off his debts for office furniture, and place all the nine-hundred-odd members of the Associated Press on an equality as regards votes, and then let him boast that the bonds have no effect upon elections!

Ten years ago Mr. Kittle made a study of the fifteen directors of the Associated Press. They were all publishers of large newspapers, and from these newspapers could be judged. Just one was a "liberal," Nelson, of the "Kansas City Star"—and he has since died. All the other fourteen were classified as "conservative or ultra-conservative." Said Mr. Kittle:

> The other fourteen papers are huge commercial ventures, connected by advertising and in other ways with banks, trust companies, railway and city utility companies, department-stores and manufacturing enterprises. They reflect the system which supports them.

There have been many changes of personality in the Associated Press in the last ten years, but there has been no change in this respect; the statement of Mr. Kittle's remains the truth about the fifteen directors. And likewise there has been no change in the policy of the organization, as Mr. Kittle reported it:

> The dispatches themselves disclose the attitude of the management. They give scant courtesy to movements for constructive legislation in the public interest. The reports, scores of which have been examined, are meager, fragmentary, isolated. Every time Tom Johnson was successful in more than fifty injunction suits, the general public in other states heard little or nothing of it. When an election recently went against him, everybody heard of the "failure" of municipal ownership. When La Follette for five years, by a continuous contest, was placing law after law on the statute-books, the matter was ignored or briefly reported in distant states; and temporary defeats were given wide publicity. When Kansas, in 1908, rejected a conservative and elected a progressive United States Senator, the general public at a distance from that state did not know the real issue involved. For more than two years, there has been a strong movement in California against the rule of that state by special and corrupt interests, but that fact, merely as news, has never reached the general public in the East. The prosecution of offenders in San Francisco has only been a part of the wider movement in California. The strong movement in New Hampshire, headed by Winston Churchill, to free that state from the grasp of the Boston and Maine Railway Company and the movement in New Jersey led by Everett Colby, which resulted in the defeat of Senator Dryden, the president of the Prudential Insurance Company, have not been given to the people adequately as matters of news.

And this is the testimony of every independent-minded newspaper man with whom I have talked about the Associated Press. Will Irwin, writing in "Harper's Weekly," shows how the old reactionary forces shape the policy of the organization. "The subordinates have drifted inevitably toward the point of view held by their masters." And again, of the average Associated Press correspondent: "A movement in stocks is to him news—big news. Wide-spread industrial misery in a mining camp is scarcely news at all." At a conference at the University of Wisconsin, the editor of the "Madison Democrat" stated that he had been a correspondent of the Associated Press for many years, and had never been asked "to suppress news or to color news in any way whatever." Reply was made by A. M. Simons: "I have had many reporters working under me, and every one of you know that you will not have a reporter on your paper who cannot 'catch policy' in two weeks."

The general manager of the Associated Press makes public boast of the high character of his employes. "Throughout the profession, employment in its service is regarded as an evidence of character and reliability." Such is the glittering generality; but investigate a little, and you find one Associated Press correspondent, Calvin F. Young, of Charleston, West Virginia, engaged in sending strike-news to his organization, and at the same time in the pay of the mine-owners, collecting affidavits against the strikers. You find a second Associated Press correspondent, E. Wentworth Prescott, of Boston, dipping into the slush funds of the New Haven Railroad, and giving an explanation of his services, so lacking in plausibility that Interstate Commerce Commissioner Anderson remarks: "I don't see why they couldn't just as well have hired you to count the telegraph poles on the street!"

The Associated Press is probably the most iron-clad monopoly in America. It was organized originally as a corporation under the laws of Illinois, but the Illinois courts declared it a monopoly, so it moved out of Illinois, and reorganized itself as a "membership corporation," thus evading the law. Today, if you wish to start a morning newspaper in the village of Corn Center, Kansas, you may get an Associated Press franchise; but if you want to start one in any city or town within circulating distance of the big "forty-one-vote" insiders, you might as well apply for a flying-machine to visit the moon. The members of the Associated Press have what is called "the right of protest"—that is, they can object to new franchises being issued; and this power they use ruthlessly to maintain their monopoly. Says Will Irwin:

> To the best of my knowledge, only two or three new franchises have ever been granted over the right of protest—and those after a terrible fight. Few, indeed, have had the hardihood to apply. When such an application comes up in the annual meeting, the members shake with laughter as they shout out a unanimous "No!" For owing to the exclusive terms of the charter, an Associated Press franchise to a metropolitan newspaper is worth from fifty thousand dollars to two hundred thousand dollars. Abolish the exclusive feature, throw the Association open to all, and you wipe out these values. The publishers are taking no chances with a precedent so dangerous.

A few years ago the editor of the "News" of Santa Cruz, California, applied for the Associated Press franchise for his paper. The San Francisco manager of the Associated Press refused it, and gave this explanation, according to a statement by the editor of the "News":

> The San Francisco daily papers owned all the Associated Press franchises for that city, and they also controlled a vast outlying territory, including Santa Cruz, eighty miles away, and would refuse to permit Associated Press dispatches to be printed by me or anyone else in Santa Cruz.

There is only one way to get by this barrier, and that is to pay the price. Joseph A. Scranton, proprietor of the "Scranton Republican," forced a man who wished to start another newspaper in Scranton to pay him ten thousand dollars before he could have the Associated Press franchise for that small city. When the "San Francisco Globe" wanted the Associated Press franchise, it had to buy the "San Francisco Post" at the price of a hundred and ten thousand dollars. Admittedly the "Post" had no value, it was not a competitor in any sense; the price paid was for the franchise alone—and it was stated by the "San Francisco Star" that the greater part of the value consisted in a lower telegraph rate, a special privilege granted by the Western Union telegraph company to the Associated Press.

Also the Associated Press, being a membership corporation or club, possesses the legal right to expel and to discipline its members. This right it has specifically asserted in its charter;

it may expel a member "for any conduct on his part, or on the part of anyone in his employ or connected with his newspaper, which in its absolute discretion it shall deem of such a character as to be prejudicial to the welfare and interest of the corporation and its members, or to justify such expulsion. The action of the members of the corporation in such regard shall be final, and there shall be no right of appeal or review of such action."

This, you perceive, is power to destroy any newspaper overnight. Not merely may a franchise worth two hundred thousand dollars be wiped out at the whim of the little controlling oligarchy; the entire value of the newspaper may be destroyed; for of course a big morning newspaper cannot exist without its franchise. The masters of the "A. P." hold this whip over the head of every member; and Will Irwin tells what use they make of it:

> Two or three liberal publishers have expressed to me, after mutual pledges of confidence, their opinion of the "A. P. cinch." And they have finished by saying something like this:
> "But for heaven's sake don't quote me in print, and don't tell anyone I've said this. The fine for such an offense runs from fifty thousand dollars up!"

In my story of the Colorado coal-strike, I showed you the "A. P." suppressing news, and the newspapers of the country, without one single exception, keeping silence about it. I showed you one bold managing editor promising to tell the truth, and then suddenly stricken dumb, and not carrying out his promise. Now I have shown you the meaning of the phenomenon.

And yet, in spite of everything, members of the Associated Press do "kick"; they "kick" repeatedly, and word of their "kicks" gets out. Fremont Older complained repeatedly, and so did Van Valkenburg, of the "Philadelphia North American." Herman Ridder complained—as Mr. Stone himself admitted when a Senate committee pinned him down. I quote a significant colloquy from a Senate "lobby" investigation:

> Senator LaFollette: Mr. Stone, has there ever been any complaint made by members of your association of unfairness on the part of the manager or the management of the Association regarding news?
> Mr. Stone: Oh, yes, sir. There is hardly—

Senator LaFollette: Have the members of your association or any member of your association complained that you suppressed important news?

Mr. Stone: Oh, yes, sir, we have had that for years.

Senator LaFollette: That you have colored news?

Mr. Stone: No, sir, I do not think anybody has ever said that. Well, I don't know about that. We have had complaints on all sides.

This is the Committee on Finance of the United States Senate, holding hearings on the subject of reciprocity with Canada (Senate Document 56, Sixty-second Congress, First Session, Vol. II). The newspapers of the country want a clause by which they can get free paper-pulp from Canada; so the Associated Press sends out full reports of the testimony of newspaper publishers before the Senate Committee. But when certain farmers appear and oppose the reciprocity scheme—listen to Senator McCumber, questioning Herman Ridder, a director of the Associated Press:

How do you account for the fact, which every senator here must have noticed, that while these farmers were giving their testimony the reporters of the Associated Press leaned back in their chairs day after day scarcely taking a note, and that the moment any man came forward to give testimony in favor of this bill every pencil came out and every pad was on the table and all of our good friends were studiously at work? And that has been the case all through these hearings.

And again:

It is a notorious fact that we have been able to get but one side of the question before the public so far as these hearings are concerned.

Also, consider the testimony brought out by the Senate Committee on the Judiciary (sixty-third Congress, First Session, Senate Resolution 92, Vol. II). It appears that the head of the Sugar Trust had issued a long statement, advocating free raw sugar, and this press-agent material had been sent out in full by the Associated Press. The senators question Melville E. Stone, to find out why, and they cannot even get the name of the Associated Press correspondent who handled the material! It is brought out that the beet sugar interests of the West, which are fighting the Sugar Trust, have made bitter complaint concerning this article, and have been to the head of the Denver office of the Associated Press to demand that their side too shall be given a hearing. You remember how I went to the head of the Denver office of the Associated Press, to try to get a hearing for *my* side—the people's side—and how completely I failed? Needless to say, it is different when a representative of Big Business makes complaint; this gentleman obtains the promise of the Associated Press to send out six hundred and fifty words, and later on Mr. Stone is found writing to his Denver manager:

Personally I am inclined to discourage the carrying of long statements of a controversial nature, but inasmuch as we carried Mr. Arbuckle's statement rather fully, my judgment is that we might have handled a little more of Mr. Hamlin's provided it was prepared as briefly as our copy here indicates.

Here, you see, we are close to the heart of a grave problem. Here are enormous sums of "easy money" in sight. If the managers and district managers and correspondents of our great press associations all sternly decline to touch this "easy money," they are all, all honorable men; also, they are different from most other men in most other branches of Big Business in America.

Do they all decline? I sincerely hope so. But I recall how Max Eastman, in the "Masses" for July, 1913, made very specific charges against the Associated Press, which thereupon caused Eastman's arrest for criminal libel. The indictment brought by the Grand Jury against Eastman and Art Young quotes a paragraph from the offending editorial, as follows:

I am told that every trust is to be encouraged to live its life and grow to such proportions that it may and must be taken over by the working public. But one trust that I find it impossible to encourage is this Truth Trust, the Associated Press. So long as the substance of current history continues to be held in cold storage, adulterated, colored with poisonous intentions, and sold to the highest bidder to suit his private purposes, there is small hope that even the free and the intelligent will take the side of justice in the struggle that is before us.

The indictment goes on to interpret the above:

Meaning and intending thereby that the said corporation intentionally withheld, suppressed and concealed from its members information of important items of news and intelligence and intentionally supplied its members with information that was untruthful, biased, inaccurate and incomplete, and that the said corporation *for and in consideration of moneys paid to it* intentionally supplied to its members misinformation concerning happenings and events that constituted the news and intelligence of the day.

Then the indictment quotes another paragraph from the editorial:

> The representative of the Associated Press was an officer in that military tribunal that hounded the Paint Creek miners into the penitentiary in violation of their constitutional liberties; and this fact is even more significant and more serious than the abrogation of those liberties. It shows that the one thing which all tribes and nations in time have held sacred—the body of Truth—is for sale to organized capital in the United States.

The indictment interprets this as follows:

> Meaning and intending thereby that the said corporation was willing to and did *in consideration of money paid to it* knowingly supply to its members information of such untruthful, biased and prejudiced nature and so distorted and incomplete *as the person paying such money might desire.*

This indictment was widely heralded in the press, and everybody thought they were going to get the truth about the Associated Press at last. But when the case was ready for trial, it was mysteriously dropped. For six years I have wondered why it was dropped. I cannot say now that I know; but I have just met Max Eastman, and heard from his lips the story of a certain eminent corporation lawyer in New York, who on several occasions has "kicked over the traces" of Big Business. This man knows a great deal about the Associated Press, and he came forward in this "Masses" case, offering to assist the defense, and to conduct the trial. It was his plan to summon the heads of high finance in New York, beginning with Pierpont Morgan, and to question them as to the precise details of their relationship to the Associated Press! Aren't you sorry that trial didn't come off? And don't you think it a very serious matter that the Associated Press did not face this precise and definite issue, which it had so publicly raised? Let me speak for myself: If any man accused me in the specific and damaging way above quoted, I would consider that my time, my money, my energy, my very life must be called to the task of vindicating my honor. And if, instead of fighting, I put my tail between my legs and sneaked away from the scene, I would expect men to conclude that there was some guilt upon my conscience.

CHAPTER XLIII

THE OWNER AND HIS ADVERTISERS

The third method by which the "kept" press is kept is the method of the advertising subsidy. This is the "legitimate" graft of newspapers and magazines, the main pipeline whereby Big Business feeds its journalistic parasites. Financially speaking, our big newspapers and popular magazines are today more dependent upon their advertisers than they are upon their readers; it is not a cynicism, but the statement of a business fact, that a newspaper or popular magazine is a device for submitting competitive advertising to the public, the reading-matter being bait to bring the public to the hook.

And of course the old saying holds, that "he who pays the piper calls the tune." The extent to which the bait used in the game of journalistic angling is selected and treated by the business fishermen, is a subject which might occupy a volume by itself. Not merely is there general control of the spirit and tone of the paper; there is control in minute details, sometimes grotesque. For example, Arthur Brisbane wrote an article on dietetics, deploring the use of package cereals. The advertising men of the "Evening Journal" came to him, tearing their hair; he had knocked off a hundred thousand dollars a year from the "Journal's" income! Brisbane wrote an editorial pointing out that stiff hats caused baldness, and the "Journal" office was besieged by the hat-dealers who advertised in the paper. Brisbane went to Europe and wrote editorials supporting a municipal subway. Said the advertising man: "Don't you know that Mr. —— at Wanamaker's is dead against that sort of thing?"

Max Sherover, in his excellent little pamphlet, "Fakes in American Journalism," writes:

The editor of a New York paper wrote an instructive editorial on the right kind of shoes to wear. The editorial was not inspired by any advertiser. It was simply the result of the editor's study and investigation of the problem of footwear. He advised against the wearing of the shoe with the curved point and urged in favor of the square-toed shoe. One of the big advertisers somehow got wind of the shoe-editorial that was intended to appear on the following day.

It so happened that this storekeeper had a shoe-sale scheduled for the following week. He called up the business manager of the newspaper on the 'phone. After five minutes of conversation the editorial went to the waste-basket.

And if the advertisers censor the general ideas, needless to say they censor news about themselves. Henry Siegel owned a department-store in New York; his wife divorced him, and nothing about it appeared in the New York papers—that is, not until after the department-store failed! Our great metropolitan dailies are, as you know, strong protectors of the sanctity of the home; you saw how they treated Upton Sinclair, when he got tied up in the divorce-courts; you saw how they treated Gorky and Herron. But how about the late C. W. Post, of "Postum" fame, when he decided to divorce his wife and marry his stenographer? Hardly a line in the newspapers throughout the country!

I have told how the Philadelphia newspapers suppressed the suicide of one of the Gimbel brothers. This same firm has a store in Milwaukee, and I have before me a letter from the District Attorney of Milwaukee County, setting forth what happened when the vice-president of this firm was indicted for bribing an alderman:

Representatives of Gimbel Brothers requested, as I am credibly informed, the newspapers in which their commercial advertisements appeared to suppress the facts connected with the proceedings of Mr. Hamburger's trial. With two exceptions, so insignificant as to justify their being entirely ignored, the English press did so. The five daily English newspapers published no account whatever of the trial, which occupied about one week and disclosed sensational matter which would have undoubtedly been published broadcast in an ordinary case. Some of these papers printed a very brief notice at the time the case was called, stating this fact, but not all of them did even this much. . . . . It was shown that all the books of account of the Gimbel Brothers, together with their correspondence and legal documents pertaining to the transaction in connection with which the bribery was alleged were burned under the direction of the defendant immediately after it was brought to his attention that the grand jury which indicted him was in session and about to investigate this case. This destruction of the books and documents occurred within the period of the statute of limitation, and less than three years after some of the entries had been made in them. The only explanation for this singular proceeding given by defendant or his business associates was that they lacked room in their vault and found it necessary to do away with papers, books and documents which they felt they could dispense with. I mention this particular line of evidence because I am satisfied that if such a showing had been made in an ordinary case of bribery the facts disclosed would have been given the widest publicity by the daily press. That the proceedings of this trial were suppressed by the English papers of this city for commercial reasons which appealed to their advertising department is unquestioned. Every newspaper man of my acquaintance to whom I have mentioned the matter has admitted the fact and deplored it.

In the same way, when Wanamaker's was detected violating the customs laws, only one Philadelphia newspaper reported the circumstances. There was organized a league for honest advertising, and you might have thought that such a league would have appealed to our highly moral newspapers; but when this league prosecuted a merchant in New York for selling furs under false names, not one newspaper mentioned the circumstances. This merchant was convicted, and again not one New York newspaper mentioned it. In Chicago various firms were prosecuted for misbranding goods, and the local papers suppressed the news. In Milwaukee four firms were prosecuted for selling a potted cheese doped with chemicals, and the newspapers withheld the names of the firms. Says Will Irwin: "I have never seen a story of a shop-lifting case in which the name of the store was mentioned." Also he makes the following statement concerning the most august of the Brahmin newspapers of New England:

The "Boston Evening Transcript" published in its issue of April 8th the fact that a workman had fallen from a tree, that an aged pauper had been found dead in bed, that the Harvard Shooting Club was about to hold a meet, but not the fact that "Harvard Beer," known to every consumer of malt liquors in Massachusetts, was in peril of the law for adulteration. Neither was the fact noted on Monday, April 10. But on Tuesday, April 11, "Harvard Beer—1,000 pure" appeared in the pages of the "Transcript"—as a half-page advertisement!

Every newspaper editor feels this pressure—even though he feels it only in his imagination. A horse that travels in harness does so, not because he likes to travel, but because he carries in his subconsciousness the memory of the whip and the bit which "broke" him in the days of his wild youth. And if, by any chance, he forgets this whip and bit, he is quickly reminded. William Winter, a dramatic critic who had served the "New York Tribune" for forty-four years, was forced to resign because his reviews of plays injured the advertising business of the "Tribune." Certain managers were making money out of producing indecent plays; Mr. Winter rebuked these plays, the advertisers protested to the "Tribune," and the managing editor of the "Tribune" censored Mr. Winter's reviews. During the controversy, Mr. Winter wrote to the managing editor that he had desired to injure the business of the producers of indecent plays; to which the managing editor replied: "My instructions with regard to that page are that the articles are not to be framed with any such purpose."

The same thing happened to Walter Pritchard Eaton, dramatic critic of the "New York Sun." I learned of it just as my book was going to press, and wired Mr. Eaton for the facts. Here is his answer:

> Syndicate withdrew ads from "Sun" after my review of Soul Kiss, demanding my discharge. Six months later I was fired, no cause given. Next Sunday all ads back in paper. No actual proof but conclusion pretty plain.

Everywhere in the world of Journalism, high and low, you see this power of the advertiser. I live in the beautiful millionaire city of Pasadena, and every afternoon I get my news of the world from a local paper, which is in some ways among the best. It publishes no scare headlines, and practically no scandal; but in its attitude toward its big commercial advertisers, the attitude of this newspaper is abject. There is a page of moving-picture advertisements, and side by side are columns of "write-ups" of these plays. Nine out of ten of these plays are unspeakable trash, but from the notices you would think that a new era of art was dawning upon Pasadena. All this is "dope," sent out by the moving-picture exploiters; such a thing as an independent and educative review of a moving-picture is not conceivable in my local newspaper. And it is the same with "write-ups" of bargain-sales, and new openings of department-stores. It is the same with the chain of leisure-class hotels; the man who manages and finances these hotels is a local god, and everything he does and says takes the top of the column.

This system of publicity in return for advertising is a fundamentally dishonest one, but it is inseparable from the business of publishing news for profit, and the legitimate and the illegitimate shade into one another so gradually that it would be hard for an honest editor to know where to draw the line. The rule will differ with every newspaper; it may differ with every editor and every mood of every editor. I have made a little study of it with my local newspaper, and had some amusing experiences. Belonging to the Socialist local in Pasadena, I several times had occasion to solicit publicity for Socialist meetings. Being a naturally polite person, I did not go to the editor and say, "I'll buy ten dollars worth of advertising space, if you'll publish a quarter of a column of news about my radical venture." What I did was to insert the advertisement, and then send to the editor the matter I wanted published, and it was published. So I thought this was a regular rule; but some time later, when the labor-men of Pasadena started a co-operative store, and I became vice-president of the enterprise, I inserted an advertisement of the store, and again presented my "copy" to the newspaper, and I did not get so much space. The advertising manager of the newspaper explained to the manager of the store that his paper could not boost a co-operative store, because the local merchants which supplied the bulk of its advertising were hostile to such an enterprise!

At the last election the people of California had to decide upon a social insurance measure, and a friend of mine wrote an article in favor of this measure, and could not get it published. I suggested that she publish it as an advertisement, but the "Pasadena Star-News" refused it, even in that form, and explained to me the reason—that the lady had referred to Christian Science as "a foolish belief"! The partisans of Christian Science are accustomed to rent a page in this paper every now and then, and to have their foolishness published without question.

A still stranger experience befell a gentleman in Boston, Sinclair Kennedy by name. In April, 1918, Mr. Kennedy learned that his state was falling far behind in the purchase of war savings and thrift stamps, and by way of helping his government in its thrift campaign, he prepared an advertisement consisting of three quotations, the first from a speech by President Wilson, the second from a speech by the Secretary of the Treasury, and the third from a speech by the Chairman of the National War Savings Committee: all three of the quotations urging that people should purchase only necessities, so that the energies of the country might go to war-production. The "Boston Herald and Journal" contracted to publish this advertisement in four issues; it published it in two issues, and then refused to publish it again, and paid to Mr. Kennedy the sum of five hundred dollars damages for breach of contract. The "Boston Post" refused to publish the advertisement at all, its manager giving the reason that it was "contrary to public policy"! I have read of many Socialists being sent to jail upon a charge of interfering with the government's war activities, but if the manager of the "Boston Post" was sent to jail, the other newspapers did not report it!

What this amounts to is a censorship of the small and occasional advertisers by the large and permanent ones; this censorship is common, and sometimes it is made to wear the aspect of virtue. The best-paying advertisements are those of automobiles and other leisure-class luxuries; as such advertisers will not publish alongside cheap patent medicine fakes, publications like "Collier's" and the "Outlook" make a boast of censoring their advertisements. But when it comes to protecting their high-priced advertisers, these publications are, as I have shown, every bit as unscrupulous as the sellers of cancer-cures and headache-powders. I, who wish to attack these high-priced advertisers, am forced to publish what I have to say in a paper which can only exist by publishing the advertisements of cancer-cures and headache-powders. This is very humiliating, but what can I do? Stop writing? If I could have my way, of course, I would write for a publication having a large circulation and publishing honest reading matter and honest advertising matter. But no such publication exists; and I have to decide the question, which does the least harm, a publication with honest advertising matter and dishonest reading matter, or a publication with honest reading matter and dishonest advertising matter.

Also, of course, there will be censorship of advertisements containing news. If the newspaper is suppressing certain facts, it will not permit you to make known these facts, even for money. The "Los Angeles Times," although it bitterly opposed single tax, was willing to take my money for an advertisement in favor of single tax; but the "Times" would not take my money for an advertisement reporting a meeting at which the truth about Russia was told. The "Times" would not sell me space to make known that the Socialists of the city had challenged the Superintendent of Schools to debate the truth of certain false statements which he had made about Russia.

In Louisville is the "People's Church," conducted by an independent clergyman in a theatre, and attended by one or two thousand people every Sunday. The "Louisville Courier-

Journal" and its evening edition, the "Times," have not contented themselves with suppressing all news about these meetings for several years; they have also refused all advertisements of this "People's Church." (Since this was written they have put the "People's Church" out of business!)

Some fifteen years ago the most important news being put before the American people was in the form of paid advertisements signed by Thomas W. Lawson. The "New York Times" refused to publish these advertisements, and tens of thousands of New Yorkers, myself among them, were obliged to buy other newspapers in consequence. It cost the "Times" large sums of money to refuse these Lawson broad-sides, but the "Times" made a virtue of it, because the broad-sides threatened the entire profit system, without which the "Times" could not exist. In the same way the newspapers of Baltimore and Boston refused advertisements of a magazine run by Thomas E. Watson in Georgia, on the ground that he was publishing in his magazine articles attacking foreign missions. If you do not believe that interests like this exercise pressure upon newspapers, just try to publish in any capitalist newspaper an advertisement of a book or pamphlet attacking the Roman Catholic Church!

Here in Los Angeles I know a man who set himself up in business as a land-appraiser, and interfered with the leading industry of our community, which is selling real estate to "come ons" from the East. He advised one client that some land in Imperial Valley was worthless, because it contained nearly three per cent of alkali; and this judgment was later vindicated by a report of the U. S. Bureau of Soils, which I have read. But it happened that this land lay perilously near to the tracts of a great land company, in which the heads of Los Angeles newspapers are interested. The three leading newspapers of Los Angeles broke their contracts with this land-appraiser, threw out his "copy" and ruined his business, and now he is working as a cowboy in the "movies." And if you think that the power of the real estate sharks is confined to the places where they prey, consider the experience of Rob Wagner, who wrote two articles about the Southern California land-sharks for the "Saturday Evening Post." The first article, being full of fun, a farce-comedy, was accepted and paid for at once; the second, giving the real story, and being full of meat, was turned down.

CHAPTER XLIV

THE ADVERTISING BOYCOTT

If the newspaper fails to protect its big advertisers, the big advertisers will get busy and protect themselves. This happens every now and then, and every newspaper editor has seen it happen. Sometimes an editor gets sick of the game and quits, and then we have a story. For example, William L. Chenery, who was editor of the "Rocky Mountain News" during the Colorado coal-strike, tells me that "the business men of Denver attempted both an advertising and a social boycott in order to prevent the publication of strike news. . . . . I was told that the owner of the paper would not be admitted to the Denver Country Club so long as our editorials seemed to support the cause of the strikers."

Or take the case of Boston. George French, managing editor of a Boston paper, told how his paper lost four hundred dollars on account of one item which the "interests" had forbidden. Says Mr. French, "That led to a little personal conversation, and to my retiring from the paper." He goes on to state:

You cannot get anything into the newspapers that in any way rubs up against the business policy of the banks and department stores, or of the public service corporations. Those three great departments of business are welded together with bands ever so much stronger than steel, and you cannot make any impression on them. News of department stores that is discreditable, or in any way attracts unfavorable attention, is all squelched, all kept out of the papers.

I have told how Otis of Los Angeles ran the "Times" as a Republican paper and an "open-shop" paper, and at the same time ran secretly the "Herald," a Democratic paper and a "closed-shop" paper. Here is a glimpse of the "Herald" office, as narrated by Frank E. Wolfe, former managing editor of the paper.

The Merchants' and Manufacturers' Association took up the proposition of an aviation meet at Domingues Field. This was managed by the walking delegate of the Merchants' and Manufacturers' Association. The manager gave out the concessions. I went to Domingues Field personally after the meet had been running a few days and found conditions so abhorrent there that I came back and personally wrote a story about fourteen or sixteen "blind pigs" running. . . . .

Immediate reprisals came through the M. and M.—which controls all the advertising placed in the newspapers of the city—by way of taking out of the "Herald" the advertising of a certain department-store—the manager or proprietor of this store being one of the chief moguls of the aviation field. They took their ad out, and the business-manager of the "Herald" came storming in to see me, as they always do in cases of this sort, to see who wrote the story. And when I told him I wrote it myself from facts I had, he wanted me to print an apology. That I have not yet done.

There is a law against workingmen getting together and enforcing a boycott; the Danbury hatters tried it, and the courts fined them several hundred thousand dollars, and took away their homes and turned them out onto the street. But if big advertisers choose to get together and boycott a magazine, the law of course would not dream of being impolite. At the very time that this Danbury hatters case was in the courts, the late C. W. Post was explaining in "Leslie's," our barber-shop weekly, how he broke the newspapers and magazines to his will.

A friend of mine once had the honor of meeting Mr. Post and standing in his private vault and being permitted to handle a package containing four million dollars worth of government bonds. All this had been made out of advertisements, which had persuaded the public to buy package cereals, of precisely the same food-value as bread, at a price several times as high as bread. On January 23rd, 1913, Mr. Post published in "Leslie's" an article, urging business men to organize and refuse to give advertisements to "muck-raking" publications; and "Leslie's" contributed an illuminating cartoon, "The Fool Who Feeds the Monster!" On April 10th Mr. Post contributed another article, describing his methods. He had his clerks go over all publications, listing objectionable matter, and he sent a form letter to offending publications, threatening to withdraw his valuable advertising unless they promised to be "good" in the future.

Mr. Post told what he was doing. There were others who preferred to work in the dark. Perhaps the most significant case was that of "Collier's Weekly" and the Ballinger "land fraud" scandals. Norman Hapgood and Robert Collier broke the Taft administration on that issue, and President Taft, a

venomous old man when he was crossed, issued a furious
denunciation of "Collier's": whereupon the National Association of Manufacturers, the most powerful organization in the
country, took the field against "muck-raking" magazines.
They not only applied the advertising boycott to "Collier's,"
they set the banks to work, as in the case of "Hampton's," and
they took away control of the magazine from Robert Collier,
and put it into the hands of a banking committee, where it
stayed. "Robbie" took to flying aeroplanes, and a year or two
ago he died, and "Collier's" published a full-page obituary of
him, telling the many services he had performed for the
public—except the one really important service, that he had
broken the Taft administration over the Ballinger "land fraud"
issue! Imagine a magazine, that, on the death of its owner,
does not dare to mention the greatest event of its owner's life!

I had an opportunity to watch, from the inside, the operation of this advertising boycott, in the case of my article, the
"Condemned Meat Industry." Many pages of advertising
were withdrawn from "Everybody's Magazine"—not merely
advertisements of hams and lard, but of fertilizers, soaps and
railways. Lawson several times tried to publish the names of
these boycotting advertisers, but "Everybody's" would not let
him. "Everybody's" possibly reflected that it might not keep
up this muck-raking business always; when it had secured
enough readers, it might let down and become respectable, and
then all the big advertisers would come back to it—as they
have done!

The few men who really did mean business knew that the
advertisers would never come back to them, so they fought
the fight through to a finish—their own finish. So it was with
"Hampton's," so it was with "Pearson's" under the old régime.
"Pearson's" tried publishing on the cheapest news-print paper
and with no advertisements, and for two or three years "Pearson's" was the only popular magazine in America from which
you could get the truth. It was the only one which dared to
fight the Railroad Trust and the Beef Trust, the only one
which dared tell the truth about the Associated Press, and
about Capitalist Journalism in general.

Early in 1914 it published a series of articles by Charles
Edward Russell: "Keeping the Kept Press," "The Magazine
Soft-Pedal," and "How Business Controls the News." Russell
told the story of the "Boston Traveller," which was bought by

a young reformer, and put under the control of a real news-paper-man, Marlin E. Pew. The young reformer died, and the Shoe Machinery Trust bought the paper and ordered Pew to be good. He refused, and stood on the contract which he had with the paper. He had a story affecting a big financial house. Threats were made, the business manager was con-fronted with ruin, the paper was tied up, and Pew was forced to sell his contract for cash. I write this story, and the name of the paper sounds familiar to me. I search my memory. Oh, yes! It was the "Boston Traveller," which, a couple of years ago, published a report to the effect that the authorities of Boston were about to confiscate copies of my magazine, and that copies had been thrown out of the library of Radcliffe College. I wrote to the librarian of Radcliffe College, and she replied that the report was a complete fabrication.

Also Russell told how someone tried to run an independent newspaper in Indianapolis, where the street-railway companies, by various manipulations, had boosted the capitalization of the railways from three million dollars to fifty-seven million dol-lars. The "Indianapolis Sun" exposed the fact that the congestion on these railways was caused by the fact that all the cars were forced to pass in front of certain big department-stores. Then the wage-slaves of the railways started to organize; the "Sun" backed them, and told how the companies had automobiles which threw their lights on the entrance to the hall where the men met, and took the name of every man who entered. Also the "Sun" reported how the railway-com-panies were having the union leaders slugged—and so the "Sun" reporter was slugged! The Merchants' Association got busy, and the "Sun" advertisers were warned of a boycott. A "safety commission" of the Chamber of Commerce was organized, and a meeting was held, at which explicit instruc-tions were given to all newspaper editors. The circulation of the "Sun" had gone up from seventeen thousand to forty thousand, but the advertising was cut off, and so the paper had to quit.

In the same way the "Akron Press" ventured to support a strike against the tire-companies, and was boycotted. The same fate befell the "Cincinnati Post," which ventured to expose a peculiar procedure engineered by a street railway corporation. There was a limitation of twenty-five years upon public franchises, so the state legislature passed a bill, permitting fifty-year franchises. The city council of Cincinnati then passed one fifty-year franchise, after which the legislature repealed the bill permitting fifty-year franchises for anybody else!

In an article in the "Atlantic Monthly" for March, 1910, Prof. Ross explained just how tight the hold of the advertiser upon the newspaper had then become:

> Thirty years ago, advertising yielded less than half of the earnings of the daily newspapers. Today it yields at least two-thirds. In the larger dailies the receipts from advertisers are several times the receipts from the readers, in some cases constituting ninety percent of the total revenues. As the newspaper expands to eight, twelve, and sixteen pages, while the price sinks to three cents, two cents, one cent, the time comes when the advertisers support the newspaper.

And in "Pearson's," Charles Edward Russell gave the figures for the magazines. He shows that at the prices then prevailing (1914), a magazine publishing four hundred thousand copies a month would support a net loss of over sixteen hundred dollars for manufacturing costs alone, not including the cost of illustrations, articles, salaries, rent, etc. All this, plus any profit from the enterprise, must come from the advertising. So largely did magazines depend upon the advertising that some of them were practically given away in order to get circulation. One large magazine was sold wholesale at an average price of three cents, another magazine was paying out a total of five dollars for every one dollar it took in through subscriptions.

And what if the advertising did not come? Why then, of course, the magazine or newspaper went out of business. One case of this sort I happened to see from the inside, as the experience befell one of my intimate friends—Gaylord Wilshire, the first of America's heroic band of "millionaire Socialists." Wilshire came from the West with a couple of hundred thousand dollars, and established a Socialist magazine in New York. He had got the figures from experts; he must have four hundred thousand circulation, and then he would be safe. So he set out to get this circulation. He had a subscription contest, with a trip around the world for a prize. He had another with a grand piano for a prize. He gave away small fortunes; also he published the truth about American public affairs, and he published the most penetrating editorial comment then to be read in America. So he got his four hundred thousand subscribers. But alas, he had reckoned without his advertisers! For some strange reason the packers of hams and bacon, the manufacturers of automobiles and ready-made clothing, of toilet perfumeries and fancy cigarettes, would not pay their money to a Socialist magazine!

POSTSCRIPT TO THE 8TH EDITION:

The following is a copy of a letter sent by the sugar trust to every country paper in the State of Utah, at the time when the sugar trust, in defiance of the law, raised the price of sugar several cents a pound:

UTAH-IDAHO SUGAR CO.
Salt Lake City, Utah, Feb. 25, 1920.

Utah Labor News,
    Salt Lake City, Utah.
Gentlemen:
    Enclosed herewith copy for display advertisement, 3 column, 3 inches deep, to be run in the next issue of your paper, as per contract for eleven weeks advertising service arranged with you by this company. Kindly send me two copies of issue carrying our "ad," and we will be pleased to accept your bill for same.
    Will also advise that this company is now planning to extend its advertising activities, and the medium we will most naturally choose is the paper that is friendly and loyal to the sugar industry, and our own organization in particular. It is our intention to read your paper with a view to learning your editorial and general attitude toward us, and we trust it will prove such as to warrant future business profitable to us both.

Yours truly,
UTAH-IDAHO SUGAR CO.
Per C. Byron Whitney.

The interests which wrote the above letter have recently bought the control of the "Salt Lake Telegram," the only newspaper in Utah which opposed their policies; and they put $100,000 into the old "Herald-Republican" in order to preserve it as a propaganda organ.

P. S. to ninth edition: It seems worth mentioning that many newspapers refused advertisements of "The Brass Check," including the "New York Times."

CHAPTER XLV

THE ADVERTISING ECSTASY

Such was the fate of a magazine which rebelled. As for those which submitted, the answer is writ large on our news-stands. "McClure's," "Collier's," "Everybody's," the "American" have survived, as a woman without virtue, as a man without honor, of whom his friends say that he would better have died. The masters of finance have taken not merely the conscience from them, they have taken the life from them. If there was a man on the editorial staff with red blood in his veins, they turned him out to become a Socialist soap-boxer, and in his place they put a pithed frog. (You know, perhaps, how the scientist takes the spinal cord out of a frog's back and puts in wire?)

Not merely have the money-masters stamped their sign upon the contents of the magazines, they have changed the very form to suit their purposes. Time was when you could take the vast bulk of a magazine, and rip off one fourth from the front and two fourths from the back, and in the remaining fourth you had something to read in a form you could enjoy. But the advertising gentry got on to that practice and stopped it. They demanded what they call "full position," next to reading-matter. One magazine gave way, and then another; until now all popular magazines are cunning traps to bring your mind into subjection to the hawkers of wares. I pick up the current number of the "Literary Digest"; there are a hundred and twenty-eight pages, and the advertising begins on page thirty-five. I pick up the current number of the "Saturday Evening Post"; there are a hundred and fifty-eight pages, and the advertising begins on page twenty-nine. You start an article or a story, and they give you one or two clean pages to lull your suspicions, and then at the bottom you read, "Continued on page 93." You turn to page ninety-three, and biff— you are hit between the eyes by a powerful gentleman wearing a collar, or swat—you are slapped on the cheek by a lady in a union-suit. You stagger down this narrow column, as one who runs the gauntlet of a band of Indians with clubs; and then you read, "Continued on page 99." You turn to page ninety-nine, and somebody throws a handful of cigarettes into your face, or maybe a box of candy; or maybe it is the crack of a revolver, or the honk of an automobile-horn that greets you. The theme of the reading-matter may be the importance of war-savings, but before you get to the end of the article you have been tempted by every luxury from a diamond scarf-pin to a private yacht, and have spent in imagination more money than you will earn in the balance of your life-time.

The culmination of this process may be studied in the supreme product of Capitalist Journalism, the "Curtis Publications"; the peerless trilogy of the "Saturday Evening Post," the "Ladies' Home Journal," and the "Country Gentleman." How many boys in college are making fortunes in their spare time, selling this trilogy to all America? I don't know, but if you write to the circulation department in Philadelphia, they will tell you, and perhaps let you join the opulent band. One hundred and thirty times every year these Curtis people prepare for their millions of victims a fat bulk of "high-class"—that is to say, high-paying—advertising. As street-urchins gather to scramble for pennies, so gather here all the profit-seekers of the country to compete for your attention; they wheedle and cajole and implore, they shriek and scream, they dance and gesticulate and turn somersaults. I say "they" do it; in reality, of course, they hire others to do it; they take the brains and vitality and eagerness of our youth—they waste in a single week enough writing talent and drawing talent to create an American literature and an American art.

The stake is a colossal one. Writing ten years ago, Hamilton Holt showed that American business was spending a hundred and forty-five million dollars a year for advertisements in periodicals. Also he stated that one Chicago department-store had spent half a million in advertising to sell fifteen million in goods. At this rate of thirty to one, the public was being persuaded, by means of advertising, to purchase four and a half billion dollars worth of goods. Allowing for the increase in extravagance and in prices today, the expenditure cannot be less than ten or twenty billions. Such is the prize to be scrambled for; and when you realize it, you no longer wonder at the raptures to which our advertisement-writers are impelled, the exhibitions of language-slinging to which they treat us.

What is your literary taste? Are you poetical? Does your temperament run to the flowery and ecstatic? If so, you will be "landed" by the full-page advertisement which I find in my evening newspaper, displaying a spreading peacock and half a dozen peacock-ladies in a whirl of ruffles and frills. "THE RAINBOW OF FASHIONS," runs the heading, and continues in this fine, careful rapture:

Other than this the impression is inadequate, that glimpse beheld of this Fashion Salon, this inimitable Third Floor of Goldstein's.

What but the Rainbow with its inexpressible sunburst of color could be the source—the inspiration from which Fashion has modeled these veritable Exquisites—these beautiful new Frocks and Suits and Coats, these Skirts and Capes—these Blouses and Hats for Milady's luxury?

Truly the Genii of Fashionery are leading us into glory Fields of Beauty never before attained, although it seemed for a time that Artists of Vogue had decided to paint indefinitely upon that picture of yesterday, with an occasional new tint perhaps to relieve somewhat the monotonous restrictions both in style and in fabric.

But now—today—at Goldstein's—the picture is a new one—startling and irresistible—to be elaborated upon each day—for it is each day that new thoughts are added as new Express Packages are opened from Fashiondom.

Come, take a pencil peek with me—and ONLY as a pencil sees them—not at all as they are—or as you may see them if you come where these "Pretties" are all assembled—where fashions are wont to congregate at Goldstein's.

Or does your taste run to humor? Are you bluff and hearty, a real fellow and a good sport? Then maybe your purse-strings will be loosened by the full-page advertisement which appears in all the magazines for August, 1919, portraying a stout and sensual gentleman with a pipe in his mouth and a wink in both eyes. Cries this gentleman:

SCRUB UP YOUR SMOKEDECKS AND CUT FOR A NEW PIPE DEAL! Say, you'll have a streak of smokeluck that'll put pep-in-YOUR smokemotor, all right, if you'll ring-in with a jimmy pipe or the papers and nail some "Devil's-dung" for packing!

Just between ourselves, you never will wise-up to high-spot-smoke-joy until you can call a pipe or a home-rolled cigarette by its first name, THEN, to hit the peak-of-pleasure you land square on that two-fisted-man-tobacco, "Devil's-dung!"

Well, sir, you'll be so all-fired happy you'll want to get a photograph of yourself breezing up the pike with your smokethrottle wide open! TALK ABOUT SMOKE-SPORT!

And now, stop and consider what proportion of the total energies of the community are devoted to the production of poisonous filth such as this. I do not count the people who read and answer the advertisements; I count only those who write them and sell them, those who set the type and manufacture the paper, those who distribute the publications and keep the accounts of the complicated operations. There cannot be less than a million people thus occupied with the advertising business in America; and all of them buried to the eyes in this poisonous filth, all compelled to absorb it, to believe it, to have their personalities befouled by it! It means, of course, that these people are permanently excluded from the intellectual life. These people cannot know beauty, they cannot know grace and charm, they cannot know dignity, they cannot even know common honesty. To say that they are bound as captives to the chariot-wheels of Mammon is not to indulge in loose metaphor, but to describe precisely their condition. They are bound in body, mind, and soul to vulgarity, banality, avarice and fraud.

You, perhaps, are not connected with the advertising business, so you think you may ignore the fate of these pitiful captives. You are a banker, perhaps; you handle the money of advertisers, and your mind is shaped by the effort to understand them and their ways. Or you are a telegrapher, and send telegrams for the advertising business; or you are a farmer, and raise food for the million advertisement-makers; or you are a steel-worker, and help to make their typewriters, the nails for their shoes, and the rails over which their products are carried.

Or perhaps you are a person of leisure; you dwell alone in an ivory tower of art. Now and then, however, you have to know something about the world in which you live; and competitive commercialism ordains that when you seek to learn this, you shall have the maniac shrieks of advertisers resounding in your brain, you shall have the whirling dervishes of this new cult of Publicity for Profit cavorting about in your ivory tower. More than that, you shall have the intellectual content of everything you read distorted by the advertisements which adjoin them; your most dignified editor, your most aloof, "art for art's sake" poet will be a parasite upon advertisements, and if he thinks the advertisements have nothing to do with him, it is only because the dignified editor and the aloof, "art for art's sake" poet are fools.

Take the "American Magazine"; that awful flub-dub I

quoted earlier in the book. What can it mean, save that the "American Magazine" had to have advertisements, and to get the advertisements it had to please the sort of people who read advertisements? Or take the "Curtis Publications"; what is the obvious fact about this colossal advertisement-distributing machine? The owner of this machine, needless to say, is not in the business of distributing advertisements for his health. On the contrary, he has lost his health and made eleven million dollars. His price for advertisements is six thousand dollars per page. To carry these advertisements, he must have reading matter, and to select this reading matter he employs a group of men and women called "editors." These "editors" are, of course, in position to offer prices such as thrill the soul of every hungry author, and cause him to set diligently to work to study the personalities of the "editors," so as to know what they want. If he doesn't find out what they want, he doesn't write for the publications—that is obvious enough. On the other hand, if he *does* find out what they want, he becomes a new star in America's literary firmament—and at the cost of pretty nearly all his ideals of truth, humanity and progress.

Take up the "Saturday Evening Post." Here is Harry Leon Wilson, who used to show signs of brains, telling a story of how a labor union tried to take control of a factory. He exhausts his imagination to make this proposition ridiculous, to pour contempt over these fool workingmen. And here is a short story writer named Patullo, solemnly setting forth that Socialism means dividing up! And here is George Kibbe Turner, who I used to think was one of America's coming novelists, with a short story, which turns out not to be a short story at all, but a piece of preaching upon the following grave and weighty theme: that the trouble with America is that everybody is spending too much money; that the railroad brotherhoods are proposing to turn robbers and take away the property of their masters; and that a workingman who is so foolish as to buy a piano for his daughter will discover that he has ruined himself to no purpose, because workingmen's daughters ought not to have pianos—they are too tired to play them when they get through with their work!

CHAPTER XLVI

THE BRIBE DIRECT

We are accustomed to the idea that in Europe there exists a "reptile press," meaning a press whose opinions are for sale, not merely to politicians and governments, but to promoters and financiers; we read of the "Bourse press" of Paris, and understand that these papers accept definite cash sums for publishing in their columns news favorable to great speculations and industrial enterprises. I have heard America congratulated that it had no such newspapers; I myself was once sufficiently naïve so to congratulate America!

Naturally, it is not so easy to prove direct bribery of the press. When the promoter of an oil "deal" or of a franchise "grab" wishes to buy the support of a newspaper, he does not invite the publisher onto the sidewalk and there count a few thousand dollar bills into his hands. But as a person who steals once will go on stealing, so a newspaper proprietor who takes bribes becomes a scandal to his staff, and sooner or later bits of the truth leak out. America has been fortunate in the possession of one bold and truth-telling newspaper editor, Fremont Older; and when you read his book, "My Own Story," you discover that we have a "reptile press" in America, a press that is for sale for cash.

The chances are that you never heard of Fremont Older's book. It was published over a year ago, but with the exception of a few radical papers, American Journalism maintained about it the same silence it will maintain about "The Brass Check." For twenty-five years Older was managing editor of a great newspaper, and now, in the interest of public welfare, he has told what went on inside that newspaper office. Older began as a plain, every-day hireling of privilege, but little by little his mind and his conscience awakened, he took his stand for righteousness in his city, and fought the enemies of righteousness, not merely at peril of his job, but at peril of his life. The first time I met Older, ten years ago, he had just been kidnapped by thugs and carried away in an automobile and locked under armed guard in a compartment of a sleeping-car, to be carried into Southern California, where the "S. P." controlled everything, and could "put him away." He told me the story, and to this day I remember my consternation. Two or three years later I happened to tell it in England, to a group of members of parliament; they were Englishmen, and were too polite to say what they thought, but I knew what they thought. It was hopeless to tell that story to Englishmen; such things did not happen—except in "movies"!

The story of the "San Francisco Bulletin," as Fremont Older tells it, is a story of corruption, systematic and continuous. The "Bulletin" was controlled in all four of the ways I have described; not merely by the owner, by the owners of the owner, and by the advertising subsidy, but by the bribe direct. The owner of the "Bulletin" was a man named Crothers, and he had an itching palm. It was itching at the beginning of the story, when it was empty, and it was still itching at the end of the story, when it was full. Says Fremont Older:

> In addition to this, the "Bulletin" was on the payroll of the Southern Pacific Railroad for $125 a month. This was paid not for any definite service, but merely for "friendliness." Being always close to the line of profit and loss, it was felt the paper could not afford to forfeit this income.

These were in the early days, you understand, when Older was playing the dirty game for his owner. He tells us, quite frankly, how he did it. For example, here is a picture of a great newspaper in politics:

> I hoped to convince Charley Fay, Phelan's manager, to accept the same plan in Phelan's fight that I used in the McKinley campaign; that is to get Phelan to buy a certain number of extra "Bulletin" editions. I suggested the idea to Fay that if I could be allowed several 10,000 editions of the "Bulletin" in addition to our regular circulation, for which we would charge $500, I thought I could hold the paper in line throughout the campaign.

But this was not enough for the itching palm, it appears:

> He (Crothers) felt that the "Bulletin's" support was worth more than an occasional $500. His pressure upon me for more money finally became so strong that I called on Charley Fay and told him that I would have to get out another extra edition to the number agreed upon between us.

And then, a year or two later:

The fight had barely started when Crothers came to me and said
that W. H. Mills, who handled the newspapers of California for
the railroad company, had agreed to raise the "Bulletin's" pay from
$125 to $250 a month if we would make only a weak support of the
new charter.

And again:

Crothers felt that the influence of the "Bulletin" was worth more
than the Southern Pacific had been paying. He insisted that I go to
Mills and demand $25,000 from the railroad for supporting Gage. I
told him that this was ridiculous, that they wouldn't consider such a
sum for a minute. He insisted that he would have $25,000 or he
wouldn't support Gage, and demanded that I tell Mills that.

In these campaigns the "Bulletin" had been supporting the
Democratic candidate; but it was supposed to be a Republican
paper, and in the next campaign the owner decided that unless
the Democrats paid him more money, he would become really
and truly "Republican." So Older went on the hunt once more.

Poniatowski said: "I will do all I can, but the best I can do personally is $500 a month for three months through the campaign. I
will put up the $1500 out of my own pocket."
    I did not dare to go to anyone else, and I hoped, but faintly, that
this would be enough. I went to Crothers with the information that
I had got $1500 to support Tobin, and he said, "It isn't enough."
    I was in despair. Only one other ruse remained by which I might
hold him. I asked former Mayor E. B. Pond, banker and millionaire; James D. Phelan, mayor and millionaire, and Franklin K. Lane,
then a rising power in California, to call on Crothers and see if they
could not prevail on him to stand by Tobin. Always greatly impressed
by wealth, I felt that their prominence and financial standing might
hold him. They called, and did their best, but made no impression.
    A few days later the railroad paid Crothers $7500. It was paid
to him by a man not openly connected with the railroad. I learned of
it almost instantly. The report was confirmed by Crothers ordering
me to support Wells.

And now Fremont Older has been forced out of the
"Bulletin," and the paper has become rancid in the cause of
reaction, and carries at the top of its editorial page this proud
slogan: "R. A. Crothers, Editor and Proprietor."
    And do you think that the owner of the "Bulletin" was
alone among San Francisco newspaper owners in the possession of an itching palm? The "San Francisco Liberator,"
organ of the reformers, showed how, in the effort to keep the
president of "United Railroads" out of jail, every crime up to
murder had been committed. Armed mobs had been organized

to resist the city's authority; thieves had been hired and safes broken open, juries had been bribed and witnesses spirited away; last, but not least, public sentiment had been corrupted through the press. The "Liberator" gives names and dates, a whole mass of detail, which would fill a chapter of this book. One example, well authenticated: One little local paper had been purchased for seventy-five dollars, and in a period of thirteen weeks had obtained thirty-two hundred and fifty dollars from the publicity-bureau of "United Railroads"!

And as I write there comes to me a letter from an editor of one of San Francisco's largest newspapers, a man who knows the game from A to Z. He tells me the sordid history of "Mike" de Young's "San Francisco Chronicle":

> The owner's brother was murdered not many years ago, because of a blackmail story run in the paper. During the war it was he who got the San Francisco Publishers' Association to charge the government full advertising rates for all war loan organizations, etc. He was a strong ally of the Southern Pacific when that road ran California, and still fights for the railroads whenever he gets a chance.

I write to others in San Francisco, to be sure that I am making no mistake. One sends me a letter by Arthur McEwen, a well-known journalist, made public twenty-five years ago. Mr. de Young, says McEwen, has a grammar of his own; he speaks of being "attackted," and he made famous the phrase, "the tout ensemble of the whole." He is a multi-millionaire, but for years had refused to pay fifteen dollars a month to keep his insane brother out of the paupers' ward of the asylum. He plunders the big corporations mercilessly, "having never been able to see why he should not share in their prosperity." Says McEwen:

> He set up in court the contention that it is legitimate for a newspaper to sell its editorial columns, and though he was reviled by his startled contemporaries for that dangerous frankness, there is no reason to doubt that he was sincere or unaffectedly astonished at the notion of there being aught disgraceful in his admission. . . . . Not until the archives of the Crocker family have been opened to the historian will it be known whether or not the common report be true which affirms that "the title deeds to his California street mansion are the intercepted love letters of a millionaire."

Another friend sends me a poem by Ambrose Bierce, entitled "A Lifted Finger." It is one of the most withering denunciations of a human being ever penned. As a sample I

quote the last stanza, in which the victim is forbidden to kill
himself:

> Pregnant with possibilities of crime,
> And full of felons for all coming time,
> Your blood's too precious to be lightly spilt
> In testimony to a venial guilt.
> Live to get whelpage and preserve a name
> No praise can sweeten and no lie unshame.
> Live to fulfill the vision that I see
> Down the dim vistas of the time to be:
> A dream of clattering beaks and burning eyes
> Of hungry ravens glooming all the skies;
> A dream of gleaming teeth and fetid breath
> Of jackals wrangling at the feast of death;
> A dream of broken necks and swollen tongues—
> The whole world's gibbets loaded with de Youngs!

Let us go to Denver, where there lives another fighter and
teller of truth, Ben Lindsey. I have made you acquainted
with the "Denver Post," and with one of its owners, Mr. F. G.
Bonfils, who made his "pile" as a lottery-promoter, and went
into partnership with another man. Now let Judge Lindsey
introduce us to this other man:

The "Post" was then as independent as a highwayman. One of its
proprietors, H. H. Tammen, had begun life as a bar-keeper, and he
would himself relate how he had made money by robbing his employer.
"When I took in a dollar," Tammen said, "I tossed it up—and if it
stuck to the ceiling, it went to the boss." He had a frank way of
making his vices engaging by the honesty with which he confessed
them; and he had boasted to me of the amount of money the newspaper made by charging its victims for suppressing news-stories of a
scandalous nature in which they were involved. He admitted that he
supported me merely because it was "the popular thing to do"—it
"helped circulation." I knew it was a very precarious support, although
the editorial writer, Paul Thieman, seemed to me an honest and public-
spirited young man.

Or come to Kansas City, where William Salisbury is working on the "Times." There is a fight on with the gas companies, which have formed a trust and doubled the price of
gas. A solitary alderman named Smith has spoken against
the ordinance.

When I returned to the "Times" office that night the city editor
came up to my desk, sat down, and said, confidentially: "We'll have
to print a favorable story on this consolidation. I wouldn't give much
space to that man Smith's remarks. I don't know what the gas people

have done here in this office, but you can guess. They've bought the Council."

Mr. Salisbury, you see, is only a reporter, so all he gets is gossip and suspicion. He notes that the Kansas City, Pittsburg & Gulf Railway is completing a line to Port Arthur, Texas; the railway company is advertising heavily in the "Times," and he is sent to write up "a two-column interview upon the beauties of Port Arthur." Again, he tells us:

> I could write columns about Cuban revolutions, and anti-cigarette and anti-high hat laws. But there were things that I couldn't write about at all, and other things that I had to write as the city editor told me, and as the owner or managing editor told him to tell me. These included street railway and paving and gas and telephone and other corporation measures, and anti-department store bills. And the City Hall reporters of the three other newspapers wrote of such things just as I did—from dictation.

Again, in Kansas City are great packing-houses, and the people of Kansas City think they should have cheaper meat. The newspapers take up the campaign, and Mr. Salisbury tells what comes of it:

> I did some detective work. At the end of several days I found that all the packing-houses were represented at a meeting each week in the Armour Building, at Fifth and Delaware Streets. I gave a negro porter five dollars to show me the room. It was his business to bring the packers wine and cigars during the sessions at which they fixed the prices of food for millions of people. He pointed out the chairs in which each of them sat. He told me their names. He was willing to arrange for me to listen in the next room when the meeting was held again.
> I returned to the "Times" office in a fever of excitement. I told what I knew. The managing editor consulted with the business manager. Then he came to me and said: "We won't print any more meat trust stories for a while."
> Several days later I saw packing-house advertisements in all the newspapers. But none of the papers published any more news about the price of meat for a very long time.

I quote this story, and then I realize that I have got out of my classification; this isn't a bribe, this is an advertisement! I can only plead that it is hard to keep to a classification, because those who are corrupting the press do not keep to it. They use various methods; and sometimes the methods shade into one another, so that only a legal expert could sort them out!

20

When is a bribe not a bribe? When it is an order for extra copies? When it is a share in a land deal? When it is a nomination for senator? When it is an advertising contract? For example, is this a bribe? Arthur Brisbane, the most highly paid and most widely read editorial writer in America, serves announcement to the public that he is going to follow with regard to the drama a policy of "constructive criticism"; he is going to tell the people about the plays that are really worth seeing, so that the people may go to see them. He writes a double-column editorial, praising a play, and two or three days later there appears in the "Evening Journal" a full-page advertisement of this play. Brisbane writes another editorial, praising another play, and a few days later there appears a full-page advertisement of this play. This happens again and again, and all play-producers on Broadway understand that by paying one thousand dollars for a full-page advertisement in the "New York Evening Journal," they may have a double-column of the "constructive criticism" of Arthur Brisbane!

Or is this a bribe? There is a fight for lower gas-rates in Boston, and Louis Brandeis, now a Justice of the Supreme Court, makes a plea in the interest of the public. One Boston newspaper gives half a column of Brandeis' arguments; no other Boston newspaper gives one word of Brandeis' arguments; but every Boston newspaper prints a page of the gas company's advertisements, paid for at one dollar per line!

If you will count these things as bribery, you are no longer at a loss for evidence. You discover that great systems of corruption of the press have been established; the bribing of American Journalism has become a large-scale business enterprise, which has been fully revealed by government investigations, and proven by the sworn testimony of those who do the work.

CHAPTER XLVII

THE BRIBE WHOLESALE

Every now and then some pillar of Capitalism is over-thrown, and a mess of journalistic worms go wriggling to cover. For example, the "New Haven" scandal: Some five years ago the Interstate Commerce Commission revealed the fact that the band of pirates who had wrecked the great "New Haven" system had been paying four hundred thousand dollars a year to influence the press; and more significant yet, the president of the railroad swore that this was "relatively less than was paid by any other large railroad in the country!" The "New Haven" had a list of reporters to whom it paid subsidies, sometimes two hundred dollars in a lump, sometimes twenty-five dollars a week. It was paying three thousand dollars a year to the "Boston Republic." "Why?" was the question, and the answer was, "That is Mayor Fitzgerald's paper." The agent of the road who had handled this money stated that "All the newspapers and magazines knew what it was for." He had paid money to over a thousand papers, among them the "Boston Evening Transcript," for sending out railroad "dope." This "New Haven," you understand, was the road which wrecked "Hampton's" for refusing to be bought. It was a "Morgan" road.

It was the same way with the Mulhall revelations, brought out by a committee of the United States Senate. Here was the "National Association of Manufacturers" and the "Merchant Marine League," spending enormous subsidies for propaganda with newspapers. When the La Follette Seamen's Law was being fought in the Senate, it was shown that the great newspapers were distributing every year two million dollars for shipping advertisements, and they claimed and got their return in the form of bitter opposition to this bill. During the Life Insurance investigations in New York, it was shown that every one of these great financial enterprises maintained not merely an advertising bureau, but a "literary bureau." The Mutual Life Insurance Company had employed a certain "Telegraphic News Bureau," which supplied newspapers with propaganda which they published as reading matter. For one item, supplied to about one hundred different papers, the agent had been paid over five thousand dollars. What the newspapers were paid was not brought out, but the agent testified that he had been paid one dollar a line, while the papers had been paid as high as five dollars a line. Also there was another agency, through which the Mutual Life was sending out what it called "telegraphic readers." The big newspapers had special advertising agents to solicit this kind of paid material, and they had regular printed schedules of rates for publishing it.

In the same way Attorney-General Monnett of Ohio brought out that the Standard Oil Company maintained the "Jennings Advertising Agency" to distribute and pay for propaganda upon this contract:

> The publisher agrees to reprint on news or editorial pages of said newspaper such notices, set in the body type of said paper and bearing no mark to indicate advertising, as are furnished from time to time by said Jennings Agency at the rate of —— per line, and to furnish such agency extra copies of paper containing such notes at four cents per copy.

In the same way the Standard Oil Company was shown to have paid from five hundred to a thousand dollars for the publication of a single article in Kansas newspapers. The Standard Oil had a subsidized press of its own—for example, the "Oil City Derrick"—and it had subsidized "Gunton's Magazine" to the extent of twenty-five thousand dollars a year.

In the same way it was brought out by Governor Hunt of Arizona, during the recent great copper strike, that the mine-owners had been bribing the local newspapers in Greenlee County for printing "plate-matter" favorable to them. It was shown that the liquor lobby had maintained an enormous "slush" fund for the press. It was shown that the great public utility interests of the Middle West had maintained a publicity bureau to send out material against municipal ownership. It was shown that the high tariff interests had been maintaining a Washington bureau and sending out "news letters," all paid for. It was shown that the railroad companies were doing the same thing; in a single office of their publicity department—that in Chicago—they had forty-three employes, and the manager stated to Ray Stannard Baker that before this bureau began its work, four hundred and twelve columns of matter

opposed to the railroads had appeared in the newspapers of
Nebraska, but after the bureau had been in operation for three
months, in one week the newspapers of Nebraska had published
two hundred and two columns favorable to the railroads, and
only four columns against them!

And year by year, as the plundering of the people increases,
this "bribe wholesale" becomes a greater menace; to-day, as
I write, it has become a nation-wide propaganda. Testifying
before the Committee on Agriculture and Forestry of the
United States Senate, January 14, 1919, Frank Heney shows
that to defeat the bill for government regulation of the packing industry now before Congress, Swift & Company alone
are spending a million dollars a month upon newspaper advertising! Heney testifies that he has had an examination made
of every newspaper in California, and every one has published
the full-page advertisements of this firm. Senator Norris
testifies that he has had an examination made in New York
State, and has been unable to find a single paper without the
advertisements—which, it is pointed out, are not in any way
calculated to sell the products of Swift & Company, but solely
to defeat government regulation of the industry. Armour &
Company were paying over two thousand dollars a page to all
the farm publications of the country—and this not for advertisements, but for "special articles"! J. Ogden Armour was
put on the stand, and some amusement developed. He had
given a banquet to the editors of these farm-journals; he did
not expect this banquet to have any influence upon the advertising, but he did have a vague hope that both banquet and
advertising might dispose the editors to look with less disfavor
upon the Armour business!

Day by day the money-masters of America become more
aware of their danger, they draw together, they grow more
class-conscious, more aggressive. The war has taught them
the possibilities of propaganda; it has accustomed them to the
idea of enormous campaigns which sway the minds of millions
and make them pliable to any purpose. They have been terrified by what happened in Russia and Hungary, and they
propose to see to it that the foreign population of America is
innoculated against modern ideas. They form the "Publishers'
Association of the American Press in Foreign Languages,"
whose purpose it is "to foster unswerving loyalty to American
ideals"—that is to say, to keep America capitalist. Then a

group of our biggest exploiters, headed by Coleman du Pont of the Powder Trust, buy the "American Association of Foreign Language Newspapers." They give a dinner to the heads of all the newspaper advertising agencies, at the Bankers' Club of New York, and explain that in future all advertising must be placed through this great association. So the massed advertising power of American corporations is to be wielded as a club, to keep the newspaper columns and the editorial columns of foreign language newspapers free from radicalism. So when there is a strike anywhere in the "Powder barony," and Poles and Hungarians are being bayonetted and shot, the powder barons will know that Polish and Hungarian newspapers are printing no news of the shooting, and giving no encouragement to the strike.

I write the above *a priori;* that is to say, I understand American Capitalism so well that I venture to guess what it plans to do with its foreign-language press machine. And six months later, as I am sending this book to the printer, I discover that I have guessed correctly! The great steel-strike is on, and the following appears in an Associated Press dispatch from Youngstown, Ohio:

> Managers of five foreign language newspapers to-day decided to publish special editions of their papers explaining to their countrymen that if they are satisfied with present mill-conditions they should meet and vote on the question of returning to work.

And, on the other hand, if the foreign-language newspapers decide to get along without advertising, and to stand by the workers, what then? Then we denounce them as Bolsheviks, and demand deportation of their editors and publishers; we raid their offices and confiscate their lists and bar them from our mails. If necessary, some of our corrupt interests "frame up" evidence against them, and throw their editors and publishers into jail.

The above may sound to you an extreme statement. But as this book is going to press I come upon definite evidence of precisely such a case, and you will find it in full in the last chapter.

CHAPTER XLVIII

POISON IVY

I have asked the difficult question, When is a bribe not a bribe? When it is "legitimate business"? When, for instance, the "New Haven" is discovered to have ordered 9,716 copies of the "Outlook" containing a boost of the "New Haven" system by Sylvester J. Baxter, a paid writer of the "New Haven"? You may read the details of this in "The Profits of Religion"; the president of the "Outlook" corporation wrote to me that the "New Haven" bought these copies "without any previous understanding or arrangement." They are so naïve in the office of this religious weekly; nobody had the slightest idea that if they boosted some railroad grafters in peril of discovery, these grafters might come back with a big order! And right now, while the railroads are trying to get their properties back, and all their debts paid out of the public treasury, the spending of millions of dollars upon advertising is perfectly legitimate—it does not have the slightest effect upon newspaper editorial policy! When the miners of Colorado go on strike, and the Rockefellers proceed to fill every daily and weekly newspaper in the state of Colorado with full-page broad-sides against the miners, this of course is not a bribe; the fact that on the page opposite there will appear an editorial, reproducing completely the point of view of the advertisements—that is a pure coincidence, and the editorial is the honorable and disinterested opinion of the newspaper editor! When the United States Commission on Industrial Relations exposes the fact that these attacks on the miners contain the most outrageous lies, and that the thousand-dollar-a-month press-agent of the Rockefellers knew they were lies—it is a pure coincidence that very little about this revelation is published in the Colorado newspapers!

This last incident is so important as to deserve fuller exposition. The thousand-dollar-a-month press-agent of the Rockefellers was a gentleman by the name of Ivy L. Lee, and after the strikers had experienced his methods for a while, they referred to him as "Poison Ivy." He took the published annual report of the Secretary-Treasurer of the United Mine Workers, which showed that the national vice-president of the union in charge of the Colorado strike had received a yearly salary of $2,395.72 and a year's expenses of $1,667.20. He put these two figures together, calling it all salary, $4,062.92; and then he added the expenses again, making a total of $5,730.12; and then he said that all this had been paid to the national vice-president for nine weeks' work on the strike—thus showing that he was paid over ninety dollars a day, or at the rate of thirty-two thousand dollars a year!

By the same method, he showed that another official was paid sixty-six dollars a day; that John R. Lawson had received $1,773.40 in nine weeks! Old "Mother" Jones was listed at forty-two dollars a day; the actual fact being that for her work as organizer she was paid $2.57 a day—and this not including the many months which she spent in jail for refusing to leave the strike-district! The "bulletin" containing these figures was published in all the newspapers, and was mailed out over the country to the extent of hundreds of thousands of copies; and when the miners exposed the falsity of the statements, "Poison Ivy" postponed correcting them until the strike was lost, and until he knew that the Walsh Commission was on his trail! Thirty-two separate "bulletins" this scoundrel sent out over the United States, and many of them were full of just such lies as this. If you want details, you may consult two articles by George Creel in "Harper's Weekly," for November 7th and 14th, 1914.

There are thousands of such press agents serving our predatory interests, but not often are we permitted to peer into their inmost souls, to watch them at their secret offices. The Walsh Commission was so cruel as to put "Poison Ivy" on the stand, and also to publish his letters to his master. An examination of these letters shows him performing functions not usually attributed to press-agents. We see him preparing and revising a letter for Governor Ammons to send to President Wilson. (You remember, perhaps, in my story of Governor Ammons, my charge that the coal operators wrote his lying telegram to the President? Maybe you thought that was just loose talk!) We see "Poison Ivy" arranging for the distribution of an enormous edition of a speech on the Colorado coal-strike by the "kept" congressmen of the coal-operators— the speech containing "Polly Pry," with the slanders against

"Mother Jones," sent out under government frank! We see him following the newspapers with minute care; for example, calling Mr. Rockefeller's attention to the fact that the Northampton, Massachusetts, "Herald" had used a part of his first bulletin as an editorial; also sending to Mr. Rockefeller an editorial by Arthur Brisbane, sneering at our "mourning pickets." Finally, this remarkable press-agent claims that he persuaded the Walsh Commission not to come to Colorado till the operators had finished strangling the strike. That he actually did this, I cannot say. Perhaps it was just a coincidence that the commission delayed to come, and "Poison Ivy" was "stringing" Mr. Rockefeller, to make sure of that thousand dollars a month!

Would you like to be such a press-agent, and get such a salary as this? If so, you can find full directions, set forth by "Poison Ivy" himself in an address to the "American Railway Guild." At this time he was prize poisoner for the Pennsylvania Railroad, and he explains that it is all a question of psychology. "Success in dealing with crowds, that success we have got to attain if we are to solve the railroad question, rests upon the art of getting believed in." And our prize poisoner goes on to give concrete illustrations of how to get the railroads "believed in." If you are opposing a "full crew" law, you will get "believed in" by changing the name of the measure to an "extra crew" law. If you are going into bankruptcy, you will get "believed in" by calling it a "readjustment of finances." If you are fighting a strike, and one small group of the strikers demands a particularly large increase in wages, you will get "believed in" by so phrasing your statement as to make it appear that all the miners are making the same unreasonable demand as the little group. "Miners Ask One Hundred and Fifty Per Cent Increase in Wages," cites "Poison Ivy." He sent a copy of this brilliant production to Mr. Rockefeller, and on the strength of it got a considerable increase in wages himself!

CHAPTER XLIX

THE ELBERT HUBBARD WORM

The Egyptians had sacred beetles, and Capitalist Journalism has sacred insects of various unpleasant and poisonous species. There was one sacred worm which all Capitalist Journalism venerated, and the Walsh Commission broke into the temple where this worm was kept, and tore away the sacred veils, and dragged the wriggling carcass out into the light of day. This was Elbert Hubbard, alias "Fra Elbertus," editor of the "Philistine," "Roycroft," and the "Fra," founder of the "Roycroft Shops," host of the "Roycroft Inn," and patron saint of East Aurora, New York. That the "Fra" was one of the high gods of Capitalist Journalism you can surely not deny. He was the very personification of the thing it calls "Success"; his books were circulated by millions, his magazines by hundreds of thousands, and all the world of hustlers and money-makers read and gloried in him. He is gone now, but they still keep his image in their Pantheon, and the corporations water his grave by free distributions of "A Message to Garcia." We are told to say nothing but good of the dead, but my concern in life is for the living, so I shall tell what I know about this sacred worm.

I have mentioned in Chapter V my early experience with him. Prices were low in these days, and I am told that Hubbard got only five hundred dollars from the packers for his slashing of "The Jungle": "Can it be possible that any one is deceived by this insane rant and drivel?" You may think that I cherish anger because of such violence to myself; you may not believe me, but I state the fact—I cherish anger because I tried to bring help to thirty thousand men, women and children living in hell, and this poisonous worm came crawling over their faces and ate out their eyes. And because again, and yet again, I saw this same thing happen! The wage-slaves of the Copper Trust went on strike, and this poisonous worm crawled over them and ate out their eyes. And then came the Colorado coal-strike—and the poisonous worm crawled on its belly to the office of the Rockefellers, looking for more eyes to eat. Thanks to Frank Walsh, we may watch him and learn how to be a worm.

First, when an eye-eating worm approaches the great ones of the earth, it applies what it calls the "human touch"; it establishes itself upon terms of equality, it gives them a hearty hand-clasp, perhaps a slap on the back—if you can imagine such actions from a worm. Listen to "Fra Elbertus," addressing young Rockefeller:

I had a delightful game of golf with your father on Saturday. How fine and brown and well and strong he is.

To which "Young John" responds with graceful cordiality:

Father has spoken of your visit to Tarrytown the other day, and of the good game of golf which you had together. He is indeed in the best of health.

These little amenities having been attended to, we proceed to the business in hand. Says the worm:

I have been out in Colorado and know a little about the situation there. It seems to me that your stand is eminently right, proper and logical. A good many of the strikers are poor, unfortunate ignorant foreigners who imagine that there is a war on and that they are fighting for liberty. They are men with the fighting habit, preyed upon by social agitators.

I am writing something on the subject, a little after the general style of my article on "The Copper Country" in the "Fra Magazine" for May. I mail you a copy of the "Fra" today. I believe you will be interested in what I have to say about the situation in Northern Michigan.

Just now it seems very necessary that someone should carry on a campaign of education, showing this country, if possible, that we are drifting at present in the direction of I. W. W. Socialism.

Are you interested in distributing a certain number of copies of the "Fra" containing my article on the Colorado situation?

Also, what do you think of the enclosed booklets? I have distributed these on my own account up to the extent of nearly a million, but I have not the funds to distribute a million more as I would like to do.

Any suggestions from you in the line of popular education will be greatly appreciated.

"Popular education," you perceive! The worm is a public worm, serving the public welfare, animated by a grand, lofty ideal, to protect "the poor, unfortunate, ignorant foreigners," who are "preyed upon by social agitators"! Mr. Rockefeller,

of course, appreciates this, and is grateful for the support of
so noble and disinterested a worm; he writes:

> Your letter of May 3rd is received. I thank you for your words
> of approval in connection with my stand on the question of the
> rights of the independent workers.

But of course, as a business man, Mr. Rockefeller has to
be cautious. He has to know what he is buying. He will pay
for the silk which a worm can make, but not until it is made.

> I have looked over the number of the "Fra" which you have sent
> me with interest, and shall be glad to see the article which you are
> proposing to write regarding the Colorado situation.

Not too cordial; but the worm has written books on Sales-
manship, explaining how you must not give up at one rebuff,
but must come back again and again, wearing the other fellow
down. He tries again:

> On May 3rd I sent you a copy of the "Copper Country" number
> of the "Fra" magazine. Our friends up north have distributed a large
> number of these, sending the magazines out from here, duly blue-
> penciled.
> I have upwards of a million names of members of Boards of
> Trade, Chambers of Commerce, Advertising Clubs, Rotarians, Jovians,
> school teachers, all judges, members of Congress, etc.
> It seems to me that we could well afford to circulate a certain
> number of copies of the "Fra" containing a judicious and truthful
> write-up of the situation in Colorado.

"Judicious and truthful," you note. Never would our
noble worm write anything that was not truthful; while as for
being judicious, it is a virtue desperately needed in this crisis,
while agitators are parading back and forth in front of the
entrance to Mr. Rockefeller's office building! The judicious
worm has observed our antics and their success and he tact-
fully reminds Mr. Rockefeller of this:

> Just here I cannot refrain from expressing my admiration for
> the advertising genius displayed by those very industrious, hard-
> working people Bill Haywood, Charles Moyer, Mother Jones, Emma
> Goldman, Lincoln Steffens and Upton Sinclair. They are continually
> stating their side of the controversy. I believe if we would state ours,
> not of course in the same way or with the same vehemence, that we
> would be benefiting the world to a very great degree.

The worm is all for benefiting the world; not for benefiting
the worm—nor even for benefiting Rockefeller! But the

worm is worthy of his hire, and would not cheapen himself
and his advertising genius in the esteem of a business man.
"The price of extra copies of the 'Fra' is $200 a thousand," he
writes. He proposes to charge Mr. Rockefeller twenty cents
apiece for magazines which he can produce and mail for ten
cents apiece. In other words, he suggests that Mr. Rockefeller shall pay him two hundred thousand dollars, from which,
after paying postage and wrapping, he will retain at least one
hundred thousand!

But alas, it is notorious how the business man fails to
appreciate genius! Mr. Rockefeller consults "Poison Ivy"
Lee, whose advice is that the worm shall be allowed to go out
to Colorado and see everything, but "have it distinctly understood that he is making this study entirely on his own initiative
and at his own expense. If, after he has produced his article
and you have read it, it seems to you something worth distributing, an arrangement for such distribution can be made
with him."

A cold, cold world for a public educator and prophet of
judiciousness! These business men haggle, precisely as if
Pegasus could be harnessed to a garbage-wagon! Says Mr.
Rockefeller, writing to the president of the Colorado Fuel &
Iron Company in Denver:

I have not seen Mr. Hubbard nor given him any encouragement
in this matter, other than as set forth in the above correspondence.

To which comes the reply from Denver:

Mr. Hubbard's price for extra copies of his publication is to my
mind high. . . . . We can determine after he has produced his
article whether or not we should go any further than we already have
in enlarging its distribution.

There was more of this correspondence. It was printed in
"Harper's Weekly" under the title, "Elbert Hubbard's Price";
the substance of the matter being summed up by "Harper's
Weekly" as follows:

Mr. Hubbard's proposal, it will be seen, had two parts. 1. To
sell his opinion. 2. Later on to make an "investigation" in support
of that opinion.

CHAPTER L

THE PRESS AND PUBLIC WELFARE

As a result of the operation of all these forces, we have a class-owned press, representing class-interests, protecting class-interests with entire unscrupulousness, and having no conception of the meaning of public welfare. These words may seem extreme, but I mean them to be taken literally. When our press says "the public," it means the property-owning class, and if in a newspaper-office you should assume it meant anything else, you would make yourself ridiculous. "We are not in business for our health," is the formula whereby this matter is summed up in the "business-office" of our newspapers. It is only in the editorial columns that any other idea is suggested.

What kind of "public welfare" will you consider? Here, for example, is William Salisbury, working for the "Chicago Chronicle," owned by a great banker. Was this banker working for the public welfare? He was working for his own welfare so diligently that later on he was sent to jail. Is Mr. Salisbury working for the public welfare? No, Mr. Salisbury is working for an actress, he tells us, and the actress is working for a diamond ring. Mr. Salisbury comes upon a "tip" that will earn him the price of the ring. A certain merchant has conceived the idea of a co-operative department store, an enterprise which might be of great service to the public; but if the big department-stores get wind of it, they will kill it. Mr. Salisbury takes the problem to his city editor, who consults owner Walsh over the telephone, and then tells Mr. Salisbury to write the story in full.

"The people who are getting this thing up are not advertisers, he added. "The big department-stores are. Besides, Walsh doesn't believe in co-operation or municipal ownership, or anything like that, so go ahead."

I wrote two columns. All the other papers copied the story.

The co-operative department-store was not started. The owners of the big emporiums in the downtown district joined forces against it. They got an option on the only available building by greatly overbidding the small merchants. The latter, whose combined capital was less than the wealth of any one of their powerful rivals, gave up the fight in despair.

Thus was nipped in the bud by the frost of publicity a project which might have revolutionized trade—and all because an actress wanted a bracelet, and a reporter wanted a scoop, and a newspaper wanted to protect its advertisers.

But sometimes the "Chronicle" was merciful, as Mr. Salisbury lets us see. All the newspapers in Chicago were pouring ridicule upon John Alexander Dowie, a fake religious prophet.

When I returned to the office I offered to write of Dowie's weeping about the birds. That was the only thing that struck me as unusual. Anything that would put Dowie in a ridiculous or unfavorable light was generally wanted by all the papers. But I was told to write nothing.

"We've just got orders to let up on Dowie," said the city editor. "Mr. Walsh wants to increase the paper's circulation among the Dowieites. Our political views have cost us subscribers lately, and we want to make up for it. If there is any good hot news about Dowie, of course we'll print it, but not unfavorably.

Maybe you distrust Mr. Salisbury. A man who could fake so much Journalism might fake one book! Very well; but here is one of the most eminent sociologists in the country, a man whose honor is not to be questioned—Prof. E. A. Ross of the University of Wisconsin. Writing in the "Atlantic Monthly" for March, 1910, Prof. Ross gives several pages of incidents of this sort. I quote:

On the desk of every editor and sub-editor of a newspaper run by a capitalist promoter now under prison sentence lay a list of sixteen corporations in which the owner was interested. This was to remind them not to print anything damaging to these concerns. In the office these corporations were jocularly referred to as "sacred cows."

Nearly every form of privilege is found in the herd of "sacred cows" venerated by the daily press.

The railroad company is a "sacred cow." At a hearing before a state railroad commission, the attorney of a shippers' association got an eminent magnate into the witness chair, with the intention of wringing from him the truth regarding the political expenditures of his railroad. At this point the commission, an abject creature of the railroad, arbitrarily excluded the daring attorney from the case. The memorable excoriation which that attorney gave the commission to its face was made to appear in the papers as the *cause* instead of the *consequence* of this exclusion. Subsequently, when the attorney filed charges with the governor against the commission, one editor wrote an editorial stating the facts and criticizing the commissioners. The editorial was suppressed after it was in type.

The public-service company is a "sacred cow." In a city of the Southwest, last summer, while houses were burning from lack of water for the fire hose, a lumber company offered to supply the firemen with water. The water company replied that they had "sufficient."

Neither this nor other damaging information concerning the company's conduct got into the columns of the local press. A yellow journal, conspicuous in the fight for cheaper gas by its ferocious onslaughts on the "gas trust," suddenly ceased its attack. Soon it began to carry a full-page "Cook with gas" advertisement. The cow had found the entrance to the sacred fold.

Traction is a "sacred cow." The truth about Cleveland's fight for the three-cent fare has been widely suppressed. For instance, while Mayor Johnson was superintending the removal of the tracks of a defunct street railway, he was served with a court order enjoining him from tearing up the rails. As the injunction was not indorsed, as by law it should be, he thought it was an ordinary communication, and put it in his pocket to examine later. The next day he was summoned to show reason why he should not be found in contempt of court. When the facts came out, he was, of course, discharged. An examination of seven leading dailies of the country shows that a dispatch was sent out from Cleveland stating that Mayor Johnson, after acknowledging service, pocketed the injunction, and ordered his men to proceed with their work. In the newspaper-offices this dispatch was then embroidered. One paper said the mayor told his men to go ahead and ignore the injunction. Another had the mayor intimating in advance that he would not obey an order if one were issued. A third invented a conversation in which the mayor and his superintendent made merry over the injunction. Not one of the seven journals reported the mayor's complete exoneration later.

And the same thing has been done in every city where radicals of any sort have gained control. Says A. M. Simons, speaking at a conference of the University of Wisconsin:

> The story of the administration of Milwaukee while it was in Socialist control was a caricature of the truth, so much so that it was found necessary to establish a weekly bulletin or press service, scarcely an issue of which did not contain a correction of some news agency story. Compare the story sent out about Mayor Shank and the public market in Indianapolis with the almost complete suppression of the fight against the ice trust by the Socialist interests in Schenectady.

One of the most incredible instances of news suppression in the interests of Big Business occurred early in 1914, during the hearings of the Interstate Commerce Commission. For three years the newspapers had carried on an elaborate campaign in favor of a five per cent increase in freight rates. Fifty million dollars a year was at stake, and the roads were spending millions in advertising their cause in the newspapers. The presidents of our biggest railroads appeared before the Interstate Commerce Commission to tell of the ruin which was threatened unless the increase were granted. The campaign was all worked out in advance, the "dope" for the newspapers

provided; but there came an unexpected hitch in the proceedings, caused by the appearance of a young man by the name
of Thorne, a member of the State Railway Commission of
Iowa. Mr. Thorne had the finances of all these railroads at
his finger-tips, and he proceeded to cross-question the railroad
presidents and tear their testimony to pieces. He showed that
in twelve years the capitalization of the roads had been
increased ninety-two per cent, and their dividends increased
three hundred and fifty-nine per cent. In the year 1912 their
dividends had been the greatest in history. In 1910 the Pennsylvania, the Baltimore & Ohio, and the New York Central
had assured the Interstate Commerce Commission that they
could not borrow money, yet in two years they had borrowed
five hundred million dollars!

Mr. Thorne showed how in their reports just submitted
they had padded their costs. Every locomotive had cost one
hundred and twelve per cent more to maintain in 1913 than it
had cost in 1912. Freight cars had increased thirty-three per
cent in cost, despite the fact that iron and steel were cheaper.
The Interstate Commerce Commission allowed Mr. Thorne to
question all the railroad presidents, and not one of them could
answer him. And what do you think the newspapers did with
this most sensational incident? I take the facts from Charles
Edward Russell, as follows: The "New York World" gave
nearly a column to the testimony of the railroad presidents,
and said not a word about Mr. Thorne! The "New York
Times" gave a full column, and not a word about Thorne!
The "Philadelphia Public Ledger" did the same, and the "Baltimore Sun"; the "Cincinnati Inquirer" gave half a column
without mentioning Thorne, and the "Chicago Herald" the
same. (This clipping marked, "By the Associated Press"!)

The hearings were continued. President Smith of the New
York Central, a Vanderbilt property, took the stand. Mr.
Thorne submitted figures showing that his road had made
eleven per cent net profit, that it had put by an eleven-million-
dollar surplus, that if its dividends had been properly figured
they would have been fifty-four per cent. President Smith
was absolutely helpless, dumb. And how do you think the
New York newspapers treated that incident? The "New York
World" gave it this headline: GOING TO THE DEVIL FAST,
SAYS HEAD OF NEW YORK CENTRAL." And not a word about
Thorne! Likewise the "New York Times" gave President

Smith's testimony in full, and nothing about Thorne! The "Philadelphia Public Ledger," the "Baltimore Sun," the "Chicago Herald" the same. ("By the Associated Press"!)

And next day came the president of the Pennsylvania Railroad. He, too, was helpless in the hands of Mr. Thorne; he admitted that he had made a stock allotment of forty-five million dollars; but again the same papers did not mention the matter. And next day came the vice-president of the "Baltimore & Ohio," and the same thing happened. All over the country the newspapers were full of articles portraying a railroad panic, our greatest roads "going to the devil," according to the sworn testimony of their officials—and never one word about State Railroad Commissioner Thorne of Iowa!

All these are positive acts; and now for a moment consider the negative—the good things that newspapers might do and don't! I could write a volume dealing with plans and social possibilities known to me, whereby the life of mankind might be made over; but you might as well start to fly to the moon as ask a capitalist newspaper to take these things up. For example, the idea of a co-operative home, as tried at Helicon Hall; or the idea set forth by Edgar Chambless in his book, "Roadtown." Did you ever hear of "Roadtown"? The chances are ninety-nine out of a hundred that you never did. If you are near a library, you may look it up in the "Independent," May 5, 1910. I will say in brief that it is a plan which won the approval of the best engineers, to build a city in a way that would save seventy per cent of the necessary labor of mankind forever after, and increase by several hundred per cent the total of human happiness. You did not find this plan "boosted" by capitalist newspapers—because its inventor sternly refused all propositions to exploit it for profit, and insisted upon preserving the idea for the free use and benefit of humanity.

CHAPTER LI

THE PRESS AND THE RADICALS

If you go into a New York club in the middle of August, you will be told in entire good faith that "everybody" is out of town. It is this "everybody" who is out of town in August that American Journalism knows and serves. Those who stay in town in August are "nobody," and have to take their chances with the newspapers, as with everything else in capitalist society. Imagine yourself a poor devil, caught in a set of circumstances which cause the city editor of some newspaper, after five minutes consideration, to make up his mind that you are guilty of a crime! Trial by a city editor in five minutes, and execution in columns of illustrated slander—that is our American system of jurisprudence. In the city of Atlanta, a Jewish manufacturer of pencils was tried for rape and murder. He was quite evidently innocent, but it happens that the "poor whites" of the South are jealous of the commercial keenness of the Jews; the politicians of the South want the votes of these "poor whites," and the "yellow" journals want their pennies; so this poor wretch was hounded by the newspapers for several months, and finally was hanged.

But it is for the poor devil become class-conscious, and protesting against injustice to his class, that our Journalism reserves its deadliest venom. It is when the Radical steps upon the scene that the hunting-pack joins in full cry. Then every prejudice, every hatred in the whole journalistic psychology becomes focused as by a burning-glass upon one centre. The hatred of the staff, men who have sold their honor, and take bold truth-telling for a personal insult; the hatred of the owner, whose life-time gains are threatened; the hatred of the advertiser who supports the paper, of the banker who handles its funds, of the politician who betrays the state to it—all these various hatreds mass themselves, they form what the foot-ball player knows as a "V," they "rush" this enemy and bowl him over and trample him under their feet.

Any kind of radical, it makes no difference; anyone who

advocates a change in anything, who expresses discontent with the system of legalized plunder and repression. Six or seven years ago Mrs. Pankhurst came from England in the interest of militant suffrage. The American people had read about Mrs. Pankhurst, and wanted to know what she looked like, and what she was going to do in America. A New York paper came out with a report to the effect that Mrs. Pankhurst, before being allowed to land in New York, had been required by the Federal authorities to give a pledge that she would not engage in militancy in America. This report was cabled to London, where it was hailed with glee by Mrs. Pankhurst's opponents; Lloyd George made a speech about it, and this speech was cabled to America by the Associated Press, and thus widely spread in the American papers. Mrs. Pankhurst stated to me personally that she had been asked for no such pledge, and had given no such pledge, and that all her efforts to have this false report corrected by the New York newspapers and by the Associated Press had been in vain.

Such was the treatment of a "militant" leader. You say, perhaps, "Well, nobody cares about those militants." If so, let us hear one of those who vehemently opposed "militancy." I write to Mrs. Alice Stone Blackwell, and she replies:

For many years, the news carried by the great press agencies on the subject of woman suffrage was habitually twisted, and the twist was almost always unfavorable to suffrage. As editor for a long time of the "Woman's Journal," and later as one of the editors of the "Woman Citizen," I had constant occasion to observe this, and I commented upon it repeatedly. The thing happened so often as to make it impossible to explain it as accident or coincidence.

As an extreme instance, take the following: Every time that the woman suffrage bill was defeated in the British House of Commons, the fact was promptly cabled to this country; but when the bill finally passed—an event which both friends and opponents of suffrage were awaiting with great interest—not one of the papers in the United States that are served by the Associated Press gave the news!

In my suffrage work, I learned beyond question that the news coming through the great press agencies was colored and distorted; and if this has been done on one subject, it has doubtless been done on others. A good many women, I think, learned a wholesome distrust of press reports during the suffrage struggle.

And now let us hear some radicals of the male sex. Hiram Johnson of California is a radical. In "Everybody's Magazine" during 1908 there appeared an interview which had been submitted to him and printed with his corrections. Sixteen newspapers published on their front page the report that Governor Johnson had repudiated this interview; and when he declared that the report was false, they refused to correct it.

Charles Zueblin is a radical—a very quiet and conservative one, who lectures on municipal ownership to ladies' clubs. I write to ask him what his experiences have been, and he tells me they are "too personal to be quoted." He gives me one illustration, which I take the liberty of quoting:

> The "Kansas City Journal" has pursued me every season I lecture there because it is an organ of the local public utilities. At one time they twisted some statement of mine in a report of a lecture which they headed: "Zueblin Believes Every Woman Should Marry a Negro." There was no doubt this was done solely to queer other things that might be said which had no connection with this invention.

Senator La Follette is a radical—and here is a public man who has been almost wiped out by deliberate newspaper boycott. The story of what was done to La Follette in the 1912 presidential campaign can hardly be made to sound like reality; it is a plot out of an old-time Bowery melodrama. La Follette was a candidate for the Republican nomination. He was conducting a tremendous campaign all through the Middle West, and the Associated Press was suppressing the news of it. At an open conference of newspaper-men, held at the University of Wisconsin, the editor of the "Milwaukee Journal," a strong capitalist paper, openly stated that the Associated Press was sending—"something, of course—but so little that it amounted to nothing." But when the governor of the state made an attack upon La Follette—"Well, the Associated Press suddenly woke up, and sent out that entire address word for word!"

Nevertheless, La Follette was winning, and stood an excellent chance to get the nomination. He was invited to a dinner of the Periodical Publishers' Association in Philadelphia, and at that dinner he told a little about the control of newspapers by the big advertising agencies—such facts as fill Chapter XLVII of this book. After the dinner was over the newspaper-men got together on the proposition, and decided that they would end the career of La Follette that night. They cooked up an elaborate story, describing how he had raged and foamed at the mouth, and rambled on and on for hours, until the diners had got up and left him orating to the empty seats and dinner-plates. It was evident, said the story, sym-

pathetically, that La Follette was suffering from over-work
and exhaustion; his mind was failing, and he would be compelled to retire from public life. After that, by deliberate
arrangement, the Washington correspondents reported not a
line of anything that La Follette wrote or said for a couple of
years!

Again, during the war, they did the same thing to him.
He made a speech before the Nonpartisan Convention in St.
Paul, denouncing bitterly the war profiteers, who were being
protected by our big newspapers. The Associated Press took
this speech and doctored it, as a means of making La Follette
odious to the country. They had to make such a slight change
in it! La Follette said, "We had grievances against the German government." And all the Associated Press had to do
was to slip in one little word, "We had *no* grievances against
the German government!" The whole country rose up to
execrate La Follette, and the United States Senate ordered
him placed on trial. When it came to a show-down, they
discovered they had nothing against him, and dropped the
case, and the Associated Press, after many months' delay and
heavy pressure from La Follette, finally admitted that it had
misquoted him, and made a public apology.

And then La Follette came before the people for their
verdict on his conduct. He carried the state by a vote of
110,064 to 70,813; but the big capitalist newspapers of Milwaukee deliberately held back the returns favorable to him,
and on election night the story was telegraphed all over the
country that the La Follette ticket had been overwhelmed.
The leading Chicago newspapers reported the election of
twenty out of twenty-six anti-La Follette delegates, and the
repudiation of La Follette by "an overwhelming majority of
Wisconsin voters." Next morning there followed editorials
in all the leading Wall Street organs, gloating over this defeat.
And, as usual in newspaper practice, this first story got all the
space that the subject was worth; the later news of La
Follette's victory was "buried."

CHAPTER LII

THE PRESS AND THE SOCIALISTS

The particular kind of radical who is most disliked by our newspapers is of course the Socialist. The Socialist meets the class-consciousness of the newspapers with another class-consciousness, almost as definite and aggressive. The Socialist is noisy; also the Socialist has a habit of printing pamphlets and leaflets, thus trespassing on newspaper profits. Every newspaper differs in the names it puts on its "son-of-a-bitch list," but every newspaper agrees in putting the most conspicuous Socialists on its "son-of-a-bitch list." The Hearst newspapers pose as friends of the people; they print a great deal of radical clamor, but there is a standing order in all Hearst offices that American Socialism shall never be mentioned favorably. All newspapers have a rule that if any Socialist get into trouble, it shall be exploited to the full; when Socialists don't get into trouble often enough to suit them, they make Socialists out of people who *do* get into trouble. Says Max Sherover:

When the King of Greece was shot by an insane and irresponsible man, the "New York Times" and hundreds of other papers ran the headline: "KING OF GREECE ASSASSINATED BY A SOCIALIST." And although it was proven conclusively that the assassin hadn't even heard of Socialism, none of these papers saw fit to retract their lie.

When the great novelist, David Graham Phillips, was shot by one Goldsborough, every paper in New York knew that Goldsborough not only was not a Socialist, but had often spoken against Socialism. They also knew that the latter had a personal grievance against the author. Notwithstanding these facts, the "New York World" and other papers came out with headlines: "DAVID GRAHAM PHILLIPS SHOT BY SOCIALIST." None of the papers retracted that lie.

When Theodore Roosevelt was shot at in Milwaukee, the Associated Press sent broadcast the news that a Socialist had assaulted the Colonel. Though it was proven by the evidence of the assailant's own statement that he was an affiliated member of a Democratic organization in New York, that he had always voted the Democrat ticket, the "New York Evening Telegram" ran the headline: "ROOSEVELT SHOT BY SOCIALIST." This the "Telegram" never retracted.

Perhaps the most tragic illustration of this kind of thing was the "Chicago Anarchists." There were one or two

Anarchists among them; the rest were Socialists, perfectly innocent working-class educators, who were railroaded to the gallows by public hysteria, deliberately incited by the newspapers of Chicago. Finley Peter Dunne, creator of "Mr. Dooley," was a reporter on one of these newspapers, and ten or twelve years ago he narrated to me some of the things he had witnessed, the most outrageous inventions deliberately cooked up. His voice trembled as he told about it. I asked him why he did not write the story, and his answer was that he had often tried to write it, but was blinded by his own tears.

The same thing was done in the Debs railway strike of 1893. Every act of violence that was committed was hailed by the newspapers of the country as part of a terrorist campaign by the labor-unions. Therefore the public permitted Grover Cleveland to smash this strike. Afterwards Cleveland's commission of investigation put the chief of police of Chicago on the witness-stand, and heard him testify that the Railway Managers' Association had hired "thugs, thieves, and ex-convicts" as their deputies, and that these men had set fire to freight-cars, and had cut the hose of the Chicago firemen.

It would not be too much to say that American capitalist newspapers sent Eugene V. Debs to jail in 1893 and made him into a Socialist. And now in 1919, when he is sent to jail again, they help to keep him there! On the day that he is sent to prison, they spread wide an interview to the effect that he will call a general strike of labor to get himself out of jail; and this interview is quoted by the Attorney-General as reason for refusing amnesty to Debs. But Debs gave no such interview. He denied it as soon as he saw it, but of course you did not see his denial, unless you are a reader of the Socialist papers.

The "Appeal to Reason" is preparing to have a suit brought against the Associated Press on this issue. It reprints a letter from Debs to the general manager of the Associated Press, written in 1912, protesting against a false story to the effect that the "Appeal" is suspending publication. This report, obviously a great injury to the "Appeal," the Associated Press refused to deny. Says Debs:

Am I to infer from your letter that the Associated Press aims to deal fairly, honestly and justly with all people, to disseminate the truth, and taboo what is false? I happen to know differently by personal experience. If there is in this country a strictly capitalist class institution it is the Associated Press.

Pardon me if I give you just an instance or two of my personal experience. During the heat of the Pullman strike, when the Pullman cars were under boycott, the Associated Press sent out a dispatch over all the country that I had ridden out of Chicago like a royal prince in a Pullman Palace car while my dupes were left to walk the ties. A hundred witnesses who were at the depot when I left testified that the report was a lie, but I could never get the Associated Press to correct it. This lie cost me more pain and trouble than you can well imagine, and for it all I have to thank the Associated Press, and I have not forgotten it.

During the last national campaign, at a time when I was away from home, the Associated Press spread a report over the country to the effect that scab labor had been employed to do some work at my home. It was a lie, and so intended. I had the matter investigated by the chief union organizer of the district, who reported that it was a lie, but I was never able to have the correction put upon the wires. That lie is still going to this day, and for that, and still others I could mention, I have also to thank the capitalistically owned and controlled Associated Press.

You might think this a pretty small lie for a big organization like the Associated Press to bother with; but if you think that, you do not know the Associated Press. Hardly ever do I mention this organization to a radical that I do not hear a new story, frequently just such a petty and spiteful story as the non-union labor in the home of Eugene Debs. In Pasadena lives my friend Gaylord Wilshire, and I mention the Associated Press to him, and he laughs. "Did I ever tell you my story of York, Pennsylvania?" "What did you do in York, Pennsylvania?" "Nothing," says Wilshire; "that's the story." It appears that he was on a Socialist lecture-tour, and the schedule was badly arranged, the trains were late, and so he cut out York, Pennsylvania, and on the date in question was up in Maine. But the Associated Press sent broadcast over the country a detailed report that the editor of "Wilshire's Magazine" had spoken in York, Pennsylvania, had denounced the courts, had offered ten thousand dollars for a debate with Mark Hanna, and had been mobbed by the citizens of York!

You will say, perhaps, that this must have been a mistake. Yes, but how comes it that the Associated Press makes all its mistakes one way? Why is there never a mistake favorable to a Socialist? Why does not the Associated Press report that Gene Debs has rescued a child from drowning; or that Gaylord

Wilshire has been awarded a gold medal by a chamber of commerce; or that Upton Sinclair has been made a bishop of the Episcopal Church for writing "The Profits of Religion"?

One of the most interesting illustrations of newspaper lying about Socialists occurred during a May-day meeting in Union Square, New York, a few years ago. It is interesting because we may go behind the scenes and watch the wires being pulled. It appears that police arrangements for this meeting were in charge of Chief Inspector Schmittberger, an old-style Tammany clubber; but he could not handle the affair in the usual fashion of the New York police, because the administration of Mayor Mitchel had ordained "free speech." Schmittberger had his clubbers hidden in an excavation of the subway, ready to sally forth when the meeting gave excuse. But the meeting did not give excuse, and some of the policemen grew impatient, and sallied out without orders and started clubbing. My friend Isaac Russell, who was reporting the day's events for the "New York Times," was standing by Schmittberger's side, and heard him shout to these unauthorized clubbers. Says Russell:

> I ran beside Schmittberger into the fracas, and he yanked and pulled cops over backwards to break up the thing. And finally he got them under control, and then gave them fits for acting without orders.

Russell, being an honest man, went back to the "Times" office, and wrote a story of how the New York police had been seized by a panic, and had broken out without orders; and that story went through. But it happened that up in the editorial rooms of the "Times" somebody was writing the conventional "Times" editorial, denouncing the Socialists for their May-day violence, and praising the police for their heroism. It never occurred to the editorial writer that the news editors could be so careless as to pass a story like Isaac Russell's! So next day here was this comical discrepancy, and an organization of magazine editors, the "Ragged Edge Club," invited Isaac Russell to come and explain to them the war between the news columns and the editorial columns of the "Times"! Russell was called up before his boss and, as he says, "roasted to a frazzle" for having written the truth. Arthur Greaves, city editor of the "Times," told him that he had "got off all wrong in that situation." But Russell's job was saved—and how do you think? The police commissioner of New York came out with a formal statement, denouncing the police, and saying that they had acted contrary to his orders!

Or take the experience of A. M. Simons, reporting an International Socialist Congress at Stuttgart, Germany, for the United Press, supposed to be a liberal organization. Simons received a dispatch from the London headquarters of his organization:

> Wire three hundred words on probable split of Congress into Bebelists, Herveists, and Laborites.

And Simons continues:

> Now, there was not a single human being in that congress that ever dreamed there would be a split. The particular question on which they were supposed to split was passed by a unanimous vote. I sent a straight news story out. At the close I put these three words: "Split talk rot." Judge of my surprise when I landed in New York to find that that story of the split of the Socialist Congress had been carried over the United Press wires to the paper I was serving!

And now, as this book is going to press, on November 11th, 1919, the Associated Press sends from the town of Centralia, Washington, a series of dispatches telling how I. W. W. members fired from windows of their meeting hall upon an Armistice Day parade of returned soldier-boys. The dispatch does not say directly that the firing was done in cold blood; it simply tells in elaborate detail about the firing, and says not one word about incidents occurring before the firing. It leaves it to be assumed that the firing was done in cold blood, and the whole country does assume that, and a perfect frenzy seizes the returned soldiers and the government authorities; they raid I. W. W. meeting rooms in a hundred places, and beat up the members and throw them into jail. And I who understand the infamies of our Journalism wait patiently, knowing that in due course the truth will begin to leak. And sure enough, three days later comes an Associated Press dispatch from Centralia, Washington, mentioning, quite casually and incidentally, that Dr. Frank Bickford, *one of the marchers,* testified at the coroner's inquest that *"the former soldiers attacked the I. W. W. hall before any shots were fired."* And the Hearst service reports the same news with the comment that "no special significance was attached to this testimony"!

Later: It appears that the soldiers were battering in the door, and the first shots were fired through it.

CHAPTER LIII

THE PRESS AND SEX

There is a whole field of problems connected with our sex-nature which we are only beginning to explore. Metchnikoff has told us something. Freud and Jung have told us more; but long after we have solved our economic problems we shall still be seeking knowledge about sex. And meantime men and women grope blindly, and are betrayed into entanglements and misunderstandings and cruel miseries. If they happen to be ordinary, respectable citizens, they keep these things under cover. If they are radicals, trying to square their preaching and their practice, they will get into weird and awful predicaments, and then there will be sport for predatory Journalism!

I have told you the stories of Maxim Gorky, of George D. Herron, of Upton Sinclair. How many such stories would you care to hear? Would you care to hear about Charlotte Perkins Gilman? About Thorstein Veblen? About Jack London, Reginald Wright Kauffman, Clarence Darrow? About Marion Craig Wentworth, Mary Ware Dennett, Gaylord Wilshire, Oscar Lovell Triggs, George Sterling? This that I am giving you is not a list of the vital spirits of our time; it is merely a list of persons of my acquaintance who happen to have been caught upon the hook of an unhappy marriage, gutted, skinned alive, and laid quivering on the red-hot griddle of Capitalist Journalism.

I will tell you a story told to me only the other day. The man asks me not to give his name; he is trying to forget. Poor fellow, as he talks about it, I see the color creep into his forehead, I see his hands begin to shake—all the symptoms I remember so well! I ask him: "Do you start in your sleep, as if someone had touched a live nerve? Do you cry aloud, and carry on long discourses through the night?"

A few years ago this man was a popular "extension" lecturer in Chicago; anywhere in the Middle West he chose to go he could have a couple of thousand people to listen to him.

332

He was unhappily married; his wife was living with another
man, and desired a divorce. When this happens in Chicago,
they usually agree upon the charge of "cruelty"; their friends,
and likewise all Chicago newspaper editors, perfectly understand that this is a conventional charge, having no necessary
relation to the facts. I have quoted the case of Mr. Booth
Tarkington, returning from Europe and saying to the newspaper reporters, with a smile, "When one's wife accuses one
of cruelty, no gentleman would think of replying." The
reporters all understood what that meant, and the public which
read it appreciated Mr. Tarkington's tact. Mr. Tarkington,
you see, is a novelist whose work involves no peril to the
profit system; therefore Mr. Tarkington's wife could charge
him with "cruelty," without Mr. Tarkington's reputation being
destroyed and the sale of his books wiped out. A recent item
sent out by Mr. Tarkington's publishers—Messrs. Harper &
Brothers, with the eight hundred thousand dollar mortgage
reposing in the vaults of J. P. Morgan & Company—stated
that they had sold a total of 1,324,900 copies of Mr. Tarkington's novels.

But it was entirely different with this Chicago lecturer;
this man, you see, was a Socialist, and therefore a menace to
mortgages. In a lecture-room the question came up of a
teacher who had switched a child; the speaker remarked play-
fully that the cave-man had been accustomed to inflict
discipline with a club, and that boys, according to biology,
were in the cave-man stage of development. So next day the
readers of a yellow journal in Chicago read a scare headline
about a "highbrow" society lecturer who was preaching "cave-
man philosophy" to his students, and applying "cave-man treatment" to his wife, so that she was divorcing him for cruelty!
Half a dozen such yarns at this were piled in quick succession
upon the head of this Socialist lecturer, with the result that his
career was ruined.

By way of contrast, let me tell you about another man—
proprietor of a great department-store in New York. I will
not name him; he is a worm, poor in everything but money.
It happened that through mutual friends I knew about his
private life; he kept numerous mistresses, and flaunted them
boldly on the "Great White Way," starting them on showy
theatrical careers, and otherwise making himself a joke to the

"Tenderloin." This man's wife divorced him for his infideli-
ties; and what do you think happened? What did the newspapers do? Not a line about the matter in any newspaper of
New York City!

To some of the rules which I lay down in this book there
are exceptions. It is sometimes possible for a radical to be
quoted honestly by a capitalist newspaper; it is sometimes possible to get news unfavorable to the profit-system into the
most reactionary sheet. But to the following two rules there
is no exception anywhere:

Rule 1. Any proprietor of a department-store anywhere
in America may divorce, or be divorced, with entire immunity
so far as concerns the press.

Rule 2. No radical in America can divorce or be divorced
without being gutted, skinned alive, and placed on the red-hot
griddle of Capitalist Journalism.

I will tell you about another Chicago Socialist whom I
have mentioned—Oscar Lovell Triggs. Fifteen or twenty
years ago Triggs was the most popular man in the faculty of
Mr. Rockefeller's University of Chicago; they had to get
extra-sized class-rooms for his lectures, and so there was
jealousy of him—camouflaged, of course, as opposition to
Socialism. Triggs was so indiscreet as to live in a radical
colony in Chicago. He was asked to give an interview on
some subject or another, and the reporter, going down the
hallway of the community building, made note of the fact
that in the next room there hung some silk stockings and a
pink kimono. So he went off and wrote a cunningly devised
and highly suggestive story about silk stockings and a pink
kimono in the room adjoining that of the Chicago college
professor.

Here was a scandal, of course; and Triggs was expected
to fight it. But, as it happened, Triggs was unhappily married,
his wife was living with an artist in Paris, and desired a
divorce. Any divorce lawyer will tell you that men who are
thus caught on the hook are prone to strange and reckless
rushes. Triggs, whose wife wanted a divorce, decided that
this story would serve as well as anything. A friend who ·
lived in the building at the time, and knew Triggs intimately,
assures me that there was not a word of truth in the insinuations, there was nothing between Triggs and the young lady

of the silk stockings and the pink kimono. Nevertheless, this
most popular professor of literature was driven out of the
university, and set to work as a common laborer on a
California chicken-ranch.

I write to ask him to verify the details of this story; I ask
him to be heroic, and let me tell the story, in the interest of
the public welfare. He gives the permission, adding the
following comment:

> In this statement, you speak of only one detail—the last one. But
> the real story involves what amounted to a conspiracy against me in
> the two years preceding my retirement from the university. This
> consisted in so reporting lectures and statements that a very quiet and
> reasonable scholar came to be regarded as a "freak professor." No
> one could stand up against this kind of attack and retain a position in
> a conventional university. I never could get to the bottom of it. It is
> a poor way to treat human material, but so be it.

Maybe you distrust the radicals; they are all "free lovers,"
you say; they deserve their marital unhappiness, they deserve
exposure and humiliation. Well, then, suppose I tell you
about some respectable person? Suppose I tell you about the
President of the United States, secure in the sanctity of the
White House? Will that convince you?

You didn't happen to know that the "Scandal Bureau" had
prepared a story on Woodrow Wilson! The "interests," which
wanted war with Germany and Mexico, had a scandal all ready
to spring on him toward the end of the 1916 campaign. They
had the dynamite planted, the wires laid; all they had to do
was to press the button. At the last moment their nerve failed
them, they did not press the button. I was told why by a
prominent Republican leader, who was present in the councils
of the party when the final decision was made. This man
pounded on the table and declared: "I'd have said I'd sooner
vote for the devil than for Woodrow Wilson, but if you start a
dirty story on the President of the United States, I'll vote for
Woodrow Wilson, and one or two million Americans will do
likewise."

Their nerve failed them; but some steps they had already
taken, and you may trace their footprints if you are curious.
There were dark hints in many newspapers, and if you saw
the Washington correspondence of London papers during the
fall of 1916, you found more than hints. For example, here

is James Davenport Whelpley, a well-known journalist, writing in the "Fortnightly Review," one of the most dignified of English monthlies:

Another issue has come to the fore in the American political campaign quite unusual in American politics. . . . . With all the freedom that is given to the American Press, and with all the pernicious intrusion into private affairs that finds expression in the columns of American newspapers, it has been many years since the personality of a candidate has played any part in the publicity work of a campaign, no matter how great the temptation may have been to use material at hand. In reading American newspapers today, however, much can be gleaned from between the lines. Something seems to be struggling against precedent and unwritten rules for clear expression, and that something finds itself articulate in the communications of man to man.

And then Mr. Whelpley goes on to tell about "elections being won and lost at the last moment by psychological waves which have swept across the national mind, swamping on their way the political hopes of one or the other candidate." So Mr. Whelpley is unable to predict the re-election of Woodrow Wilson!

More definite even than this, there was a story in "McClure's Magazine," which had already gone to press, and could not be recalled. "McClure's," now a tool of the "interests," was conducting a raging campaign for "preparedness," and Wilson stood in the way. The story was called "That Parkinson Affair," by Sophie Kerr, and was published in the issue of September, 1916—just when the scandal was ready to be sprung. It is ostensibly a piece of fiction, but so transparent that no child could fail to recognize it. It is the vilest piece of innuendo in American political history, and remains on our library shelves as a monumental example of the depths to which our predatory interests have been willing to drag their "kept" magazines.

When the big magazines were bought up by the "interests," we were solemnly assured that the purpose was to put an end to "scandal-mongering." But now it appears that the purpose was not to lay the "muck-rake" on the shelf, but merely to turn it against the friends of human progress!

CHAPTER LIV

THE PRESS AND CRIME

You guess that this chapter will show how the press exploits crime for its profit; and that sounds tiresome, you know all about that. You know how the yellow journals take up murder cases and divorce cases and sexual irregularities, and carry on campaigns of scandal, lasting for months. You know how they send out their amateur sleuths, and work up a case against some one, and make it a matter of journalistic prestige that this person shall be hounded to jail.

No; this chapter does not deal with the crimes which the press exploits, nor yet with the crimes which it invents. I could tell a hilarious anecdote of a group of New York reporters assigned to the immigration service, shy of news and bored to death, who cooked up a tale of an imaginary murder by an imaginary Austrian countess, kept all New York thrilled for a week, and "got away with it." But all that is comparatively nothing. The theme of this chapter is the crimes which the press commits.

What is a crime? The definition is difficult; you have to know first who commits it. Many things are crimes if done by workingmen, which are virtuous public services if done by great corporations. It is a crime when workingmen conspire to boycott; but it is no crime when newspapers do it, when advertisers do it. It is a crime when an individual threatens blackmail; but when a great newspaper does it, it is business enterprise. For example, in Los Angeles there was started a municipal newspaper, which was thriving. Gen. Harrison Gray Otis of the "Times" sent agents to various advertisers to notify them that if they continued to advertise in this paper they would be boycotted, black-listed, and put out of business. So the big advertisers deserted the municipal paper.

I have told in this book about many crimes committed by newspapers against myself; not metaphorical crimes, but literal, legal crimes. It was a crime when a Philadelphia reporter broke into my home and stole a photograph. It was a crime when the "New York Evening Journal" sent forged cablegrams to Dr. James P. Warbasse and Mrs. Jessica Finch Cos-grave. It was a crime when the newspapers of New York bribed a court-clerk to give them the testimony in my divorce case. Any lawyer will tell you that these things are crimes, yet they are a recognized part of the practice of American Journalism, and follow logically and inevitably from the competitive sale of news.

[Nietzsche says of the soul of man that it "hungers after knowledge as the lion for his food." Just so the yellow journals hunger after news, and just so their proprietors hunger after profits. When profits are at stake, they stop at nothing. I have quoted Hearst's telegram to Frederick Remington: "You make the pictures and I'll make the war." I have told of Hearst's ruffian conduct towards myself in the case of Adelaide Branch. Do you think that a man who would commit such acts would stop at anything? When Hearst ventured to run for governor of New York State, his enemies brought out against him a mass of evidence, showing that he had deliberately organized his newspapers so that the corporations which published them owned no property, and children who had been run down and crippled for life by Mr. Hearst's delivery-wagons could collect no damages from him.]

Mr. Hearst poses as a friend of labor, but he keeps his newspapers on a non-union basis, and when his employes go on strike, he treats them as other corporations treat their strikers. And all newspaper corporations do the same. I could name not one, but several cities in which newspapers have hired thugs to break the strikes of newsboys; or where they have hired strikes against their rivals. During the Colorado coal-strike the "Denver Express" was publishing the truth about the strike, and the other newspapers organized a boycott of the dealers who handled the "Express." When the "Express" hired its own newsboys, mysterious gangs of rowdies appeared, and beat up these newsboys and scattered their papers in the streets. And no interference from the police, no line about these riots in any Denver newspaper—except the "Express," which could not get distributed!

Wherever you dig in the cellars of these great predatory institutions, you find buried skeletons. I have dragged some of them into the light of day; I would drag others—but the test here is not what I know to be true, but what I can prove in a court of law. And it is so easy for a great newspaper to buy witnesses; so easy for a great newspaper to terrorize witnesses! I came upon one typical story that I could prove, and prove to the hilt; I prepared to tell the story, with names and places and dates, but while I was collecting the evidence, a friend of the victim exclaimed: "You will ruin him! You will set the newspaper after him again!"

This man, a former city official, an honest public servant, had been deliberately ruined by a newspaper conspiracy, and brought to utter despair. The thing happened six years ago, and only now is he beginning to recover his practice as a lawyer. If now I revive this story, he will take up his morning paper and read something like this: "The defendant was represented by John Jones, who a few years ago was indicted—etc." Or: "The striking carpenters have retained John Jones, who was once city prosecutor, and concerning whom several witnesses testified—etc., etc." Shall I inflict this upon a man, in spite of his wishes? I thought the matter over from many angles, and decided to ask the reader to accept the story on my word. Really, it is too incredible a story to be an invention! Listen:

John Jones, city prosecutor, caused the arrest of the proprietor of a great and powerful newspaper for printing salacious advertisements. He forced this newspaper to make abject public apology, and to promise reform. Later he caused the arrest of the proprietor for criminal libel; whereupon this proprietor set out to "get" the city prosecutor. The paper had a "literary editor," a man who has since become well-known as a critic and novelist, author of perhaps a dozen books. At this time his salary was thirty dollars a week, and he was told by the proprietor of the newspaper to go and "get" John Jones, using either wine or women.

A woman was brought on from the Middle West, a woman just one month under twenty-one, which is the "age of consent" in the state in question. This woman sought a city position from John Jones, came to his office, threw her arms about his neck, and screamed. Instantly the door was broken in, and it was made known that "sleuths" had bored a hole through the office-wall, and were prepared to testify that they had seen John Jones committing a crime with this woman under age.

Now, I hear you say, with a knowing smile, "That's the story John Jones tells!" No, reader, I assure you I am not so naïve; I did not get this story from John Jones, I did not get it from any friend of John Jones. It happens that I know the "literary editor" fairly well, and I know a dozen of his friends. To one of these, an intimate friend of mine, this "literary editor" told the entire story. Two friends of mine were present at a club dinner, when the man was confronted by accident with his victim, and admitted what he had done, and begged pardon for it. It was his "job," he said—his "job" of thirty dollars a week! And that is how I came on the story!

I go over in my mind the newspapers concerning which I can make the statement that I know, either from direct personal knowledge, or from the evidence of a friend whom I trust, that the owner or manager of this paper has committed a definite act of crime for which, if the laws were enforced, the owner or manager would be sent to the penitentiary. I count a total of fifteen such papers, located in leading American cities, such as New York, Boston, Philadelphia, Chicago, San Francisco, Los Angeles. Each one of these criminals sits in a seat of power and poisons the thinking of hundreds of thousands of helpless people. I ask myself: In what respect is the position of these people different from that of the peasantry of mediæval Germany, who lived and labored subject to raids from robber knights and barons whose castles they saw upon distant cliffs and mountain tops?

CHAPTER LV

THE PRESS AND JACK LONDON

I once had the pleasure of hearing Jack London express his opinion of American Journalism; it was a picturesque and vivid experience, a sort of verbal aurora borealis. Not wishing to trust to my memory of the incidents, I write to Mrs. London, and she sends me a huge scrap-book, the journalistic adventures of Jack London during the year 1906. I open it, and the first thing I come upon is a clipping from the "St. Louis Post-Dispatch," with a picture of Mrs. London which is not Mrs. London! Then, a couple of pages on, a clipping from the "New Haven Palladium," with a picture of Jack London which is not Jack London!

They just take any old picture, you understand, and slap your name under it. I have seen Jack London's picture serving for me, and I have seen my own picture serving for a vaudeville actor. As I write, the "Los Angeles Times" comes to my desk, with a scare-headline all the way across the page: "BRITAIN DEFIES UNION LABOR THREAT OF REVOLUTION." It appears that the miners are preparing a general strike, and the "Los Angeles Times," wishing to make them odious, publishes on its front page a large portrait, with this caption: "TRYING TO THROW BRITAIN OFF BALANCE. Robert Smillie, Brains of the Triple Alliance of Powerful Labor Unions, Seeking Social and Economic Revolution in the United Kingdom." The portrait shows a foreign-looking individual with straggly beard and tousled hair, wearing a Russian blouse. It is Abram Krylenko, commander-in-chief of the Russian Bolshevist armies! If you are near a library you may find the picture in the "Outlook," Vol. 118, p. 254; or in the "Independent," Vol. 93, p. 405; or in the "Metropolitan Magazine" for October, 1919. A picture of Smillie appears in "Current Opinion" for August, 1919—an entirely conventional-looking Englishman!

To return to Jack London: This was the year that Charmian and Jack got married. It was in Chicago, and the Hearst paper of that city reported it in this chaste fashion:

JACK LONDON WINS IN BATTLE FOR A BRIDE.

Messenger-boys, Telephones, Korean Valet, Political Influence, Plead-
ings, Many Explanations, and a Special Dispensation
Finally Won a Marriage License on
Sunday for Jack London.

And then next day the Hearst reporters discovered that
this marriage was not legal; Jack was liable to three years in
jail; so, as a matter of precaution, he was going to be married
in every state in the Union! All over the country this story
was telegraphed; such trifling with a sacred institution dis-
pleased certain women's clubs in Iowa, which canceled their
engagements to hear Jack London lecture! Returning to his
home after these excitements, I find Jack being interviewed by
the "Oakland Herald."

That report was all the imagination of the Chicago reporters who
were scooped on the wedding story. There was nothing in that at all.

Later on Jack took another trip to the East, and delivered
his famous address, "Revolution," which you may find in his
volume "Revolution and Other Essays." He is describing
the feelings of a Colorado workingman under the régime of
the militia general, Sherman Bell, whose orders were, "To hell
with the Constitution." Says London:

Nor does the Constitution of the United States appear so glorious
and constitutional to the workingman who has experienced a bull pen
or been unconstitutionally deported from Colorado. Nor are this
particular workingman's hurt feelings soothed by reading in the newspapers that both the bull pen and the deportation were preeminently
just, legal, and constitutional. "To hell, then, with the Constitution,"
says he, and another revolutionist has been made—by the capitalist
class.

And next morning here comes the "New York Times," not
quite saying that Jack said "To hell with the Constitution," but
carefully implying it; which dishonesty, of course, takes wings,
and from one end of the country to the other Americans read
that Jack London has said, "To hell with the Constitution."
Jack is on his way home, and cannot answer; here am I, as
vice-president of the Intercollegiate Socialist Society, under
whose auspices the meeting had been held, writing to the
"Times" to call attention to the injustice it has done to a great
American novelist. The "Times" puts my letter under the
title:

THE CALL OF THE WILD

Jack London Puts an "If" in the Condemned Constitution.

And here is the "New York Evening Sun," denouncing Jack; here is the "Chicago Inter-Ocean," in an editorial:

If Jack London speaks only for himself, he is either a cheap seeker after notoriety or a pestilential agitator. If the latter, he is more dangerous than the agitators whose fulminations led to the assassination of President McKinley, and assassination is as likely to follow his diatribes.

Our laws prevent the importation of foreign Anarchists. Are the laws and public sentiment not strong enough to suppress the exploiter of sensationalism who preaches treason to the flag and war on the Government?

And here is the "Rochester Post Express," with the headline: "A LITERARY ANARCHIST." Here is the "Milwaukee Sentinel": "LONDON BELCHES MORE FIRE." Here is the "Chicago Inter-Ocean": "ASSASSINATION PET JOY OF MR. LONDON."

And here are various public libraries, rushing to defend our imperiled institutions by barring the books of Jack London from their shelves: Derby, Connecticut; Des Moines, Iowa; Pittsburgh, Pennsylvania. And here is Jack, writing to Gaylord Wilshire: "Thanks for the enclosures. You bet they amuse me! I leave it to you if my situation isn't amusing!" In a letter to me, Mrs. London explains this amusement: "Down went his royalties!" And she adds:

Several years ago Jack learned, from one newspaper man and another, what he had often suspected—that the standing instructions in practically every newspaper office on the Pacific Coast were to give Jack London the worst of it whenever possible. Of course this meant no matter what the occasion, whether slamming his work, or wilfully misrepresenting his personal actions. And they only subsided, as I have said above, when they adjudged he had a bank account, and therefore must needs be less radical.

This trick played upon Jack London is a favorite one with our newspapers—to take some quotation, and put it in the mouth of the quoter. What a sordid man is William Shakespeare; he said: "Put money in thy purse!" What a vainglorious man is the apostle Matthew; he said: "All these things will I give thee, if thou wilt fall down and worship me!" What a violent man is James H. Maurer, president of the Pennsylvania Federation of Labor; he said: "Down with the Stars and Stripes!"

Mr. Maurer came to New York to tell the people about the state constabulary, a public strike-breaking agency organized by the big capitalists of his state. The big capitalists of New York wanted the same thing, and the big newspapers of New York were boosting for it, and of course ridiculing and slandering all who opposed it. At the Washington Irving High School, on April 19, 1916, Mr. Maurer addressed a public meeting and read a passage from his book, "The American Cossack." The incident he read was a funeral; a Spanish war-veteran had died during the miners' strike in Westmoreland County, and was being buried by the striking miners with military honors. Members of the state constabulary came riding up. They objected to these lousy strikers using the American flag, and ordered that the flag be lowered. The strikers refused, whereupon the Cossacks threatened to shoot unless the flag was lowered and furled. Maurer quoted them: "Down with the Stars and Stripes!" So next day the newspapers reported Maurer as saying, "Down with the Stars and Stripes!" The "New York Times" went farther yet, and reported him as saying, "To hell with the Stars and Stripes!" I quote Maurer's letter:

Mayor Mitchel of New York ordered the school-board to investigate these charges at once and they did so. At the hearing twelve witnesses were heard. Eleven swore that I said nothing of the kind and repeated what I did say. One, a "New York Sun" reporter by the name of Lester S. Walbridge, contended that I had said, "Down with the Stars and Stripes!" but admitted that there had been much cheering at the time and that he did not catch all that I said. Three others wrote and telegraphed their testimony, all saying that I said nothing of the kind. Some of the witnesses were people favorable to the State Police. The verdict of the School-board was to the effect that I said nothing of the kind, but had simply told my audience what the State Police had said; that it was the State Police who said, "Down with the Stars and Stripes," and not Mr. Maurer. A clear vindication.

The day the story first appeared in the New York papers, charging me with the flag slander, the story was used to stampede the New York senators into voting for the State Police Bill then pending, and it worked. Although I was vindicated, the story is still used; every now and then someone editorializes about it.

In my effort to verify this story, I write to a reporter who was on the job at this time. He answers:

As a matter of fact all the reporters were out getting a drink when Maurer spoke, and they took their version of what he said from the Real Estate Association's provocateurs at the meeting.

In connection with this Maurer episode, there is a curious story which should be told. You remember "Collier's Weekly," a magazine "run on a personal basis," and the many young writers who had been debauched by "Collier" prosperity. One of these writers was Richard Harding Davis, and you would have to hunt a long time to find a more perfect incarnation of capitalist prosperity and success in literature. It happened that Davis was at his country home when he read in the "New York Times" that Maurer had said, "To hell with the Stars and Stripes!" Davis flew into a rage, and drafted a telegram to the mayor of New York, calling upon him to use the power of the government to put down these preachers of sedition. He went to the telephone to dictate the message, and before he was half-way through, fell dead of an apoplectic stroke!

Ten years ago I produced in California a one-act play called "The Indignant Subscriber." The editor of a great newspaper is found walking on the shore of an imaginary lake. A stranger invites him for a row in a boat—the "boat" consisting of two chairs and a board tied together, the "oars" being brooms. The stranger rows the editor out into the middle of the lake, and then announces himself as the Indignant Subscriber. "For twenty-five years," he says, "I have listened helplessly, while you set forth your views on every subject under the sun. Now for once I mean to tell you my views on one subject—yourself!" So he speaks his mind, and at the end upsets the boat and swims away, leaving the editor floundering in the water.

Now I am the Indignant Subscriber, who has been taking the "New York Times" for twenty-five years. I propose to give the "Times" a taste of its own medicine—by writing some headlines and letting the "Times" see just how it feels. Here goes:

"NEW YORK TIMES" KILLS FAVORITE AUTHOR

Death of R. H. Davis Caused by Reporter Seeking High-ball
Lie Occasions Fatal Shock
Reads "Times" Incitement, Drops Dead in Home

Now, how's that?

CHAPTER LVI

THE PRESS AND LABOR

I have told many stories of newspaper lies about myself, and perhaps you thought that was just one person who was wronged, and it didn't make much difference; but when it comes to lying about the labor movement, thousands and even millions of people are wronged, and that surely does make a difference. When newspapers lie about a strike, they lie about every one of the strikers, and every one of these strikers and their wives and children and friends know it. When they see deliberate and long-continued campaigns to render them odious to the public, and to deprive them of their just rights, not merely as workers, but as citizens, a blaze of impotent fury is kindled in their hearts. And year by year our newspapers go on storing up these volcanic fires of hate—against the day when labor will no longer be impotent!

Imagine, if you can, the feelings of a workingman on strike who picks up a copy of the "Wall Street Journal" and reads:

We have a flabby public opinion which would wring its hands in anguish if we took the labor leader by the scruff of his neck, backed him up against a wall, and filled him with lead. Countries which consider themselves every bit as civilized as we do not hesitate about such matters for a moment.

Whenever it comes to a "show-down" between labor and capital, the press is openly or secretly for capital—and this no matter how "liberal" this press may pretend to be. Says Professor Ross:

During labor disputes the facts are usually distorted to the injury of labor. In one case (Chicago), strikers held a meeting on a vacant lot enclosed by a newly-erected billboard. Forthwith appeared, in a yellow journal professing warm friendship for labor, a front-page cut of the billboard and a lurid story of how the strikers had built a "stockade" behind which they intended to bid defiance to the blue-coats. It is not surprising that when the van bringing these lying sheets appeared in their quarter of the city, the libeled men overturned it.

During the struggle of carriage-drivers for a six-day week, certain great dailies lent themselves to a concerted effort of the liverymen to win public sympathy by making it appear that the strikers were interfering with funerals. One paper falsely stated that a strong force of police was being held in reserve in case of "riots," and that policemen would ride beside the non-union drivers of hearses. Another, under the misleading headline, "Two Funerals Stopped by Striking Cabmen," described harmless colloquies between hearse-drivers and pickets. This was followed up by a solemn editorial, "May a Man Go to His Long Rest in Peace?"—although, as a matter of fact, the strikers had no intention of interfering with funerals. . . . .

That was in Chicago, ten years ago. And now, as I write, the employes of the packing-houses, my old friends of "The Jungle," are on strike again, and the Chicago newspapers are at their usual game of deliberate lying: "Violence is Expected," "Situation is Critical," and so on. It happens that an honest man, Alfred W. McCann, is on the scene. He writes:

I say it isn't true. To the shame of the press, no foundation can be discovered for the wild stories now filling their columns, spreading public anxiety and inciting labor to outbursts of indignation against what is called "the deliberate misrepresentation of the press."

The packers advertise heavily in Chicago newspapers; and so also do the Chicago department-stores. Says Prof. Ross:

In the same city (Chicago), during a strike of the elevator men in the large stores, the business agent of the elevator-starters' union was beaten to death, in an alley behind a certain emporium, by a "strong-arm" man hired by that firm. The story, supported by affidavits, was given by a responsible lawyer to three newspaper men, each of whom accepted it as true and promised to print it. The account never appeared.

Try, for a moment, to put yourself in the position of a girl-slave of one of these big department-stores. You resist the flirtatious advances of the floor-walker, and continue to eat your twenty-cent dinners; but after a few years you grow desperate, and in the face of the heaviest pressure you organize and declare a strike for better pay. How much chance do you stand for fair play from the newspapers? Why, they won't even print the names of the stores against which you are striking! Says Max Sherover:

While addressing a street meeting, held under the auspices of the Retail Clerks' Union, in front of Stern Brothers' department-store, Miss Elizabeth Dutcher was arrested at the instigation of one of the store-managers. Miss Dutcher is highly prominent in social and labor circles, and the papers did not dare to be entirely silent about the arrest. Every paper in New York, except one—and that one does not carry department-store advertising—spoke of a meeting at the doors of a "large retail establishment." They also referred to an earlier incident as a disturbance at the doors of a "Sixth Avenue Store," not daring to mention the name, Gimbel's.

Or again, Prof. Ross:

In New York the salesgirls in the big shops had to sign an exceedingly mean and oppressive contract, which, if generally known, would have made the firms odious to the public. A prominent social worker brought these contracts, and evidence as to the bad conditions that had become established under them, to every newspaper in the city. Not one would print a line on the subject.

And not only do they exclude the news; they keep watch over the general ideas which go into their columns, to make sure there is nothing to injure the sensibilities of department-stores, or to favor the girl-slaves of department-stores. Would you think I was absurd if I were to declare that there is a whole set of philosophical ideas which the newspapers forbid you to know about, because the department-stores ordain? Yes, even so! You must believe in free will, you must not believe in economic determinism! You must think that prostitution is a sexual phenomenon; you must not learn that prostitution is an economic phenomenon. Anybody who advocates the heretical, anti-department-store doctrine that white-slavery is caused by low wages will be suppressed, and if necessary will be slandered as an immoral person. You remember the "New York World," its solemn editorial about twenty-cent dinners? Some years ago the "World" was under contract to publish every week a short story by O. Henry. They received the manuscript of what posterity has come to recognize as O. Henry's masterpiece, "The Unfinished Story"; they refused to publish this "Unfinished Story," because it was injurious to department-stores!

Or consider what happened when the Illinois Vice Commission made an investigation of the causes of prostitution, and submitted one of the best reports on this subject ever written. The report was highly sensational, also it was highly important; it was news in every possible sense of the word. But it attributed prostitution to low wages, and therefore only one Chicago newspaper gave an adequate account of this report!

You saw the "Boston Herald" and "Journal," and also the "Boston Post," forbidding you to know that President

Wilson was urging you not to spend money on luxuries. In the same way, when there is a crisis of unemployment, the department-stores and other advertisers command that false-hoods shall be told you. If you know that business is bad, you may be cautious and save your money; whereas the department-stores want you to spend your money, and the kept press wants its share of this money for advertisements. Says Prof. Ross:

> The alacrity with which many dailies serve as mouth-pieces of the financial powers came out very clearly during the recent industrial depression. The owner of one leading newspaper called his reporters together and said in effect, "Boys, the first of you who turns in a story of a lay-off or a shut-down, gets the sack." Early in the depression the newspapers teemed with glowing accounts of the re-sumption of steel-mills and the revival of business, all baseless. After harvest-time they began to cheep "Prosperity," "Bumper Crops," "Farmers Buying Automobiles." In cities where banks and employers offered clearing-house certificates instead of cash, the press usually printed fairy tales of the enthusiasm with which these makeshifts were taken by depositors and workingmen. The numbers and sufferings of the unemployed were ruthlessly concealed from the reading public. A mass meeting of the men out of work was represented as "an-archistic" or "instigated by the Socialists for political effect." In one daily appeared a dispatch under the heading "Five Thousand Jobs Offered; Only Ten Apply." It stated that the Commissioner of Public Works of Detroit, misled by reports of dire distress, set afoot a public work which called for five thousand men. Only ten men applied for work, and all these expected to be bosses. Correspondence with the official establishes the fact that the number of jobs offered was five hundred, and that three thousand men applied for them.

That was twelve years ago, in the Middle West. Six years ago we had another unemployment crisis, and I watched the newspapers handling it in New York. You might have thought they would not have been able to fool *me;* but they did! A boy out of this unemployed army, Frank Tanenbaum by name, led a number of starving men to the Catholic Church of St. Alphonsus to request shelter on a winter's night. I read several newspapers, in the hope of getting the truth from one of them; on this occasion all the papers agreed that the un-employed men and their leader abused and threatened the priest, and were noisy and blasphemous in their behavior. I was heartsick about it. Oh, what a pity! If only those poor devils had had the sense to go to the churches in a quiet and respectful way, their position would have been impregnable. Christian churches would not have dared to turn out starving men on a winter's night!

But Christian churches did! And the capitalist press backed them up! The leader, Frank Tanenbaum, was arrested, and he called as witnesses the very newspaper men who had written the stories of his "raid." These men had been willing to lie in what they wrote—that was part of the newspaper game; but they were unwilling to lie under oath—that was *not* part of the game! So they testified that these unemployed men had been entirely peaceful in their conduct, that Tanenbaum had addressed the priest with politeness and respect, and that the crowd had left the church when told that they must do so!

Some years ago there was a strike of the hotel-workers in New York, an I. W. W. strike—and of course there is nothing with which the newspapers deal more freely than the I. W. W. They quoted Joe Ettor as having advised the strikers to put poison in the soup which they served to hotel patrons; also as having insulted the American flag. Ettor denied vigorously having made any such statements, but of course his denial went for nothing. Some of us who knew Ettor thought that the public ought to get a little of the truth about conditions under which these hotel-workers were forced to live—conditions menacing not only to themselves, but to the public they served. Therefore the Intercollegiate Socialist Society called a meeting in Carnegie Hall to hear the I. W. W. leaders. A fiery little New York politician who held the office of sheriff saw an opportunity to leap into the lime-light. He would attend that meeting with a large force of deputies, and protect the American flag from insult! He brought some thirty deputies, to whom the county paid three dollars each; and we provided them with seats on the platform, and all the orators made speeches to them, and the young ladies who passed the collection-plates took away a part of their three dollars. And next morning the newspapers reported that the gallant sheriff had protected the American flag and tamed the seditious fury of the I. W. W.!

You remember, perhaps, my story of the Paterson silk-strikers, and how the "New York Times" quoted me as telling them that they "had the police at their mercy." Here is another glimpse of this strike, through the eyes of Max Sherover:

At the I. W. W. pageant held about two years ago at Madison Square Garden, New York, for the benefit of the Paterson, N. J., silk-strikers, the writer was an eye-witness to the following scene: A reporter, whose identity we were unable to learn, in the basement of the Garden hurriedly printed the following words on an improvised banner, "No God and No Master, I. W. W." One of the illiterate strikers was asked to hold the banner aloft and pose while a newspaper photographer was taking a flashlight photo.

This Paterson pageant was a result of the effort of a few literary men and women in New York, who saw the shameless lying of the press and the shameless violation of law by the authorities in Paterson. A group of people, including Ernest Poole, Hutchins Hapgood, Leroy Scott, John Reed, Thompson Buchanan, Margaret Sanger, and myself worked for weeks, giving all our time and energy and a great deal of money, and brought about a thousand strikers to New York City to rehearse the story of their sufferings before an audience in Madison Square Garden. This was so sensational that the newspapers could not suppress it; therefore what they did was to ridicule and betray it. They always make out that labor-movements are rolling in wealth, and that "agitators" are making fortunes. In this case they said that we were planning to finance the strike by this pageant. Every newspaper man knew this was absurd, for they knew the seating capacity of the Garden and could figure the possible gross receipts. The enterprise suffered a deficit of one or two thousand dollars; so of course the poor, starving strikers, who had read in the newspapers that they were to be "financed," were bitterly disappointed. The "New York Times" thus had a chance for a story to the effect that the strikers were accusing us of having robbed them; and this while we were engaged in making up the deficit out of our own pockets!

Or take the Lawrence strike. I have told the story of how conspirators of the great Woolen Trust planted dynamite in the homes of strike-breakers as a "frame-up" to discredit the strikers. The man who was convicted of this was a school commissioner and a prominent Catholic, a close friend of the mill-owners. When this dynamite was found, the Associated Press sent the story fully. When the plot was exposed, it sent almost nothing. These statements were made publicly at a conference at the University of Wisconsin by A. M. Simons, and never challenged by the Associated Press. And at this same conference it was stated by George French that the department-stores served notice upon all the Boston news-papers that if they featured this strike they would get no more Sunday advertising!

Or take the present struggle of the railroad brotherhoods for a living wage. The "Saturday Evening Post" published a series of articles by Edward Hungerford, full of gross false-hoods regarding the wages of railroad workers and managers under the Federal administration. These, mind you, were flat misstatements of facts officially recorded and available to any one. The brotherhoods asked a certain United States railroad administration official to prepare from official records a state-ment concerning these misrepresentations. This was formally submitted to the "Saturday Evening Post," and was abso-lutely ignored.

Or take the case of Tom Mooney. The capitalist news-papers of San Francisco tried Tom Mooney, with the help of a million dollar corruption fund, raised by the Merchants and Manufacturers Association of the city. They found him guilty, but the prosecuting authorities didn't have enough evi-dence to make good the verdict in court, so they manufactured the evidence. Mooney was a Socialist and a well-known labor organizer, so the case was taken up by the Socialists and the unions of the country, and became the great labor issue of the time—all without one word getting into the capitalist newspapers of the East! There were two or three million copy "protest editions" of the "Appeal to Reason" issued—and still not a word about it in the capitalist newspapers out-side of California! Finally the Anarchists in Petrograd took up the matter; they attacked the American embassy, and the news was cabled back to New York that the attack was on account of a certain "Tom Muni." The newspapers of New York didn't know anything about the case, and couldn't find out about it in time; they had to publish the name as it came over the cables—thus laying bare their shame to the whole world! Could any writer of farce-comedy have invented a greater satire upon New York Journalism than the fact that it had to get its San Francisco labor-news misspelled from Petrograd?

CHAPTER LVII

THE ASSOCIATED PRESS AND LABOR

Great strikes are determined by public opinion, and public opinion is always against strikers who are violent. Therefore, in great strikes, all the efforts of the employers are devoted to making it appear that the strikers are violent. The greatest single agency in America for making it appear that strikers are violent is the Associated Press. How does this agency perform its function?

In the first place, by the wholesale method of elimination. There are some violent strikers, needless to say, and Capitalist Journalism follows this simple and elemental rule—if strikers are violent, they get on the wires, while if strikers are not violent, they stay off the wires; by which simple device it is brought about that nine-tenths of the telegraphic news you read about strikes is news of violence, and so in your brain-channels is irrevocably graven the idea-association:

Strikes—violence! Violence—strikes!

What about the millions of patient strikers who obey the law, who wait, day after day, month after month, starving, seeing their wives fading, their little ones turning white and thin—and still restrain themselves, obeying the laws of their masters? What about the strike-leaders who plead day in and day out—I have heard them a hundred times—"No violence! No violence!"—what about them? Why, nothing; just nothing! The Associated Press will let a big strike continue for months and never mention it—unless there is violence! For example, the great coal-strike in West Virginia. It happens, through a set of circumstances to be explained in the next chapter, that I have before me the sworn complete file of all the dispatches which the Associated Press sent out during the sixteen months of this strike. The strike began April 1, 1912. The first dispatch sent by the Associated Press was on April 6; a very brief dispatch, telling of threats of violence. The second dispatch was on June 1; this also very brief, to the effect that "serious rioting is imminent." The third dispatch was on July 23; also brief, telling of rioting, and of state troops sent in. Thus it appears that during one hundred and thirteen days of a great strike the Associated Press considered it necessary to send only two brief items—and these containing not one line about the causes of the strike, not one line about the demands of the miners, not one line about the economic significance of a ferociously bitter labor struggle! I have before me the affidavit of Thomas Cairns, president of the United Mine Workers' West Virginia district, stating that during these sixteen months, which brought West Virginia to a state of civil war, not once did the correspondent of the Associated Press come to him for information about the strike!

And now, in 1919, there is more trouble in this district, and I pick up my morning paper and read that three thousand miners of Cabin Creek have taken up arms and are marching to battle against machine-guns. The strike has been going on for weeks, says the report; but this is the first hint I have heard of it—I who read four Associated Press newspapers, the "Los Angeles Times" and "Examiner," and the "New York Times" and "World"!

The first point to be got clear is that in cases of big strikes the Associated Press is getting its news through its local newspaper member. I have shown that in Los Angeles it is content to co-operate with the unspeakable "Times." In San Diego it works with the "Union," personal organ of John D. Spreckles, the "sugar-king"; and a few years ago, when a murderous mob of bankers, lawyers and merchants was engaged in shooting, clubbing, tarring and feathering, throwing into prison, and there torturing, drugging, and starving the radicals of that city, the "San Diego Union" paid editorial tribute to the fact that the Associated Press was handling this situation to the satisfaction of the murderous mob of bankers, lawyers and merchants. The "San Diego Union," which had done most of the inciting of this mob, stated editorially:

> Great credit is due the Associated Press for the manner in which it has handled the news end of this matter.

In city after city, you will find the Associated Press thus tied up with the worst reactionary influences. In Louisville, for example, it co-operates with the "Courier-Journal," whose serio-comic story I have told in detail. In St. Paul, Minnesota, we saw the Associated Press misquoting Senator La Follette in a manner calculated to ruin him. It sought at first to put

the blame upon its "member paper," the "St. Paul Pioneer
Press." You recall the charges made against this paper by
Walter W. Liggett, quoted on page 268. Note that the Associated Press did not cease taking its news through a paper
which had failed to resent such grave charges as these.

I cannot find that the "A. P." ever did raise this issue
with one of its member-papers. An interesting light is thrown
on this very important subject by a controversy between the
"Sacramento Bee" and the "San Francisco Star." The "Bee"
printed a long defense of the Associated Press, and the "Star"
discussed it as follows:

> Another damaging admission is that the Associated Press doesn't
> care a picayune what manner of pirates buy a newspaper that has an
> Associated Press franchise. It mentions the case of the "San Francisco
> Globe," which bought the special privilege news service of the "Post"
> when it bought the name of that paper. The franchise went with the
> name to a band of industrial pirates who wanted a special privilege
> news service to supplement their special privilege traction service in
> this city.

The "San Francisco Star" is a weekly, and so its editor
does not need to be afraid of the Associated Press. I have
a letter written by this editor, James H. Barry, to Prof. Ross
of the University of Wisconsin:

> You wish to know my "confidential opinion as to the honesty of
> the Associated Press." My opinion, *not* confidential, is that it is the
> damndest, meanest monopoly on the face of the earth—the wet-nurse
> for all other monopolies. It lies by day, it lies by night, and it lies
> for the very lust of lying. Its news-gatherers, I sincerely believe, only
> obey orders.

In great labor centers, from which strike-news comes,
you find this situation: that even if the Associated Press
wished to deal with a fair newspaper, there is no fair newspaper to deal with. In Lawrence, Massachusetts, in Paterson,
New Jersey, in Trinidad, Colorado, in Bisbee, Arizona, the
newspapers are owned by the local industrial magnates and
their financial and political henchmen. In Montana the
Anaconda Mining Company, a Rockefeller concern, owns or
controls practically every newspaper in the state; so of course
the Associated Press sends no fair labor news from Montana.
I asked Ex-Governor Hunt of Arizona how the Associated
Press had treated him while he was giving the miners a

square deal during the big copper strike. He answered: "They were so unfair that I quit dealing with them at all." I said: "What paper in your state capital do they work with?" He answered: "There are only two—one owned by a millionaire land-speculator, the other owned by the 'Ray'!" (The "Ray" is a copper company, one of the most powerful and most corrupt.) Said Ex-Governor Hunt: "I proposed a law in Arizona requiring that papers should carry the line: 'This paper owned by the "Ray," or the "Copper Queen," or whatever the case might be.'" No wonder this ex-governor is an "ex"!

He comes to see me, and brings a clipping from the "Messenger," an independent weekly of his state capital. It appears that the wealthy bandits of the copper companies, who two years ago seized over a thousand miners and deported them from their homes, are now being tried for their crime. Says the "Messenger":

Associated Press reports from Bisbee and Douglas relative to the preliminary trial of alleged kidnappers are enough to condemn that service forever. It was bad enough to withhold service on July 12, 1917, the day of deportation, but the present stuff—

And then the "Messenger" goes on to explain in detail what is happening; the reporters of the local, copper-owned dailies of Bisbee and Douglas are acting as Associated Press correspondents, and are sending out "doctored stuff" to the country. Three times during one week of the trial at Douglas the "Bisbee Review" has had to apologize and correct statements attributed to a woman witness; these errors, "telegraphed broadcast" by the Associated Press, have been corrected "only by local mention"!

And here is the Central Trades Council of Tucson adopting a resolution, denouncing the "brazen one-sidedness" of the Associated Press reports of the trial:

Resolved, That to date we have not seen a single article that did not feature some silly remark made by some foreigner or illiterate witness for the state, and the vital news parts omitted.

In the case of the Colorado coal-strike, I have shown you what the Associated Press did in New York and in Denver. What was it doing meantime in the actual strike-field? In Walsenburg the publisher was "Jeff" Farr, whiskey-magnate, coal company sheriff and organizer of assassination, popularly known as the "King of Huerfano County." In Trinidad there

were two dailies owned by the chief attorney of the Colorado
Fuel and Iron Company, whose son took command of one of
the gunmen armies, and seized a United States mail-train to
transport them. The "A. P." day man was the editor of the
evening paper; the "A. P." night man was the telegraph-
editor of the morning paper! Max Eastman tells me of interviewing one of them—introducing himself as a Chautauqua
lecturer, desirous of getting the truth about the strike. The
editor was in a mood of frankness, and said:

> There's no use coming to me for the truth. A man in my posi-
> tion naturally gets only one side, the operators' side.

And, of course, he sent out that side. During the latter
part of the strike the "Rocky Mountain News" of Denver sent
its own correspondent to the field, and one of the editors told
me of a conversation with the Associated Press representative in Denver. Said the latter, "Why do you keep a man
down there?" Said the editor, "Because you people refuse to
send me the news." And it was exactly the same during a
strike in another part of the state, the "Northern field," where
several score labor leaders were thrown into jail, but when it
came to trial were nearly all acquitted. George Creel writes:
"The Associated Press furnished the newspapers with accounts of these cases, but lost interest when the verdicts were
returned."

As I write, there is a great steel strike, and from the
"Panhandle" of West Virginia comes the following special
dispatch to the "New York Call":

> The capitalist press representatives have so falsely reported the
> existing strike conditions that steel strike leaders here now refuse to
> make any statements at all to them. Several times, after having
> promised to write, without alterations, the reports which the strike
> leaders had given, the Associated Press representatives deliberately re-
> versed the statements.

So much for steel. And now hear what Charles Edward
Russell has to say (Pearson's for April, 1914) concerning the
conduct of the Associated Press in the Calumet copper-strike.
In a letter to me he writes:

> I may say that the Associated Press made a loud squeal on the
> story and blacklisted me for some years afterward, so you will see
> that the subject is one on which they are sensitive.

I quote from the article, "The Associated Press and Calumet":

Some of the richest copper deposits in the world are in the Upper Peninsula of Michigan, most of them purporting to be owned or controlled by a great corporation called the Calumet and Hecla. This is a mining company that is also the holding concern for seventeen other mining companies, owns a railroad or two, some smelting works, some other profit-making devices and an organized system of politics the equal of any.

It is one of the richest and most profitable enterprises in the world. Except for a few railroads like those of Mr. Hill, the Calumet and Hecla has made more money on a smaller investment than any other corporation that ever existed. In the sixteen years ending with 1912 the smallest annual dividend has been 80 per cent, and in other years it has been as much as 400 per cent.

As these dividends were declared upon a capital stock less than half of which was ever paid for, a nominal dividend of 400 per cent was an actual dividend of 800 per cent.

On every dollar ever invested in this company more than one hundred dollars have been paid in dividends, while millions of dollars of other profits have been diverted to the purchase of additional profit-making ventures. With a par value of $25.00 on which only $12.00 was paid in, the shares have now a value of $540.00 each.

This gigantic cornucopia is owned by the Shaws, Agassizs and Higginsons, leading families of Boston; and besides their dividends, they pay themselves enormous salaries as officers and directors of Calumet and Hecla, and of the seventeen subsidiary companies. Says Russell:

The Calumet and Hecla barony comprises one hundred and seventeen miles. There is every reason to believe that it occupies and has occupied this land without rightful title, and all the vast wealth it has taken therefrom really belongs to the people of the United States.

There is also good reason to believe that it has consistently violated its charter, and is now engaged in doing so every day and every hour of every day: a fact that will not in the least astonish you when you come to learn of some of its other activities, but that adds a rarely piquant taste to the pious exclamations of its attorneys on the subject of law-breaking.

And now, what of the men who worked for these copper barons? They were ill-paid and ill-treated, badly housed, worked for long hours at peril of life and limb; they lived in a community absolutely dominated by their masters; there was no other industry or source of wealth, and the politicians and the courts, the newspapers and the churches—everything was owned by "Copper." It is the old, sickening story of the overthrow of American institutions, the subjection of political democracy to industrial autocracy.

The copper miners of the "Upper Peninsula" went on strike. They stayed on strike for many months, and during that time they were slugged and beaten up by imported gunmen, their offices raided, their leaders shot or jailed. During this entire affair the Associated Press sent out to the country a string of subtle and knavish falsehoods, of which Charles Edward Russell gives seven pages, printing them in parallel columns, first the falsehood, and then the result of careful investigations, backed by numerous affidavits. (I might add that the Congressional investigation vindicated these affidavits in every detail.)

The parallel columns which Russell gives would fill about twenty pages of this book. I give four samples, and the reader may take my word that these samples are typical of the rest:

THE ASSOCIATED PRESS

(From Washington Post.)
Calumet, Mich., Sept. 1.—The copper strike situation took a serious aspect today as a result of the fatal shooting of Margaret Faxakas, aged 15, daughter of a striker, at the North Kearsarge mine, when a picket of strikers and women clashed with deputy sheriffs guarding a mine.

THE FACTS

Her name was Margaret Fazekes. She was not the daughter of a striker, and had no connection with the strike. There was no clash with any picket. A Labor Day procession was being held at Kearsarge. It had nothing to do with the strike. A band of armed guards without excuse or occasion attacked the procession and broke it up, firing about 100 shots from their revolvers. This girl was not in the procession. She was walking along the sidewalk, and a bullet from a gunman's revolver pierced her skull.

THE ASSOCIATED PRESS

Calumet, Mich., October 22, 1913.
To the Associated Press,
Chicago, Ill.

As a measure of precaution against possible disorder, the troops have kept on the move bodies of strikers who collect while men are going to work in the morning, but this is not construed as interference with any of the rights of the strikers.

THE AFFIDAVITS

For instance, Victor Ozonick swears that on July 31st he was walking quietly along the public road when he was arrested, taken to Houghton and thrust into jail. After a time he was taken into the sheriff's office and searched. A deputy sheriff struck him in the face with his clenched fist and then kicked him. He was then asked if he was a member of the miners' union. When he said "yes" he was dragged back to a cell and locked up for twenty-four hours. After that he was released. No warrant was issued for his arrest, no charge was made against him, no proceedings of any kind were had.

There are sheafs of such affidavits relating the manner in which the armed guards proceeded to obey the orders to "start something." The results of their efforts to obey their orders was a reign of terror throughout the strike zone. Men, women and children were shot at, beaten, ridden down by armed guards, or pursued along the highways. At the road intersections shacks were erected, from the windows of which the guards could command every house in a village, and the inmates could not stir out of their dwellings except under the watchful eyes of the gunmen and the muzzles of rifles.

THE ASSOCIATED PRESS

(From Chicago Record-Herald.)

Calumet, Mich., Dec. 11.—Guerrilla warfare, which raged in the South Range district of the copper miners' strike zone, was ended today when a force of deputy sheriffs invaded several towns there and made 39 arrests. The only person injured was Timothy Driscoll, a deputy sheriff, who was shot and seriously wounded when he and other officers attempted to force an entrance into a union hall.

The trouble this morning centered around the hall of the Western Federation of Miners in the town of South Range. Here Driscoll was shot and several of the arrests made. Henry Oski, a striker, was specifically charged with wounding the officer, and he is said to have implicated by his confession two other members of the union.

THE ASSOCIATED PRESS

(From the Washington Post.)

Calumet, Michigan, Dec. 26.—Charles H. Moyer, president of the Western Federation of Miners, was put on a train and sent out of the copper strike district tonight. The deportation was the

THE AFFIDAVITS

A mob composed chiefly of the gentlemen of the Citizens' Alliance gathered in Houghton and went by special train to South Range. There the mob attacked the hall of the South Range branch of the Western Federation of Miners, broke down the door, smashed all the furniture, seized all the books, papers and records, and destroyed several thousand relief coupons that had been prepared for the miners' families. Henry Koski, the secretary of the branch, lived over the hall. When the work of destruction had been completed the mob rushed upstairs and began with rifles to beat down the door to Koski's rooms. He warned the rioters that if they did not desist he would fire. They continued to batter the door, whereupon he fired two shots, one of which passed through the belly of one of the rioters.

THE FACTS

A mob broke into the room in Scott's Hotel, Hancock, occupied by Mr. Moyer and Charles Tanner, general auditor of the Western Federation of Miners, seized them both, beat and kicked them, shot Moyer in the back and direct result of a refusal of families stricken by the Christmas Eve disaster here to accept relief from a committee, the majority of whose members belonged to the Citizens' Alliance, an organization combatting the five months' strike of the federation.

At the local federation headquarters Moyer's departure was called "a kidnapping by the Citizens' Alliance." The action was said to have caused no great surprise, as it was said that threats of such a possibility had been received two weeks ago.

The relief committee, which had collected $25,000, found itself unable to give away one cent when it started today to deliver the fund.

Every bereaved household that was approached told the men and women in charge of the distribution that they had been promised adequate aid by the Western Federation of Miners, and nowhere was there any assistance wanted.

dragged them, both wounded, from the hotel into the street.

The two prisoners were held so that they could not defend nor protect themselves, and in this position were dragged through the streets and across the bridge to Houghton, being incessantly kicked and beaten. Mr. Moyer was bleeding and weak from a revolver shot, and Mr. Tanner was bleeding from a wound just be'ow his right eye.

In this condition they were placed upon a train and under armed guard taken out of the state, being threatened with lynching if they should return.

Nobody has been indicted nor arrested for these assaults, although the persons that committed them are perfectly well known in Hancock.

But Mr. Moyer has been indicted for conspiracy.

It might be worth while to summarize Russell's narrative of the outcome of this last matter. The leader of the mob was an eminent Bostonian, James MacNaughton, vice-president and general manager of "Calumet and Hecla." When he was accused, the Associated Press took the trouble to send out a dispatch explaining that he could not possibly have been the man, because of an elaborate and complicated alibi—which alibi was later proven to prove nothing. Mr. MacNaughton was never prosecuted in this matter; nor was the Associated Press prosecuted—except by Charles Edward Russell. We may believe the statement in Russell's letter, that "the Associated Press made a loud squeal on the story!" I would ask: Why did they not prosecute Russell? Why is it that the general manager of the Associated Press makes nothing but a "loud squeal"? Why does he content himself with easy victories before church forums and chambers of commerce banquets? Why does he not come into court and vindicate his honor in an open contest before a jury?

CHAPTER LVIII

"POISONED AT THE SOURCE"

I have been privileged to examine a mass of material, some three or four million printed and typewritten words, the evidence collected for the defense of Max Eastman and Art Young, when they were indicted for criminal libel in November, 1913, at the instance of the Associated Press. These three or four million printed and typewritten words enable us to enter the offices of the Associated Press, and to watch its work hour by hour. They enable us to study the process whereby the public opinion of America is "poisoned at the source."

Three hundred miles from our national capital, in the lonely mountains of West Virginia, exists an empire of coal, governed in all respects as Russia was governed in the days of the Tsardom. I take up two printed volumes of testimony given before the investigating committee of the United States Senate, a total of 2,114 closely printed pages; I turn these pages at random, and pick out a few heads that will give you glimpses of how things are managed by the coal barons of West Virginia: "Check weighmen guaranteed by law, but not allowed to the miners." "Men paid in scrip which they could not cash." "Men discharged and put out of their houses, as fast as they talked unionism." "Mail burned by store manager." "Law of West Virginia relieves coal owners from liability for injuries in the mine, no matter how they occur." "Independent store-keeper refused his goods at the express office which was on company grounds." "Men not allowed to approach postoffice on company property." "Provost Marshal imprisoned nine men without trial." "No mine guard has ever been tried for participating in any battle." "Machine-guns and guards turned on peaceful crowd coming from meeting."

In "King Coal" I have portrayed the conditions in Colorado. In West Virginia conditions were in all respects the same, and for the same reason. When the sixteen months' strike in West Virginia had been smashed, the same mine guards, with the same rifles and machine-guns, were shipped to Colorado, and under the direction of the same Baldwin-Felts Detective Agency they smashed the fourteen months' strike in Colorado. And both in West Virginia and Colorado the same Associated Press was made use of to send to the country the same misrepresentations and suppressions of truth.

In the "Independent" for May 15, 1913, after the West Virginia strike had lasted more than a year, there appeared an article by Mrs. Fremont Older, describing the farcical military trial of some union officials at Paint Creek Junction. Mrs. Older, the only impartial person who was able to get into this court-room, made the statement: "The Provost Marshal was not only the ruling officer of Paint Creek Junction; he was the Associated Press correspondent. He had the divine gift for creating darkness." In the next issue of the "Independent" appeared a letter from the assistant general manager of the Associated Press, declaring: "The Provost Marshal was not the Associated Press correspondent, and never had been."

Nevertheless, this rumor would not down, and in the "Masses" for July, 1913, appeared a cartoon: "Poisoned at the Source," representing the president of the Associated Press engaged in pouring the contents of a bottle labeled "Lies" into a reservoir labeled "Public Opinion." Accompanying the cartoon was an editorial, one sentence of which read: "The representative of the Associated Press was an officer in that military tribunal that hounded the Paint Creek miners into the penitentiary in violation of their constitutional liberties." The answer of the Associated Press to this was the indictment for criminal libel of Max Eastman and Art Young. The "Masses," presumably by advice of counsel, did not discuss the case, and continued to maintain silence, even after the case was dropped. The facts are here made public for the first time—possibly because in preparing this book I have not taken the trouble to consult counsel. Here are certain facts which the public should have; and if I have to hand them to the public through the bars of a jail, it will not be the first time that has happened in history.

Was the Provost Marshal of the West Virginia State Militia a correspondent of the Associated Press? He was, or he was not—according to whether you care about truth or technicality.

You are, doubtless, a loyal American. You believe in the constitution and laws of your country, and you do not understand just what it meant to be Provost Marshal of the West Virginia State Militia during the coal strike of 1912-13. If you think that it meant to be a public official, performing a public service in the interest of the public, you are naïve. To have had anything to do with the West Virginia State Militia during that strike meant to be a creature of the mine operators, in the pay of the mine operators, owned body and soul by the mine operators. It meant that you were setting aside, not merely the laws of the state of West Virginia, but the Constitution of the United States. It meant that you were beating and flogging and shooting strikers, kicking their wives and children out of their homes to freeze in the mountain snows, turning machine-guns upon their tent-colonies, throwing their leaders into jail without trial, and torturing them there for months on end. It meant this, whether you were the lowest Baldwin-Felts mine-guard taken out of a city slum and put into the militia uniform; or whether you were Capt. Lester, an official of militia, who testified under oath before the Senate committee that it was not his business to know if miners had a legal right to organize or not—he was sent there to prevent their organizing, and he did what he was sent there to do.

And now, just what was the relationship of the Associated Press to this prostituted State Militia? Was the Provost Marshal of Militia the Associated Press correspondent in this field? He was, or he was not—according as you care about truth or technicality.

The Associated Press correspondent at Charleston, who covered all the strike, and who had been officially appointed and acknowledged, was a man named Cal Young, and he had his office in the office, or connected with the office, of the Adjt. General of Militia. This Cal Young had an intimate friend by the name of John C. Bond, who was Provost Marshal of Militia, and also was correspondent for several newspapers. Cal Young did not trouble himself to travel about in the strike field, which was widely scattered, occupying a number of mountain valleys. Bond, however, was compelled by his militia duties to travel to the scene of all troubles; therefore Bond and Young had an arrangement whereby Bond telephoned news from wherever he was, and Young sent this news, not only over the Associated Press wire, but to the papers which Bond represented.

The above was stated from first-hand positive knowledge by Jesse Sullivan at the State House to an attorney for whom I can vouch. Also it was sworn to by W. Bruce Reid, reporter for the "Charleston Gazette" and the "Kanawha Citizen." Reid swore that he knew Young intimately; that Young maintained his offices in the Adjt. General's office without charge; that Young from this office transmitted orders for the movements of the State Militia, and for these services was paid out of the Governor's contingent fund; that he acted as official reporter for the state administration; that anyone who called at the State House for news was referred by the Governor and the Adjt. General to Young; that Young received news of military doings and of strike incidents from J. C. Bond, who was a printing clerk in the Secretary of State's office, and also captain and paymaster of militia; that Bond was made Provost Marshal, with absolute authority over the strike territory, and tried a number of citizens, ninety-eight in all, by military tribunal; that Bond had a regular arrangement with Young whereby he furnished Young with news reports; and that Young had an understanding with the military department whereby all news was given out through him.

Reid further testified that he was instructed by the militia authorities to distort news, and also to write editorials for his paper, supporting the military policy; that when he refused to do this, the editors of his paper were called up and practically instructed to write such editorials, and that they did this; that furthermore Reid was threatened if he failed to distort news as directed; that all these things were well known to Young, correspondent of the Associated Press; that Young was "extremely bitter against the miners' cause"; that he continually so expressed himself before Reid; that a correspondent of the "Baltimore Sun," who came to Charleston, was so impressed with Young's prejudice that he went into the field for himself, and wrote an entirely different account of the events. It was known that Young, while Associated Press representative, was seeking employment from the state administration, and he had since obtained such employment.

So much for outside evidence. And now let us hear from

Young himself. The attorney sent by the "Masses" called upon Cal Young, who told him that after the strike he had been discharged from the Associated Press by W. H. French, manager of the Pittsburgh division, and that French had stated to him that the reason was that Fremont Older and others had made complaint concerning the news that the Associated Press had furnished from West Virginia. Young admitted practically everything as stated by Reid: his desk in the Adjt. General's office, his relations with the administration, and his arrangement with Bond, whereby Bond furnished him regularly and continually with news from the field. I note three sentences from the investigator's report:

> Young also stated that before martial law he got most of his information from the Sheriff or Deputy Sheriff, or from telegraph operators who were in the employ of the railroad company or the mine owners. He stated that although he went up the Creek a few times, he obtained most of the information through official reports. Young stated that through the Senatorial investigation he had to cover other territory and that during that time Bond covered the investigation for the A. P.

Such are the facts. I have taken the trouble to give them at length, so that you may judge for yourself. And in the light of these facts, what do you think of the letter published in the "Independent" over the signature of Frederick Roy Martin, assistant General Manager of the Associated Press? Do you think that Mr. Martin was entirely ingenuous when he stated: "The Provost Marshal was not the Associated Press correspondent, and never had been"?

W. H. French, manager of the Pittsburgh division of the Associated Press, was subpoened by the "Masses" editors, and gave his deposition in advance of the expected trial. It was a trial all in itself, and the stenographic record of it lies before me. For the light it throws on Mr. French's sincerity, let it be noted that he swore he could remember nothing whatever of his conversation with Cal Young when he discharged Young from the employ of the Associated Press. The discharge had taken place less than a year previously, and Mr. French had taken a special trip from Pittsburgh to Charleston, West Virginia, to attend to the matter. But he could not remember why he had discharged Young, nor what he had said to Young. He could not remember having mentioned Fremont Older's complaints. He vaguely thought that he had mentioned Bond, but he couldn't be sure in what connection he had mentioned Bond!

Mr. French explained in detail the methods by which the Associated Press handled its news, and the principles upon which he and his subordinates "edited" it. He produced a bulky mass of typewritten sheets, containing all the dispatches dealing with the West Virginia strike sent out by the Associated Press during sixteen months. Mr. French swore that this record was complete; and you will readily understand that in studying the reports it is of the utmost importance whether Mr. French was telling the truth. If the Associated Press sends out hundreds of dispatches about a strike, and if, before such dispatches are offered in evidence, they are carefully gone over and those which are flagrantly untrue and damaging to the reputation of the Associated Press are extracted and destroyed—then obviously the Associated Press has poisoned the evidence of the trial at the source.

Can I say that the officials of the Associated Press did thus poison the evidence by which they endeavored to send Max Eastman and Art Young to the penitentiary? No, I cannot say that. All I can say is, that Mr. French submitted this record under oath, as the original record, and a correct and complete record, and testified under oath that there was no possibility of its being incorrect or incomplete. Also I can say that an investigation made in the bound files of two Associated Press newspapers revealed the fact that these papers had published dispatches, marked as sent by the Associated Press, which did not appear in the correct and complete record offered under oath by the Associated Press. Such a dispatch may be found in the "Los Angeles Times," September 9, 1912, marked "(by A. P. Night Wire to the Times)." Another such dispatch may be found in the "Nashville American," September 22, 1912, marked "(By Associated Press)."

Let us take the five hundred and thirty-seven exhibits that the Associated Press did submit. By means of them we are enabled to enter the Associated Press' Pittsburgh office and watch step by step the process of poisoning the news at the source. Mr. French, it appears, was not satisfied with the bitterly prejudiced reports which his correspondent, Young, and Young's partner, Bond, sent in to him. He found it necessary to go over their dispatches, and to put in still more poison. The dispatches, as submitted in evidence, contained numerous pencil-marks, excisions and revisions; and all these were initialed, so that it was possible to tell whether Mr. French or one of his assistants had done the work.

Mr. French, under cross examination, explained exactly upon what principles this "editing" had been done. Thus there had been cut out a sentence: "That mine-guards have resorted to unlawful practice is generally conceded." Mr. French explained that this sentence was editorial opinion; the dispatch did not say *who* conceded it. Mr. French declared that he used this same system of editing all through the dispatches. But in the same dispatch his attention was called to the sentence: "Contrary to expectations, the miners did not go to the meeting armed with rifles." This clearly prejudiced sentence stayed in the dispatch—in spite of the fact that the dispatch did not reveal *whose* expectations were referred to! And Mr. French testified that such cutting out of a sentence favorable to the miners and leaving in of a sentence injurious to the miners did not in his judgment render the dispatch unfair. Mr. French repeated the words twice: "I do not say unfair. I do not say unfair." So we are provided with a precise measure of the sense of fairness of an Associated Press manager in charge of strike-news!

In one case the story of an ambush by miners came to the Pittsburgh office, with the qualification: "According to the story which reached here this afternoon." These words were cut out—the effect of the alteration being to make a rumor into a statement of fact. Mr. French could give no justification for this proceeding. From another dispatch the sentence had been cut: "The workers were ready to stick to the last." That seemed to Mr. French a superfluous sentence! Again he had altered a dispatch which interviewed the President of the United Mine Workers of America. "He declared that the miners of West Virginia were groaning under oppressive methods." Mr. French's office had altered it to read that the miners *had been* groaning; and he could see no difference in this change of tense!

I have taken the trouble myself to study the dispatches; and how I wish that I might have Mr. French upon the witness-stand! I would like to go through the five hundred and thirty-seven dispatches and point out how utterly false is his claim that hearsays and opinions were not admitted. There are literally hundreds of hearsays and opinions! For example, the miners are threatening trouble, and "it is thought that on account of this situation the martial law zone may have to be extended." Again: "In some quarters the opinion was expressed that the miners had retired into the mountains." Again: "All the prisoners, it was reported, have been removed from box-cars and were being made as comfortable as possible." Again: "This afternoon there was considerable shooting at Holly Grove. It is said that men employed in the mines were accosted by strikers." Again: "Armed miners have taken possession of the strike territory, according to reports." Such hearsays and opinions as this you find in every other dispatch. Certain testimony is introduced before a commission of the Governor of the State, and the Pittsburgh office of the Associated Press is so in love with hearsays and opinions that it takes some of the evidence introduced and deliberately turns it into hearsay and opinion! I quote one paragraph, first as it was sent in by the correspondent in the field, and second as it was altered in the Pittsburgh office:

> The evidence introduced all tends to show that the prices at the company stores have been much higher than at independent stores, and that there had been no trouble until the mine-guards were brought into the district.
> *According to the miners* the prices at the company stores have been much higher than at independent stores. *They say* there would have been no trouble if the mine-guards had not been brought into the district.

On November 20, 1912, the Charleston correspondent sent a long dispatch about the fighting, and whole paragraphs of this dispatch were cut out in the Pittsburgh office. I note that in these paragraphs were many hearsays and opinions; but I note that Mr. French's assistants were not content to cut out the hearsays and opinions—they also cut out the news. Here, for example, is one paragraph that never saw the light:

> During the first period of military control the sympathy, it is claimed of a majority of the West Virginians, was with the miners. Since that time many of the union miners have left this section, taking their families into other coal fields. Then, it is alleged, the contention was the removal of the mine-guard system maintained by the coal operators, which had become obnoxious to the miners.

Or these two sentences, cut from the same dispatch:

24

Many strike-breakers imported into the trouble zone have deserted. Today hundreds of these men reached this city from the mining district and walked the streets.

It is especially interesting to note that the date of the dispatch from which the above two paragraphs were cut corresponds exactly with a date when Mr. French, according to his own testimony, sent a special correspondent to Charleston to report the news more fully. He sent a special man, and when this special man sent news favorable to the miners, Mr. French or his assistants sliced out whole chunks from his dispatches—practically everything giving the miners' side!

On September 25, 1912, the Associated Press correspondent in Charleston was moved by some unaccountable impulse to tell the world the precise mechanism of the blacklist which the companies maintained—while insisting, of course, that they had never heard of a blacklist. Says the dispatch:

This it was shown was accomplished through a personal description of a miner on the back of house leases. If the miner was dismissed as undesirable other operators were given a copy of the description.

But was this dangerous information allowed to go out to the world? It was not!

Or again, take the dispatch of February 10, 1913, which tells how, whenever the militiamen came after the strikers, the strikers would dodge trouble; they would "defeat the purpose of the authorities by quietly retiring into the mountains." Mr. French's office makes such a slight change; it merely cuts out one word—the word "quietly"—thus turning a joke into a military operation! Or take the night dispatch of April 22, 1913, which tells how the Governor of West Virginia made a speech to the miners' delegates. Among other things the Governor said: "I assure you that the laboring world has no better friend in public office than myself." The Pittsburgh office of the Associated Press cut out this incendiary sentence from the Governor's speech!

A still more illuminating method of approaching the problem is to compare the Associated Press dispatches as they actually reached the public with the facts as developed by sworn testimony of hundreds of witnesses before the Senate committee. I have made many such comparisons; I will give one.

Among the men who testified before the Senate committee was Lee Calvin, a mine-guard of the Baldwin-Felts Detective Agency. Calvin later made an affidavit, in the course of which he told of his experiences on board the "Bull Moose Special," an armored train which was taken up and down the railroads of these valleys, to shoot up the homes and tent-colonies of the strikers with a machine-gun. This "Bull Moose Special" was at the disposal, not merely of the state militia and of the mine-guards, but of the mine-operators as well. Calvin tells how he was invited by Quinn Morton, the largest coal-operator in the Kanawha Valley, to join a shooting party on the night of February 7, 1913. There were two or three dozen men with several boxes of guns; also the machine-gun. I quote from an affidavit by Calvin:

When we got near Holly Grove the brakeman commenced turning down the lights. When the engineer came in front of Holly Grove he gave two short blasts from the whistle. I was leaning out of the window and they commenced firing out of the baggage car. Flashes, lights, reports and cracks from the machine-gun took me all at once, and the train was a long stream of fire which commenced coming out of the Gatling gun. In about twenty or thirty seconds there came a flash here and there from the tents. About four came from the tents altogether, and they were about 100 feet apart, it would seem to me. No shots had been fired from the tents prior to the time the shots were fired from the train.

Do not imagine that these incidents rest upon the credibility of Lee Calvin alone. They were sworn to by numerous persons of all classes. Mr. Quinn Morton himself admitted before the Senate committee that he had called up the superintendent of the Chesapeake and Ohio Railroad and ordered the "Bull Moose Special" for that night; also that he had gone to a hardware store and purchased thirty Springfield rifles and taken them in a taxi-cab to the train. He objected to the train being referred to as "his" train—explaining that by the objection he meant that he did not own the train!

Also there was introduced the evidence of many persons who happened to be at the muzzle-end of Mr. Morton's thirty Springfield rifles: for example, Mrs. Estep, wife of a miner in Holly Grove:

Senator Kenyon: "Had there been any disorder in the settlement that night? Had you heard any shooting before that time?"
Mrs. Estep: "No, sir."

Senator Kenyon: "Could you hear this train coming?"
Mrs. Estep: "We heard it after it commenced shooting. We had not heard it before. We had our doors closed."
Senator Kenyon: "Could you see the train?"
Mrs. Estep: "No, sir; I never went out the front way at all."
Senator Kenyon: "When did you know your husband was shot?"
Mrs. Estep: "I didn't know he was killed until after the train quit shooting, and I heard some of them speak to him and call his name, and I never heard him answer."

And now, put yourself in the place of the Associated Press correspondent, with your office in the Adjt. General's office in the State House. This train, you understand, starts from Charleston, and comes back to Charleston, and militia officers are on it, and deputy sheriffs are on it. You know Quinn Morton well; you know everybody concerned well; you are in the midst of the gossip and excitement, you see the warriors come back from the fray, boasting of their achievements, laughing and "kidding" one another. You know that they have done this thing several times before, and intend to go on doing it. It is your duty to furnish the American people with news concerning their doings.

The matter is a ticklish one, because Quinn Morton is the largest coal operator in the Kanawha Valley. Of course you cannot mention his name in such a connection; you cannot imply that any mine-operator ever had anything to do with violence, nor must you admit that a striker was killed during a machine-gun attack upon a village at night. You cover the death of Mrs. Estep's husband in one clever sentence as follows:

According to information received here late today, Robert Estep, a miner, was killed last night during the rioting at Mucklow.

The above sentence is from an Associated Press dispatch. And here are the three dispatches in which the news of the "Bull Moose Special" was sent out to the world. I give them exactly as they stand, with all the telegraph marks and technicalities. I might mention that the word "correct," which has been inserted, is an "A. P." mark; I do not know its relation to the dispatch. Also I might add that the words "passenger train" are Associated Press euphemism for "Bull Moose Special." You may not recognize the events, but this is really the same "Bull Moose" expedition that Lee Calvin and Quinn Morton and Mrs. Estep have just told us about:

BULLETIN

Charleston, W. Va., Feb. 7.

Conditions are critical tonight in Paint and Cabin Creeks, Kanawha County, where a coal strike has been on over a year. A Chesapeake and Ohio passenger train was shot up late tonight; the town of Mucklow, W. Va., was riddled with bullets and a physician, with a man dying driving through the district, was fired upon. When the physician with his patient arrived at the hospital, the patient was dead.

Will Be Add,

H.

A T J—12:55 A. M.

BULLETIN

Charleston, W. Va., Feb. 7.

(Add bulletin.)

The Chesapeake and Ohio passenger train ran for half a mile under fire, but no one was injured. At Mucklow a majority of houses bear marks from rifles, but in this place no one was injured.

Late tonight a conference was held with Governor Glasscock, during which Sheriff Bonner Hill asked the governor that troops be sent into the strike territory. Sheriff Hill notified the governor that the Chesapeake and Ohio Railroad would have a special train ready to move the troops at once.

Will Be Add,

H.

A 2 J—1:11 A. M.

BULLETIN

Charleston, W. Va., Feb. 7.

(Add bulletin.)

At midnight striking miners were gathering from Paint and Cabin Creeks in the vicinity of Mucklow. There is anxiety here as to the next move of the strikers.

The engineer and two passengers were injured when the passenger train on the Chesapeak and Ohio was fired upon. (CORRECT.)

Deputy sheriffs waiting for such an attack as occurred tonight were prepared. The officers directed bullets into Mucklow from rapid fire guns and rifles. The miners' camp was subjected to a heavy fire and whether the shots were effective is not known.

Mucklow is surrounded by mountains and the fighting between strikers and the authorities is difficult.

H.

A 2 J—1:22 A. M.

These are your night dispatches. Next day more details come in, and you send a message to the effect that the sheriff and his deputies cannot get into the miners' camp to see if any of the campers have been killed or injured. Then, realizing that serious trouble is coming, you wonder whether you may not have distorted the news a little more than is permitted, even to an Associated Press correspondent. You fear that you have put in a fatal dose of poison, and decide to protect yourself by sending a small quantity of antidote—such a wee, small quantity of antidote! You write:

Shooting from the train, attacked on the Chesapeake and Ohio Railroad during the night, *was in the direction of the camp,* and it was feared that if any of the women and children had been hurt the sheriff and his men would be unable to restrain the angry men as they outnumber the posse ten to one, and are said to be well armed.

Such is the news, and all the news which the Associated Press sent to the public about that exploit of the "Bull Moose Special" on the night of February 7, 1913. And now do you think, or do you not think, that the editors of the "Masses" were justified in their cartoon alleging that this news was "Poisoned at the Source"? I think so; also I think that Senator John W. Kern of Indiana was justified in his statements made in the United States Senate three months later, regarding the suppression of other news from this coal strike:

But to me the most startling fact bearing on the subject under discussion was this: Here was a proceeding not only unusual but almost unheard of being carried on almost in sight of the capital of West Virginia and within 300 miles of the National capital. One of the best-known women in America—a woman past her eightieth year—a woman known and loved by millions of the working people of America for the promotion of whose welfare and for the ameliora-tion of whose condition she had dedicated her life—a woman so honored and beloved by these millions that she was known to all of them in every humble home as Mother Jones, was being tried in this unusual way before this mock tribunal.

The fact of the trial was sensational. The subject matter of the trial was of the deepest interest. The incidents of such a trial would be of necessity, not only sensational, but would interest the country.

And yet the great news-gathering agencies of the country, active, alert, with a large, intelligent force searching everywhere for items of news, were not able to furnish a line of information to their news-paper patrons concerning this astonishing proceeding.

This fact speaks volumes as to the conditions in that terror-stricken country. A zone had been established for these infamous proceedings for the purpose of suppressing information concerning them.

I was informed by a representative of the greatest of all these news-gathering agencies that the proceedings were not reported because the conditions there were such that it was not safe for newspaper men to enter the field to secure the facts for publication.

This same agency has had a representative in the City of Mexico throughout the period of the recent revolutions. He was not afraid to remain there and report faithfully the news while the streets were being plowed and mowed by the deadly missiles from the cannons of contending armies. But in West Virginia the situation was such that the American reading public was kept in profound ignorance of the startling happenings there because of a reign of terror which could not be braved by the dauntless representatives of the American Press associations.

This single fact alone will justify fully the most searching investigation.

I have discussed in Chapter XLII the mystery of why the Associated Press dropped the case against the "Masses." I always prefer to give both sides of a question, and it was my hope that I might be able to give the Associated Press explanation of this mystery. My hope was roused by Mr. Stone himself, who entered into correspondence with me, and made the flat-footed statement: "I am glad to give anyone information respecting this organization." I, being a trusting person, took Mr. Stone at his word, and wrote him a courteous letter, putting to him four questions, as follows:

1. Was any investigation made of my wife's complaint to you of the false report sent out by the Associated Press that she was arrested on April 29, 1914, in New York City? And why was no correction of this false report ever made, in spite of my wife's written request? Every New York newspaper and every other press association in America sent out a correct report of my arrest, only the Associated Press reported that my wife was arrested.

2. What was the result of the investigation which you promised to make concerning my article published in the "Appeal to Reason" in the latter part of May, 1914, telling of the refusal of the Associated Press to send out a report of a deliberate lie told by Gov. Ammons of Colorado to President Wilson? Mr. John P. Gavit of the "New York Evening Post" showed me your letter, promising to investigate this matter.

3. What was the reason the Associated Press decided to drop the libel suit against the "Masses"?

4. What action, if any, did the Associated Press take concerning the charges published in "Pearson's Magazine" by Charles Edward Russell, dealing with its gross and systematic misrepresentation of the Calumet strikers?

I put these four questions politely, and in entire good faith, and instantly my correspondence with Mr. Stone comes to an end! I wait day by day; I wait with sorrow and yearning, but no answer comes from Mr. Stone. I delay sending my book to the printer for more than two months, hoping to get a reply from Mr. Stone; but I get no reply!

I now publicly address to Mr. Stone one final communication. I implore him, for the sake of the honor of the great institution which he represents, for the sake of the good name of all American Journalism, not to swallow in silence the charges published in a book called "The Brass Check." I implore him to have the author of that volume arrested for criminal libel—and when the case is ready for trial, not to drop it!

My wife reads this chapter and asks me to omit the last paragraph. She says I am "bow-wowing" at Mr. Stone.

I think it over and decide to accept the metaphor. I picture a big dog walking down the street, a stately and dignified dog, and a very little dog comes up behind him and says "bow-wow," and the big dog puts his tail between his legs and runs. However we may think about this incident, one thing certainly has been accomplished—the big dog has been robbed of his pose. Never again will we regard him as a stately and dignified dog!

P. S. to ninth edition: The Associated Press ignored this challenge. But the public clamor became so great that something had to be done. The annual convention of the Associated Press is a great state occasion, when delegates come from every A. P. paper, and propaganda is handed out concerning the immaculateness of the organization. At the 1921 convention, sixteen months after the publication of "The Brass Check," the A. P. gave to the press a statement that it had appointed a committee to investigate my charges, and that "a mass of evidence" had been collected, and would soon be published. The delegates accepted this assurance and adjourned. A month later I wrote to the A. P. asking when the evidence was to appear. No answer. I sent a copy of my letter to every delegate who had attended the convention, and to every A. P. newspaper. Not a word from any one. For several years thereafter I sent a copy of my letter and challenge to the delegates to every A. P. annual convention, but I was never able to get a reply. I have never seen the "mass of evidence," and neither has the American people ever seen it.

CHAPTER LIX

THE PRESS AND THE WAR

War came upon the world, and the writer, as a student of Journalism, watched the great tide of public opinion. There had been newspapers in America which had kept a careful pretense of impartiality; under the pressure of war this pretense was forgotten. For example, the "New York Times." Everyone would admit that the editorial page of the "Times" is class-propaganda, but the "Times" tries not to let you know that its news-columns are class-propaganda. It avoids the cruder blunders, such as false headlines. But when the threat of war came, and the "Times" was trying to force the country into war, the "Times" forgot even that precaution. On Thanksgiving Day, 1915, some twelve hundred clergymen in New York preached sermons. The "Times" selected eleven of these sermons and put them all under this headline:

PREPAREDNESS FROM MANY PULPITS

Thanksgiving Sermons Justify War for Defense of American Liberty and Ideals

Then you read the sermons, and what did you find? Three of them contained utterances which might be construed as urging preparedness; the other eight contained not a word in reference to preparedness!

And the same with the magazines. There had been magazines which in the old days would give excuses for not publishing this or that—they were concerned with questions of dignity, of art; they could not lend their columns to propaganda. But now these magazines became frankly organs of propaganda. Long before America entered the war, "McClure's" turned all its energies to a campaign for "preparedness." The "American," the "Metropolitan," the "Outlook" did the same. "Current Opinion" abandoned its policy of reprinting from other publications, and introduced propaganda of its own. The "Literary Digest," supposed to be an impartial survey of public opinion, became a partisan organ of hate. Says a writer in "Reedy's Mirror":

The standardizing of the press had already proceeded to inordinate lengths before the war. As one sectional bookcase may differ from another of the same pattern only in its greater or lesser number of sections, so differs one American newspaper from another American newspaper. However, some small opportunity for individuality, for thought or pretense of thought, still existed, but even this has ended. With the opening of the war the American press ceased to think. The abstention has been so complete and prolonged that it may never be possible to resume the habit of thinking.

Look over these newspapers as they come in from the mails. Flag-waving of the cheapest, most brainless sort, Liberty Bonds, Thrift Stamps, Red Cross. This is the gamut that has countless repetition from New York to San Francisco, supplemented only by supercensored, mercilessly standardized stuff from the fighting fronts.

The writer of this book gave his support to the war against Germany, and has no apology to make for that course. He believed that the world would be a safer place for radicals to work in when the Kaiser had been overthrown; he still believes this—even though at the moment it seems that the result of our fighting has been to set up new imperialisms in Italy, France, England and America.

But my support of the war did not mean that I had given myself into the hands of war-profiteers. I saw that the old-time plunderers of America were among the war's most ardent supporters, and they went right on with their plundering—becoming "dollar-a-year" men in Washington, with a great cry of patriotism, and letting themselves contracts out of which hundreds of millions of profit were made! The Beef Trust, the Steel Trust, the Oil Trust, the Powder Trust, multiplied many times over the profits they were taking from the necessities of the people; also they dictated legislation which spared their profits, and saddled the cost of the war upon future generations. A war has to be won with materials then existing in the world, or immediately produced; it manifestly cannot be won with materials produced a generation later. The only question is, shall the necessary materials be taken from the owners by means of taxes, or shall they be borrowed, shall the labor of future generations be pledged in exchange? This is clear and simple; but if you tried to explain it to the people during the war you would be lynched, or sent to jail for twenty years.

It was the grand chance for the plunderers of America to put their enemies, the radicals, out of the way. Many of these radicals opposed the war, but others were put out of the way merely for opposing the profiteers, and they received sentences which, for ferocity, exceed anything in the records of the Russian Tsardom. Some two thousand of them are still in jail, their sentences aggregating twenty-five thousand years.

It would have been a simple matter to persuade the Socialists to support the war. We know today that Nicholas Lenine asked only a promise of support from America, offering to repudiate the Brest-Litovsk treaty and join the war on Kaiserism. As to labor at home, an intelligent army officer showed the way in the Northwest; he gave the lumbermen an eight-hour day, decent living conditions, and generous wages, and so turned the I. W. W. of the spruce country into a patriotic society. But elsewhere the army officers were less intelligent, and the profiteers had their way; in the oil country of Kansas they threw scores of I. W. W. organizers into jail without trial, and held them there for a couple of years. They are holding some thirty of them still, and my mail is full of pitiful letters from poor devils who are asked to raise ten thousand dollars bail. All over the country this was done— in a frenzy of public excitement, deliberately created by the capitalist press.

The story of what the newspapers did to American radicals in this crisis would be unbelievable—if you had not read the rest of this book. Thus, for example, the case of Bannwart, a Boston pacifist, one of a committee which called upon Senator Lodge to protest against the declaration of war. Senator Lodge lost his temper and struck Bannwart in the face; and all over the country went the report that Senator Lodge had been assaulted in his office by a pacifist! The Senator became a national hero; the Boston newspapers printed columns and columns about the incident, and when Bannwart called upon the Senator to admit the truth, he not only refused to admit it, but gave out for publication many telegrams congratulating him upon his heroism. No newspaper would publish Bannwart's side, and he was helpless for two years, until his suit for damages was about to come up in court; then the Senator gave way, and admitted in writing that he had struck the first blow. You have been acquainted with the "Evening Transcript," organ of Boston's aristocracy of wealth and culture, which publishes half-page advertisements of "Harvard Beer 1,000 pure," and full-page advertisements of the arguments of gas company attorneys, and sends out "dope" for the "New

Haven" plunderers; so you will be prepared to hear that the "Transcript" buried this apology of Senator Lodge in a remote corner, and without comment!

Or take the experience of my friend Feigenbaum, Socialist Assemblyman of New York State. The Socialist assemblymen had been protesting against the custom of the machine gang to drive through bills without consideration. They resolved to put a stop to the custom; whereupon the machine leaders set a little trap for the Socialists. A bill was introduced, without being read, and the speaker asked unanimous consent to advance it to the second reading. The leader of the Socialist group immediately objected. The bill had not been read, he declared, no one on the floor knew what was in the bill, no one even knew the name of the bill. The speaker cut him short: "No explanation is necessary. Your objection is sufficient." So the bill, under the rules, went over to the next day. Says Feigenbaum:

> The members drifted out to the cloak-rooms, or they remained at their desks. They didn't know what the bill was about, because nine-tenths of them hadn't read it, and not more than four or five were in the secret of the day's mysterious doings.

But next morning the Socialists found out what had happened. The bill was to turn over certain lands in Saratoga County to the War Department, and the Socialists had been guilty of stopping war legislation which was desperately needed! The "New York Tribune" carried an elaborate account of a tempestuous scene, in which the speaker had "scathingly rebuked, the Socialist leader. The members had swarmed around the Socialists, shaking their fists in their faces, threatening them with physical violence; also, the Socialist leader had refused to stand at the playing of the national anthem. Says Feigenbaum: "The whole story was a fabrication, pure and simple, out of whole cloth." And he tells what happened afterwards—

> A campaign of vilification hitherto unheard of. It went so far that Albany papers called for the raiding of the rooms we occupied, called for a boycott of us by shop-keepers and restaurant-men in Albany, and gave high praise to a drunken ruffian, an ex-prizefighter, member of the Assembly, who in a drunken fit of temper called for the lynching of the Socialists. This speech was highly praised editorially in Albany and Troy.

During the war our industrial autocracy has learned to

organize for propaganda; it has learned the arts of hate. Today all the energies which were directed against the Kaiser have been turned against the radicals; also the spy-system which the government developed for the war has been turned against the radicals. Government agents raid their offices and seize their letters, and these letters are spread broadcast in the capitalist press—duly doctored, of course, and supplied with commentaries to distort their meaning.

For example, the "Lusk Committee" of the New York State Legislature holds a secret session with the executives of the New York newspapers (June 3, 1919, at the Murray Hill Hotel), and lays out its campaign in detail. It then proceeds, with a carload of soldiers and detectives, to raid the Rand School of Social Science; taking along a secret service agent of the British government, which is shooting radicals in Ireland and India, and wishes to find out all it can about their supporters in America. They find a manuscript, outlining a plan for propaganda among negroes. It was a rejected manuscript, as it happens; but the Lusk Committee "accepts" it, and spreads it broadcast. I shiver, contemplating the day when they raid my office, and publish all the queer manuscripts that arrive in my day's mail! Manuscripts of health-cures, manuscripts of bible-prophecies, manuscripts of plans to abolish money, to communicate with Mars, to exterminate the vermin in the Los Angeles County Jail!

Also they find a circular of the Rand School, saying that the Socialists "must prepare to take over the government." They publish this in the newspapers with horrified clamor: Sedition! Treason! Let the charter of the Rand School be annulled! As if there were any political party or political association in America which does not propose to take over the government! As if there were anything else which any political party or political association could propose!

Among the other seditious documents are some copies of "The Profits of Religion," which gives occasion for sarcasm from the investigators. They propose to investigate "the profits of agitation"; so they spread broadcast the fact that Scott Nearing was paid six hundred dollars by the Rand School—and deny Nearing an opportunity to testify that part of this was payment for lectures delivered outside of the school, for which the school had collected the money on a percentage basis; and the balance for lecturing at the school, at a rate approximating ten cents per week for each student!

They lie about the pacifists and those whom they call Bolsheviks; they lie equally about a man like myself, who supported the war, and is opposing Bolshevism. In the accounts of the proceedings of the Senate Committee investigating "Bolshevism in America," there was submitted, according to newspaper accounts, a long list of writings "urging the overthrow of the United States government by violence"; among the writers named being Upton Sinclair. I at once wrote to Solicitor Lamar of the postoffice department, to Major Humes, and to Senator Overman—these being the parties who had compiled the writings in question. I explained to these gentlemen that for twenty years I had been writing for the precise purpose of avoiding "the overthrow of the United States government by violence," and I requested to know what writings of mine could have justified their charge. I have letters from all three of these parties, stating that nothing of mine was included, or had been included in the list; the published report of the Overman Committee reveals that this statement is correct; yet the dispatch including my name was sent broadcast over the country by the Associated Press— and I am without redress!

The listing of anecdotes of this sort is merely a question of the amount of space one is willing to give. The United States government is deporting Hindu revolutionists to be executed by the British government when they reach India. Prof. Richard Gottheil of Columbia University writes to the "New York Times" denying that this is so. Robert Morse Lovett, editor of the "Dial," writes to the "Times," citing case after case, upon British official authority. And the "Times" refuses to print Mr. Lovett's letter! A friend of mine writes to Prof. Gottheil about it, and he answers that he wishes the "Times" would print Mr. Lovett's letter, because he believes in fair play. But the "Times" does not believe in fair play!

In the same way, the "Times" attacks "Jimmie Higgins." In the last chapters of this story an American soldier is represented as being tortured in an American military prison. Says the "Times":

Mr. Sinclair should produce the evidence upon which he bases his astounding accusations, if he has any. If he has simply written of

hearsay evidence, or, worse still, let himself be guided by his craving
to be sensational, he has laid himself open not only to censure but
to punishment.

In reply to this, I send to the "Times" a perfectly respectful letter, citing scores of cases, and telling the "Times" where
hundreds of other cases may be found. The "Times" returns
this letter without comment. A couple of months pass, and
as a result of the ceaseless agitation of the radicals, there
is a congressional investigation, and evidence of atrocious
cruelties is forced into the newspapers. The "Times" publishes an editorial entitled, "Prison Camp Cruelties," the first
sentence of which reads: "The fact that American soldiers
confined in prison-camps have been treated with extreme
brutality may now be regarded as established." So again I
write a polite letter to the "Times," pointing out that I think
they owe me an apology. And how does the "Times" treat
that? It alters my letter without my permission! It cuts out
my request for an apology, and also my quotation of its own
words calling for my punishment! The "Times," caught in a
hole, refuses to let me remind its readers that it wanted me
"punished" for telling the truth! "All the News that's Fit to
Print!"

Or take the case of Henry Ford, who brings suit against the
"Chicago Tribune" for libel, and cites five lies in one single
news item:

Lie No. 1. That guardsmen employed by Ford would lose their
places.
Lie No. 2. That no provision would be made for their dependents.
Lie No. 3. That their families could get along as best they might.
Lie No. 4. That when they returned they would have to apply
for their old jobs as strangers.
Lie No. 5. That this rule applied to the Ford plants everywhere.

At the trial it was proven that all these statements were
false. All the Ford workers who were drafted to Mexico had
their wages paid to their families while they were away. On
the other hand it was shown, through the testimony of Joseph
Medill Patterson, one of the editors of the "Tribune," and a
renegade Socialist, that he had ordered the stopping of the pay
of all those "Tribune" men who were drafted to Europe! I
quote the testimony.

"How many of your employes went to the great war?"
"About two hundred and sixty-eight."

"None of them drew salaries?"

"No."

"But you drew your salary when you went over-seas, didn't you?"

"Yes."

"And your salary is about twenty thousand dollars a year, isn't it?"

Witness admitted that it was.

"The World's Greatest Newspaper."

Or take the Nonpartisan League of North Dakota. All through the war the newspapers strove to make this appear a disloyal organization. The League held a convention at St. Paul, at which hundreds of speeches were made; and the Associated Press found it possible to make one of the speakers, La Follette, appear disloyal by misquoting him. So it featured La Follette—and reported the other speakers hardly at all. As this book is going to press, the League bank is raided, and the farmers by thousands come pouring into Fargo in the rain, and at two enormous gatherings they pledge themselves to make their bank the biggest in the state. The bank is reopened, and on the first day forty-five thousand dollars is put in and only nine thousand taken out. And how is all this handled by the Associated Press? Hear the "Idaho Leader":

Several newspaper representatives from St. Paul and Minneapolis were present to send as unfavorable reports of the great meeting to their papers as they could, and the Associated Press, the news agency which supplies the "Boise Statesman" with its daily fables from North Dakota, evidently fearing that their local manager was not capable of falsifying in the manner which big business demands, sent a special representative out from St. Paul to report the meeting. And this "A. P." representative did himself proud, or rather he did the bidding of his masters.

Among other highly colored and untrue statements which the Associated Press representatives made was that "when the speaking was ended in the auditorium and a recess taken before the evening meeting, the crowds made a rush for the doors to get away so that they would not have to subscribe for stock in the Scandinavian bank!"

The crowd *did* make a rush but it was not for the doors. The crowd rushed, jostled, and pushed, in the anxiety of dozens of men to reach the front of the building, where a number of persons took subscriptions for stock. Those handling the subscriptions were swamped, and many men were forced to stand in line for a long time before they were waited on.

CHAPTER LX

THE CASE OF RUSSIA

But the perfect case of journalistic knavery, the case which in the annals of history will take precedence over all others, past or present, is the case of Russia. You might say that all previous experience of the capitalist press of America in perverting and distorting news was but training for what it was to do to the Russian revolution. Say to yourself as follows: American Journalism did thus and so to an American author who advocated the abolition of privilege and exploitation; what would this Journalism do to a hundred and eighty million people who rose up and actually put an end to privilege and exploitation upon the half of two continents?

Let me make clear at the outset my point of view, oft repeated. I am not a Bolshevik, and have never been a Bolshevik. I understand that a Bolshevik is one who repudiates political action, and wishes to accomplish the social revolution by mass action of the proletariat, the direct overthrow of our present capitalist government and the setting up of a government by councils of the workers, something corresponding to our present trade union councils and conventions. For my part, I agree with the syndicalists in thinking that the best way to govern industry is through trade unions; that is the only real industrial democracy. But I believe that the trade unions can get this power by the ballot, backed by the mass strike. I don't believe that it will be necessary for the workers to seize guns and turn the politicians out of office; I believe that they can elect their own politicians, or force even capitalist legislatures to pass laws recognizing union control of industry.

I am well aware that this method will be slower, but I believe it will be quicker in the long run, because it will avoid the waste incidental to civil war, and the possibilities of failure and temporary reaction. Anybody can see that, as a matter of business, it would pay the workers better to continue working for the capitalists a few months or even a few years longer, than to take a course which might result in burning down the factories and getting the best leaders of the movement stood up against a wall and shot.

But such a program, of course, can be effective only in a country where political rights are recognized. Russia was not such a country. The Russian people had been held down by an utterly ruthless and utterly corrupt despotism, deprived of all opportunity to organize and to educate themselves, to acquire experience in government affairs; so, when they rose, they turned upon their oppressors the weapons they had been taught to understand. We, who were born in a more fortunate land, and have learned to use, if only half successfully, the ballot and public discussion in the settlement of our affairs— what attitude were we to take towards the Russian people, striking out blindly against their oppressors, groping for liberty and life?

The first revolution, the Kerensky revolution, was a political one, and that suited us fairly well; it made no threat against property, and it proposed to support our war. Our capitalist newspapers had no difficulty in getting the news about it, and had no objection to letting us read this news. But then came the second revolution, the Bolshevik revolution, and that did threaten property, and proposed to withdraw from our war. How did we treat that?

We had been training ourselves for a generation, so as to be instantly ready; we had been training ourselves in the office of Mr. Hearst's "Cosmopolitan Magazine," where Mr. Hearst had a twenty-five-thousand-dollar-a-year journalistic wizard by the name of Edgar Sisson. When we needed a molder of opinion for Russia, we sent this Hearst wizard across the seas, where he came upon a set of documents proving that Lenin and Trotsky were German agents. These documents had been examined and rejected as forgeries by Raymond Robins, also by the British Embassy, none too favorably disposed to the Bolsheviks; but matters like that do not trouble Hearst editors, who have learned to think in headlines. The "Sisson documents" were shipped to Washington, and issued under the authority of the United States government, and published in every newspaper in America.

We know today who were the real pro-Germans in Russia. Viscount French, in his recently published book, has told us that the Russian Court was rotten with pro-Germanism, and that if it had not been for treason among the Russian aristocracy, the war would have been won two years earlier. As for Lenin and Trotsky, not only were they bitter enemies of the German government, they were at this time offering to reject the Brest-Litovsk treaty, if America would support them; but America was a virtuous capitalist nation, and the entire capitalist press of America was a unit in proclaiming that our country should have no relations with men who refused to pay interest on the Tsar's debts to J. P. Morgan & Company.

All the lying power of our Journalism was turned against the Russian Soviets; and if you have read this book without skipping, you know what that lying power is. No tale was too grotesque to be believed and spread broadcast. In the same week we would read that Trotsky had fled to Spain, that he had been put in jail by Lenin, that he had been seeking a job on the "Appeal to Reason," Girard, Kansas! They published so many inventions that they couldn't keep track of them. Here are two paragraphs from a single issue of one newspaper:

Nicolai Lenin, the Bolshevist Premier, is the only prominent Bolshevist left who appears to lead an austere life.—"New York Times," February 26, 1919.

Premier Lenin, refugees say, is not affected by the food problem. His bill for fruit and vegetables in a recent month amounted to sixty thousand rubles.—"New York Times," February 26, 1919.

In his book, "Russia in 1919," Arthur Ransom tells how in Finland he read detailed accounts of mutiny and revolt in Petrograd, the city being bombarded by naval guns. He went into Petrograd and found the city peaceful, and everybody laughing at his tales. Returning to England he found that the tales had been forwarded to England, and published and universally believed. As I write these words, I read in my paper every other day of the fall of Petrograd. The accounts are detailed, some of them are "official," and they continue for weeks. But finally I read that the anti-Bolshevik armies are in retreat from Petrograd!

Or take the "nationalization of women," the most grotesque scare-crow ever constructed to terrify a highly moral people. I have shown you how the imagination of "kept" journalists runs to foul tales about sex orgies of radicals. A comic paper in Moscow published such a "skit" on Bolshevism, and the outcome is explained in the following from the "Isvestija," the official organ of the Central Soviet Government, May 18, 1918:

Moscow Soviet decision.—The Moscow newspaper, the "Evening Life," for printing an invented decree regarding the socialization of women, in the issue of the 3rd of May, No. 36, shall be closed for ever and fined 25,000 roubles.

And then again, in the city of Saratov, in central Russia, the Anarchists were making trouble, and some wag, to discredit the Anarchists, invented an elaborate decree, signed, "The Free Association of Anarchists of Saratov." This decree was discovered one morning, posted in several parts of the city. An American writer, Oliver M. Sayler, who was in Saratov, wrote the story in the "New Republic," March 15, 1919. He visited the Anarchist clubs, and found them boiling with indignation—calling it a "Bolshevist plot"! Needless to say, of course, the decree had no relation to reality; the Anarchists never had any power to enforce any decree, whether in Saratov or anywhere else in Russia; several hundred Anarchists had been jailed by the Bolsheviki. But that, of course, made no difference to the editors of capitalist newspapers in America, to whom Anarchists, Bolsheviki, and Socialists were all the same; from one end of the country to the other this decree took the front page. The "Los Angeles Times" published it with a solemn assurance to its readers that the authenticity of the decree might be accepted without question. And forthwith all our capitalist clergymen rose up in their pulpits to denounce the Bolsheviki as monsters and moral perverts, and a good part of the moving picture machinery of Southern California has been set to work constructing romances around this obscene theme.

The "New Europe," which had first published the story, made a full retraction and apology. Harold Williams, who had sent the story to England, also apologized. The American State Department denied the story officially, February 28, 1919. Jerome Davis, of the American Red Cross, denied it from first-hand knowledge in the "Independent," March 15, 1919. But did you read these apologies and denials in American capitalist newspapers? You did not! It would not be too much to say that nine people out of ten in America today firmly believe that women have been "nationalized" in Russia, or at any rate that the Bolsheviki attempted it. In the "World Tomorrow," for July, 1919, I come upon a letter signed Remington Rogers, Tulsa, Oklahoma. I find something very quaint and pathetic about this letter. How does it strike you?

I find that like most radical papers, you assume that your reader knows a great many things that may be trite in the discussion of parlor Socialists, but with which the average citizen is not in the least familiar. For example, in your May issue, page 141, I find the assertion that the reports purporting to show how family life had been officially demoralized in Russia are "now happily proved false." If this is the fact, no such proof has leaked into the newspapers or other periodicals to which I subscribe, and in view of the fact that we have what purport to be authentic copies of the official edicts and decrees, I cannot believe that these reports have been proved false.

And here is a letter from Alice Stone Blackwell, which, needless to say, could only be published in some radical paper. It appeared in the "Public," New York:

Catherine Breshkovsky "the Grandmother of the Russian Revolution," is getting badly misquoted. She is astonished to see how different some of the press reports are from what she really said. She tells me she declared the other day that she would work twenty years longer to keep Russia from having another Tsar, and she was reported as saying that she would work twenty years longer to get the Tsar back.

She also denied that women have been "nationalized," or "made common property," or that the Government puts any compulsion upon them in matters of sex. She said to me: "Women have more freedom in Russia now than they ever had before." As Madame Breshkovsky is strongly opposed to the Bolshevist régime, her denial of this particular accusation may be accepted as conclusive.

I have at several places in this book portrayed the degeneracy of "McClure's Magazine," since it has become an organ of privilege; also I have mentioned Newell Dwight Hillis, agent of the Clerical Camouflage, and his knavish pamphlet against the Colorado strikers. Now we see "McClure's" hiring Hillis to vilify the Russian Soviets. After all these denials have been published, and are available to all honest men, this agent of the Clerical Camouflage contributes to "McClure's" (June, 1919) a long article calling for the blood of the Russian people. "McClure's" puts over the article a picture representing a hideous fiend with a torch and bomb; also this editorial statement:

Dr. Hillis's articles have brought in a flood of letters of commendation. He writes as he preaches, fearlessly, truthfully.

I ask: Could the re-crucifixion of Christ go farther than the application of the words "fearlessly, truthfully," to the following dastardly lie:

It is now conceded that the interior towns and cities of Russia have gone over to this nationalization of women.

This agent of the Clerical Camouflage of course portrays Russia as a chaos of murder and bloodshed; in which our whole capitalist press agrees. We now know that most of the time Petrograd and Moscow were the most orderly capitals in Europe; but our newspaper correspondents in Stockholm and Copenhagen and Odessa and Omsk, meeting in the cafés with exiled Russian noblemen, thought nothing of standing a few thousand Russians against the wall of the Kremlin and shooting them in a news despatch. For weeks they harrowed us with a projected "St. Bartholomew's Eve Massacre," in which all the bourgeoisie in Russia were to be destroyed. Bartholomew's Eve came, and next morning I looked in the papers, and saw that there had been a general amnesty for political prisoners in Russia—something for which I am still petitioning the President of my own country! I saw no mention of the massacre; but this did not surprise me. I, too, have been lied about by Capitalist Journalism on the front page, and have seen the retraction buried in small print among the advertisements.

That there was much killing in Russia, I do not doubt; but whether there was more killing than under the government of the Tsar—that is the real question. Frazier Hunt tells us that in the first fourteen months of their rule, the Bolsheviki executed four thousand, five hundred persons, mostly for stealing and speculation; whereas, in twelve months after the 1905 revolution, Stolypin, minister of the Tsar, caused the execution of thirty-two thousand, seven hundred and seventy-three persons. That is about the usual proportion of the White Terror to the Red, and the proportion that would have prevailed had the Allies succeeded in their plan of getting Kolchak to Moscow.

Our papers were giving us lurid accounts of the Bolsheviki advancing in the Baltic provinces, burning and slaying as they went; but the conspiracy slipped a cog, and there crept into an Associated Press dispatch a little paragraph which gave the game away. In reading it, understand that these provinces are a part of Russia, which the Russians were taking back from the Germans:

Warsaw, Dec. 29.—The Bolsheviki are advancing rapidly toward

Vilna, and are favored by mild weather. Their advance guards are said to be orderly, well clothed and well armed. *They have committed no depredations except where they met with resistance.*

And here is another from Berlin, Feb. 15, 1919, which gives us the real reason for the world-wide dread of the Bolsheviki. Ralph Rotheit, correspondent of the Berlin "Vossische Zeitung," visited the Bolshevik line at Vilna.

He pictured the situation as extremely pessimistic, although so far the Bolsheviki have always been defeated by the Germans whenever they ventured skirmishing. However, Rotheit writes, the Bolsheviki do not rely so much on fighting as on corrupting opponents by never-ceasing wireless propaganda, and by sending emissaries into the districts still occupied by the Germans, and by Bolshevik literature with which the latter's positions are flooded. Rotheit says unfortunately the effect of this propaganda at Kovno, headquarters of the German commander, was only too evident, as in many other places on German territory, as well as the Russian and Polish.

Here we have the real quarrel with the Soviets, the real reason why they must not, cannot be permitted to survive. They are propagandists; day and night they agitate, they preach and they print—and for some reason, the more loudly we proclaim that their propaganda is false, the more deeply we seem to dread its success! Since when have we lost our faith in the might of truth? Since when have we decided that error must be fought with bullet and machine-gun? Surely there must be some dark secret here, some skeleton in our family closet!

The truth is that we have seen in Russia a gigantic strike, an I. W. W. strike, if you please; and it has been successful. The workers have seized the factories, and now we call for the militia to drive them out. The very existence of capitalism depends upon their being driven out; as the phrase is, they must "be made an example of." And so the capitalist press is called in, our great lying-machine is given the biggest job in its history. The Associated Press does for Russia precisely what Charles Edward Russell showed it doing for Calumet, what I showed it doing for Colorado. All our newspapers, big and little, do what they are accustomed to do whenever there is a strike in America—telling everything evil about the strikers and nothing good about them, clamoring for violence against them, justifying every crime committed against them in the name of "law and order."

Recently the Soviets, pressed by starvation, have bowed so

far to the will of world-capitalism as to agree to pay interest
on the Tsar's debts; they have offered to pledge some of the
vast natural resources of Russia to pay for the machinery and
supplies they must have. So Allied diplomacy hesitates and
falters; dare the diplomats risk the terrors of Bolshevist
propaganda, that mysterious black magic? Dare they allow
the world to see a prospering social revolution, a government
of the workers, by the workers, for the workers, which does
not perish from the earth?

They decided upon a conference with the Bolsheviki, on a
remote island in Turkish waters. Our newspapers printed the
fact that the invitation had been extended to the Bolsheviki:
but they did not print the Bolshevik acceptance. They did not
print the text of the Russian foreign minister's appeal to the
French Socialist, Longuet, as to the meaning of the Allied
proposals. They did not print the fact that the conference was
abandoned because William Allen White, American delegate
and man of honor, insisted upon full publicity.

President Wilson sent a confidential mission to Russia,
composed of William C. Bullitt and Lincoln Steffens. They
came back and reported that there was order in Russia; that
the Russian people were satisfied with the Soviet régime; that
the "nationalization of women" in Russia was an absurd yarn;
that the cause of the starvation and misery in Russia was the
allied blockade; and that Lenin wanted peace, and was willing
to do almost anything to get peace. President Wilson, for
reasons presumably known to him, turned down the advice of
this commission. Steffens made a public statement as to his
position, which was reported in the "London Daily Herald,"
but in no American newspaper or magazine. Bullitt resigned
from the Peace Commission, and addressed to President
Wilson a brief and dignified letter, explaining his reasons:
which letter was published in the "New York Nation," but in
no capitalist newspaper in America, so far as I could find out.

Then Bullitt was summoned before the Senate committee,
and the Associated Press sent out a brief and inadequate
report of his testimony. Next day he submitted the confidential report about Russia which he had delivered to President
Wilson. This was the most important information about
Russia yet available to the American people; and the "Los
Angeles Times," from which I get my first news of the world,
gave not a line of this report! More than that, in order to

avoid having to mention the report, the "Times" cut out that day every word of its news about the struggle over the peace treaty in the Senate! Instead, it gave two columns, of which I quote the headlines:

ROOSEVELT SCORES REDS
"Smash 'Em!" Cries Teddy, Jr., in Talks Telling of Perils in Radicalism

That was on Sunday morning. On Monday morning again, the "Times" had not a word about Bullitt, and not a word about the agitation over the peace treaty in Washington, the most important news of the day; the reason being simply that Washington was talking about the Bullitt report, and about nothing else! But on Tuesday, the British government issued a denial of some of Bullitt's statements—one of those evasive denials whereby the gigantic trading corporation tells lies without quite telling them; so once more the "Los Angeles Times" was willing to mention William C. Bullitt!

I call up the "Los Angeles Examiner," to ask if the Associated Press handled the Bullitt report. The "Los Angeles Examiner," you understand, gets the Associated Press service—is one of the "forty-one vote" newspapers. Both the city editor and the telegraph editor assure me that the Associated Press did not send the "Examiner" a word of it—the most important news about Russia yet made available to the American people! Says the "Nation":

> No newspaper has printed Mr. Bullitt's testimony in full or even in generous part; there were only three press representatives present when he testified, and he has had the invariable experience of having his testimony misquoted and altered, and interviews attributed to him which he never gave.

The Social Revolution came in Hungary. It came in an orderly and sensible way, without terror, without bloodshed; and how was it treated by Capitalist Journalism? It was treated just as the Russian Soviets had been treated—as an outcast and outlaw. All the power of World Capitalism was turned against the Hungarian Communist government. Poland, Roumania, the Ukraine, all made war upon it, with French officers and British tanks and American money; and at the same time the great lying-machine was put to work. The news agencies brought the report that Bela Kun had fled to the Argentine; and two days later that he was about to be overthrown in Budapesth! All the power of American Journalism was set to keeping the workers from realizing that a nation of fifteen or twenty million people had overthrown the profit system, and was making a success of the Co-operative Commonwealth.

I have before me some letters from a correspondent in Budapesth, representing one of the most influential and supposed-to-be-respectable of the great New York newspapers. This correspondent explains that she sends her articles with the instructions that they shall be published as written or not at all—and they are not published. "One of my confrères here had an article twisted and turned about so badly that it meant exactly the opposite of what he knew and wrote to be true." And there is a group of correspondents in Budapesth, all having the same experiences, it appears:

> Their economic sentences are cut out of articles and their radical articles are paid for but never printed. There isn't a day passes that we don't have an indignation meeting. One man wrote a long article for one of the prominent magazines two months ago alluding to the new order. He received a fat check with the letter announcing that the article could not be used; they wished him to write more *moderately*. Since my trip to Hungary and my conviction that Budapesth is the only honest place in Europe outside Russia, I am not any longer willing to write "moderately."

Only once before in modern history was there a crime like this—when the kings and emperors of Europe went to war to wipe out the French revolution, which their hired propagandists described in precisely the same terms as we now see applied to the Bolsheviki. Then it was political revolution, now it is social revolution; but the program is the same—the earth is to be soaked with the blood of revolutionists, their new ideal is to be corrupted in the military campaign necessary to its defense, and the world is to be made safe for another Holy Alliance—this time of the profit-system, of Industrial Exploitation. It is for the people, who pay for all privilege and maintain all parasites, to decide whether history shall repeat itself to the full; whether the Holy Alliance of World Capitalism is to crush for another century the hopes of the working masses of the world.

CHAPTER LXI

"BOLSHEVISM" IN AMERICA

And what of those American radicals who have ventured to protest against this policy, and to expose this campaign of falsification? Here again it is only a question of how much space one is willing to give to anecdotes.

My friend Rose Pastor Stokes is a pacifist, under sentence of ten years in jail for pacifist activities; again and again the New York newspapers report her as calling for a bloody revolution in America, and refuse to publish her protest that this is false. You may not like pacifists; I myself admit that during the war I found some of them extremely trying to my patience. But do you believe that the proper way to treat them is to lie about them? Listen to the experiences of Mrs. Stokes on a lecture trip in the Middle West. The "Kansas City Star," a one-time "liberal" paper, sent a special writer to interview her on the laundry-workers' strike then in progress; but finding that this interview put her in a good light, they suppressed it, and sent another reporter to write up her address to the "Women's Dining Club." Says Mrs. Stokes:

The "Star" so garbled and twisted my speech that it was actually unrecognizable. For example, one of the things I was quoted as having said was that the Red Cross was a war camouflage. It so happened that I did not mention the Red Cross during the entire speech.

Then she went to speak in Springfield, Missouri, and the "Star" had a lurid account of how she had been arrested in Springfield, and admitted to bail, and has stolen out of the city at day-break, forfeiting the hundred-dollar bond of a Socialist comrade. Says Mrs. Stokes:

Except for the arrest, the story was a fabrication. I had left Springfield at a respectable hour, wholly cleared; and no bond was forfeited.

She came back to Kansas City, and a "Star" reporter was sent to interview her; she asked him to deny this Springfield story, and he turned in a denial, but not a word of it was published. As a direct result of this newspaper misrepresentation,

Mrs. Stokes was arrested by the Federal authorities and sentenced to ten years in jail. She tells me how this trial and sentence were reported, and points out the obvious motive of the falsifications:

Anything to frighten people away from Socialist meetings! If you want to see this motive running through the capitalist press of the entire country as a single thread, come and read the hundreds of editorials on my ten-year sentence. Every state and every important industrial community is represented. The wording is almost as if one man, let alone one spirit, had dictated them all.

And here is Judson King, writing to members of Congress:

For your information permit me to state that at the meeting at Poli's Theatre Sunday afternoon at which I presided there was no advocacy of anarchy or violence, no attack upon the American form of government, and no propaganda that Bolshevism be adopted in our country. The well-nigh unanimous sentiment of audience and speakers was that American troops be withdrawn and Russia be permitted to settle her own fate in her own way.

The article in Monday's "Washington Post" headed, "Urge Red America," is an absurd perversion of the truth and a gross violation of journalistic ethics. Discussions in Congress regarding this meeting, based apparently upon this article, have proceeded under a misapprehension of facts. Whether any attempt was made to verify the truth of the article I do not know. No inquiry was made of me.

Mr. King goes on to state that the address of Albert Rhys Williams at this meeting was read from a typewritten text, and a carbon copy handed by him to a reporter of the "Washington Post." The falsification of Williams' remarks by the "Post" was therefore deliberate.

At this same time Max Eastman was touring the country, addressing enormous meetings. The meeting in Los Angeles was reported by the "Examiner" as follows:

RADICAL'S TALK BRINGS POLICE

Max Eastman Stops Address When Disgusted Auditors Leave and Officers Arrive

Cutting his lecture short, when many of his auditors left Trinity Auditorium in disgusted anger, probably saved Max Eastman, editor of a radical Socialist publication, from a police intervention last night.

Before the speaker had entered far upon his subject, "Hands Off Russia," his remarks were deemed so unpatriotic and his unwarranted attack upon the administration so vitriolic that scores left the auditorium and telephoned the Federal authorities and the police, denouncing Eastman and demanding his arrest.

Apparently scenting trouble, Eastman effected a sudden diminuendo, his anti-climax coming when he left the rostrum to conduct a canvassing of his audience for prospective subscribers to his magazine and purchasers of stock in same. When the police officers appeared on the scene, nothing of treasonable nor anarchistic nature was heard.

Eastman's address contained many statements so preposterous that even the most gullible refused to believe them. He demanded that Eugene Debs, Thomas J. Mooney and all I. W. W.'s in jail should be freed and advised his hearers to emulate the Russian Bolsheviks and rise in revolution.

Only a scant audience heard the address.

As it happens, I do not have to ask the reader to take either my word or Eastman's about this meeting. Here is part of a letter written to Max Ihmsen, managing editor of the "Los Angeles Examiner," by Rob Wagner, artist and author of "Film Folk."

Mar. 2, 1919.

Dear Max Ihmsen:

The other night Mrs. Wagner, Charlie Chaplin and I, seeking light on darkest Russia, went to hear Max Eastman's lecture. During what we thought was a very thoughtful and unimpassioned address, he made the statement that the press of the country was in a deliberate conspiracy to withhold or color all news from that country.

We all felt that he was unfair in including *all* the papers with those notorious offenders, such as the "Times," from which one could expect nothing else. But the next morning we read an account of the lecture in the "Examiner" that was false from the headline to the final sentence, which said: "Only a scant audience heard the address."

The lecture was not broken up by the police; in fact if there were any police present no one even saw them. The chairman announced that Mr. Eastman would speak on Russia; then Mr. McBride would tell them about their magazine; and then at the end Mr. Eastman would answer questions. The program was finished exactly that way, without the slightest interruption, and to the very sympathetic applause of some twenty-five hundred auditors.

Nor did Mr. Eastman insult the President. In urging the withdrawal of American troops from Russia—a policy vigorously urged by Hearst papers—he simply stated that there was a striking inconsistency between President Wilson's words and his deeds; for when the President addressed his memorandum on the Marmora conference he assured the delegates that America had absolutely no interest in the internal affairs of Russia, and would not take sides; while at that moment he was commander-in-chief of an army that was at war with the Russians on two fronts.

Rob Wagner went on to explain that he wrote this protest "in the kindliest spirit"; and Mr. Ihmsen in reply expressed his regret, and promised to investigate the matter. You remember how it was with the express companies in the old days; they would lose your package, and promise to "investigate"—which meant that they filed your complaint away with five hundred thousand others of the same sort. Six months later I am preparing the manuscript of this book, and I write to Mr. Ihmsen that I desire to verify every charge I bring against American Journalism. Will he inform me if he has ever published a correction of this falsehood? Mr. Ihmsen replies that he has unfortunately overlooked the matter, but will be glad to publish a correction now. He does—the very next day! I wonder if this will seem as funny to the reader as it seems to me. Mr. Ihmsen brands Max Eastman in the public mind as a coward and a blatherskite, and for six months he lets that brand remain, though he knows it is undeserved. But then suddenly he learns that he himself is to be branded as a character-assassin; and so he makes a quick jump. But even so, he cannot be really fair. He gave the original story half a column; he gives the correction two inches of space, in a corner so remote that I, who read the "Examiner" every morning, do not see it until he sends me a marked copy!

A month or two after Max Eastman's lecture came Louise Bryant, freshly returned from Russia, and gave one of the most interesting talks I have ever heard; and next morning not a line in any Los Angeles newspaper! The following evening she spoke again, and I came upon the platform, and called the attention of the audience to this case of newspaper suppression, and asked for funds to get the truth to the people of Los Angeles. Before I had finished speaking, money began to shower upon the stage, and the total collection amounted to twelve hundred and forty dollars. I interviewed the assistant managing editor of the "Los Angeles Examiner," and he agreed to publish a report of the meeting, and allowed me to dictate a column to a reporter—of which he published two inches! A committee called upon the managing editor of the "Los Angeles Times," and this gentleman not only refused to publish a line, but refused to accept a paid advertisement giving the news; incidentally he flew into a rage and insulted the ladies of the committee. The money collected at the meeting was expended upon an edition of fifty thousand copies of a local radical paper, the "New Justice," containing an account of the whole affair; and when an attempt was made to distribute these papers among the ship-yard workers in the harbor, the distributors were arrested, and the judge declared that he wished he could get the editors of the paper.

In connection with this meeting, there was a humorous incident which ought to be mentioned. Among the statements made by Miss Bryant was that the Bolsheviki had taken Odessa because the French troops had refused to fight them; several companies had gone over to the enemy. This statement was published in the "New Justice," and was among those which the Los Angeles newspapers refused to admit to their columns. Louise Bryant had travelled all over the country making the statement, and almost everywhere the capitalist press refused to print it. But two months later came an Associated Press despatch from Paris; the Odessa incident had become the subject of interpellations in the French parliament—so at last the news was out that French troops had mutinied when ordered to fight the Bolsheviki!

Now comest the joke of the matter. To the Associated Press despatch, the "New York Times" added the following comment:

> The account of the mutiny of the seamen on the French Black Sea Fleet, given by M. Goude in the French Chamber, rationally explains *for the first time* the extraordinary events which took place at Odessa on April 8, the day the city was evacuated by the Allies and by all the population who could get away.

Don't you think those words, "for the first time," are funny? Almost as funny as the story of "Tom Muni" from Petrograd!

And then President Wilson comes to Los Angeles, and there is held in the largest music auditorium in the city a mass meeting of two thousand citizens, which unanimously submits to the President a request for amnesty for political prisoners. The "Los Angeles Times" gave this meeting not one word. I am invited to address the City Club of Los Angeles, and I tell them of this failure of the "Times" to report the news. Whereupon the "Times" starts a campaign to have me put in jail! I quote its first editorial; they have followed it up, every other day for a couple of weeks—they are quite determined that I shall go to jail!

> Get the I. W. W. Seditionists! And lock them up. Tight! Right! But why let Upton Sinclair roam at large? He spits more poison than the cheap skate. It is villainy to promote anarchy in these ticklish times· Blood will be on the heads of some of the civic club managers,

male and female. It is a crime for them to invite disloyal speakers to spout for them; just for amusement. The City Club and some of the women's clubs have boosted the Red cause. Bolshevism is no toy to play with, ladies and gentlemen. An "open forum" should not be open to mobocracy and treason.

As I have said, I know several of the men and women who help to edit the newspaper in which the above murderous raving is published. These men and women will read this book, and I now request the general public to step outside for a few moments, while I address these editors privately. I speak, not in my own voice, but in that of an old-time journalist, venerated in his day, John Swinton, editor of the "New York Tribune." He is answering, at a banquet of his fellow-editors, the toast: "An Independent Press":

There is no such thing in America as an independent press, unless it is in the country towns.

You know it and I know it. There is not one of you who dares to writes his honest opinions, and if you did you know beforehand that it would never appear in print.

I am paid one hundred and fifty dollars a week for keeping my honest opinions out of the paper I am connected with—others of you are paid similar salaries for similar things—and any of you who would be so foolish as to write his honest opinions would be out on the streets looking for another job.

The business of the New York journalist is to destroy the truth, to lie outright, to pervert, to vilify, to fawn at the feet of Mammon, and to sell his race and his country for his daily bread.

You know this and I know it, and what folly is this to be toasting an "Independent Press."

We are the tools and vassals of rich men behind the scenes. We are the jumping-jacks; they pull the strings and we dance. Our talents, our possibilities and our lives are all the property of other men. We are intellectual prostitutes.

PART III

THE REMEDY

CHAPTER LXII

CUTTING THE TIGER'S CLAWS

Every day the chasm between the classes in America grows wider; every day the class struggle grows more intense. Both sides become more conscious, more determined—and so the dishonesty of American Journalism becomes more deliberate, more systematic. And what is to be done? It must be evident to any sensible man that the conditions portrayed in this book are intolerable. Mankind will not consent to be lied to indefinitely.

William Marion Reedy discussed the question ten years ago, and his solution was pamphleteering. We must return to the custom of the eighteenth century, printing and circulating large numbers of leaflets, pamphlets and books. And for the past ten years we have been doing this; the Socialist party, for example, is a machine for the circulating of pamphlets and leaflets, and the holding of public meetings to counteract the knaveries of the capitalist press. There are innumerable other organizations which serve the same purpose: the "People's Council," the "Civil Liberties Bureau," the "International Workers' Defense League," the I. W. W. groups, "The Rand School," the "People's College," the "Young People's Socialist League," the "Intercollegiate Socialist Society." But, obviously, this can only be a temporary solution. The workers of the country are in the condition of a frontier settlement besieged by savage Indians. They defend themselves with such weapons as they find at hand; but sooner or later, it is evident, they will organize a regular force, and invade the woods, and be done with those Indians once for all.

Take the Moyer-Haywood case, the Mooney case, the Ludlow massacre, the Bisbee deportations; and consider what happens. For days, for weeks, perhaps for years, the Associated Press and its thousand newspapers prepare a carefully constructed set of falsehoods, and twenty or thirty million copies per day of these falsehoods are sold to the public. Whereupon men and women of conscience all over the country are driven to protest. They call mass-meetings, they organize a new league and raise defense funds, print leaflets and pamphlets and devise a system of house-to-house distribution, call big strikes and parades of protest; by this prodigious mass of effort they succeed in conveying some small portion of the truth to some small portions of the population. Is it not obvious that society cannot continue indefinitely to get its news by this wasteful method? One large section of the community organized to circulate lies, and another large section of the community organized to refute the lies! We might as well send a million men out into the desert to dig holes, and then send another million to fill up the holes. To say that William Marion Reedy, after a study of our journalistic dishonesty, could find no better solution of the problem than pamphleteering, is merely to say that bourgeois thought is bankrupt.

The first remedy to which every good American takes resort is the law. We pass fifty thousand new laws in America every year, but still we cling to the faith that the next thousand will "do the business." Let us have laws to punish the lying of the press!

I, as a good American, have thought of laws that I would like to see passed. For instance, a law providing that newspapers shall not publish an interview with anyone until they have submitted the interview and had it O.K.'d; or unless they have obtained written permission to quote the person without such O.K.

Also, a law providing that when any newspaper has made any false statement concerning an individual, and has had its attention called to the falsity of this statement, it shall publish a correction of the statement in the next edition of the publication, and in the same spot and with the same prominence given to the false statement.

For example, the press sends out a report that the Rev. Washington Gladden is about to resign his pulpit. His mail is full of letters from people all over the country, expressing regret. Says Dr. Gladden:

The trouble with such a report is that you can never get it corrected. I have done my best to get such correction, but in this I have signally failed. Anything which discredits a man is "good stuff," which most newspapers are ready to print, provided it is not actionable; any correction which is made of such a report is not so apt to find a place on the wires, and is pretty sure to be blue-pencilled by the telegraph editors.

It happens, while I am preparing this book for the printer, that I visit a friend, and mention what I am doing; he says: "There was one newspaper story which almost caused me to despise you. I wonder how much truth there was in it." He explains that he was in Chicago in the early days of the war, attending a conference of the People's Council, and in a Chicago newspaper he read that I had denounced Emma Goldman to the government, and had turned over some of her private letters to the government.

I tell my friend what happened. An insane man had threatened my life, and I had applied to the Los Angeles police department for permission to carry a revolver. They promised to keep secret my application, but within half an hour there were two newspaper reporters after me. I refused to talk about the matter; so, as usual, they made up a story. It happened that I had given to the chief of detectives what information I had as to the insane man's past conduct; among other things, that he had caused a disturbance at a meeting of Emma Goldman's. That was the way her name came in, and the only way. I barely know Emma Goldman, having met her twice at public meetings; I knew nothing whatever about her activities at this time, and had no letters from her in my possession. I now have one, for immediately I wrote to her to say that the published story was false, and she replied that I need not have worried; she had known it was false.

Now, I sent a denial of that story to every newspaper in Los Angeles, and also to the Associated Press; but my denial went into the waste-basket. And why? At this time the capitalist press was engaged in hounding Emma Goldman to prison; the lie was useful to the hounders, so it stood, in spite of all my protests.

Obviously enough, here is a gross injustice. Common sense dictates a law that any newspaper which prints a false statement shall be required to give equal prominence to a correction. The law should provide that upon publication of any false report, and failure to correct it immediately upon receipt of notice, the injured party should have the right to collect a fixed sum from the newspaper—five or ten thousand dollars at least. At present, you understand, the sum has to be fixed by the jury, and the damages have to be proven. If the "Los Angeles Times" calls Upton Sinclair an "Anarchist writer," if the "Chicago Tribune" calls Henry Ford an "Anarchist," it is up to the plaintiffs to prove just how and to what extent they have been damaged. The newspaper has the right to question their character and reputation, to examine them about every detail of their lives and opinions. Was Upton Sinclair justified in divorcing his wife? Does Henry Ford know how to read? If not, then it is all right to call them "Anarchists."

Also there is the problem of the Associated Press, the most powerful and most sinister monopoly in America. Certainly there will be no freedom in America, neither journalistic freedom nor political freedom nor industrial freedom, until the monopoly of the Associated Press is broken; until the dis-· tributing of the news to American newspapers is declared a public utility, under public control; until anyone who wishes to publish a newspaper in any American city or town may receive the Associated Press service without any formality whatever, save the filing of an application and the payment of a fee to cover the cost of the service. Proceedings to establish this principle were begun a year ago by Hearst before the Federal Trade Commission. Hearst had been barred from getting the "A. P." franchise in certain cities, and I venture to guess that his purpose was to frighten his enemies into letting him have what he wanted. At any rate, he found himself suddenly able to buy the franchises, so he dropped his proceedings against the "A. P." The attorney in this case was Samuel Untermyer, who writes me about the issue as follows:

If the prevailing opinion is right, the monopoly of the Associated Press over the news of the world is complete. Unless the courts will hold, as I think they will, when the question comes before them, that news is a public utility; that the Associated Press is engaged in interstate commerce, using the cables, telegraph lines and telephones and that it is, therefore, bound to furnish its service on equal terms to all who choose to pay for it. If that is not the law, it should be the law, and can readily be made the law by Federal legislation. Until this is done, the monopoly of the Associated Press will continue intolerable.

I have fought it for years and thus far in vain, but I shall continue to fight until it is broken. The little clique that controls the Associated Press is in turn under the complete domination of a few of the most narrow-minded and reactionary of the great capitalists of the country. If our Government fails to stand the strain of these terrible times and if revolution and blood-shed follow—which God forbid!— the responsibility will rest at the doors of men like Gary and lawbreakers like the U. S. Steel Company who lack all vision and sense of justice.

Also there should be a law forbidding any newspaper to

fake telegraph or cable dispatches. At present, this is a universal custom in newspaper offices; the most respectable papers
do it continually. They clip an item from some other newspaper, re-write it, and put it under a "telegraphic headline."
They will take the contents of some letter that comes to the
office, and write it up under a "London date-line." They will
write their own political propaganda, and represent it as having come by telegraph from a special correspondent in Washington or New York. In "Harper's Weekly" for October 9,
1915, there was published an article, "At the Front with Willie
Hearst." Mr. Hearst's "Universal News Bureau" was shown
to be selling news all over the country, purporting to come
from "more than eighty correspondents, many of them of
world-wide fame." Every day, if you read this "Universal
Service," you became familiar with the names of Hearst correspondents in London, Paris, Vienna, Rome, Berlin, Petrograd. All these correspondents were imaginary persons; all
this news was written in the Hearst offices in New York,
being a re-hash for American afternoon papers of the news
of the London morning papers. This is obvious fraud, and
the law should bar it, precisely as it bars misbranded maple
syrup and olive oil and strawberry jam.

Such laws would help; and I could suggest others that
would help; nevertheless, the urging of such laws is not the
purpose of this book. It is a problem of cutting the claws of
a tiger. The first thing you have to do is to catch your tiger;
and when I undertake the hard and dangerous job of invading
a jungle and catching a tiger and chaining him down, am I
going to be content with cutting off the sharpest points of
the beast's claws, and maybe pulling one or two of his teeth?
I am not!

CHAPTER LXIII

THE MENTAL MUNITION-FACTORY

A solution that comes at once to mind is state-owned or municipal-owned newspapers. This is the orthodox Socialist solution, and is also being advocated by William Jennings Bryan. Fortunately, we do not have to take his theories, or anyone's theories; we have facts—the experience of Los Angeles with its public paper, the "Municipal News," which was an entire success. I inquire of the editor of the paper, Frank E. Wolfe, and he writes:

The "Municipal News"? There's a rich story buried there. It was established by an initiative ordinance, and had an ample appropriation. It was launched in the stream with engines going full steam ahead. Its success was instantaneous. Free distribution; immense circulation; choked with high-class, high-rate advertising; well edited, and it was clean and immensely popular.

Otis said: "Every dollar that damned socialistic thing gets is a dollar out of the 'Times' till." Every publisher in the city re-echoed, and the fight was on. The chief thing that rankled, however, was the outgrowth of a clause in the ordinance which gave to each political party polling a three per cent vote a column in each issue for whatsoever purpose it might be used. The Socialist Labor Party nosed out the Prohibitionists by a fluke. The Socialists had a big margin in the preceding elections, so the Reds had two columns, and they were quick to seize the opportunity for propaganda. The Goo-goos, who had always stoutly denied they were a political party, came forward and claimed space, and the merry war was on. Those two columns for Socialist propaganda were the real cause for the daily onslaught of the painted ladies of Broadway (newspaper district of Los Angeles). There were three morning and three evening papers. Six times a day they whined, barked, yelped and snapped at the heels of the "Municipal News." Never were more lies poured out from the mouths of these mothers of falsehood. The little, weakly whelps of the pornographic press took up the hue and cry, and Blanche, Sweetheart and Tray were on the trail. Advertisers were cajoled, browbeaten and blackmailed, until nearly all left the paper. The "News" was manned by a picked staff of the best newspaper men on the coast. It was clean, well edited, and gave both sides to all controversies—using the parallel column system. It covered the news of the municipality better than any paper had ever covered it. It was weak and ineffective editorially, for the policy was to print a newspaper. We did not indulge in a clothes-line quarrel—did not fight back.

The "News" died under the axe one year from its birth. They used the initiative to kill it. The rabble rallied to the cry, and we foresaw the end.

The paper had attracted attention all over the English-reading world. Everywhere I have gone I have been asked about it, by people who never dreamed I had been an editor of the paper. Its death was a triumph for reaction, but its effect will not die. Some day the idea will prevail. Then I might want to go back into the "game."

City-owned newspapers are part of the solution, but not the whole part. As a Socialist, I advocate public ownership of the instruments and means of production; but I do not rely entirely upon that method where intellectual matters are concerned. I would have the state make all the steel and coal and oil, the shoes and matches and sugar; I would have it do the distributing of newspapers, and perhaps even the printing; but for the editing of the newspapers I cast about for a method of control that allows free play to the development of initiative and the expression of personality.

In a free society the solution will be simple; there will be many groups and associations, publishing their own papers, and if you do not like the papers which these groups give you, you can form a group of your own. Being in receipt of the full product of your labor, you will have plenty of money, and will be surrounded by other free and independent individuals, also receiving the full product of their labor, and accustomed to combining for the expression of their ideas. The difference is that today the world's resources are in the hands of a class, and this class has a monopoly of self-expression. The problem of transferring such power to the people must be studied as the whole social problem, and not merely as the problem of the press.

Fortunately there are parts of America in which the people have kept at least a part of their economic independence, and have gone ahead to solve the problem of the "kept" press in true American fashion—that is, by organizing and starting honest newspapers for themselves. The editor of the "Nonpartisan Leader," Oliver S. Morris, has kindly written for me an account of the experiences of the Nonpartisan League, which I summarize as follows:

The League commenced organization work early in 1915 in North Dakota. By the summer of the next year it had forty thousand members, yet no newspaper in the state had given, even as news, a fair account of the League's purposes. Every daily paper in the state was filled with "gross misinfor-- mation and absurd lies." So the League started a little weekly paper of its own. With this single weekly, against the entire daily press of the state, it swept the primaries in June, 1916.

Then the League decided to have a daily paper. The "Courier-News" of Fargo had been for sale, but the owners would not sell to the League. The League went ahead to start a new paper, actually buying machinery and taking sub-scriptions; then the "Courier-News" decided to sell, and its circulation under League ownership now exceeds the total population of Fargo.

The League at present has weekly papers in seven states, with a total circulation of two hundred thousand, and another weekly, the "Non-partisan Leader," published in St. Paul, with a circulation of two hundred and fifty thousand. It is starting co-operative country weekly papers, supervising their editorial policy and furnishing them news and editorial service; over one hundred of these weekly papers are already going. There is another League daily in Grand Forks, North Dakota, and one at Nampa, Idaho. Finally, the League is going ahead on its biggest venture, the establishment of a daily in Min-neapolis. This paper is to be capitalized at a million dollars, and the stock is being sold to farmer and labor organizations throughout the state. Says Mr. Morris: "Many wealthy pro-fessional and business men, disgusted with the controlled press, have purchased stock, and are warm boosters for the League publications." Also he says:

One of the chief results of the establishment of a League press is a different attitude on the part of many existing papers. With com-petition in the field, many publishers who have hitherto been biased and unfair have been forced to change their tactics. Few of these papers have gone over to the League side of political and economic questions, but they have been forced at least to print fair news reports on both sides of the question in their news columns, reserving their opposition to the movement for their editorial columns. That, of course, is fair enough. The menace of the controlled press in America is due to the fact that as a rule this press does not confine its argu-ments and opposition to the editorial columns, but uses the news columns for propaganda, and, failing to print the news, printing only a part of it, distorting it or actually lying, sways opinion through the news columns.

Such is the procedure in places where Americans are free.

But what about our crowded cities, with their slum popula-
tions, speaking forty different languages, illiterate, unorganized,
and dumb? Even in these cities there have been efforts made
to start newspapers in the interest of the people. I know few
more heroic stories than the twenty-year struggle to establish
and maintain the "New York Call." It began as a weekly,
"The Worker." Even that took endless campaigns of begging,
and night labor of devoted men and women who earned their
livings by day-time labor under the cruel capitalist grind. At
last they managed to raise funds to start a daily, and then for
ten years it was an endless struggle with debt and starvation.
It was a lucky week when the "New York Call" had money
enough to pay its printing force; the reporters and editors
would sometimes have to wait for months. A good part of
the space in the paper had to be devoted to ingenious begging.

The same attempt was made in Chicago, and there bad
management and factional quarrels brought a disastrous
failure. At the time of writing, there are Socialist dailies in
Butte, in Seattle, and in Milwaukee, also a few foreign-
language Socialist dailies. There are numerous weeklies and
monthlies; but these, of course, do not take the place of newspapers, they are merely a way of pamphleteering. The people
read falsehoods all week or all month, and then at last they
get what portion of the truth the "Appeal to Reason" or the
"Nation" or the "Liberator" or "Pearson's" can find room for.
In the meantime the average newspaper reader has had his
whole psychology made of lies, so that he cannot believe the
truth when he sees it.

There are a few millionaires in America who have liberal
tendencies. They have been willing to finance reform campaigns, and in great emergencies to give the facts to the people;
they have been willing now and then to back radical magazines,
and even to publish them. But—I state the fact, without
trying to explain it—there has not yet appeared in America a
millionaire willing to found and maintain a fighting daily paper
for the abolition of exploitation. I have myself put the proposition before several rich men. I have even known of cases
where promises were made, and plans drawn up. My friend
Gaylord Wilshire intended to do it with the proceeds of his
gold-mine, but the gold-mine has taken long to develop. I had
hopes that Henry Ford would do it, when I read of his purchase of the "Dearborn Independent." I urged the matter

upon him with all the eloquence I could muster; he said he meant to do it, but I have my fears. The trouble is his ignorance; he really does not know about the world in which he finds himself, and so far the intellectual value of the "Dearborn Independent" has been close to zero.

So our slum proletariat is left to feed upon the garbage of yellow journalism. Year by year the cost of living increases, and wages, if they move at all, move laggingly, and after desperate and embittered strife. In the midst of this strife the proletariat learns its lessons; it learns to know the clubs of policemen and the bayonets and machine-guns of soldiers; it learns to know capitalist politicians and capitalist judges; also it learns to know Capitalist Journalism! Wherever in America the workers organize and strike for a small portion of their rights, they come out of the experience with a bitter and abiding hatred of the press. I have shown you what happened in Colorado; in West Virginia; in Paterson, New Jersey; in Calumet, Michigan; in Bisbee, Arizona; in Seattle, Washington. I could show you the same thing happening in every industrial center in America.

The workers have come to realize the part which the newspapers play; they have come to know the newspapers as the crux of the argument, the key to the treasure-chamber. A modern newspaper, seen from the point of view of the workers, is a gigantic munition-factory, in which the propertied class manufactures mental bombs and gas-shells for the annihilation of its enemies. And just as in war sometimes the strategy is determined by the location of great munition-factories and depots, so the class-struggle comes to center about newspaper offices. In every great city of Europe where the revolution took place, the first move of the rebels was to seize these offices, and the first move of the reactionaries was to get them back. We saw machine-guns mounted in the windows of newspaper-offices, sharp-shooters firing from the roofs, soldiers in the streets replying with shrapnel. It is worth noting that wherever the revolutionists were able to take and hold the newspapers, they maintained their revolution; where the newspapers were retaken by the reactionaries, the revolution failed.

In Petrograd the "Little Gazette," organ of the "Black Hundreds," became the "Red Gazette," and has remained the "Red Gazette." The official military organ, the "Army and

Fleet," became the "Red Army and Fleet." The "Will of Russia," organ of Protopopov, last premier of the Tsar, became the "Pravda," which means "Truth." In Berlin, on the other hand, the "Kreuz-Zeitung," organ of black magic and reaction, became for a few days "Die Rothe Fahne," the "Red Flag"; but, alas, it went back to the "Kreuz-Zeitung" again!

Will it come this way in America? Shall we see mobs storming the offices of the "New York Times" and "World," the "Chicago Tribune," the "Los Angeles Times"? It depends entirely upon the extent to which these capitalist newspapers continue to infuriate the workers, and to suppress working-class propaganda with the help of subservient government officials. I personally am not calling for violent revolution; I still hope for the survival of the American system of government. But I point out to the owners and managers of our great capitalist news-organs the peril in which they place themselves, by their system of organized lying about the radical movement. It is not only the fury of resentment they awaken in the hearts of class-conscious workingmen and women; it is the condition of unstable equilibrium which they set up in society, by the mass of truth they suppress. Today every class-conscious workingman carries about with him as his leading thought, that if only he and his fellows could get possession of the means of news-distribution, could take the printing-offices and hold them for ten days, they could end forever the power of Capitalism, they could make safe the Co-operative Commonwealth in America.

I say ten days, and I do not speak loosely. Just imagine if the newspapers of America were to print the truth for ten days! The truth about poverty, and the causes of poverty; the truth about corruption in politics and in all branches of government, in Journalism, and throughout the business world; the truth about profiteering and exploitation, about the banking graft, the plundering of the railroads, the colossal gains of the Beef Trust and the Steel Trust and the Oil Trust and their hundreds of subsidiary organizations; the truth about conditions in industry, the suppression of labor-revolts and the corrupting of labor movements; above all, the truth about the possibilities of production by modern machinery, the fact that, by abolishing production for profit and substituting production for use, it would be possible to provide abundance for all by two or three hours' work a day! I say that if all this legitimate truth could be placed before the American people for ten successive days, instead of the mess of triviality, scandal, crime and sensation, doctored news and political dope, prejudiced editorials and sordid and vulgar advertisements upon which the American people are now fed—I say that the world would be transformed, and Industrial Democracy would be safe. Most of our newspaper proprietors know this as well as I do; so, when they read of the seizing of newspaper offices in Europe, they experience cold chills, and one great newspaper in Chicago has already purchased half a dozen machine-guns and stored them away in its cellar!

For twenty years I have been a voice crying in the wilderness of industrial America; pleading for kindness to our laboring-classes, pleading for common honesty and truth-telling, so that we might choose our path wisely, and move by peaceful steps into the new industrial order. I have seen my pleas ignored and my influence destroyed, and now I see the stubborn pride and insane avarice of our money-masters driving us straight to the precipice of revolution. What shall I do? What can I do—save to cry out one last warning in this last fateful hour? The time is almost here—and ignorance, falsehood, cruelty, greed and lust of power were never stronger in the hearts of any ruling class in history than they are in those who constitute the Invisible Government of America today.

CHAPTER LXIV

THE PROBLEM OF THE REPORTER

One important line of attack upon Capitalist Journalism occurred to me some five years ago, after the Colorado coal-strike. I have saved this story, because it points so clearly the method I wish to advocate. You will find the story in "Harper's Weekly" for July 25, 1914; "Hearst-Made War News," by Isaac Russell.

You remember how Hearst "made" the war with Spain. Sixteen years later, in 1914, Hearst was busy "making" another war, this time with Mexico. President Wilson, trying to avoid war, had arranged for arbitration of the difficulty between Mexico and the United States by delegates from Argentine, Brazil and Chile. This was the Niagara Conference, and to it the "New York American" sent an honest reporter. It did this, not through oversight, but because the usual run of Hearst reporters had found themselves unable to get any information whatever. One Mexican delegate had taken the card of a Hearst reporter, torn it to pieces, and thrown the pieces into the reporter's face. The delegates for the United States refused to talk to the Hearst representatives, the other newspaper-men refused to have anything to do with them. So the managing editor of the "New York American" selected Mr. Roscoe Conklin Mitchell, a man known to be honest.

Mr. Mitchell came to Niagara, and got the news—to the effect that all was going well at the conference. He sent a dispatch to that effect, and the "New York American" did not publish this dispatch. Day by day Mr. Mitchell sent dispatches, describing how all was going well at the conference; and the "American," which was determined that the Conference should fail, doctored these dispatches and wrote in false matter. Mr. Mitchell had to explain to the delegates and to the other reporters how he was being treated by his home office. On two occasions Mr. Mitchell forced the "American" to send up another man to write the kind of poisoned falsehoods it wanted; and on each occasion these men were forced to leave, because no one would have anything to do with them, they could get no information. Finally, in the midst of Mr. Mitchell's dispatches, the "New York American" inserted a grand and wonderful "scoop": "PRESIDENT CARRANZA'S CONFIDENTIAL MESSAGE TO THE MEDIATORS." Mr. Mitchell had sent no such dispatch, and upon inquiry he learned that the document was a fake; no such "confidential message" had been received from President Carranza. So Mr. Mitchell wired his resignation to the "New York American."

The managing editor of the "American" protested. "Please be good soldier and good boy," he telegraphed. Again he telegraphed: "Come home comfortably, be philosophical. Good soldiers are patient, even if superior officers make mistakes. Be resigned without resigning." When the news of Mitchell's resignation reached the other reporters, they formed an impromptu committee and rushed in automobiles to his hotel to congratulate him. The American delegates to the convention held a reception, during which the head of the delegation made to Mr. Mitchell a speech of congratulation. Summing up the story, Isaac Russell puts this question to you, the reader: Will you leave it to the men on the firing line, the reporters, to fight out alone the question of whether you are to receive accurate information concerning what is going on in the world? Or will you help to find means whereby both you and your agent, the reporter, may be less at the mercy of the unscrupulous publisher, who finds that lying and misrepresentation serve his personal ends?

Isaac Russell, you recall, was the reporter for the "New York Times" who had stood by me through the struggle over the Colorado coal-strike. This struggle was just over, and both Russell and I were sick and sore. Russell was fighting with his editors day by day—they objected to his having written this "Hearst-made War News," by the way, and took the first opportunity thereafter to get rid of him. Russell had word of an impending break between Amos Pinchot and Theodore Roosevelt, and wrote it up. Gifford Pinchot, brother of Amos, made a furious denial, whereupon the "Times" fired Russell. But very soon afterwards Amos Pinchot broke with Theodore Roosevelt!

Russell and I talked over the problem of the reporter and the truth. Must a reporter be a cringing wretch, or else a man of honor in search of a job? Might not a reporter be a

member of an honored profession, having its own standards, its
sense of duty to the public? Obviously, the first trouble is
that in his economic status the reporter is a sweated wage
slave. If reporting is to become a profession, the reporters
must organize, and have power to fix, not merely their wage-
scale, but also their ethical code. I wrote an article calling for
a "reporters' union," and Russell began to agitate among New
York newspaper-men for this idea, which has now spread all
over the country.

What would be the effect upon news-writing of a reporters' union? What assurance have we that reporters would
be better than owners? Well, in the first place, reporters are
young men, and owners are nearly always old men; so in the
newspaper-world you have what you have in the world of
finance, of diplomacy, of politics and government—a "league
of the old men," giving orders to the young men, holding the
young men down. The old men own most of the property, the
young men own little of the property; so control by old men is
property control, while control by young men would be control
by human beings.

I have met some newspaper reporters who were drunken
scoundrels. I have met some who were as cruel and unscrupulous as the interests they served. But the majority of newspaper reporters are decent men, who hate the work they do, and
would gladly do better if it were possible. I feel sure that
very few of the falsehoods about Helicon Hall would have
been published if the reporters who accepted our hospitality
had been free to write what they really thought about us. I
know that throughout our "Broadway demonstration" a
majority of the reporters were on our side. They took us
into their confidence about what was going on in their newspaper offices; they went out of their way to give us counsel.
Again and again they came to my wife, to plead that our
mourning "stunt" was "petering-out," and could we not think
up some way to hold the attention of the public? Would not
my wife at least rescind her request that they omit descrip-
tions of that white military cape? After the last assault upon
the street speakers in Tarrytown, it was a reporter who warned
my wife that the situation was getting out of hand; the authorities would not listen to reason, there was going to be violence,
and she had better persuade me to withdraw.

27

I have before me a letter from C. E. S. Wood, poet and lawyer:

You doubtless know more newspaper men than I do, but I know a great many—fine fellows personally; themselves writhing in the detestable position of moral bandits, the disgrace of which they feel as keenly as any, and yet economic determinism keeps them there. They are in a trap. They are behind the bars, and as the thief said to Talleyrand, or some minister of France, "One must live." I know of no other profession that deliberately trains its neophytes to lying and dishonor, which makes it a part of the professional obligation to ruin man or woman by deliberate lies; which never honestly confesses a mistake, and never has the chivalry to praise an adversary.

And again, William Marion Reedy:

To one who has lived all his life in cities, to one who has spent most of his days and nights with the men who write the great daily papers of the cities, it is perfectly evident that ninety out of one hundred editorial writers on the press today are men who are in intellectual and sympathetic revolt against present-day conditions. You will find the average editorial writer a Socialist, and as for the reporter, he is most likely to be an Anarchist. The reason of this is plain enough. The men who make the newspapers are behind the scenes—they see the workings of the wires—they note the demagogy of politicians, they are familiar with the ramifications by which the public service corporations control the old parties down to the smallest offices, and even at times finance reform movements, which always stop at the election of some respectable figurehead or dummy, but never proceed to any attack upon the fundamental evils of our social and economic system. It is my firm belief that were it not for the capitalists at the head of the great daily newspapers, if it were possible for the men who write the news and the editorials of all the newspapers in the United States, to take absolute charge of their publications and print the news exactly as they see it, and write their views exactly as they feel them, for a space of three days, there would be such a revolution in the United States of America as would put that of France to shame. The only possible reason why this might not occur is that the editorial writers and reporters actually believe in nothing—not even in the various remedies, rational or wild-eyed, which occasionally, in private, they proclaim.

And here is another letter, written by Ralph Bayes, for many years city editor of the "Los Angeles Record," and now laid up in a sanitarium with tuberculosis.

I wonder as you gallop gaily along the way, throwing rocks in gypsy-like abandon at the starched and frilled little children of privilege—I wonder whether you will give your readers just one glimpse of the tragedies that are the lives of the men hired by the system to do the work you condemn. It isn't merely that we journalists must prostitute our own minds and bodies in answer to the call of that inexorable tyrant, our collective belly. Every man who toils and sweats for a wage is perforce doing the same thing. The bitterness of our portion is this precisely: that we are hired poisoners, whose lot it is to kill the things we love most. To kill them, not as bold buccaneers in a stand-up fight, but to slay them artfully, insidiously, with a half-true head-line or a part suppression of fact. In my ten years of experience on various sheets as reporter, editor and Associated Press representative, I have come to know the masses with whom I had to deal. Their intellects were the pawns with which I must learn to play the editorial game. I knew for instance, sitting at my desk, just how many extra papers I could sell with a scare-line on a police scandal. I knew to how many men on the street the filthy details of some married woman's shame would prove a lure to buy. And as I watched the circulation rise or fall, day by day, like a huge beating pulse, I became familiar, somewhat, with the mental processes of the average human animal. It was my tragedy, as it is the tragedy of the majority of my fellows, that this knowledge, acquired always at a tremendous cost of our life's energies, must be used not for the uplift, but for the further enslavement, the drugging of the minds of men. How many times have I sat at my desk, and in apparently heartless fashion, cut the big truth out of the stuff that honest reporters wrote. Sometimes there were other moments in my life, as in the lives of the rest of my kind, when there were opportunities for sly sabotage—when we thought by the ridiculous speciousness of our alleged facts, to make the pseudo-truths which we pretended to propound stand forth in their gaunt shamelessness for the things they actually were. Do you remember Harwood, of the "Los Angeles Times"? If I were only with you now, I could point out to you in that daily concatenation of lies, a few truths about things, peering covertly through the mass of corruption, and seeming almost to be holding their figurative noses in disgust. How we used to chuckle when he would succeed in passing a sly sentence—a word—over the sleepy night editor at the desk! Poor intellectual Pierrots that we were! Literary Pantaloons!

But out of the tragedy of my own experience, and out of the tragedies of the experiences of the fellows I have known, I can glimpse a great light ahead. For I'm an optimist, you see. I was talking the other day to the editor of one of the sheets which poison public opinion in Phoenix, Arizona. He is a thoroughly fine and likable chap, but I had always known him for an ultra-conservative—a kept man entirely. The conversation drifted to Russia, and to my utter astonishment he quite frankly, but confidentially, told me that he didn't believe a word of the dispatches put forth by the Associated Press—the Associated Press which hitherto had been Almighty God to him. I glanced at him curiously, and then: "You're not a radical?" I said, dubiously. "I don't know what I am," he replied. "I've lost my perspective and I haven't anchored to any economic philosophy as yet, but sometimes my thoughts are so bitter that I'm afraid of them. I've just seen a man sent to jail for twenty days," he continued. "He had been in town but half an hour, and his only crime was that he couldn't obtain work and that he had run out of money. God," he said, "some day I may be that man. I feel his feelings now, and I must hide them or lose my job." Poor fellow, his wife is dying of tuberculosis, and he is almost distracted with the burden of his financial troubles.

It was just another journalistic tragedy I had seen, but joy burst in upon me as I listened to him talk. "Things aren't so bad after all," I thought, "for the press, at least, isn't any more rotten or venal than the rest of the system." In the editorial rooms of the country there are good fellows and true, sheer tired of the daily assassination in which they participate. Their fine delusions are spent. Their faith in the old is waning. And when the big day comes, I think you will find the press full ripe—riper perhaps than most of our institutions—for the change.

On page 149 I stated that the publisher of the "New York Times" gave a dinner to his staff, and my friend, Isaac Russell, corrected me, saying: "WE REPORTERS PAID FOR THAT DINNER." Now let me give you another glimpse into a reporter's soul:

I can understand it now. We were trying to get together in an association, but the big bosses always got in, and Mr. Ochs always came TO OUR DINNER, and always made the principal speech, and always dismissed the gathering after vaudeville stunts by "old vets." I remember that at that dinner I PAID, but sat away at the foot of a horseshoe table, and the BIG GUNS of the "Times" all sat around the center of the horse-shoe, and the big guns thundered and sent us away —me boiling, that we writers had to sit mute and dumb at our own dinner, and could never talk over our affairs—the bosses rushed so to every gathering we planned.

I wish you could print the menu card for that dinner—the illustration on the cover. I kept it as the most humiliating example I ever saw of the status of the news-writer. . . . . The illustration showed Adolph S. Ochs as a man with his coat off wielding a big sledgehammer. He was knocking one of those machines where you send the ball away up in the air, and get a cigar if the bell rings at the top of the column. Well, a little figure stood behind the redoubtable plutocratic owner of the "Times." This little figure was labeled "THE STAFF."

"STAFF" WAS FLUNKEYING IT FOR OCHS—holding the great man's hat and coat, if you will—while he hit the circulation ball a wallop!

CHAPTER LXV

THE PRESS SET FREE

Some years ago Allan Benson told me of his troubles as an honest journalist; I asked him to repeat them for this book, and he answered:

I doubt if my experiences as a daily newspaper editor would serve your purpose. When I was a daily editor I edited. I printed what I pleased. If I could not do so, I resigned. I didn't resign with a bank account to fall back upon—I resigned broke.

I am sorry that I struck my friend Benson in an uncommunicative mood. It doesn't in the least interfere with my thesis to learn that some editors resign; it is plain enough to the dullest mind that it doesn't help the public when an honest man resigns, and a rogue or a lickspittle takes his place.

I am not one of those narrow radicals who believe that the pocket-nerve of the workers is the only nerve, or even the principal nerve, by which they will be moved to action. I know that the conscience of newspaper men is struggling all the time. Now and then I come on a case of truth-telling in a capitalist newspaper, which cannot be explained by any selfish, competitive motive. What does it mean? If you could go inside that office, you would find some man risking the bread that goes into his children's mouths, the shoes that go onto their feet, in order that the knavery of Capitalist Journalism may be a little less knavish; going to his boss and laying down the law: "I won't stand for that. If that goes in, I go out." As a rule, alas, he goes out—and this reduces the inclination of others to fight for honesty in the news.

One purpose of this book is to advocate a union of newspaper workers, so that they may make their demands as an organization, and not as helpless individuals. Events move fast these days; while I write, I learn that there is already a "News-Writers' Union" in Boston, and one in New Haven; there is one being formed in Omaha, one in Louisville, one in Seattle, one in San Francisco. In Louisville the "Courier-Journal" and "Times" served notice on their staff that joining the union would automatically constitute resignation. In San

Francisco, I am told by an editor of that city, the movement "was carried through swiftly and silently at the start, the evening papers being one hundred per cent organized, the morning papers about fifty per cent." Then the publishers got wind of it, and held a secret meeting in the St. Francis Hotel. "That fearless backer of organized labor and the rights of the working classes, to wit: William Randolph Hearst, preferred to carry out his great program of betterment without consulting his handmaidens and bondmen." The "Chronicle," the paper of "Mike" De Young, took the same stand; so—

Upon the morning after the meeting every man on both papers who had signed the charter roll of the proposed association was told to recant with bended knee, or to go forth and earn his bread with a pick and shovel. Some did and some did not—all honor to the latter. . . . . It is certain that the publishers of the morning papers will fight to the last ditch.

My informant goes on to tell about his own position. You remember the immortal utterance of President Eliot of Harvard, that the true "American hero" of our time is the "scab." How does this true "American hero" feel about himself? Listen:

And I? Well, old man, I somewhat shamefully admit that I am at present guarding my bread and butter, and looking to the future with one eye on the boss's and my own opportunities, and in my heart damning the conditions that make me an undoubted renegade. I am drawing a little better than forty per, am in the best of standing, being now —— and with the possibility of being its head shortly, and with certain advancement coming in both pay and rating. Now what the deuce? Shall I tell Polly to support us and get in on the big game, or shall I eat my bitter bread?. . . .
I do know this, that there is going to be no present big success of the union movement, that whoever joins it too prominently is going to fight the owners for the rest of his life, and that the union can do me myself no good at all from any standpoint.

You will remember that in my story of the "Los Angeles Times" I mentioned a young reporter, Bob Harwood, who had told me of the "Times" knaveries. Harwood is now in San Francisco, where you may have another glimpse of him.

Bob told 'em all to go to hell, and is now organizing actively. There is an addition coming to the Harwood family shortly. Why comment further?

And then, let us see what is happening on the other side of the continent. In New Haven the "News-Writers' Union" goes on strike, and while they are on strike, they publish a paper of their own! In Boston the "News-Writers' Union" declares a strike, and wins all demands. Incidentally they learn—if they do not know it already—that the newspapers of Boston do not publish the news! They do not publish the news about the News-Writers' strike; when the strike is settled, on the basis of recognition of the union, not a single Boston newspaper publishes the terms of the settlement!

In every union there is always a little group of radicals, occupied with pointing out to the men the social significance of their labor, the duty they owe to the working-class, and to society as a whole. So before long we shall see the News-Writers' Union of Boston taking up the task of forcing the Boston newspapers to print the truth. We shall see the News-Writers' Union taking up the question: Shall the "Boston Evening Transcript" permit its news-columns to be edited by the gas company, and by "Harvard Beer, 1,000 Pure"? We shall see the union at least bringing these facts to public attention, so that the "Transcript" can no longer pose as a respectable newspaper.

I quote one paragraph more from my San Francisco letter:

All three evening papers, I am told, are one hundred per cent organized; a charter is on the way from the I. T. U. and the movement has the full backing—or is promised the full backing—of the A. F. of L. and the local labor organizations. Just what that is worth is yet to be learned.

This man, you see, is groping his way. He doesn't know what the backing of organized labor is worth. But the newspapermen of Boston found out; they won because the type-setters and the pressmen stood by them. And the New York actors won because the musicians and the stage-hands stood by them. And this is the biggest thing about the whole movement—the fact that workers of hand and brain are uniting and preparing to take possession of the world. One purpose of this book is to urge a hand-and-brain union in the newspaper field; to urge that the news-writers shall combine with the pressmen and type-setters and the truckmen—one organization of all men and women who write, print and distribute news, to take control of their own labor, and see to it that the newspapers serve public interests and not private interests.

What I ask at the very outset is a representative of the News-Writers' Union, acting as one of the copy-readers of every newspaper. This man will say, in the name of his organization: "That is a lie; it shall not go in. This news-item is colored to favor the railroad interests; it must be re-written. To-night there is a mass-meeting of labor to protest against intervention in Russia. That meeting is worth a column." Such demands of the copy-reader will, if challenged, be brought before a committee of the workers of the paper—the workers both of hand and brain. If any demand is not complied with, the paper will not appear next day. Do you think that lying about the labor movement would continue under such conditions?

I recognize the rights of the general public in the determining of news. I should wish to see a government representative sitting in all councils where newspaper policy is laid down. The owner should be represented, so long as his ownership exists; but unless I mis-read the signs of the times, the days of the owner as owner are numbered in our industry. The owner may best be attended to by a government price-fixing board, which will set wages for newspaper work and prices of newspapers to the public at a point where interest, dividends and profits are wiped out. So the owner will become a worker like other workers; if he is competent and honest, he will stay as managing director; if he is incompetent and dishonest, he will go to digging ditches, under the eye of a thoroughly efficient boss.

Little by little the workers of all industrial nations are acquiring class-consciousness, and preparing themselves for the control of industry. In America they seem backward, but that is because America is a new country, and the vast majority of the workers have no idea how the cards are stacked against them. I have just been reading an account of the general strike in Seattle, the most significant labor revolt in our history, and I observe how painfully chivalrous the Seattle strikers were. Because they did not permit the capitalist papers of their city to be published, therefore they refrained from publishing their own paper! This was magnificent, but it was not war, and I venture to guess that since the Seattle strikers have had the capitalist newspapers, not merely of their city, but of all the rest of the world telling lies about them, they will be more practical next time—as practical as those they are opposing.

How all this works out, you may learn from the Syndicalist movement of Italy—only, of course, Capitalist Journalism has not allowed you to know anything about the Syndicalist movement of Italy! The glass-workers were beaten in a terrific strike, and they realized that they had to find a new weapon; they contributed their funds and bought a glass-factory, which they started upon a co-operative basis. When this factory had its product ready for sale, strikes were called on the other factories. By applying this method again and again, the union broke its rivals, and bought them out at a low price, and so before the war practically the entire glass-industry of Italy was in the hands of co-operative unions, and the glass-workers were getting the full value of their product.

The same thing was being done before the war by the agricultural workers in Sicily. The strikers had been shot down by the soldiery, their own brothers and sons; they bought several estates and worked them co-operatively, and when harvest-time came there was labor for the co-operative estates, and there were strikes against the absentee landlords, who were spending their time in Paris and on the Riviera. So the landlords made haste to sell out, and the agricultural unions were rapidly taking possession of the land of Sicily.

The same methods were recently tried out in the newspaper field by strikers in the Argentine Republic; I quote from an account in the "Christian Science Monitor," a Boston newspaper which gives fair accounts of radical happenings abroad, and which may some day give fair accounts of radical happenings in America. The "Christian Science Monitor" is interviewing a United States embassy official, just returned from Buenos Aires:

An incident of the latter strike shows the unique control, as Mr. Barrett puts it, that they exercise over the newspapers. During the seventy-three days the port was closed, the only goods handled were shipments of newsprint. The newspapers represent the workers. If a paper dares to send to its composing-room an item opposed to the interest of the labor element, the compositors probably will refuse to put it in type. If they do set it up and it appears, the paper can expect no more newsprint from the docks.

I hear the reader says: "These strikers don't represent the public; they represent themselves. You are only substituting one kind of class-interest for another." Ah, yes—dear reader of capitalist opinion!

This at least you admit; the class represented by the
strikers is vastly larger than that represented by the owners;
we are that much nearer to democracy. But you demand one
hundred per cent pure democracy—dear reader of capitalist
opinion!

Well, the workers offer you the way; they cheerfully
permit all owners to become workers—either of hand or
brain—and to receive their full share with all other workers
of hand or brain; whereas, in the nature of the case, the
owners do not welcome the workers as owners, and are doing
all in their power to make sure that no one shall be owners
but themselves. This is the fundamental and all-determining
fact about the class struggle, and the reason why he who serves
the interest of the workers is serving the interest of all society,
and of the Co-operative Commonwealth which is to be. To
the argument that the taking of power by the workers is the
substitution of one kind of class tyranny by another kind of
class tyranny, the answer, complete and final, is that there is no
need of the capitalist class as a class and that the world will be
a happier place for all men when the members of that class
have become workers, either of hand or brain. When that has
been done, there will be no classes, therefore no class tyranny,
and no incentive to class lying. Thus, and thus only, shall we
break the power of the capitalist press—by breaking the power
of capitalism. And so it is that I, an advocate of pure democracy, am interested in this story from the Argentine Republic,
and tempted to cry to the American dockers, the American
typographers, the American newswriters: "Help! Help against
the lying, kept press!"

And as I am reading the final proofs of this book, I hear
the answer to my cry. I read the following in the "New York
Times":

Boston, Oct. 28.—Pressmen employed by the Chapple Publishing
Company, Ltd., on discovering in a cartoon in "Life" which is being
printed here during the New York strike, what they considered a re-
flection on organized labor, suspended work and refused to return
until the objectionable cartoon was taken out. The cartoon was elimi-
nated, and the men returned to work.

The drawing depicts a room apparently meant to typify conditions
existing in a city tenement district. The artist portrays a man beating
his wife over the head with the leg of a chair. The woman is shown
lying on the floor; the man has one knee on her body and one hand
clutching her throat. A child about two years old is shown in bed

watching the scene. Its face is expressive of horror. Another child, evidently a little older, is stretched on the floor, face downward. At the door is standing a patrolman in full uniform. He is talking with a captain of police, who has rushed on the scene with drawn revolver. The patrolman with hand upraised says: "It's all right, Captain, he's got a union card."

You may think my remedy drastic; but, honestly, do you think that any remedy could be too drastic for an infamy such as this?

Here, as everywhere, the salvation of the world rests upon you, the workers of hand and brain. I took up half this book telling how the capitalist press lied about one man; you said, perhaps, that I liked to be in the "limelight"; anyhow, I was only one writer-fellow, and it didn't matter to you what the newspapers did to a writer-fellow. But now I make my appeal for yourself, for your wives and your children. I have shown you how this knavish press turns the world against you; I have shown how it turns you against yourself—how it seduces you, poisons your mind, breaks your heart. You go on strike, and it plays upon your fears, it uses your hunger and want as weapons against you; it saps your strength, it eats out your soul, it smothers your thinking under mountain-loads of lies. You fall, and the chariot of Big Business rolls over you.

These men who own the world in which you struggle for life—what is it that they want? They want power, power to rule you. And what is it that you want? You want power to rule yourself. Between those two wants there is eternal and unending and irreconcilable war—such is the class struggle, and whether you will or not, you take your part in it, and I take mine. I, a writer-fellow who wants to write the truth, appeal to you, the laboring fellows of hand and brain, who want to read the truth, who *must* read the truth, if civilization is not to perish. I cry to you: "Help! Help against the lying, kept press!"

I cry to you for the integrity of your calling, for the honor and dignity of Journalism. I cry to you that Journalism shall no longer be the thing described by Charles A. Dana, master-cynic of the "New York Sun," "buying white paper at two cents a pound and selling it at ten cents a pound." I cry to you that Journalism shall be a public ministry, and that you who labor in it shall be, not wage-slaves and henchmen of privilege, but servants of the general welfare, helping your fellow-men to understand life, and to conquer the evils in nature outside them, and in their own hearts. Why cannot the men and women of this great profession form a society with a common mind and a common interest and a common conscience, based upon the fact that they are all necessary, they have each, down to the humblest office-boy, their essential part in a great social service?

By the blindness and greed of ruling classes the people have been plunged into infinite misery; but that misery has its purpose in the scheme of nature. Something more than a century ago we saw the people driven by just such misery to grope their way into a new order of society; they threw off the chains of hereditary monarchy, and made themselves citizens of free republics. And now again we face such a crisis; only this time it is in the world of industry that we have to abolish hereditary rule, and to build an industrial commonwealth in which the equal rights of all men are recognized by law. Such is the task before us; go to it with joy and certainty, playing your part in the making of the new world, in which there shall be neither slavery nor poverty, in which the natural sources of wealth belong to all men alike, and no one lives in idleness upon the labor of his fellows. That world lies just before you, and the gates to it are barred only by ignorance and prejudice, deliberately created and maintained by prostitute journalism.

CHAPTER LXVI

A FRAME-UP THAT FELL DOWN

In concluding this, the most important and most dangerous book I have ever written, I have a personal word to leave with the reader. I have here attacked the most powerful interests in America, and it seems to me hardly conceivable that they will permit the attack to go out to the world, to be circulated among the general public, without some attempt at interference.

What will they do? I cannot say. There are things on every page of this book which are libelous unless they are true. If I am brought into court and required to prove them, I may be facing a judge who has been appointed by the interests I have exposed, a jury which has been selected by the interests I have exposed, a prosecuting attorney who is looking to these interests for his campaign-funds and his publicity at the next election. The trial will be conducted on this simple basis—that everything favorable to me is kept from the public, and everything that can be made to seem unfavorable to me is sent by telegraph and cable all over the world.

I would not mind losing what little property I own in the world; I would not mind going to jail for this book. There are only two things I would mind—first, having the book barred from circulation, and second, being discredited in the eyes of those I seek to influence in favor of Social Justice. So in this, the last word I may be able to get to you on the subject, I wish to warn you of one crucial fact, which is this:

Our police and prosecuting authorities, our political machines and Big Business interests, are many of them practiced in the art of producing in court whatever testimony may be required in an emergency. There are few traction interests or other public service corporations in America which do not regularly employ perjured witnesses in case of need; and those which have given up the custom have done so merely because they have got the courts and the jury system so completely in their hands that they no longer care what evidence is introduced against them. We have seen Tom Mooney

429

held in jail for three years, entirely upon the basis of perjured testimony. Even the trial judge has written that he is satisfied that Tom Mooney is innocent—but still Tom Mooney stays in jail!

I am doing what I can to get this book to the people. I intend to go on doing what I can to that end. Meantime I say to you, my readers, what I said to my wife when I went out to Colorado on behalf of the coal-strikers: "Whatever you read about me, don't worry. If there is any scandal, pay no attention to it, for that is the way they fight in Denver."

That is the way Big Business fights all over America.

The above was written in August. In November I am reading the page proofs of the book, and "Big Business" steps forward to prove me a prophet. A plot is laid against me, so wanton and so utterly without basis of truth that no less than an assassin could have planned it. I escaped—but by a margin so narrow that it is unpleasant to think about it. Literally by a minute or two of time I missed having printed on the front page of every big newspaper in America convincing evidence that I am a secret German conspirator, contriving underhand plots for the undermining of my country! My wife remarks: "I have been watching the radical movement for seven or eight years, and I have heard much about 'frame-ups.' I always thought it was foolish talk, cheap melodrama; but now I know that the 'frame-up' is a real thing, and it has changed my whole view of the class struggle."

I have mentioned on page 399 how I made a speech before the City Club of Los Angeles, exposing the dishonesty of the "Los Angeles Times," whereupon the "Times" opened up a furious attack upon me, demanding that I should be put in jail. I have quoted one sample of its ravings. Every day or so for a week it printed similar abuse, and it continues the attack, both editorially and in its news columns. I have stated publicly in the "Appeal to Reason" that I am collecting evidence against the "Times," and preparing a book exposing it; so the "Times" proclaims me as "the trumpet of Bolshevism," and will be satisfied with nothing short of a life sentence for me.

There is in Los Angeles a returned soldiers' paper, the "Dugout." The editor, Sydney R. Flowers, is an American citizen who was in South Africa at the outbreak of the war, and was so anxious to fight the Kaiser that he left his wife and baby and enlisted. Invalided to England, he tried again to enlist, and finally enlisted in Canada, and served for three years in Belgium and France. He was twice wounded and once gassed, and has only one lung as a result. Returning to his home in Los Angeles with his wife and child, he found the war veterans' organization being courted as a strike-breaking agency by the Merchants' and Manufacturers' Association of the city. Flowers rebelled, and started a rival organization, the Allied World War Veterans, and with the support of these veterans he started the "Dugout." I met him, and heard him speak several times, and gave him my support to the extent of raising some money. He told me of the efforts of the "M. and M." to bribe him, and of their plots against him; he knew, and I knew, that there were spies in his office.

There came to the office a letter from a stranger who signed himself "Paul Rightman." The envelope bore a Chicago return address, but had been mailed in Los Angeles. It was typewritten, and the type was bad, the ribbon double, with traces of red showing here and there. "Paul" suggested to Flowers that he should send sample copies of his paper to Socialist and labor papers abroad. Flowers, who is out to prevent the next war by the spirit of international fraternity, thought this a good idea; his impulse was encouraged by a mysterious Austrian who happened into his office a few minutes after the letter arrived, and suggested to him exactly the sort of letter he should write to these foreign editors—most of whom, by a curious coincidence, happened to be in Silesia, where American troops are going!

Flowers wrote the letters and mailed them, and an hour or two after he had mailed them, two men who have been seen frequently in the offices of the "M. and M.," called upon Flowers' wife and terrified her by the announcement that her husband had committed a crime which would cause him to be sent to jail for life; his only chance was to drop the "Dugout," and he had one hour in which to make his decision. Flowers was summoned by a telephone call, purporting to come from the United States District Attorney's office. He obeyed this call, and in the hallway of the Federal Building was met by two mysterious persons who exhibited shields of authority, and informed him that he had three minutes in which to decide whether he would drop the "Dugout" or be sent to jail for life.

He refused to decide so quickly, and telephoned me for advice. I advised him to stand firm. I went to his office, and in my hearing he gave orders over the telephone for the printing of the next issue of his paper. In less than one hour after he had given that order, someone, identity unknown, came to the United States Attorney with "definite" information that Flowers was in relation with enemy publications abroad, and a search warrant was issued and served. I happened to be present in the office of the "Dugout" and witnessed the events, and can testify that the Federal agents, in defiance of the law, refused to permit Flowers to read the search warrant; that they held him against his will in violation of the law; that they raided the office of the Allied World War Veterans, which they had been given no authority to enter; and finally that they left the place a wreck.

Next morning there appeared in the "Los Angeles Times" a front page two-column story about the uncovering of a nest of treason. Among other things, it was stated that Flowers had been publishing seditious material before the armistice, and had been warned by the Federal authorities and forced to change his tone; the fact being that at this time Flowers was in the trenches in France, and did not start the publication of the "Dugout" until four or five months after the armistice!

I have said that the raid was brutally conducted. I might mention that I protested to one of the Federal agents against the unnecessary rowdyism, and this man remarked concerning the other man, his chief: "He's a rough-neck. I don't believe in rough-house business myself, there's no sense at all in it." Also I might mention that I brought two assistant U. S. Attorneys to the scene, and they arrived five minutes after their agents had left, and admitted to me that the proceedings were wholly unwarranted; one of them called up Flowers' home and very angrily ordered the agents to desist from the search they were making of that place. But next morning the "Los Angeles Times" reported:

VIOLENCE FAKED

The government agents disturbed no property in the office, simply carrying away the papers they desired. After the inspectors had gone, witnesses say that certain known followers of Flowers took possession of the offices, tore down an American flag which was on the wall, threw it on the floor, and generally wrecked the place. Then they sent for a "Los Angeles Examiner" photographer to make a photograph of the offices, with the apparent desire to have the publication of the photograph give the impression that the Federal officers had desecrated the flag and destroyed the office property.

Prior to this episode I had been too busy with my own writings to have even read a copy of the "Dugout" through. But I knew the record of Flowers in the war, and I knew his purpose since the war, and when I saw this plot to destroy his magazine, I made up my mind to stand back of him. I engaged a lawyer for him, and I sent long telegrams about the case to the "Appeal to Reason" and other Socialist papers over the country. So the masters of Los Angeles decided to get me in the same net with Flowers.

There came to Flowers' office a second letter signed by the mysterious "Paul." This letter was written on the same bad typewriter, with a double ribbon showing traces of red. But this time the return address on the envelope was not "Paul Rightman, Chicago, Illinois"; this time it was "Upton Sinclair, Pasadena, California!"

Flowers called me on the 'phone, and said: "Did you mail me a letter yesterday?" I answered, "No, I haven't written you any letter." "Well," said Flowers, "here is a letter with your name on the envelope. Evidently somebody wants it to appear that you are writing me letters signed with an assumed name." "What is in the letter?" I asked, and Flowers started to read it to me over the 'phone. It was a letter of violent denunciation of the government, full of the most venomously treasonable sentiments, and offering to supply Flowers with more names of papers in Germany with which he might correspond. I waited to hear only about half of it, then I cried: "Get that letter out of your office!"

"But wait—" said Flowers.

"Don't wait for anything," I insisted. "Drop what you are doing and take that letter to my lawyer as quickly as you can run."

Flowers promised me he would do that, and I hung up the receiver. Two or three minutes after he left his office with the letter in his pocket there were two agents of the District Attorney's office of Los Angeles County looking for him at his office. When he returned there were four of them on hand, and they held him up and proceeded to make another

raid. The man in charge, I might mention, was C. E. Sebastian, once mayor of the city, prosecuted for a sexual crime,
kicked out of office by the people, and now working as a
detective for the District Attorney's office!

The first thing this man did was to examine all Flowers'
letters—letters on his desk, letters in the drawers of his desk,
letters in his pockets. There were some hundred and fifty
letters altogether, and they went over them all several times,
studying the return addresses on the envelopes. They spent
something like an hour and a half at it, and their balked
anger was comically evident. In their whispered consultations
Flowers heard them mention my name several times, and once
he heard Sebastian say: "He's a slick one."

Flowers was haled before the Grand Jury, indicted under
the Criminal Syndicalism law, and thrown into jail at once.
The authorities fixed the bail at fifteen thousand dollars, which
they hoped would be prohibitive, and denied Flowers the right
to see his counsel that night. They have taken every scrap
of paper belonging to the magazine. They have frightened off
one printer and raided another, and so they think they have
smashed the "Dugout."

Come to my lawyer's office for a minute and examine this
mysterious "Paul" letter. It is a long letter, very abusive and
stupid, and I won't waste space on it, except to point out one
more of the subtle traps that were placed in it. One sentence
denouncing the acts of the government agents adds the phrase:
"as I stated in the papers." It so happens that out of the half
million population of Los Angeles, just one person had been
quoted in the newspapers as protesting against the raid on
the "Dugout," and that one person was myself. So when this
letter was published, the newspapers would be able to say:
Upton Sinclair is carrying a secret correspondence with a pro-
German conspirator, using the alias "Paul." But you see, he
forgets and puts his name on the envelope! And also he gives
himself away in the text of the letter—he identifies himself as
the mysterious conspirator!

If you have any doubt that this was the plan, you have
only to look at the "Los Angeles Times" next morning; a
double-column, front page story about this second raid on the
"Dugout," giving the full text of the first "Paul" letter as a
part of Flowers' "conspirings" with the enemy—and without
any hint that this mysterious "Paul" might be an imaginary

person! If the second "Paul" letter had been found, that too would have been published in full, and the entire country would have read a story to the effect that both letters had come from Upton Sinclair, who was thus caught red-handed in a vile German conspiracy against his country!

Maybe you are like my wife; maybe you never believed in the "frame-up." But study this case, and see what else you can make of it. Ask yourself: How comes it that the raids of both the Federal agents and of the Los Angeles County officers are so precisely timed to the arrival of letters from a mysterious "Paul" whom nobody has ever seen? And how comes it that this mysterious "Paul" puts the name of Upton Sinclair on his envelope? If "Paul" is afraid to put his own name on the envelope, why does he not mail it without return address, as millions of letters are mailed every day? And why does he employ the words: "As I stated in the papers"— when he hasn't stated anything whatever in the papers, and when Flowers must know he hasn't stated anything? Is it not plain that some dark agency is here working behind the scenes, plotting to ruin Upton Sinclair, and "tipping off" both the Federal authorities and the county authorities at the precise critical moment?

What is this agency? I do not know, and my lawyer, who takes this conspiracy very seriously, will not permit me to guess in public. But he admits my right to study these "Paul" letters, and to point out a peculiar bit of internal evidence. It would seem that this dark agency which is plotting to ruin Upton Sinclair is also interested in injuring the "Los Angeles Examiner." The first "Paul" letter offers to supply Flowers with the names of more German papers, if he will insert a request in the personal columns of the "Examiner"; and the "Times" publishes this letter in full, calling particular attention to the damaging mention of the "Examiner." Day after day the "Times" is attacking the "Examiner," calling it a pro-German sheet; and here is a German conspirator using this pro-German sheet as a medium for his schemes!

The above is what is done to me before this book comes out. What will be done after my enemies have actually read the book, I cannot imagine. All I can do is to repeat my warning to you. Twenty years ago old "One-hoss" Wayland told me he had made it the rule of his life never to write a letter that he would not publish in the "Appeal to Reason."

And that is the principle upon which I have always carried on my propaganda. I have no secrets. What I have to say is said once a week in a full page of the "Appeal," and the opposition to violence and conspiracy in the class struggle which I there write in public I advocate just as vigorously in private, and all my friends know it. So, if at any time you read that a carload of dynamite bombs has been found in my home, or that I have been carrying on a cipher correspondence with some foreign assassins, or that I have poisoned my wife and eloped with a chorus girl, or that I have taken a job on the "Los Angeles Times"—please go back and read this warning, and understand what is being done to both of us.

CONCLUSION

When I first talked over this book with my wife, she gave me a bit of advice: "Give your facts first, and then call your names." So throughout this book I have not laid much stress on the book's title. Perhaps you are wondering just where the title comes in!

What is the Brass Check? The Brass Check is found in your pay-envelope every week—you who write and print and distribute our newspapers and magazines. The Brass Check is the price of your shame—you who take the fair body of truth and sell it in the market-place, who betray the virgin hopes of mankind into the loathsome brothel of Big Business. And down in the counting-room below sits the "madame" who profits by your shame; unless, perchance, she is off at Palm Beach or Newport, flaunting her jewels and her feathers.

Please do not think that I am just slinging ugly words. Off and on for years I have thought about this book, and figured over the title, and what it means; I assert that the Brass Check which serves in the house of ill-fame as "the price of a woman's shame" is, both in its moral implications and in its social effect, precisely and identically the same as the gold and silver coins and pieces of written paper that are found every week in the pay-envelopes of those who write and print and distribute capitalist publications.

The prostitution of the body is a fearful thing. The young girl, trembling with a strange emotion of which she does not know the meaning, innocent, confiding and tender, is torn from her home and started on a road to ruin and despair. The lad, seeking his mate and the fulfilment of his destiny, sees the woman of his dreams turn into a foul harpy, bearer of pestilence and death. Nature, sumptuous, magnificent, loving life, cries: "Give me children!" And the answer comes: "We give you running sores and bursting glands, rotting lips and festering noses, swollen heads and crooked joints, idiot gabblings and maniac shrieks, pistols to blow out your brains and poisons to still your agonies." Such is the prostitution of the body.

But what of the mind? The mind is master of the body, and commands what the body shall do and what it shall become; therefore, always, the prostitution of the mind precedes and causes the prostitution of the body. Youth cries: "Life is beautiful, joyous! Give me light, that I may keep my path!" The answer comes: "Here is darkness, that you may stumble, and beat your face upon the stones!" Youth cries: "Give me Hope." The answer comes: "Here is Cynicism." Youth cries: "Give me understanding, that I may live in harmony with my fellow-men." The answer comes: "Here are lies about your fellow-men, that you may hate them, that you may cheat them, that you may live among them as a wolf among wolves!" Such is the prostitution of the mind.

When I planned this book I had in mind a sub-title: "A Study of the Whore of Journalism." A shocking sub-title; but then, I was quoting the Bible, and the Bible is the inspired word of God. It was surely one of God's prophets who wrote this invitation to the reading of "The Brass Check":

Come hither; I will shew unto thee the judgment of the great whore that sitteth upon many waters;
With whom the kings of the earth have committed fornication, and the inhabitants of the earth have been made drunk with the wine of her fornication.

For eighteen hundred years men have sought to probe the vision of that aged seer on the lonely isle of Patmos. Listen to his strange words:

So he carried me away in the spirit into the wilderness: and I saw a woman sit upon a scarlet colored beast, full of names of blasphemy, having seven heads and ten horns. And the woman was arrayed in purple and scarlet color, and decked with gold and precious stones and pearls, having a golden cup in her hands full of abominations and filthiness of her fornication:

And upon her forehead was a name written, MYSTERY, BABY-LON THE GREAT, THE MOTHER OF HARLOTS AND ABOMI-NATIONS OF THE EARTH.

Now, surely, this mystery is a mystery no longer! Now we know what the seer of Patmos was foreseeing—Capitalist Journalism! And when I call upon you, class-conscious workers of hand and brain, to organize and destroy this mother of all iniquities, I do not have to depart from the language of the ancient scriptures. I say to you in the words of the prophet Ezekiel:

So the spirit took me up, and brought me into the inner court; and behold, the glory of the Lord filled the house.
And I heard him speaking unto me out of the house:
Now let them put away their whoredom, and the carcases of their kings, far from me, and I will dwell in the midst of them forever.

PUBLISHER'S NOTE

Two years ago I finished "The Profits of Religion," and offered it to publishers. They said it could not be sold; no book on religion could be sold, it was the deadest subject in the world. I believed that "The Profits of Religion" could be sold, and I published it myself. In less than a year I have sold forty thousand copies, and am still selling them.

One reason, of course, is the low price. Everybody told me that a book could not be published at that price. I would report on the figures if I could, but I gave the book as a premium for my magazine, and never made any attempt to separate the two ventures. All that I can report is that since February, 1918, when I started the magazine, I have taken in for magazines and books a total of $14,269, and I have paid out for printing, postage, labor and advertising, a total of $20,995. This deficit represents some two hundred thousand magazines sent out free for propaganda purposes; the deficit was made up by donations from friends, so it cost me nothing but my time, which I gladly gave. And I am willing to give it again; I can't expect either royalty as author or profit as publisher from "The Brass Check." The cost of book manufacturing has increased fifty per cent in the past two years, and to make matters worse, "The Brass Check" is exactly twice as long as "The Profits of Religion." If this book were published in the ordinary way, to be sold to book-stores, it would be priced at $2.00, postage extra; or possibly even

$2.50. Sold, as it is, at $1.20, postpaid, it is an appeal to the conscience of every reader to do his part in helping to get it widely distributed.

"The Profits of Religion" was practically boycotted by the capitalist press of America. Just one newspaper, the "Chicago Daily News," reviewed it—or rather allowed me space in which to review it myself. Just one religious publication, the "Churchman," took the trouble to ridicule it at length. Half a dozen others sneered at it in brief paragraphs, and half a dozen newspapers did the same, and that was all the publicity the book got, except in the radical press. That this was a deliberate boycott, and not the fault of the book, is something which I leave for my readers to assert.

"The Brass Check," of course, will be treated in the same way. If it gets any publicity, it will be only because of a libel suit or something sensational. If the great mass of the people ever hear of the book, it will be because you, the reader, do your part. If it seems to you an honest book, and one which the public ought to know, get busy. If you can afford it, order a number of copies and give them to your friends. If you can't afford that, make up a subscription list among your friends. If you need to earn money, turn agent, and sell the book among your neighbors, in the shop where you work, on the road. If your experience is the same as mine, you will find nearly everybody distrustful of Capitalist Journalism, and willing at least to consider the truth about it.

POSTSCRIPT TO SECOND EDITION.—A letter from E. J. Costello, managing editor of the "Federated Press":

"Let me say in this very first sentence that the 'Brass Check' is the, most remarkable book that has ever been published in America. It is one that should, in the quickest possible manner, be placed in the hands of every American who can read, and read to every American who cannot read.

"I have been in this newspaper game for about twenty years, and I know from my own experience that your story is the absolute truth. For dozens of the incidents of 'kept press' rottenness I can cite counterparts. Your story of the Associated Press is without doubt the most concise exposé on record of the despicable methods which prevail in that organization."

Mr. Costello goes on to tell me that he was for seven years a staff correspondent and editor for the Associated Press. He was in charge of its Des Moines bureau at the time I was trying to get out the truth from the Colorado coal strike. One day there came through on the

Associated Press wire instructions from the New York office "that henceforth Upton Sinclair must be kept out of the Denver office, and that no relations with him might be had by any employe of the Denver bureau. I remember that my operator copied the message and brought it to me, and that I determined to keep it for possible future reference.

"Within fifteen minutes after the message had been sent the chief operator at Chicago asked the Des Moines operator if he had copied it, and on being informed affirmatively he ordered the copy sent to Chicago. The operator asked me for the message, but I declined to let him have it. I placed it in a locked compartment of my desk, where it remained for several weeks, when one day it turned up missing. I have never been able to ascertain just how it disappeared, but I am quite positive that other keys fitted my desk, and that there was a reason for its disappearance. It wasn't so many months after this occurrence that I was ordered in to the Chicago office, presumably because it was thought I would bear watching. My radical views led finally, in 1916, to my leaving the Associated Press service entirely.

"Perhaps you have not heard that it was because of his efforts to do the square thing by you in the Ammons matter that Rowsey was discharged by Superintendent Cowles upon the orders of Melville E. Stone. Yet that was what was currently reported in inner 'A. P.' circles at the time."

Mr. Costello goes on to tell me that he left the Associated Press with his mind made up as to what was to be his life's work, "the establishment of a press association which would represent the people who work, as against the eight or ten millionaire publishers, who, through the ownership of Associated Press bonds, outvote nearly 2,000 other members of the organization, and absolutely control the channels through which the great public gets its poisoned news."

The "Federated Press" had its inception at a convention of the Labor Party in Chicago, November, 1919. It is a co-operative non-profit-making organization of working class newspapers, and maintains an admirable service of vital news from all over the world. It publishes a weekly four-page bulletin, which it will mail to you for five dollars a year, and which you will find worth the price many times over. The address of the "Federated Press" is 166 West Washington Street, Chicago, Illinois.

POSTSCRIPT TO EIGHTH EDITION.—In the first seven editions of "The Brass Check," a total of some 110,000 copies, there was printed a plan for the establishing of an honest weekly newspaper entitled the "National News," serving no party or cause, but giving the facts to the people. At the end of six months I had received a large number of subscriptions to this paper, but the amount of money pledged was not sufficient, and I had to choose between going out and raising the money, and staying at home and writing other books. I have chosen the latter alternative; and as I do not wish to cause my readers to continue collecting subscriptions for a non-existent "National News," I have cut out the plan from future editions of "The Brass Check," and am substituting in place of it an index to the book, something for which many readers have expressed a wish.

INDEX

Arabic numerals refer to pages, Roman numerals to chapters.
Newspapers are entered under names of cities where published.

441